COMING NEXT VOLUME:

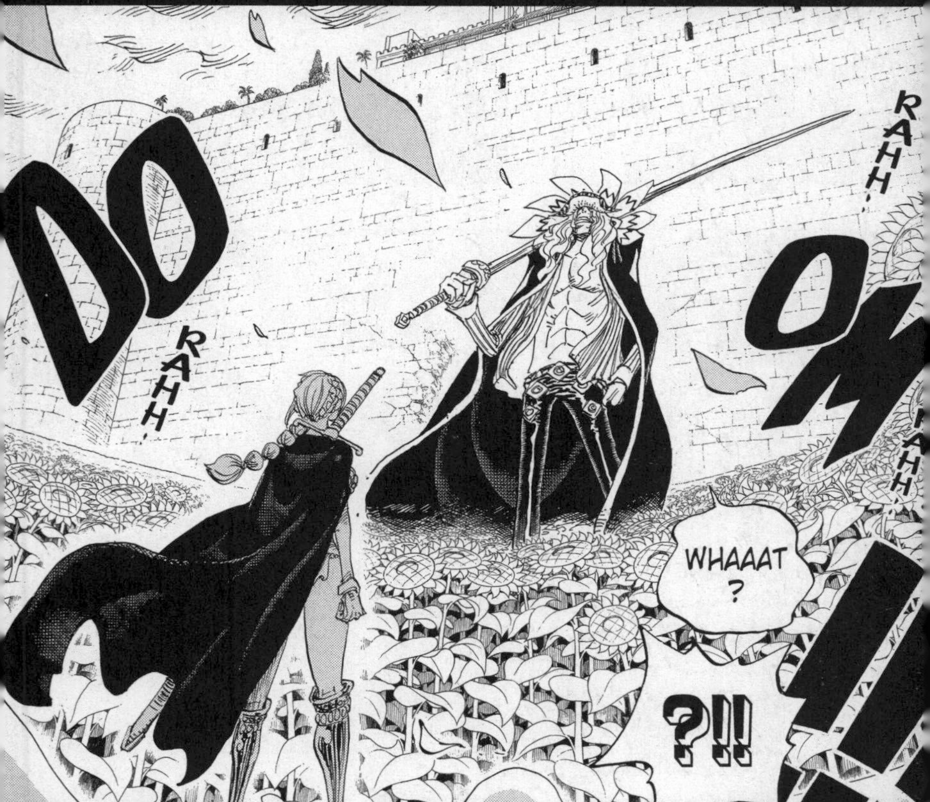
RAHH
ON
WHAAAT ?
?!!
DO
RAHH

The Straw Hats and their allies are now trapped on Dressrosa, and their only way off the island is to defeat Doflamingo. But that's easier said than done as the Doflamingo family members start flexing their muscles. Meanwhile, what is the secret behind Law and Doflamingo's tragic past? The truth is finally revealed!

ON SALE NOVEMBER 2015!

Reading in the Wrong Direction!!

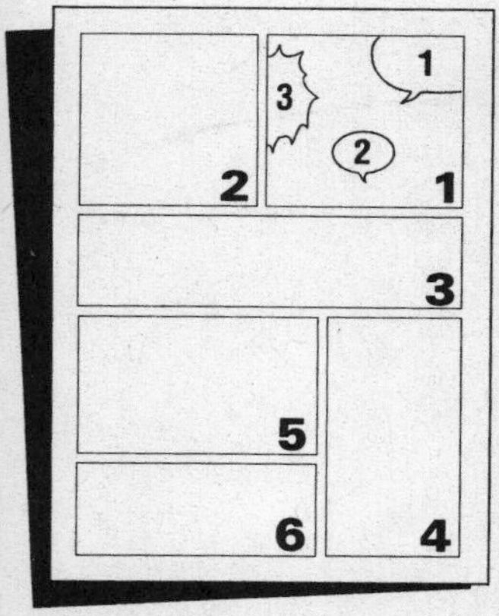
1
2
3
1
2
3
4
5
6

Whoops! Guess what? You're starting at the wrong end of the comic!

...It's true! In keeping with the original Japanese format, **One Piece** is meant to be read from right to left, starting in the upper-right corner.

Unlike English, which is read from left to right, Japanese is read from right to left, meaning that action, sound effects and word-balloon order are completely reversed...something which can make readers unfamiliar with Japanese feel pretty backwards themselves. For this reason, manga or Japanese comics published in the U.S. in English have sometimes been published "flopped"—that is, printed in exact reverse order, as though seen from the other side of a mirror.

By flopping pages, U.S. publishers can avoid confusing readers, but the compromise is not without its downside. For one thing, a character in a flopped manga series who once wore in the original Japanese version a T-shirt emblazoned with "M A Y" (as in "the merry month of") now wears one which reads "Y A M"! Additionally, many manga creators in Japan are themselves unhappy with the process, as some feel the mirror-imaging of their art skews their original intentions.

We are proud to bring you Eiichiro Oda's **One Piece** in the original unflopped format. For now, though, turn to the other side of the book and let the journey begin...!

—Editor

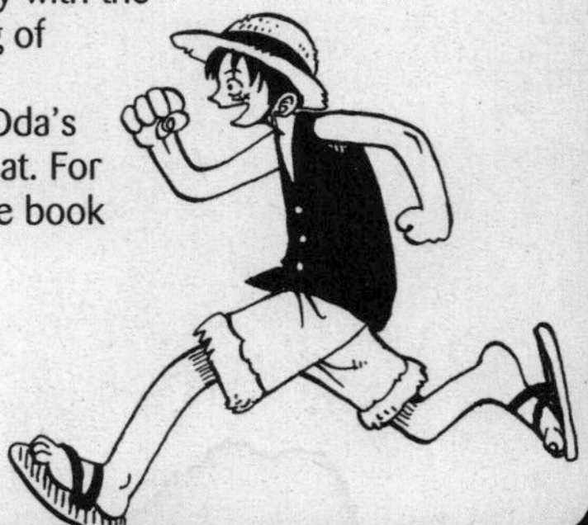

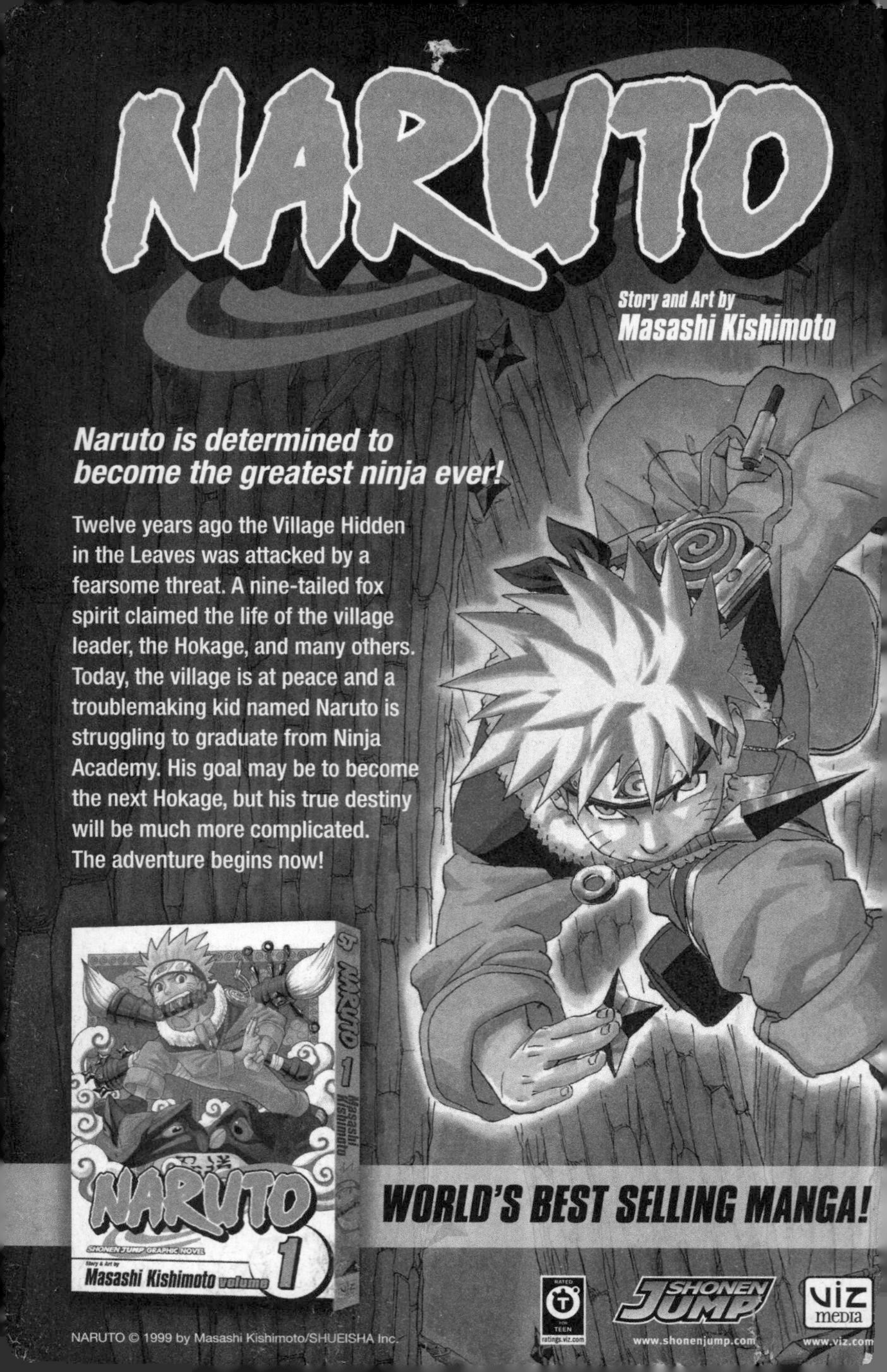
NARUTO
Story and Art by
Masashi Kishimoto
Naruto is determined to become the greatest ninja ever!
Twelve years ago the Village Hidden in the Leaves was attacked by a fearsome threat. A nine-tailed fox spirit claimed the life of the village leader, the Hokage, and many others. Today, the village is at peace and a troublemaking kid named Naruto is struggling to graduate from Ninja Academy. His goal may be to become the next Hokage, but his true destiny will be much more complicated. The adventure begins now!
NARUTO
1
SHONEN JUMP GRAPHIC NOVEL
Story & Art by
Masashi Kishimoto volume 1
WORLD'S BEST SELLING MANGA!
RATED T FOR TEEN
ratings.viz.com
SHONEN JUMP
www.shonenjump.com
VIZ MEDIA
www.viz.com
NARUTO © 1999 by Masashi Kishimoto/SHUEISHA Inc.

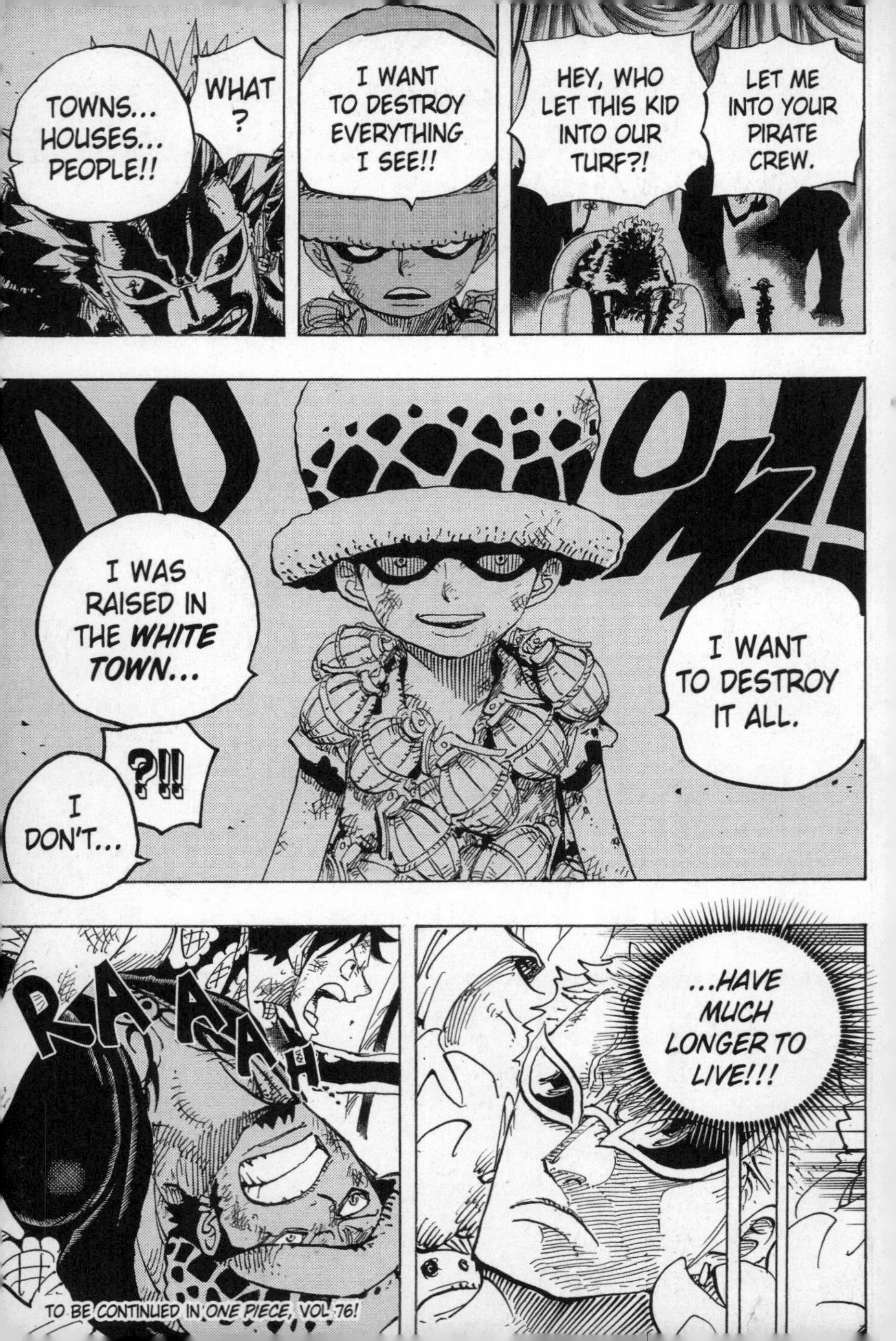
LET ME INTO YOUR PIRATE CREW.
HEY, WHO LET THIS KID INTO OUR TURF?!
I WANT TO DESTROY EVERYTHING I SEE!!
WHAT?
TOWNS... HOUSES... PEOPLE!!
DOOM
I WANT TO DESTROY IT ALL.
I WAS RAISED IN THE *WHITE TOWN*...
?!!
I DON'T...
...HAVE MUCH LONGER TO LIVE!!!
RAAAH
TO BE CONTINUED IN *ONE PIECE*, VOL. 76!

尾田栄一郎

Lately, it seems like companies don't use regular color names for their products. Instead of brown, they'll say "chocolate," or "rose" instead of red. It's very fashionable and nice. There's "champagne gold," "mint," "wine," "ruby," "cherry," "chocolat," "caramel," "natto," "rice," "miso soup," "pickled plums," "and now," "booger-colored," "volume," "75," will begin!!

–Eiichiro Oda, 2014

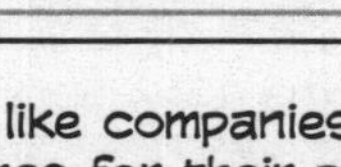

E iichiro Oda began his manga career at the age of 17, when his one-shot cowboy manga **Wanted!** won second place in the coveted Tezuka manga awards. Oda went on to work as an assistant to some of the biggest manga artists in the industry, including Nobuhiro Watsuki, before winning the Hop Step Award for new artists. His pirate adventure **One Piece**, which debuted in **Weekly Shonen Jump** in 1997, quickly became one of the most popular manga in Japan.

**ONE PIECE VOL. 75
NEW WORLD PART 15**

SHONEN JUMP Manga Edition

STORY AND ART BY EIICHIRO ODA

Translation/Stephen Paul
Touch-up Art & Lettering/Vanessa Satone
Design/Fawn Lau
Editor/Alexis Kirsch

Printed in the U.S.A.

Published by VIZ Media, LLC
P.O. Box 77010
San Francisco, CA 94107

10 9 8 7 6 5 4 3 2 1
First printing, August 2015

www.viz.com

THE WORLD'S
MOST POPULAR MANGA

www.shonenjump.com

SHONEN JUMP MANGA

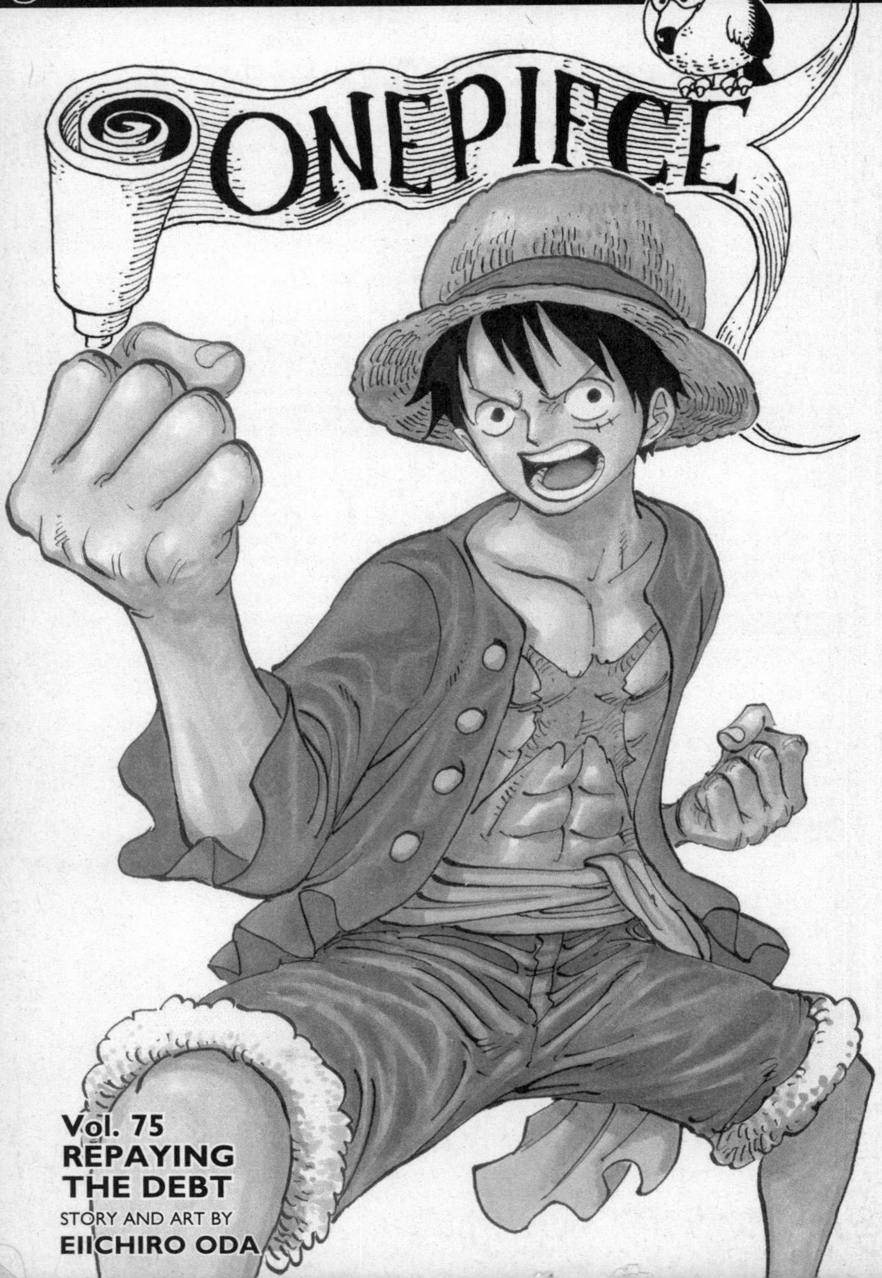

ONE PIECE

Vol. 75
REPAYING THE DEBT

STORY AND ART BY
EIICHIRO ODA

The Straw Hat Crew

Tony Tony Chopper

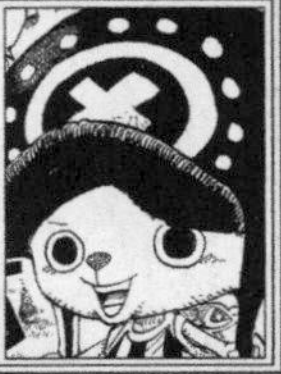

After researching powerful medicine in Birdie Kingdom, he reunites with the rest of the crew.

Ship's Doctor, Bounty: 50 berries

Monkey D. Luffy

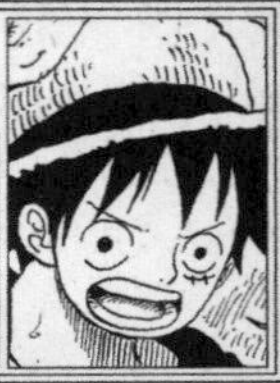

A young man who dreams of becoming the Pirate King. After training with Rayleigh, he and his crew head for the New World!

Captain, Bounty: 400 million berries

Nico Robin

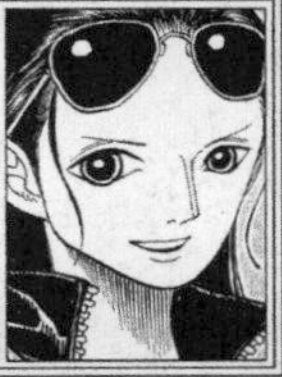

She spent her time in Baltigo with the leader of the Revolutionary Army: Luffy's father, Dragon.

Archeologist, Bounty: 80 million berries

Roronoa Zolo

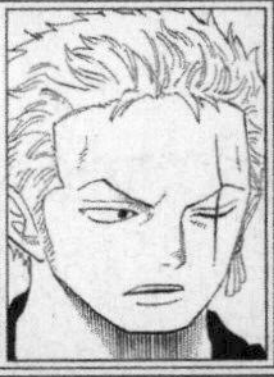

He swallowed his pride and asked to be trained by Mihawk on Gloom Island before reuniting with the rest of the crew.

Fighter, Bounty: 120 million berries

Franky

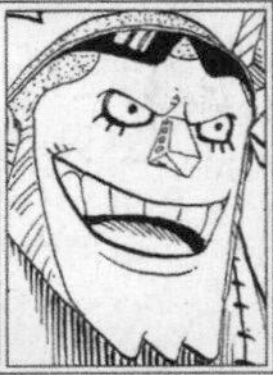

He modified himself in Future Land Baldimore and turned himself into Armored Franky before reuniting with the rest of the crew.

Shipwright, Bounty: 44 million berries

Nami

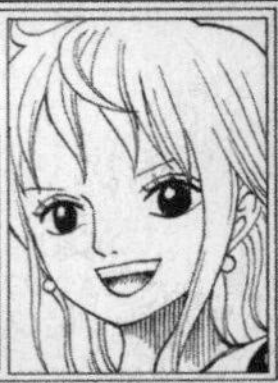

She studied the weather of the New World on the small Sky Island Weatheria, a place where weather is studied as a science.

Navigator, Bounty: 16 million berries

Brook

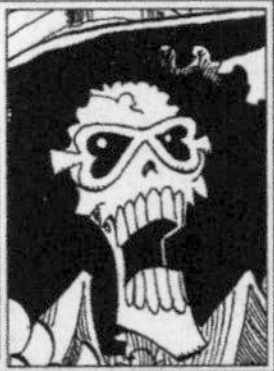

After being captured and used as a freak show by the Longarm Tribe, he became a famous rock star called "Soul King" Brook.

Musician, Bounty: 33 million berries

Usopp

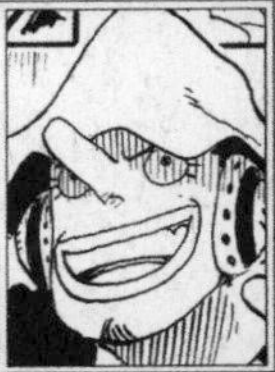

He trained under Heracles at the Bowin Islands to become the King of Snipers.

Sniper, Bounty: 30 million berries

Shanks

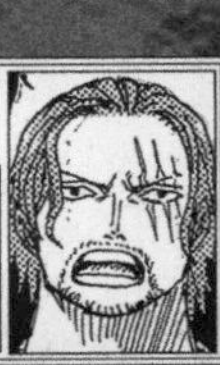

One of the Four Emperors. Waits for Luffy in the "New World," the second half of the Grand Line.

Captain of the Red-Haired Pirates

Sanji

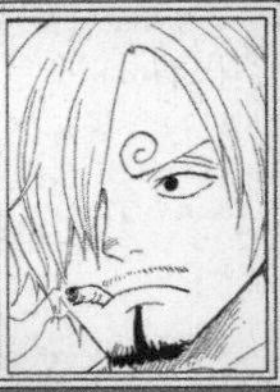

After fighting the New Kama Karate masters in the Kamabakka Kingdom, he returned to the crew.

Cook, Bounty: 77 million berries

the crew meets a one-legged toy soldier who informs them of the nation's hidden darkness, and they decide to help the little Tontattas in their fight for freedom. Luffy leaves to rescue Law, and Usopp tracks down Sugar to free those who have been turned into toys. Despite his best-laid plans, Usopp's scheme fails before the might of the officers. But in his most desperate moment, he "miraculously" succeeds in knocking out Sugar...

Don Quixote Pirates

Don Quixote Doflamingo (Joker)

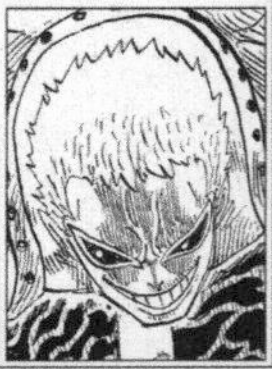

One of the Seven Warlords of the sea and a weapons broker. He works under the alias of "Joker."

Pirate, Warlord

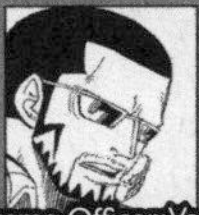

Supreme Officer: Vergo

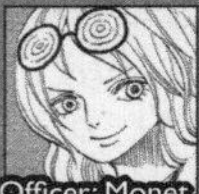

Officer: Monet

Pica Army

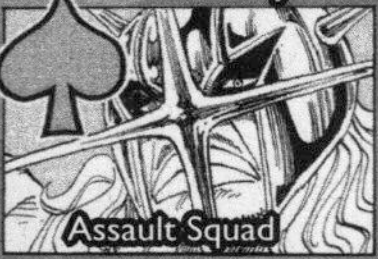

Assault Squad

Diamante Army

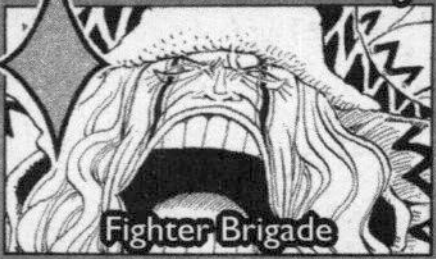

Fighter Brigade

Trebol Army

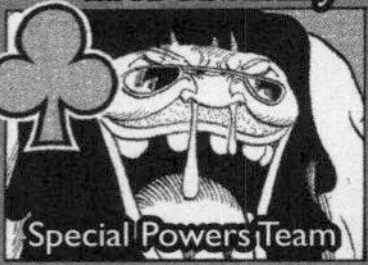

Special Powers Team

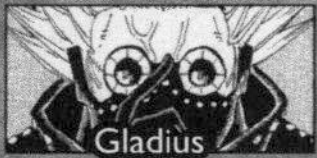

Gladius

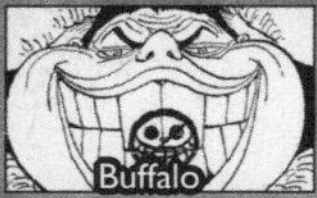

Buffalo

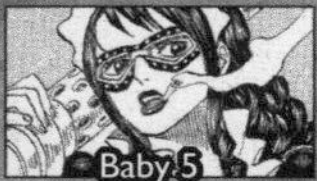

Baby 5

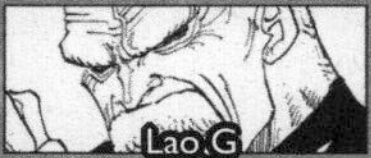

Lao G

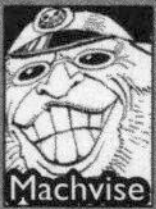

Machvise

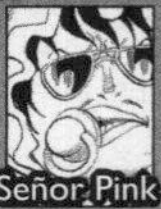

Señor Pink

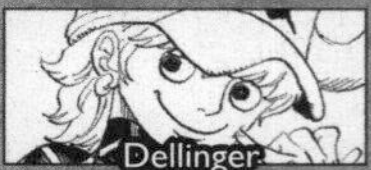

Dellinger

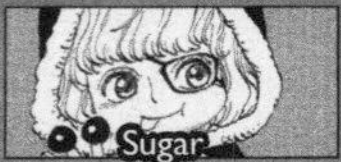

Sugar

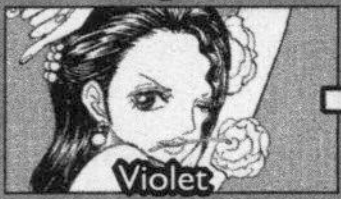

Violet

→ Viola
Former Princess, Rebecca's Aunt

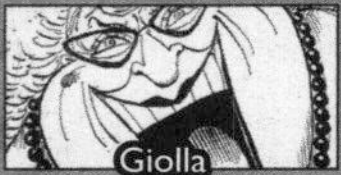

Giolla

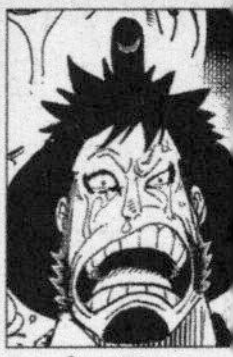

Foxfire Kin'emo

Samurai of Wano

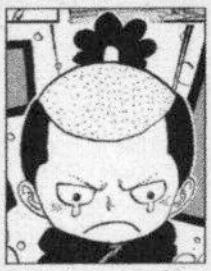

Momonosuke

Kin'emon's Son

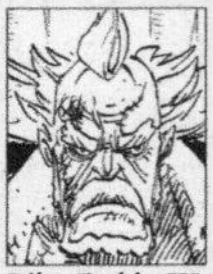

Riku Doldo III

Former King of Dressrosa

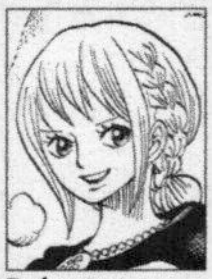

Rebecca

Gladiator (Riku's G.Daughter)

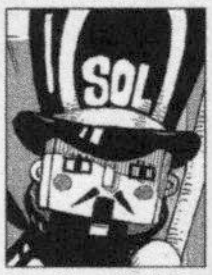

One-Legged Soldier

Toy

Fujitora (Issho)

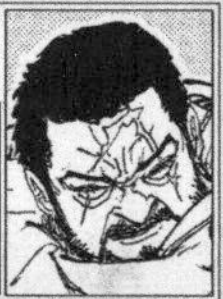

A blind swordsman. One of the Three Admirals after Aokiji's departure.

Naval HQ Admiral

Trafalgar Law

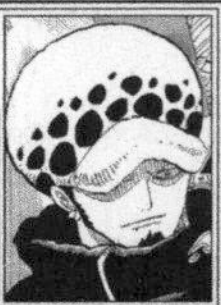

The Surgeon of Death, wielder of the Op-Op Fruit's powers. Currently allied with Luffy.

Pirate, Warlord (Tentative)

Story

After two years of hard training, the Straw Hat pirates are back together, first at the Sabaody Archipelago and then through Fish-Man Island to their next stage: the New World!!

The crew happens across Trafalgar Law on the island of Punk Hazard. At his suggestion, they form a new pirate alliance that seeks to take down one of the Four Emperors. The group infiltrates the kingdom o Dressrosa in an attempt to set up Doflamingo, but Law is abducted after falling into a trap. The rest o

Vol. 75
Repaying the Debt

CONTENTS

Chapter 743:
DRESSROSA TREMBLES

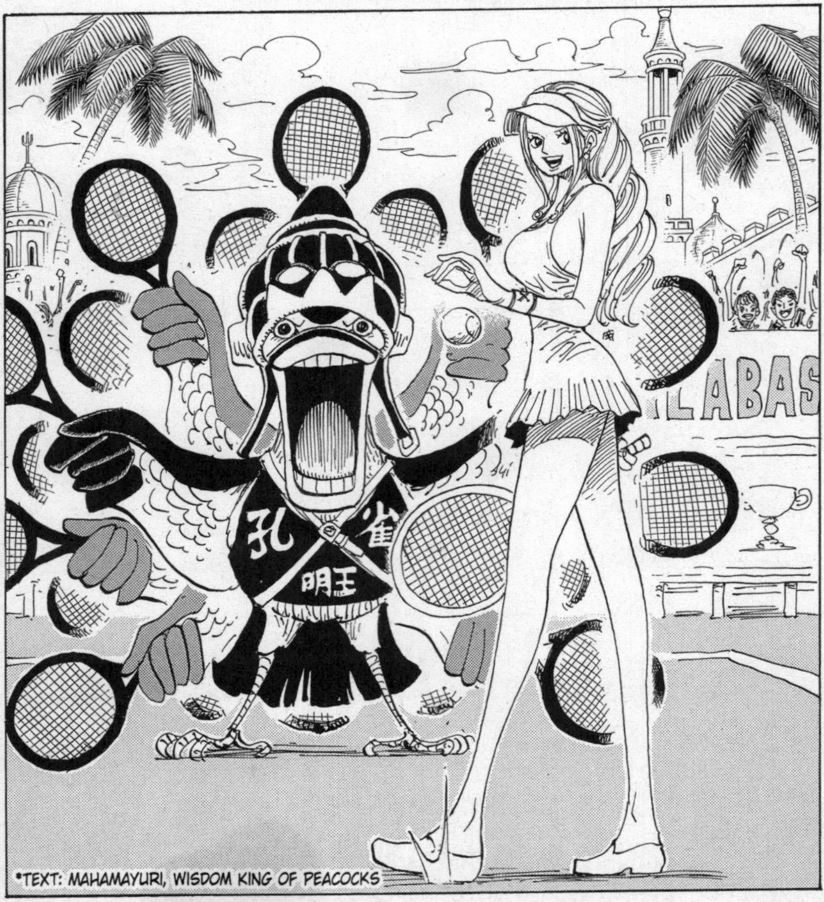

孔雀
明王
ALABAS
*TEXT: MAHAMAYURI, WISDOM KING OF PEACOCKS

REQUEST: "KAROO AND VIVI PLAYING TENNIS"
BY MOKUKU FROM AICHI

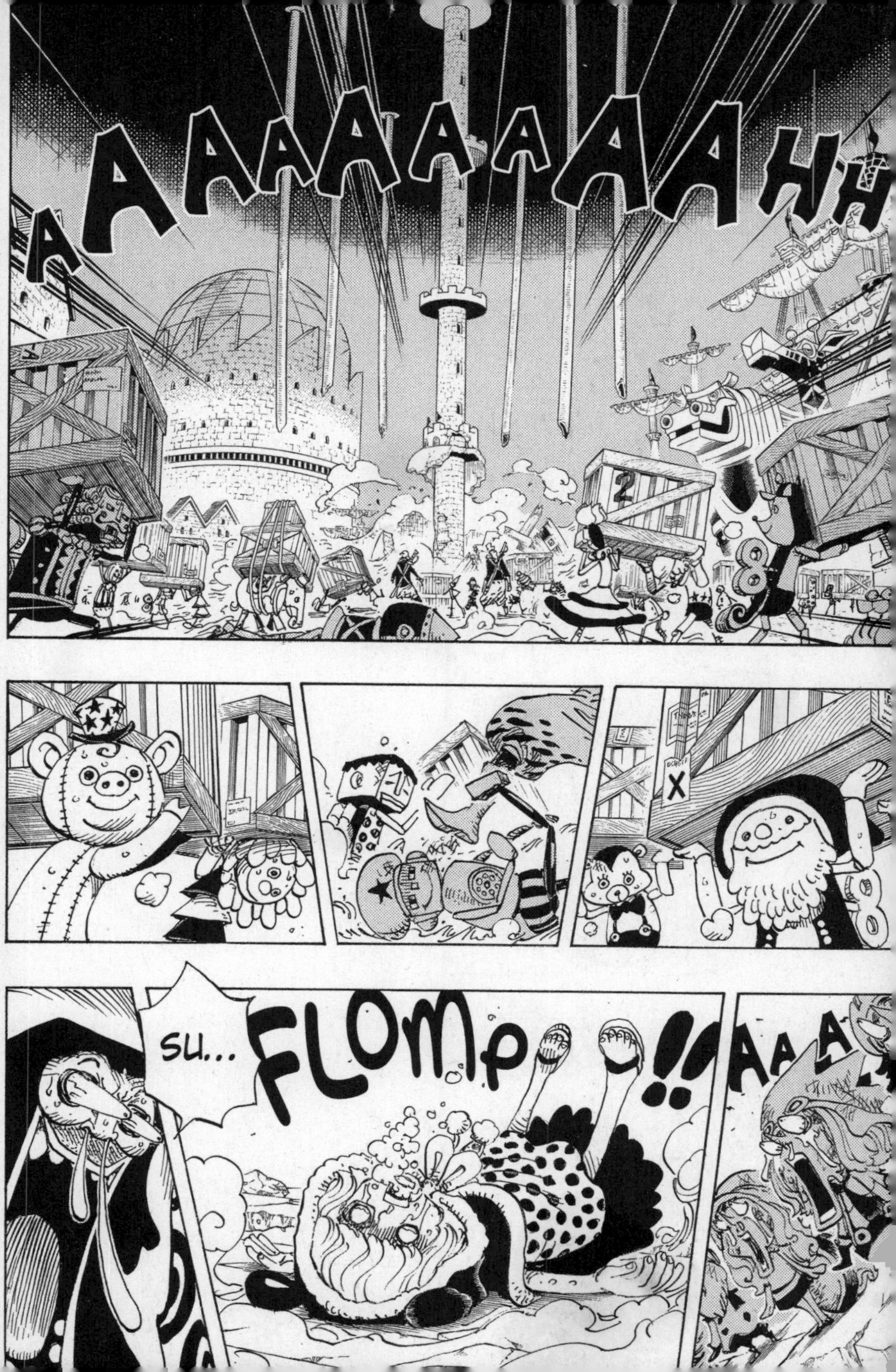
AAAAAAAAAAHH
AAA
su...
FLOMP!!

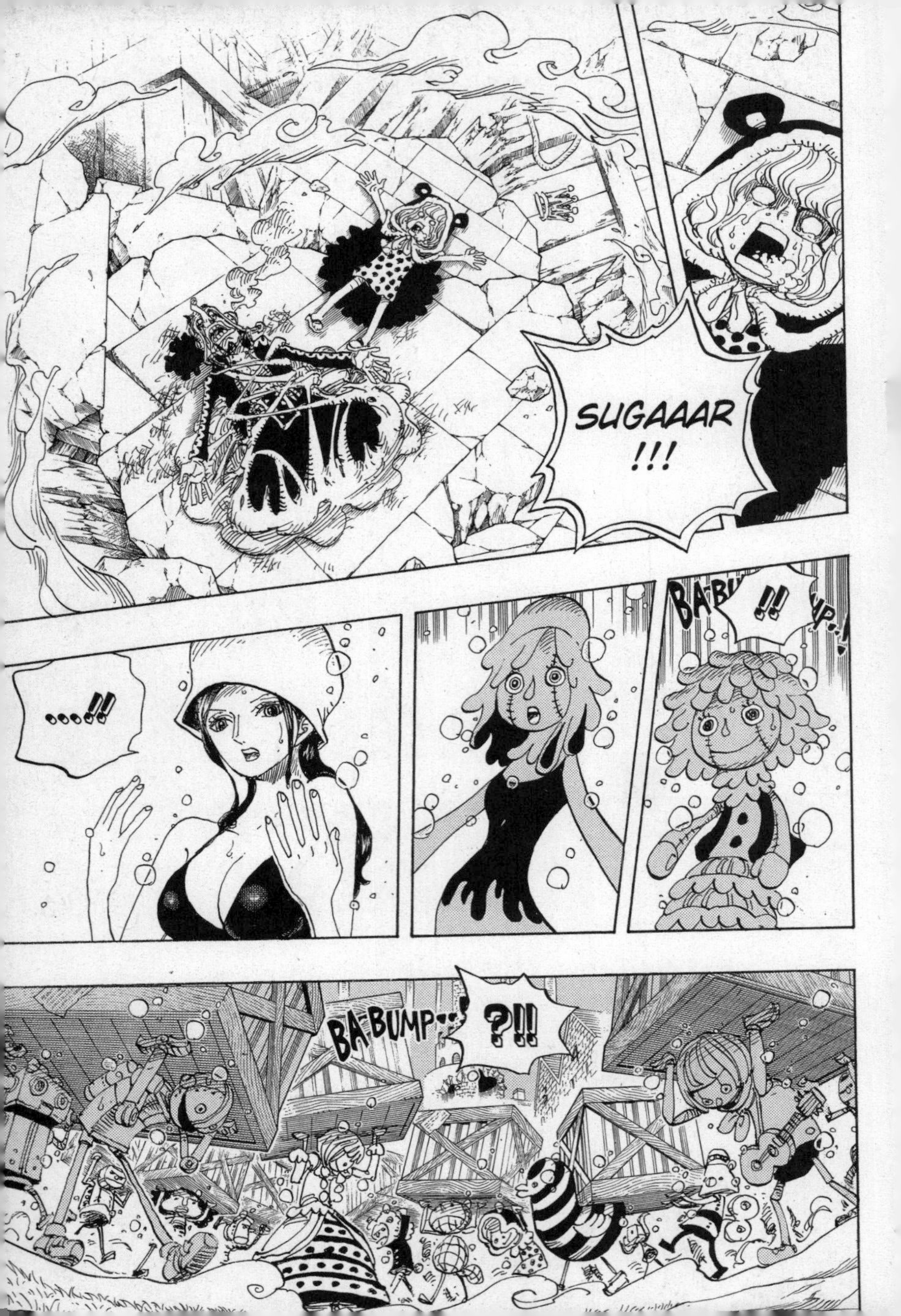
SUGAAAR !!!
!!
....!!
BA-BUMP...
?!!

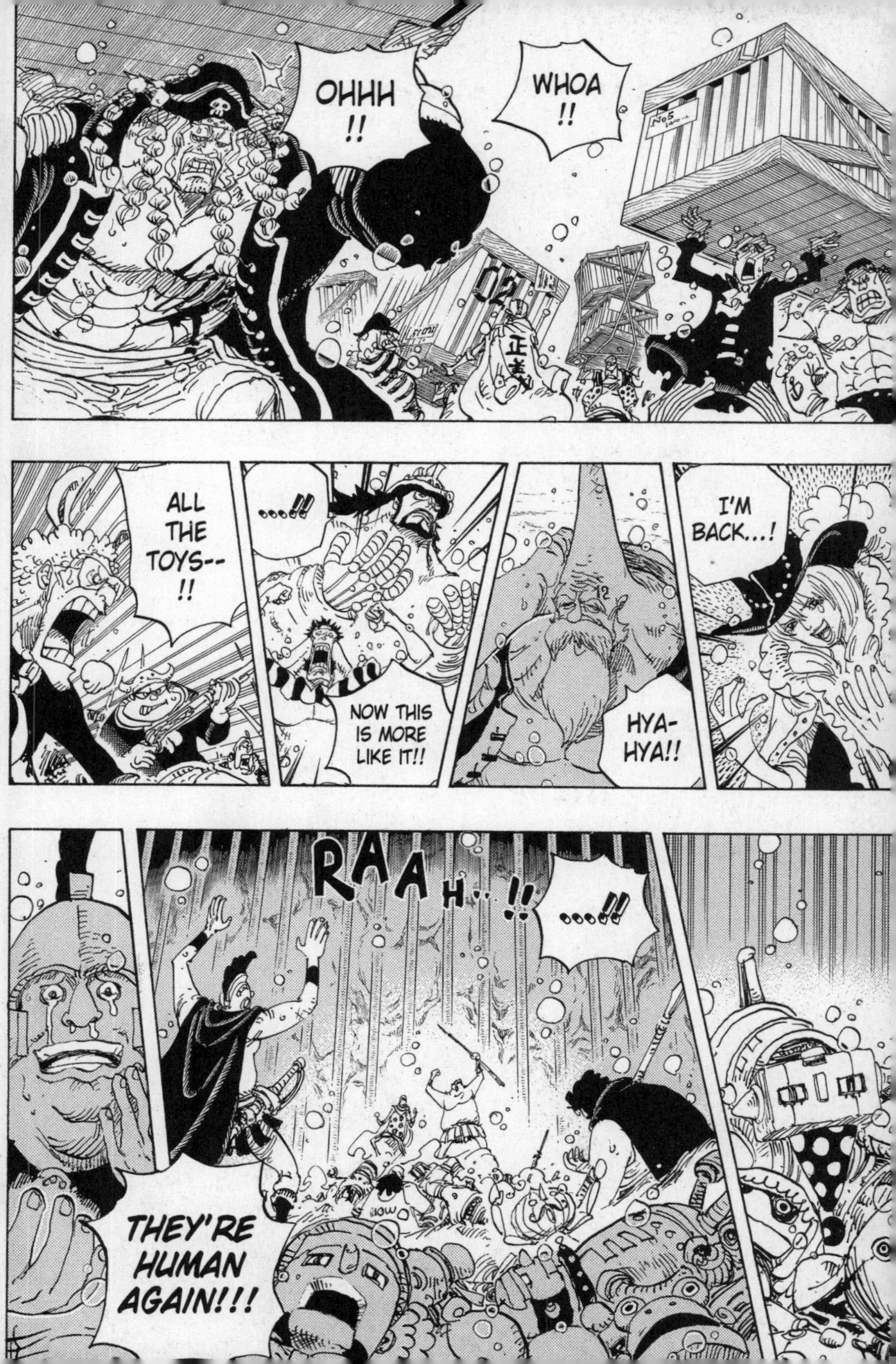
WHOA !!
OHHH !!
I'M BACK...!
HYA-HYA!!
...!!
NOW THIS IS MORE LIKE IT!!
ALL THE TOYS-- !!
...!!
RAAH..!!
THEY'RE HUMAN AGAIN!!!

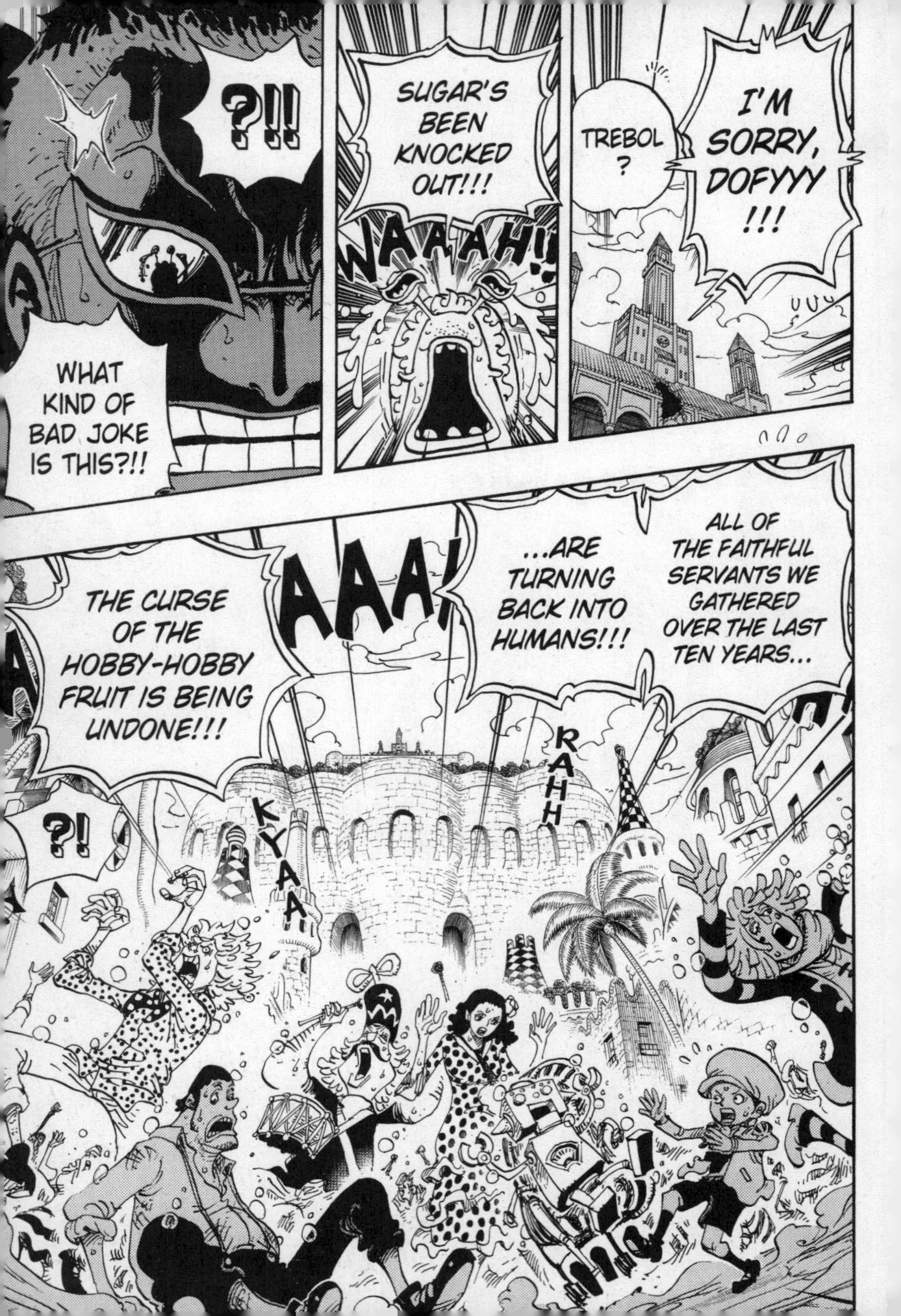
I'M SORRY, DOFYYY!!!
TREBOL?
SUGAR'S BEEN KNOCKED OUT!!!
WAAAH!!
?!!
WHAT KIND OF BAD JOKE IS THIS?!!
ALL OF THE FAITHFUL SERVANTS WE GATHERED OVER THE LAST TEN YEARS...
...ARE TURNING BACK INTO HUMANS!!!
AAAA
THE CURSE OF THE HOBBY-HOBBY FRUIT IS BEING UNDONE!!!
RAHH
KYAAA
?!

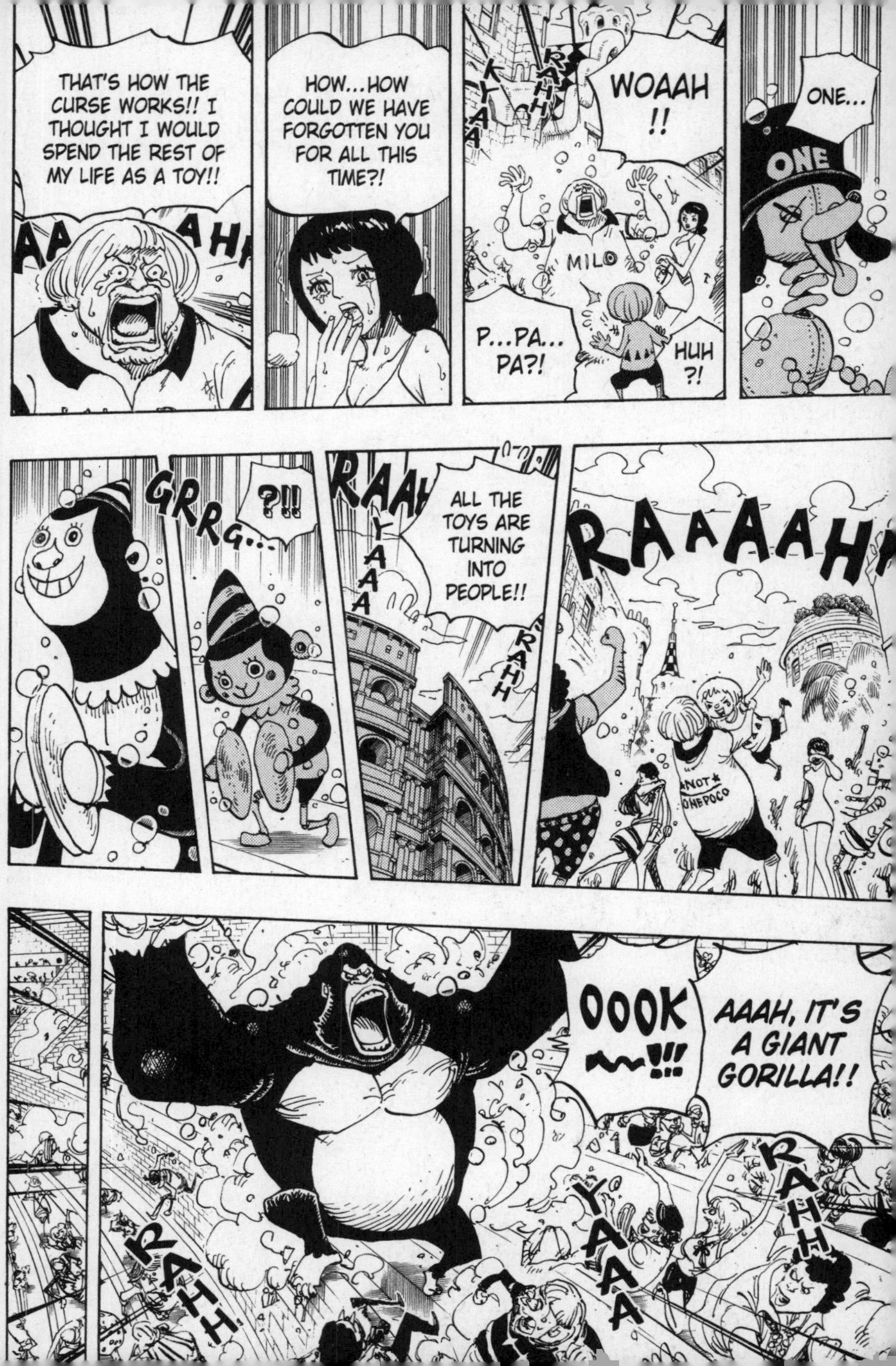
ONE...
ONE
WOAAH!!
RAHH
KYAAA
MILO
P...PA...PA?!
HUH?!
HOW...HOW COULD WE HAVE FORGOTTEN YOU FOR ALL THIS TIME?!
THAT'S HOW THE CURSE WORKS!! I THOUGHT I WOULD SPEND THE REST OF MY LIFE AS A TOY!!
AAAHH
RAAAAAHH
NOT ONEPOCO
ALL THE TOYS ARE TURNING INTO PEOPLE!!
RAAH
YAAAA
RAHH
?!!
GRRRG...
AAAH, IT'S A GIANT GORILLA!!
OOOK~!!!
RAHH
YAAAA
RAHH

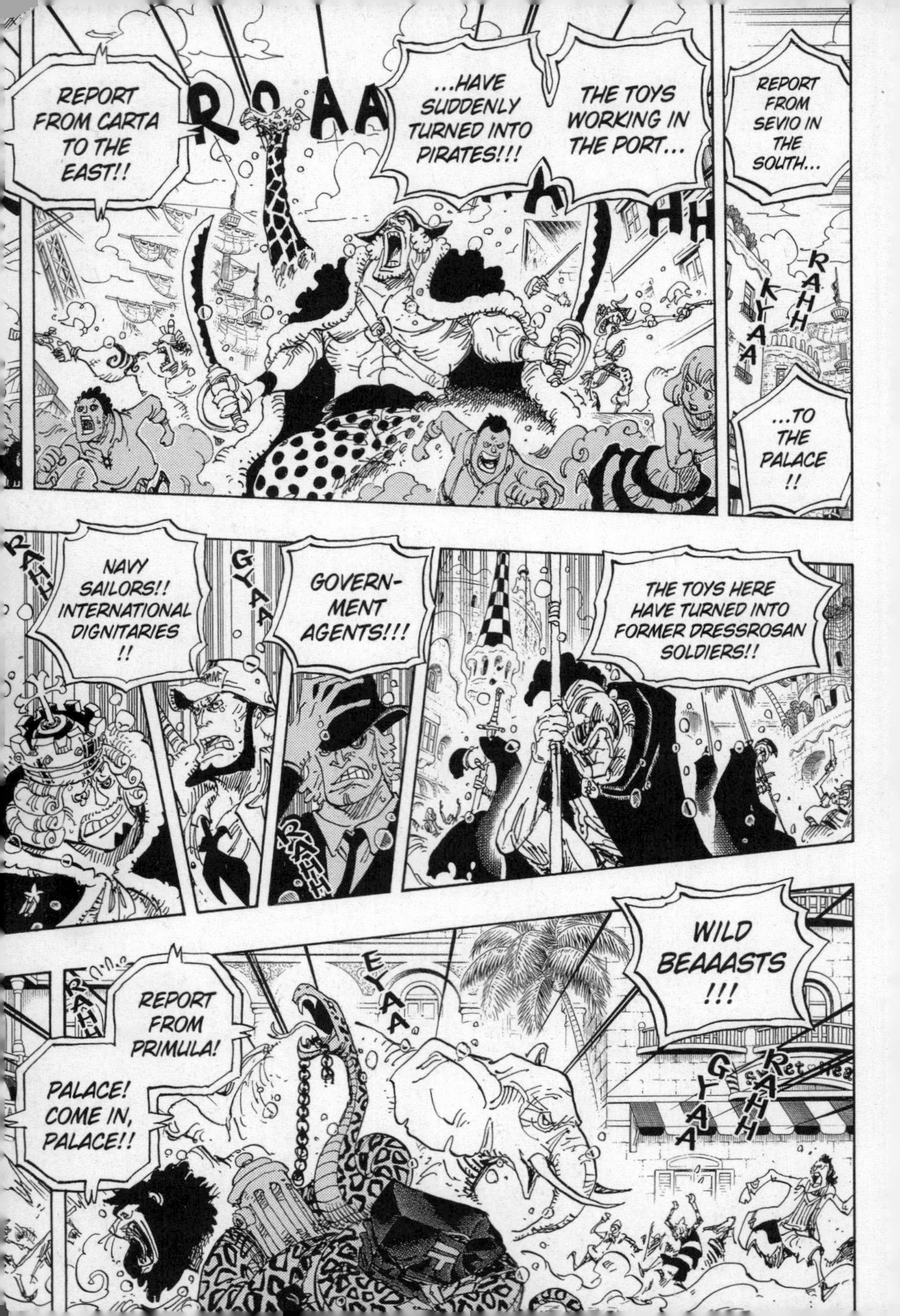
REPORT FROM SEVIO IN THE SOUTH...
RAHHH
KYAA
...TO THE PALACE!!
THE TOYS WORKING IN THE PORT...
...HAVE SUDDENLY TURNED INTO PIRATES!!!
REPORT FROM CARTA TO THE EAST!!
ROAAAHHH
THE TOYS HERE HAVE TURNED INTO FORMER DRESSROSAN SOLDIERS!!
GOVERN-MENT AGENTS!!!
GYAA
NAVY SAILORS!! INTERNATIONAL DIGNITARIES!!
RAHH
WILD BEAAASTS!!!
KYAHHH
GYAA
EYAA
REPORT FROM PRIMULA!
PALACE! COME IN, PALACE!!
RAHH

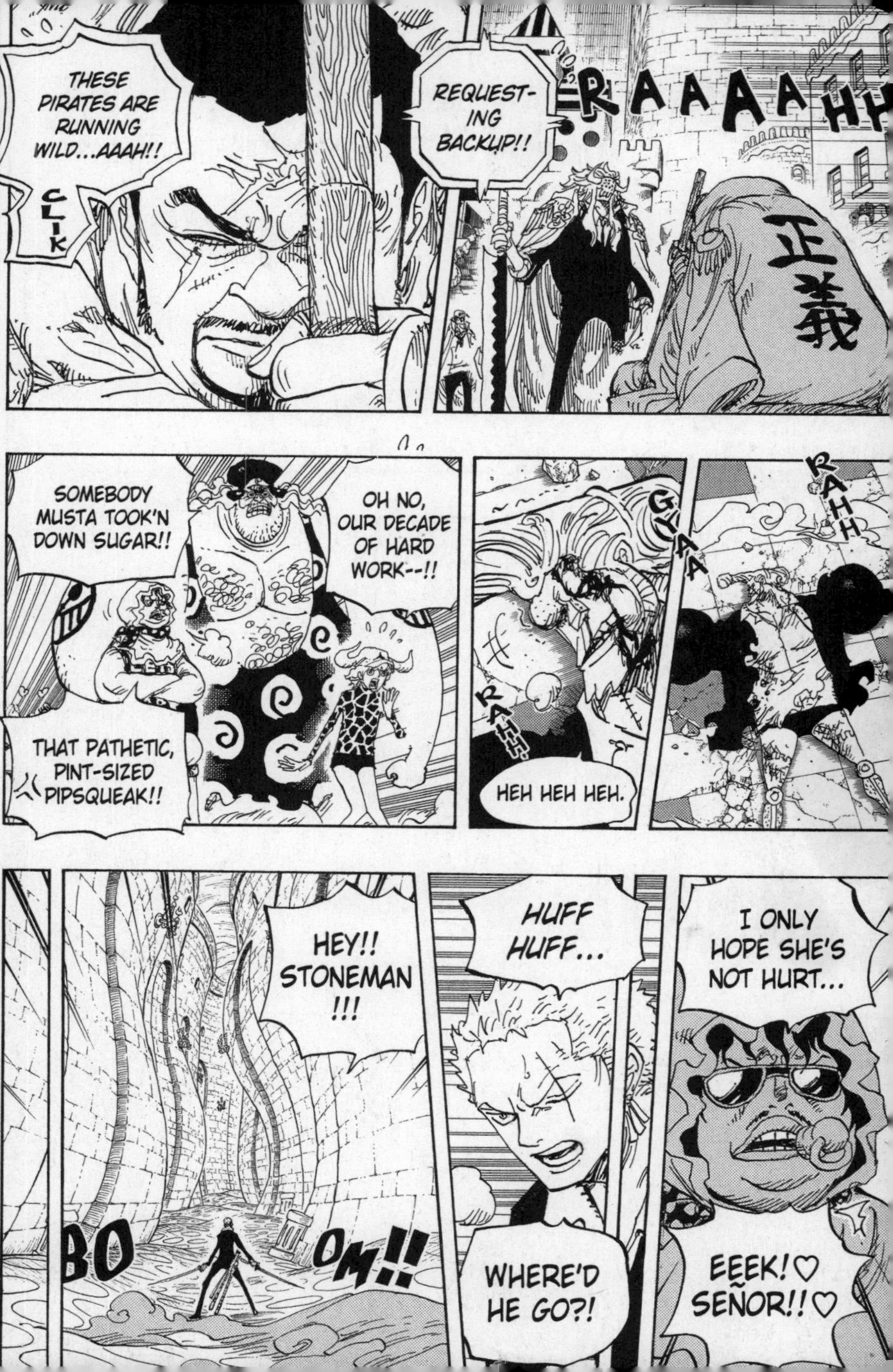
RAAAAHH
REQUEST-ING BACKUP!!
THESE PIRATES ARE RUNNING WILD...AAAH!!
CLIK
RAHH
GYAA
RAHH
HEH HEH HEH.
OH NO, OUR DECADE OF HARD WORK--!!
SOMEBODY MUSTA TOOK'N DOWN SUGAR!!
THAT PATHETIC, PINT-SIZED PIPSQUEAK!!
I ONLY HOPE SHE'S NOT HURT...
EEEK!♡ SEÑOR!!♡
HUFF HUFF...
WHERE'D HE GO?!
HEY!! STONEMAN!!!
BOOM!!

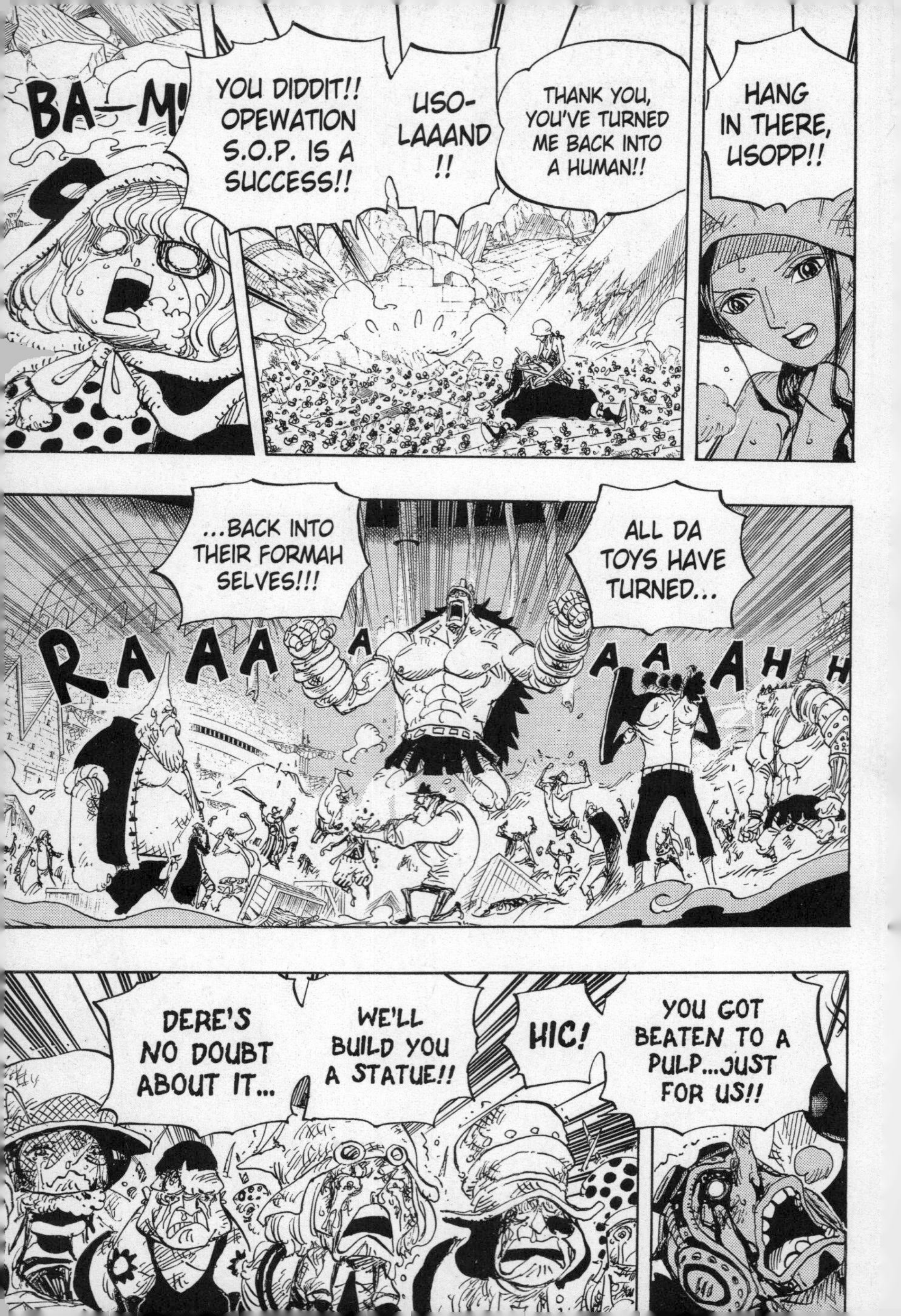
HANG IN THERE, USOPP!!
THANK YOU, YOU'VE TURNED ME BACK INTO A HUMAN!!
USO-LAAAND!!
YOU DIDDIT!! OPEWATION S.O.P. IS A SUCCESS!!
BA-M!
ALL DA TOYS HAVE TURNED...
...BACK INTO THEIR FORMAH SELVES!!!
RAAAAAAAHH
YOU GOT BEATEN TO A PULP...JUST FOR US!!
HIC!
WE'LL BUILD YOU A STATUE!!
DERE'S NO DOUBT ABOUT IT...

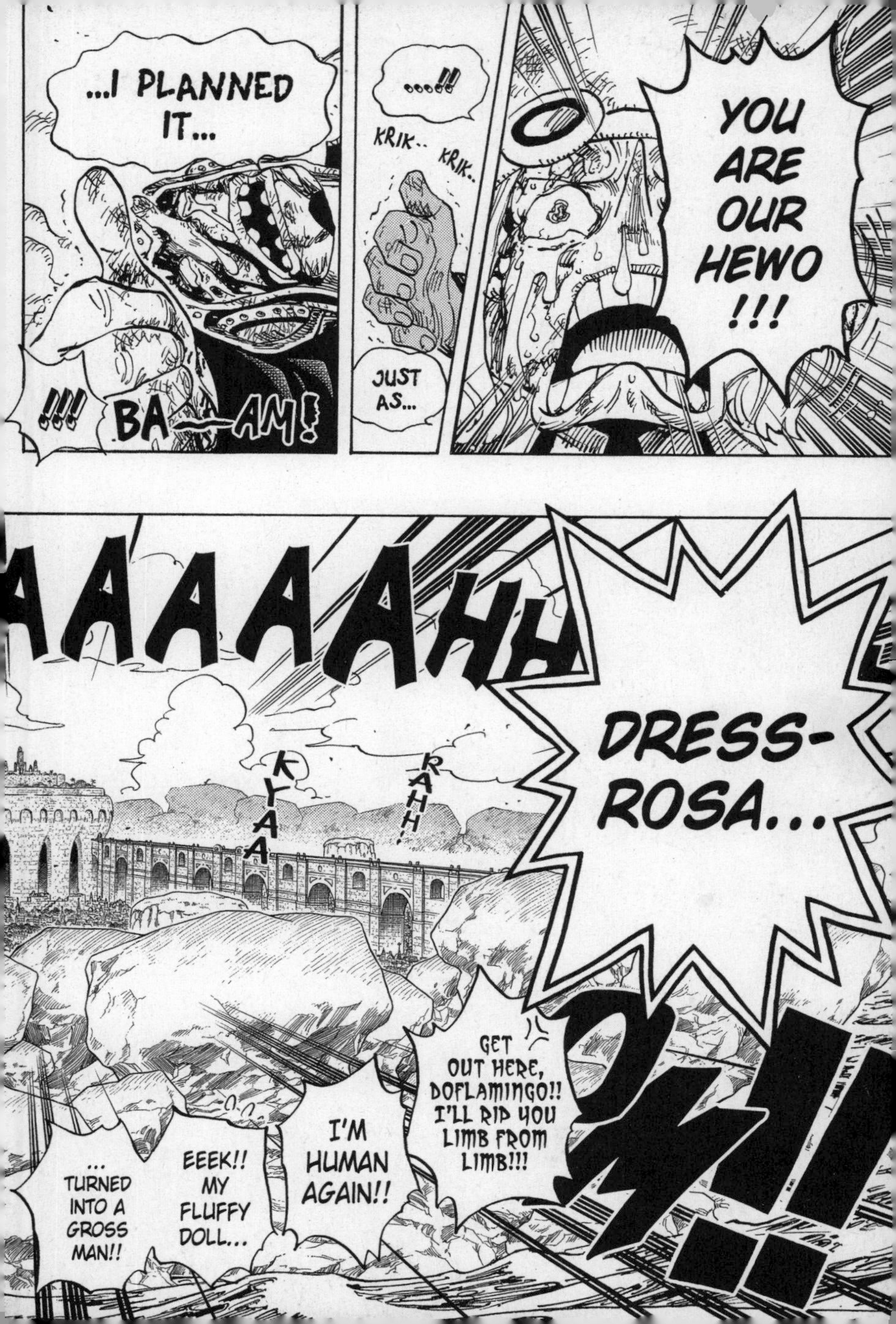
YOU ARE OUR HEWO !!!
...!!
KRIK.. KRIK..
JUST AS...
...I PLANNED IT...
!!!
BA—AM!
DRESS-ROSA...
AAAAAHH
RAHH
KYAAA
GET OUT HERE, DOFLAMINGO!! I'LL RIP YOU LIMB FROM LIMB!!!
I'M HUMAN AGAIN!!
EEEK!! MY FLUFFY DOLL...
... TURNED INTO A GROSS MAN!!

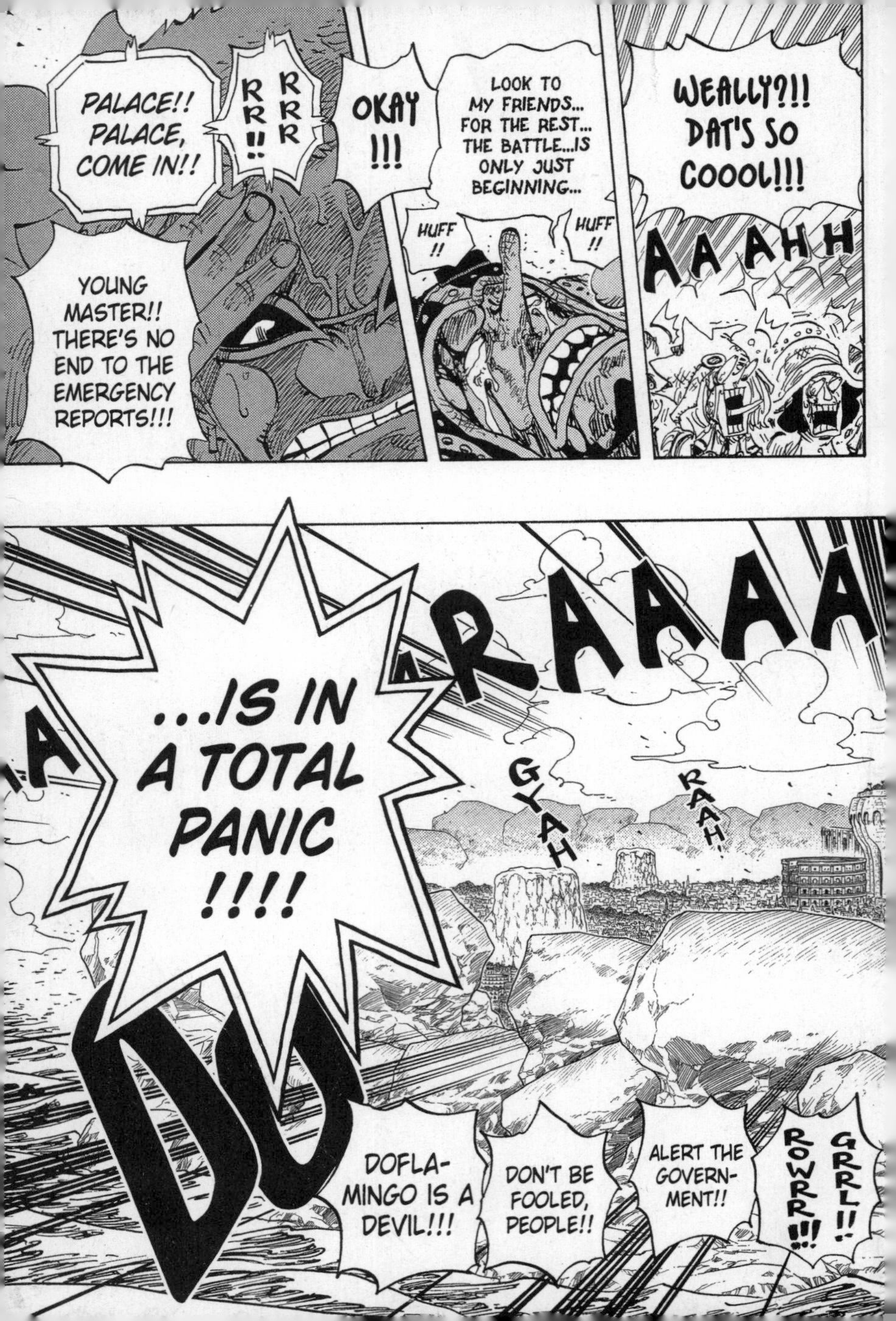
WEALLY?!! DAT'S SO COOOL!!!
AAAHH
LOOK TO MY FRIENDS... FOR THE REST... THE BATTLE...IS ONLY JUST BEGINNING...
HUFF!!
HUFF!!
OKAY!!!
RRR
RR!!
PALACE!! PALACE, COME IN!!
YOUNG MASTER!! THERE'S NO END TO THE EMERGENCY REPORTS!!!
RAAAAA
A
...IS IN A TOTAL PANIC!!!!
RAAH
GYAH
DU
GRRL!!
ROWRR!!!
ALERT THE GOVERN-MENT!!
DON'T BE FOOLED, PEOPLE!!
DOFLA-MINGO IS A DEVIL!!!

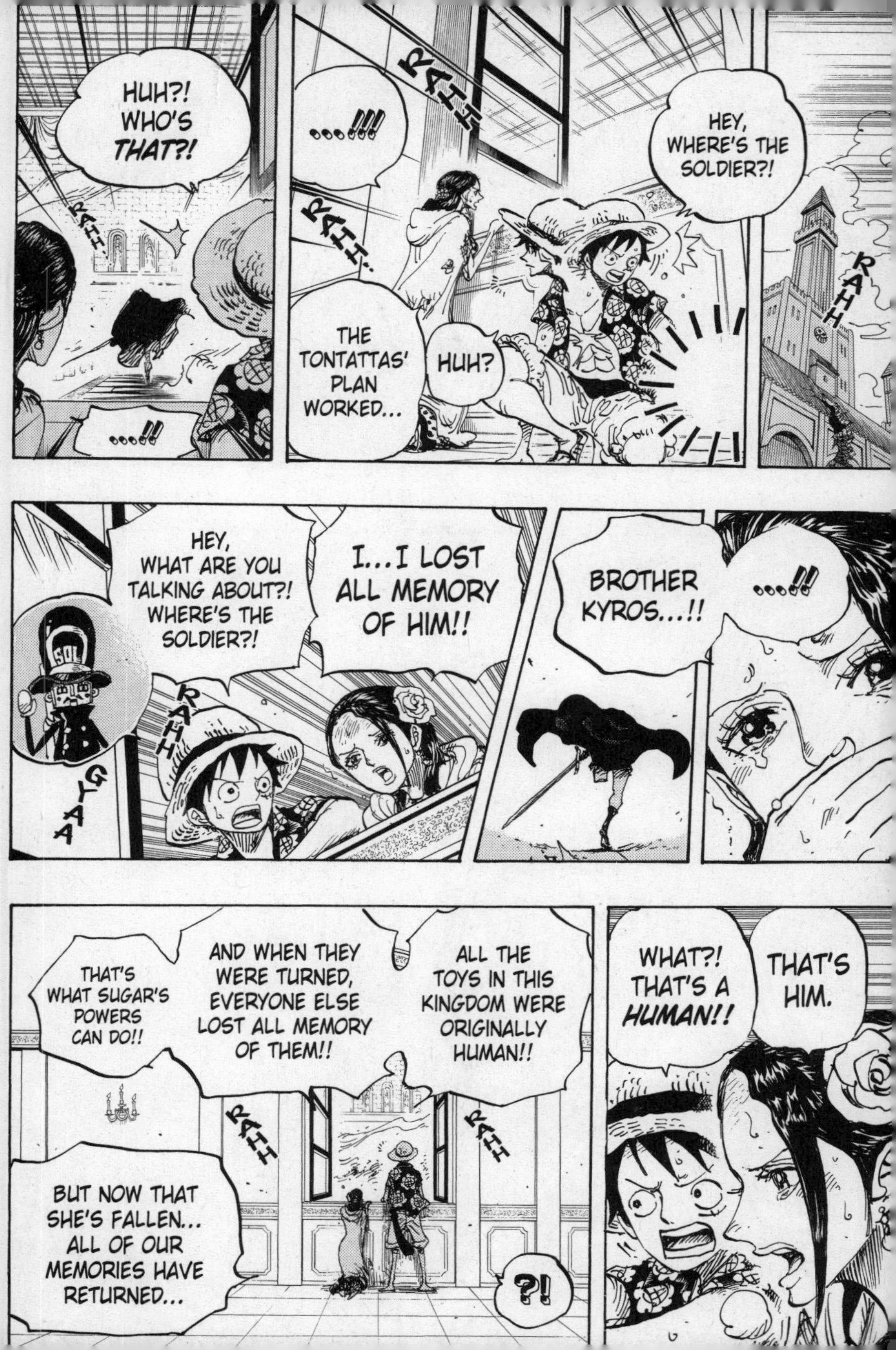
HEY, WHERE'S THE SOLDIER?!
RAHH
RAHH
...!!!
RAHH
HUH?
THE TONTATTAS' PLAN WORKED...
HUH?! WHO'S THAT?!
RAHH
...!!
...!!
BROTHER KYROS...!!
I...I LOST ALL MEMORY OF HIM!!
HEY, WHAT ARE YOU TALKING ABOUT?! WHERE'S THE SOLDIER?!
RAHH
SOL
GYAA
THAT'S HIM.
WHAT?! THAT'S A HUMAN!!
ALL THE TOYS IN THIS KINGDOM WERE ORIGINALLY HUMAN!!
AND WHEN THEY WERE TURNED, EVERYONE ELSE LOST ALL MEMORY OF THEM!!
THAT'S WHAT SUGAR'S POWERS CAN DO!!
RAHH
RAHH
?!
BUT NOW THAT SHE'S FALLEN... ALL OF OUR MEMORIES HAVE RETURNED...

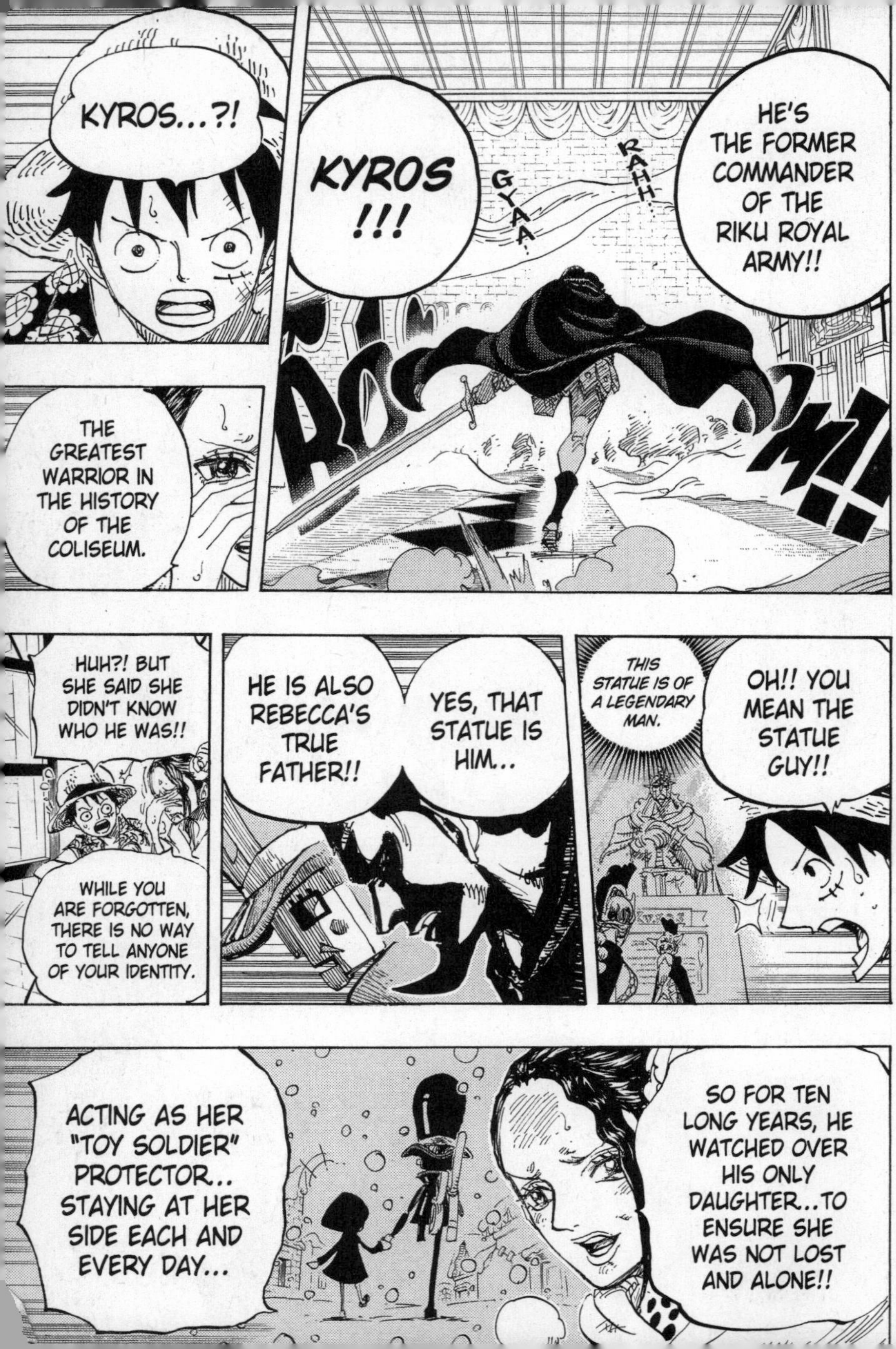
HE'S THE FORMER COMMANDER OF THE RIKU ROYAL ARMY!!
RAHH...
GYAA...
KYROS!!!
BO
M!!
KYROS...?!
THE GREATEST WARRIOR IN THE HISTORY OF THE COLISEUM.
OH!! YOU MEAN THE STATUE GUY!!
THIS STATUE IS OF A LEGENDARY MAN.
YES, THAT STATUE IS HIM...
HE IS ALSO REBECCA'S TRUE FATHER!!
HUH?! BUT SHE SAID SHE DIDN'T KNOW WHO HE WAS!!
WHILE YOU ARE FORGOTTEN, THERE IS NO WAY TO TELL ANYONE OF YOUR IDENTITY.
SO FOR TEN LONG YEARS, HE WATCHED OVER HIS ONLY DAUGHTER...TO ENSURE SHE WAS NOT LOST AND ALONE!!
ACTING AS HER "TOY SOLDIER" PROTECTOR... STAYING AT HER SIDE EACH AND EVERY DAY...

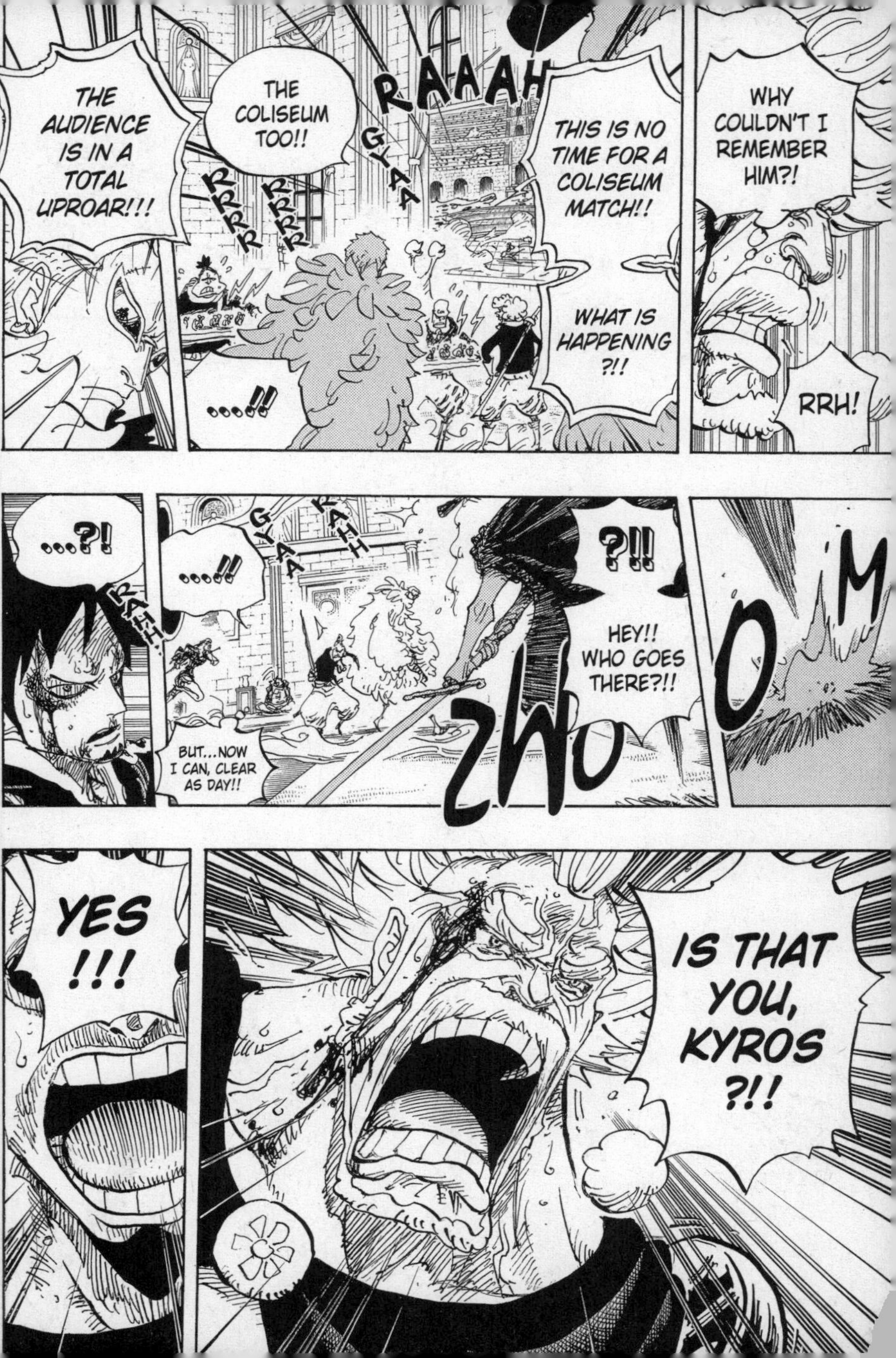
WHY COULDN'T I REMEMBER HIM?!
RRH!
RAAAH
THIS IS NO TIME FOR A COLISEUM MATCH!!
WHAT IS HAPPENING ?!!
GYAA
THE COLISEUM TOO!!
RRRR
RRRR
...!!
THE AUDIENCE IS IN A TOTAL UPROAR!!!
ZHOOM
?!!
HEY!! WHO GOES THERE?!!
RAHH
GYAA
...!!
BUT...NOW I CAN, CLEAR AS DAY!!
...?!
RAHH
IS THAT YOU, KYROS ?!!
YES !!!

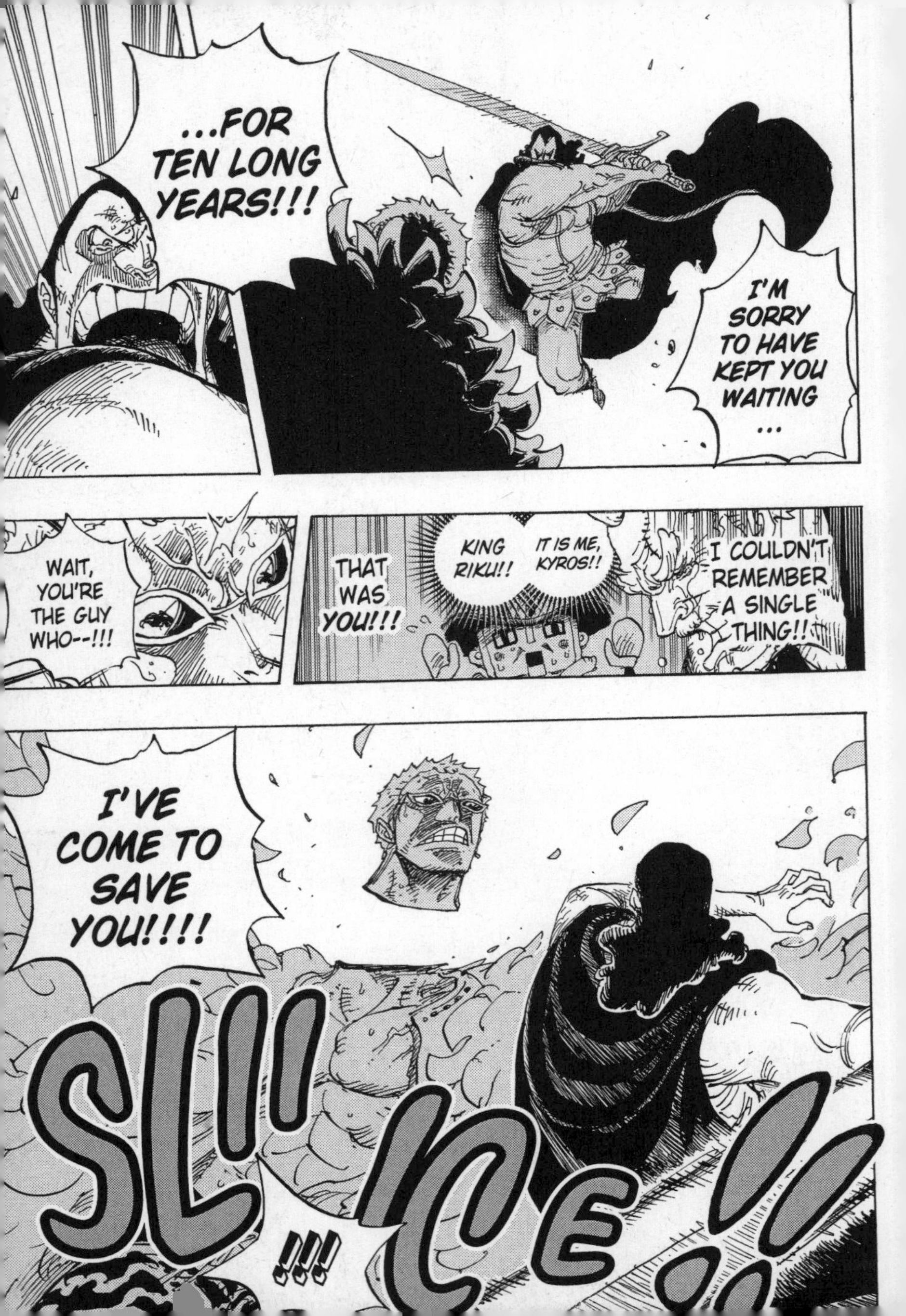
I'M SORRY TO HAVE KEPT YOU WAITING ...
...FOR TEN LONG YEARS!!!
I COULDN'T REMEMBER A SINGLE THING!!
IT IS ME, KYROS!!
KING RIKU!!
THAT WAS YOU!!!
WAIT, YOU'RE THE GUY WHO--!!!
I'VE COME TO SAVE YOU!!!!
SLIICE!!!

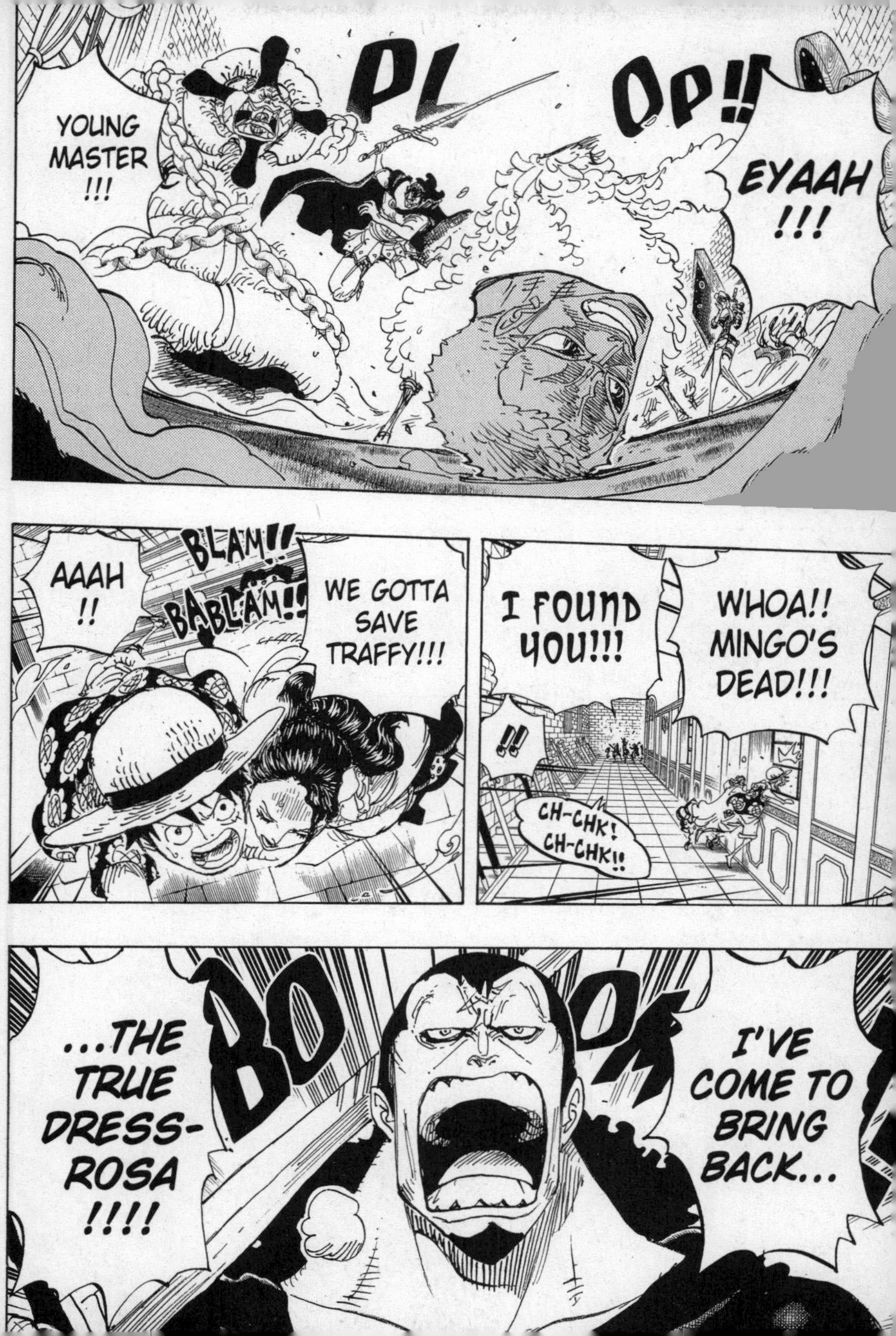

EYAAH !!!
PLOP!!
YOUNG MASTER !!!
WHOA!! MINGO'S DEAD!!!
I FOUND YOU!!!
!!
CH-CHK! CH-CHK!!
WE GOTTA SAVE TRAFFY!!!
BLAM!!
BABLAM!!
AAAH !!
I'VE COME TO BRING BACK...
...THE TRUE DRESS-ROSA !!!!

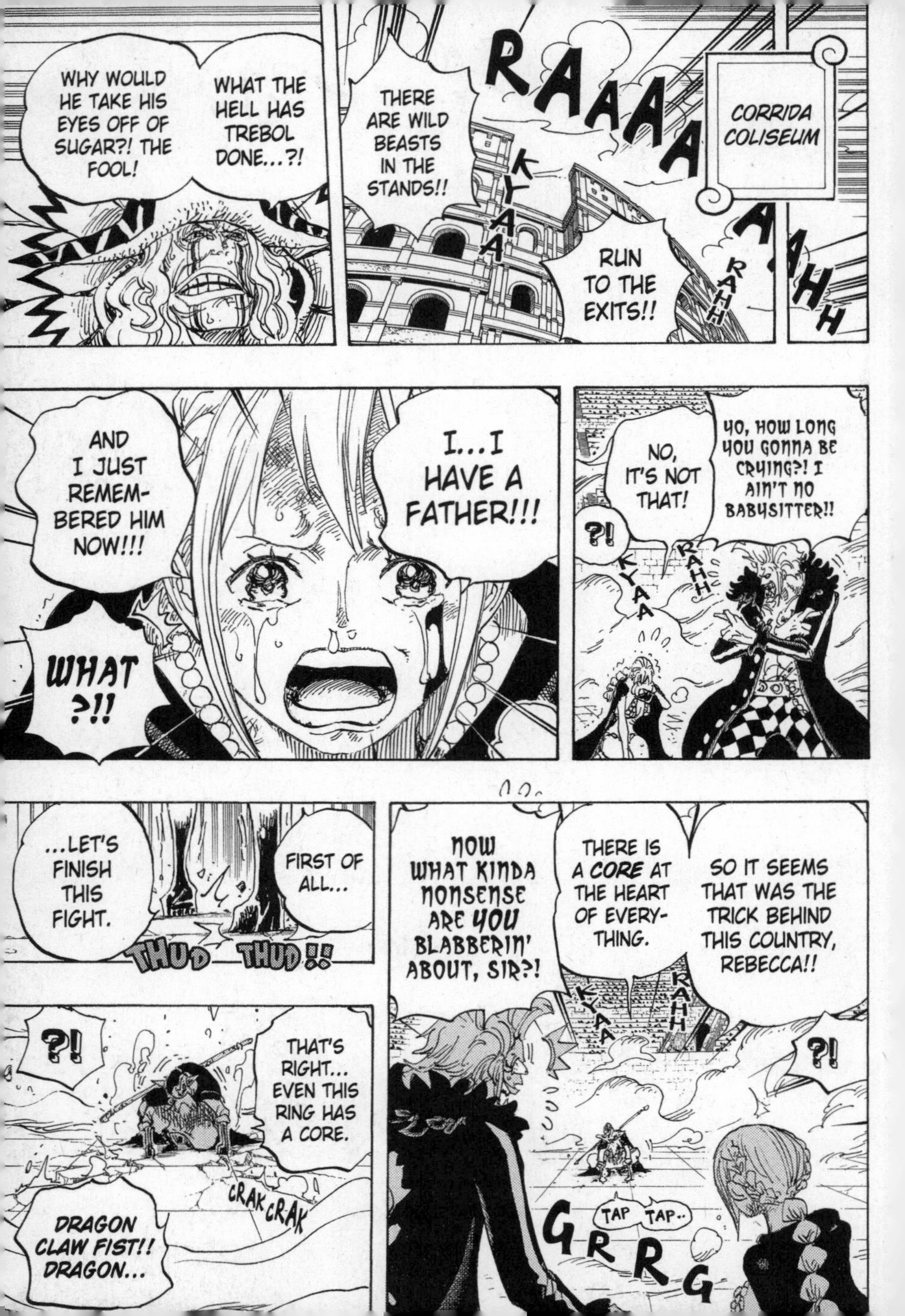
CORRIDA COLISEUM
RAAAAAAHH
THERE ARE WILD BEASTS IN THE STANDS!!
KYAAA
RUN TO THE EXITS!!
RAHH
WHAT THE HELL HAS TREBOL DONE...?!
WHY WOULD HE TAKE HIS EYES OFF OF SUGAR?! THE FOOL!
YO, HOW LONG YOU GONNA BE CRYING?! I AIN'T NO BABYSITTER!!
NO, IT'S NOT THAT!
?!
RAHH
KYAA
I...I HAVE A FATHER!!!
AND I JUST REMEM-BERED HIM NOW!!!
WHAT?!!
SO IT SEEMS THAT WAS THE TRICK BEHIND THIS COUNTRY, REBECCA!!
THERE IS A CORE AT THE HEART OF EVERY-THING.
NOW WHAT KINDA NONSENSE ARE YOU BLABBERIN' ABOUT, SIR?!
RAHH
KYAA
?!
TAP TAP..
GRRRG
FIRST OF ALL...
...LET'S FINISH THIS FIGHT.
THUD THUD!!
THAT'S RIGHT... EVEN THIS RING HAS A CORE.
?!
CRAK CRAK
DRAGON CLAW FIST!! DRAGON...

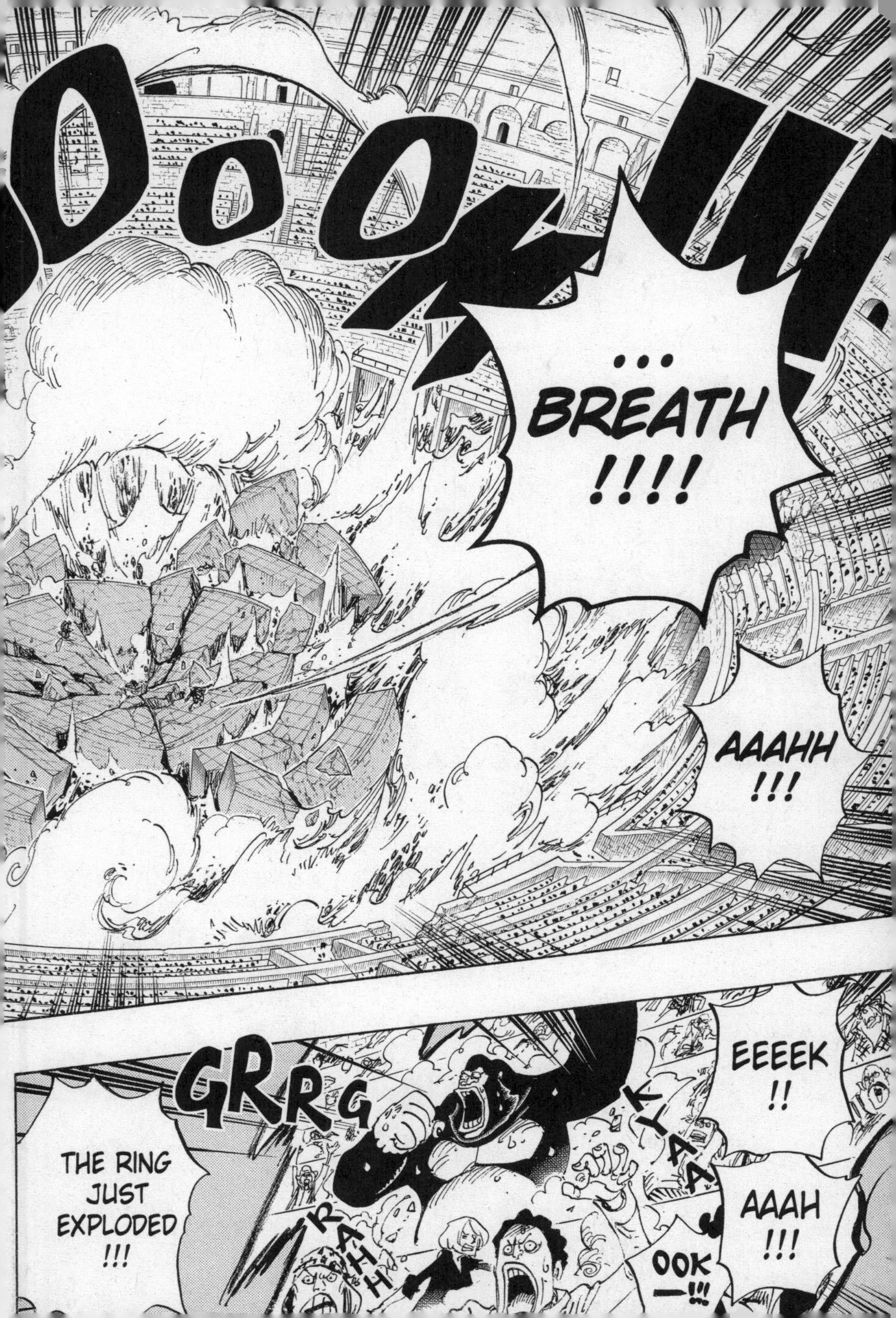

... BREATH !!!!
AAAHH !!!
EEEEK !!
AAAH !!!
OOK—!!!
KYAA
GRRG
RAHH
THE RING JUST EXPLODED !!!

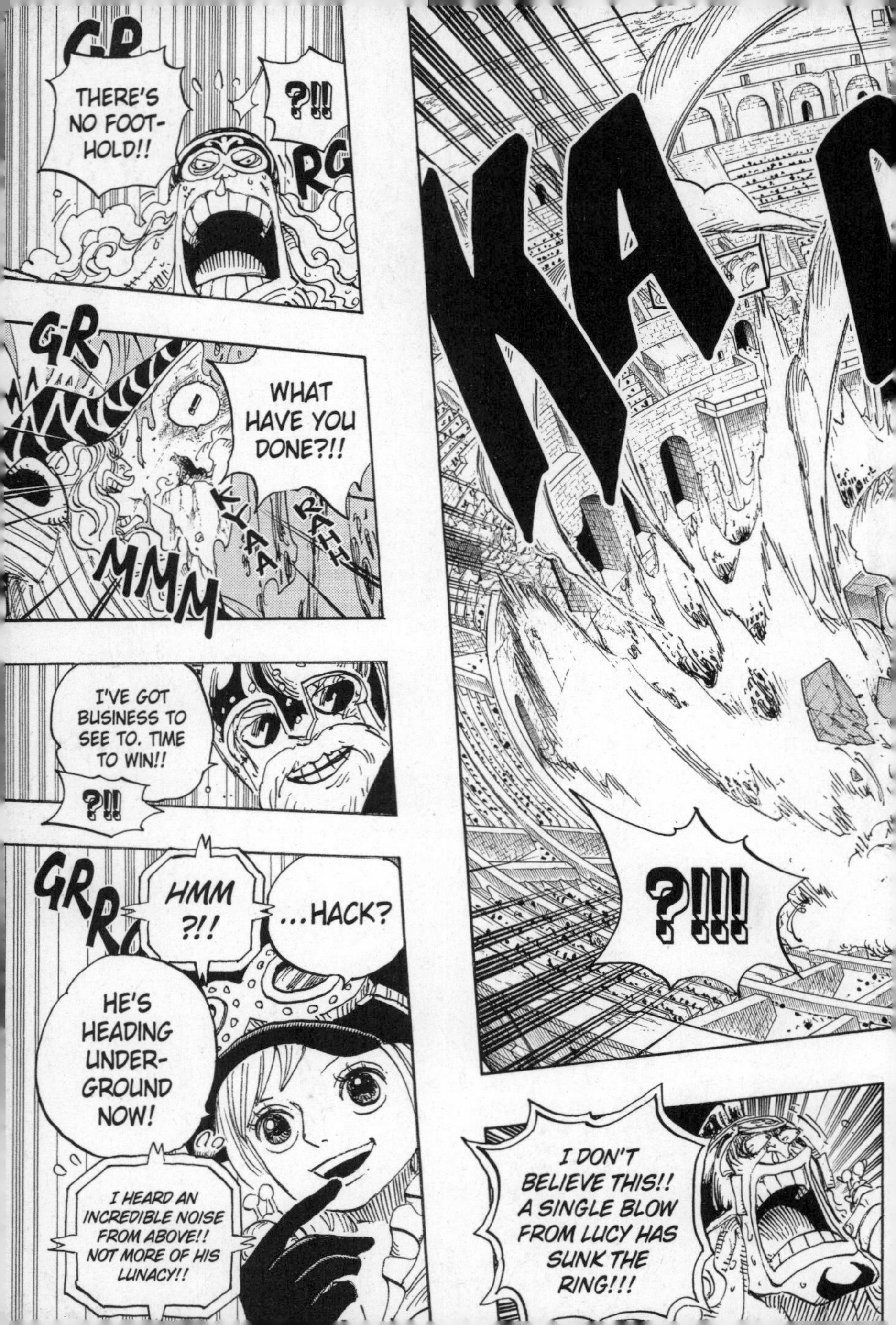
KA
?!!!
I DON'T BELIEVE THIS!! A SINGLE BLOW FROM LUCY HAS SUNK THE RING!!!
GR
THERE'S NO FOOT-HOLD!!
?!!
RG
GR
WHAT HAVE YOU DONE?!!
KYAA
RAHH
MMM
I'VE GOT BUSINESS TO SEE TO. TIME TO WIN!!
?!!
GR
HMM ?!!
...HACK?
HE'S HEADING UNDER-GROUND NOW!
I HEARD AN INCREDIBLE NOISE FROM ABOVE!! NOT MORE OF HIS LUNACY!!

SBS Question Corner

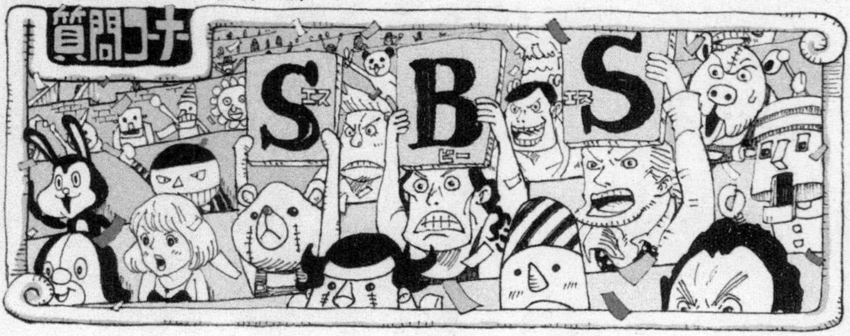

質問コーナー
S
B
S

(Captain, Tochigi)

Q: Odacchiii!
Let's begin the PTA!!
--Oriori

A: The Parent-Teacher Association!!!
The parents are taking over! Why would they do that?! It's the SBS, silly! Okay, let's get started.

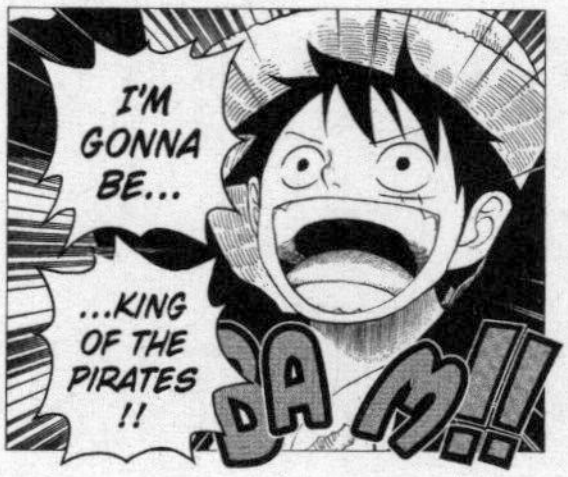

I'M GONNA BE...
...KING OF THE PIRATES !!
DAM!!

Q: Now that the midterms are nearly here, there's only one thing for me to do.
I'm gonna be king of the pirates!!
--Momota-ro

A: That's not right!! That's not right... Right?!
You're making a big mistake with your life, sonny.

Q: Odacchi! Hello. Remember when you introduced the sexy dynamite Naval Admiral Momousagi in the section on page 86 of Volume 74? Well, how about this design for Admiral Chaton (Brown Pig), who asked her out a hundred times and got shot down a hundred times? ➡
--Hideyan of Akaike

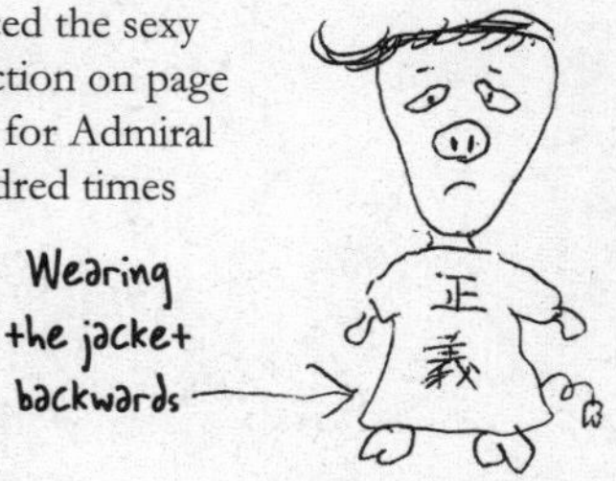

Wearing the jacket backwards
正義

A: Um, since he's not actually an admiral...he must be one of the potential admirals who were in the running along with Momousagi. You're talking about this ➡ Vice Admiral Chaton, right?! I found him in my sketchbook. As a matter of fact, for a time I was considering making the next group of admirals based on a pig and kappa, the water imp. That way, I'd have monkey, pig and kappa, just like in Journey to the West. Instead I went with the tiger and bull I'm using now. There's a reason for that, but I'm not saying.

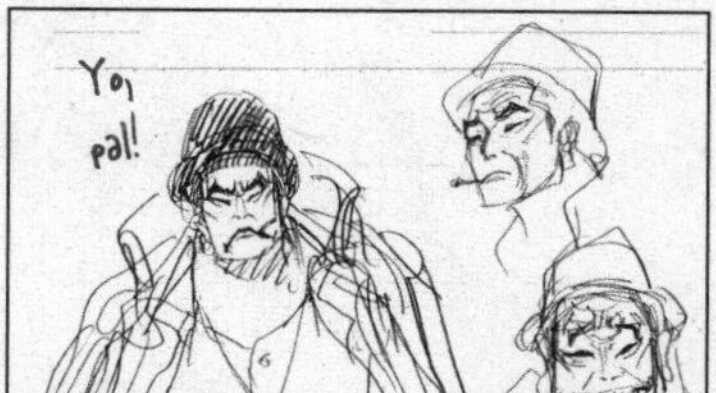

Yo, pal!
Vice Admiral Chaton

Chapter 744:
REVOLUTIONARY ARMY CHIEF OF STAFF

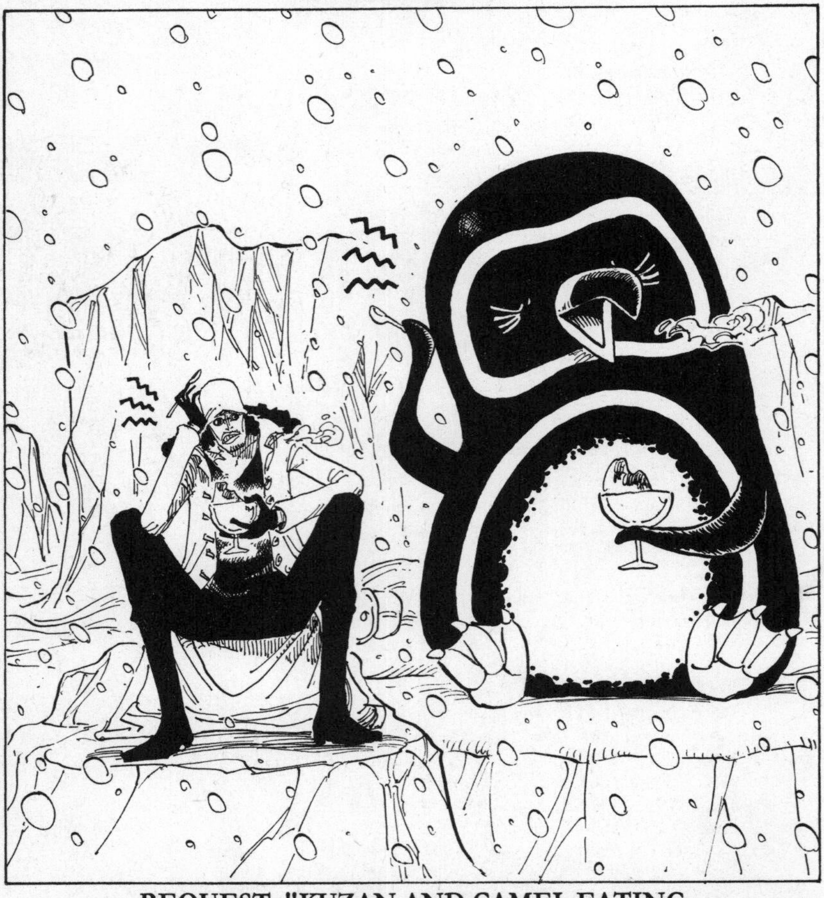

REQUEST: "KUZAN AND CAMEL EATING SHAVED ICE AND GETTING BRAIN FREEZE" BY LOVE ONE PIECE FROM HIROSHIMA

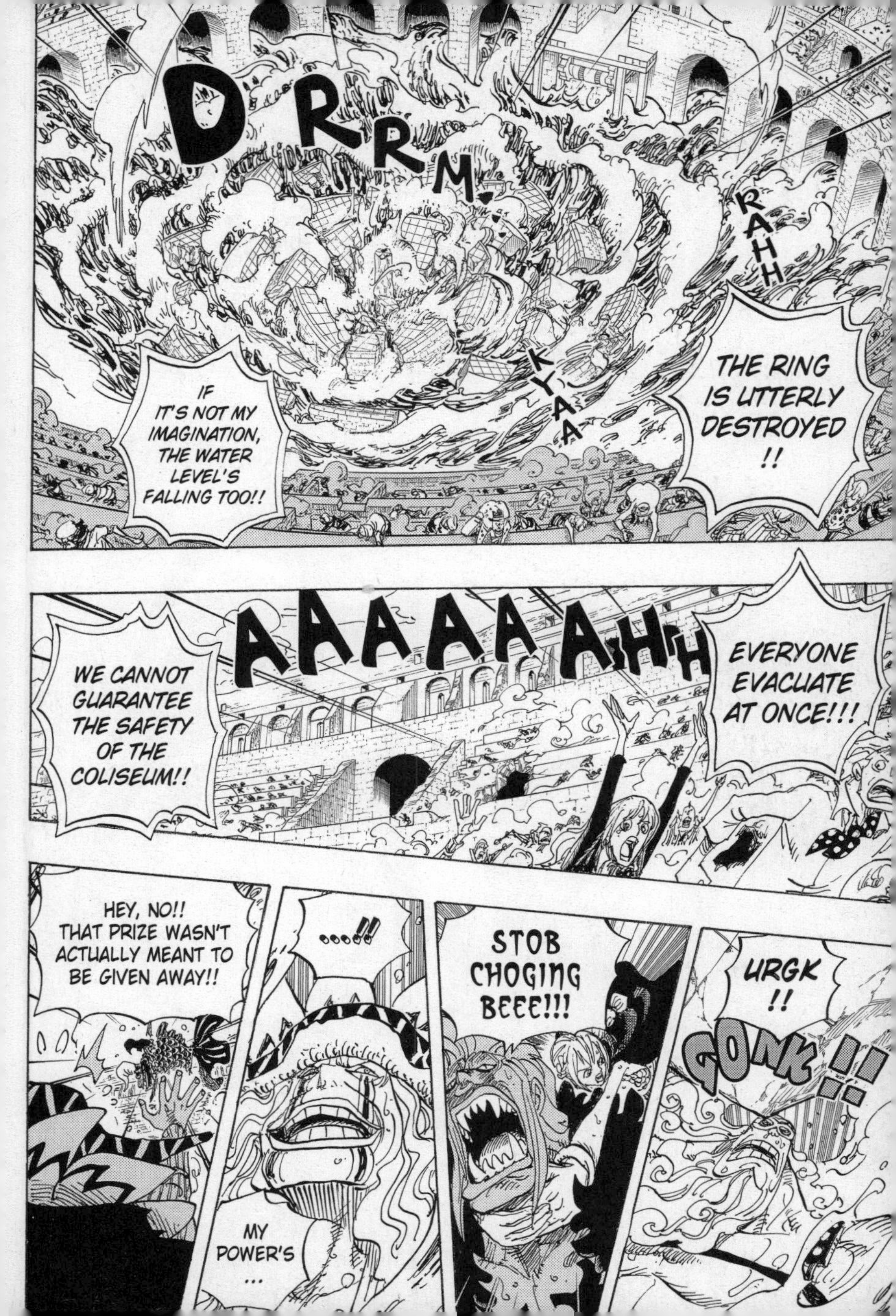
RAHHH
THE RING IS UTTERLY DESTROYED!!
DRRM
KYAA
IF IT'S NOT MY IMAGINATION, THE WATER LEVEL'S FALLING TOO!!
EVERYONE EVACUATE AT ONCE!!!
AAAAAAHH
WE CANNOT GUARANTEE THE SAFETY OF THE COLISEUM!!
URGK!!
GONK!!
STOB CHOGING BEEE!!!
...!!
MY POWER'S...
HEY, NO!! THAT PRIZE WASN'T ACTUALLY MEANT TO BE GIVEN AWAY!!

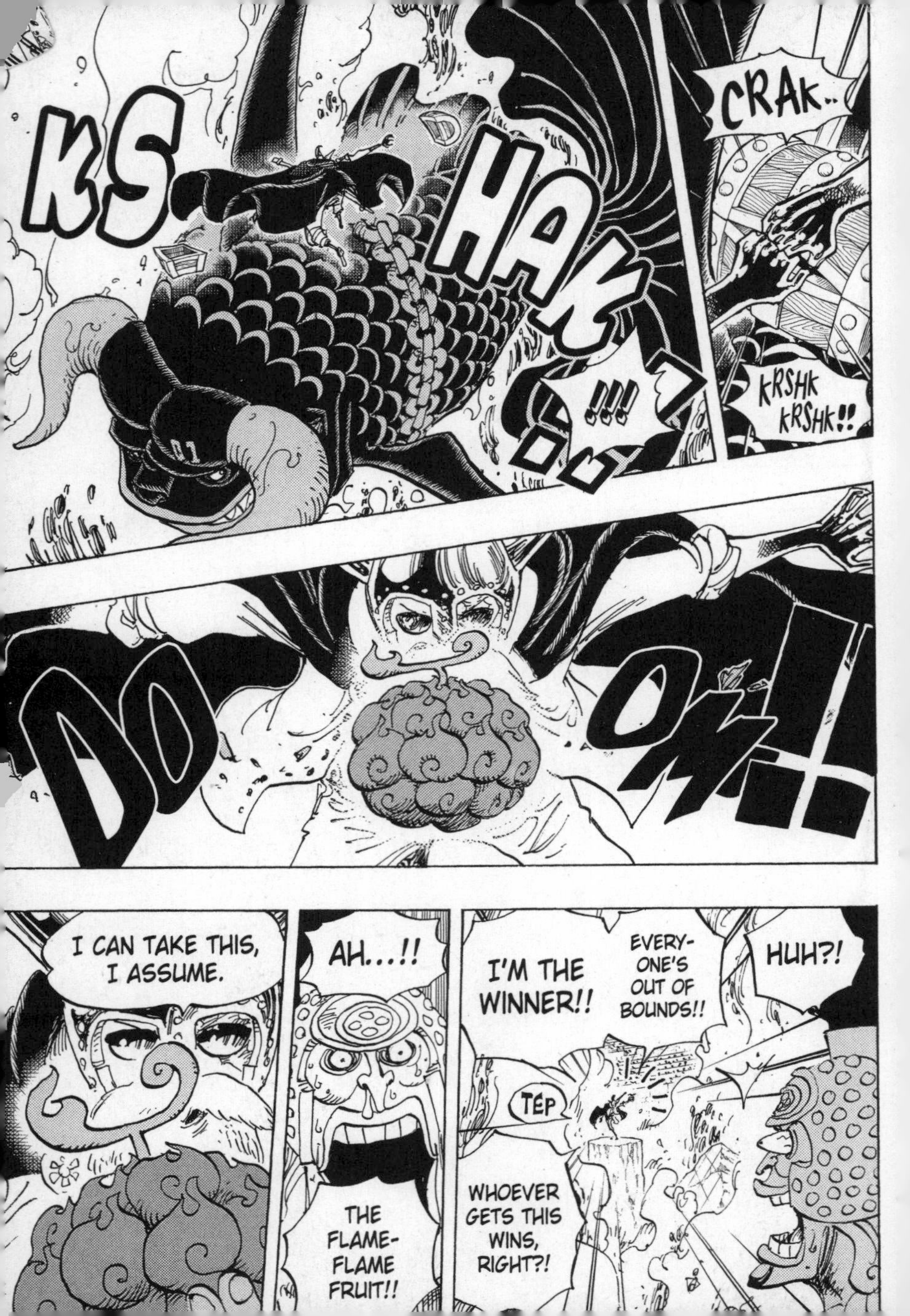
CRAK..
KRSHK KRSHK!!
KS-HAK!!!
DOOM!!
HUH?!
EVERY-ONE'S OUT OF BOUNDS!!
I'M THE WINNER!!
TEP
WHOEVER GETS THIS WINS, RIGHT?!
AH...!!
THE FLAME-FLAME FRUIT!!
I CAN TAKE THIS, I ASSUME.

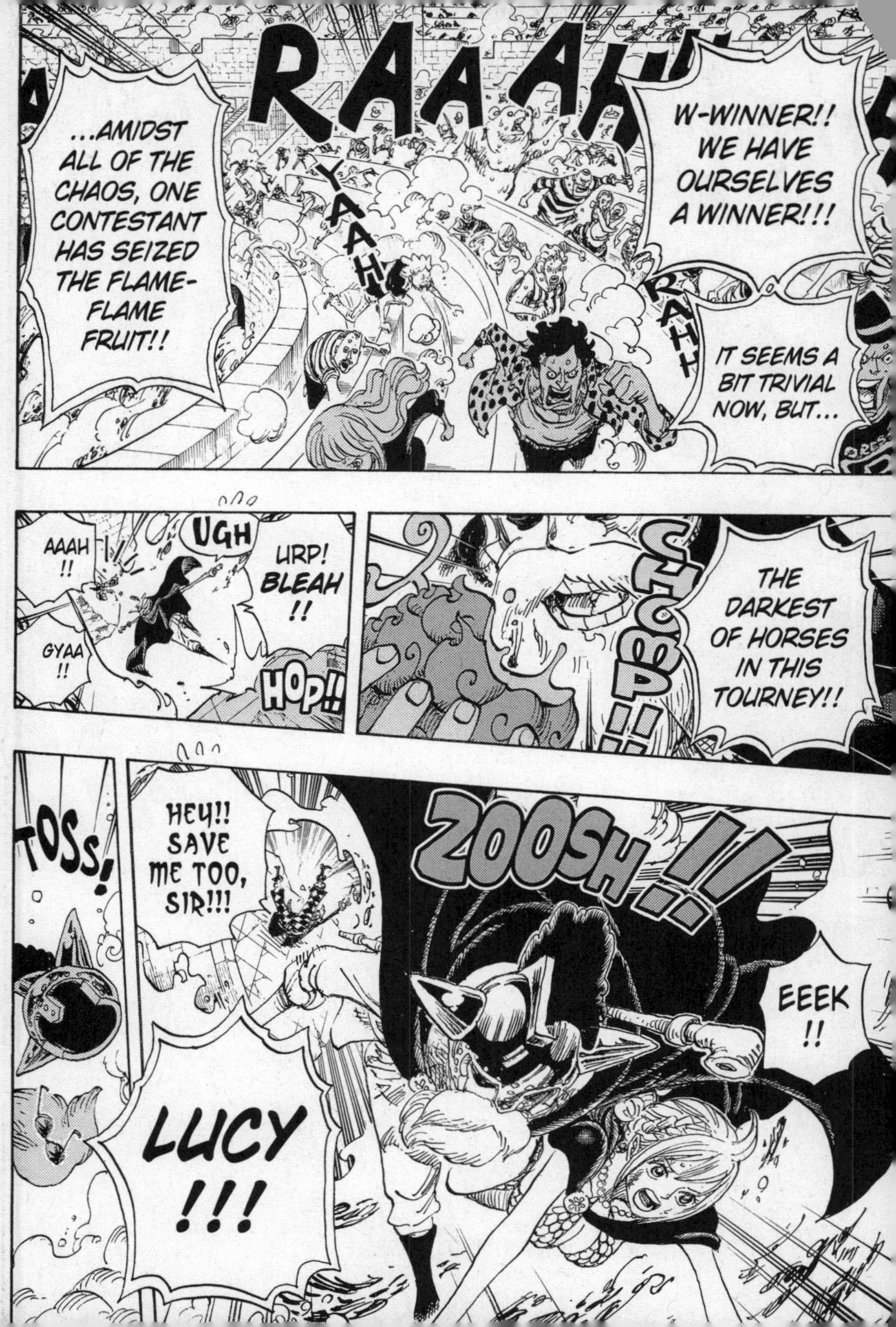
RAAAH
W-WINNER!! WE HAVE OURSELVES A WINNER!!!
IT SEEMS A BIT TRIVIAL NOW, BUT...
...AMIDST ALL OF THE CHAOS, ONE CONTESTANT HAS SEIZED THE FLAME-FLAME FRUIT!!
YAAAH
RAHH
THE DARKEST OF HORSES IN THIS TOURNEY!!
CHOMP!!
UGH
URP! BLEAH!!
AAAH!!
GYAA!!
HOP!!
ZOOSH!!!
EEEK!!
HEY!! SAVE ME TOO, SIR!!!
TOSS!
LUCY!!!

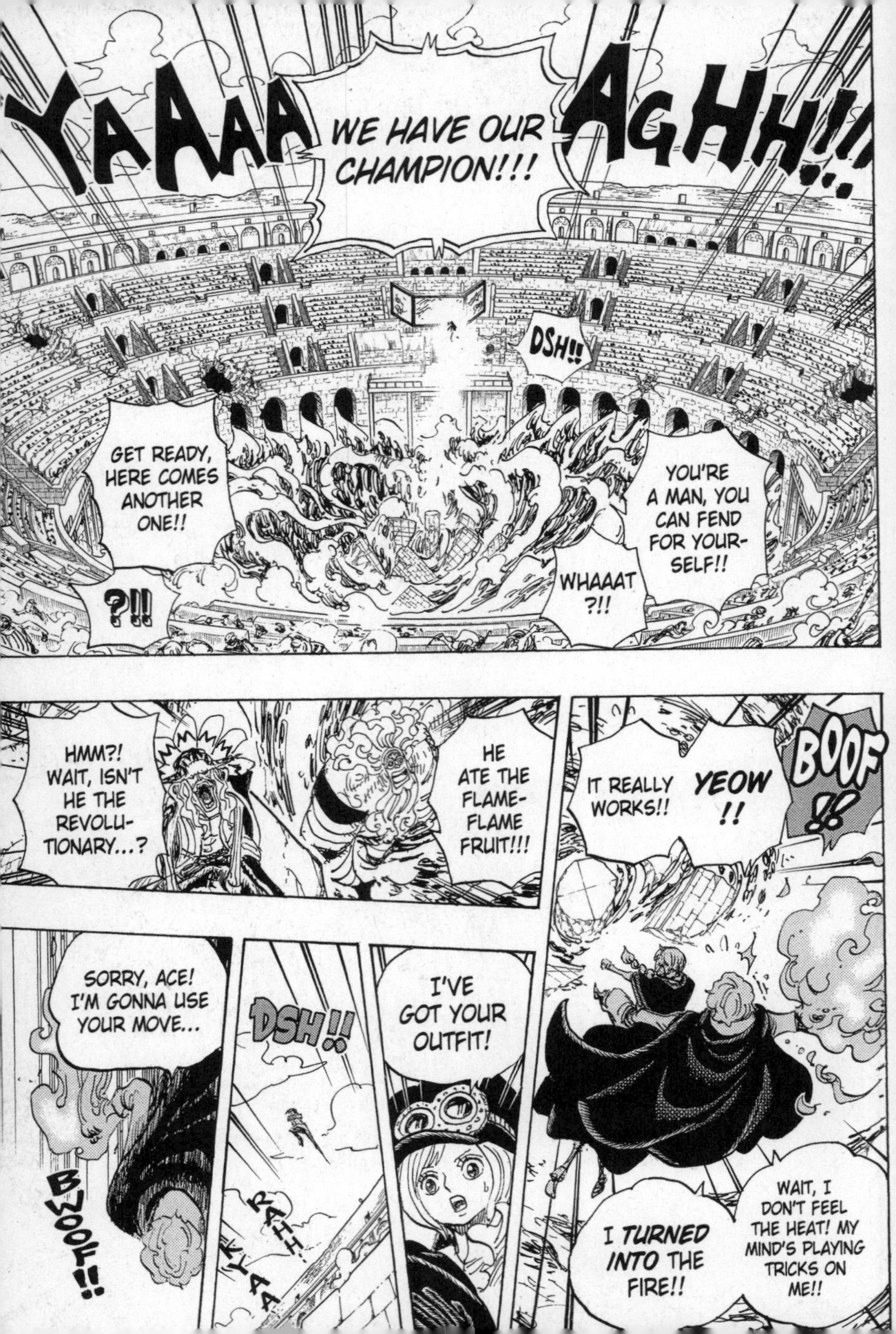

YAAAA
AGHH!!!
WE HAVE OUR CHAMPION!!!
DSH!!
YOU'RE A MAN, YOU CAN FEND FOR YOUR-SELF!!
WHAAAT?!!
GET READY, HERE COMES ANOTHER ONE!!
?!!
BOOF!!
YEOW!!
IT REALLY WORKS!!
WAIT, I DON'T FEEL THE HEAT! MY MIND'S PLAYING TRICKS ON ME!!
I TURNED INTO THE FIRE!!
HE ATE THE FLAME-FLAME FRUIT!!!
HMM?! WAIT, ISN'T HE THE REVOLU-TIONARY...?
I'VE GOT YOUR OUTFIT!
DSH!!
RAHH!
KYAA
SORRY, ACE! I'M GONNA USE YOUR MOVE...
BWOOF!!

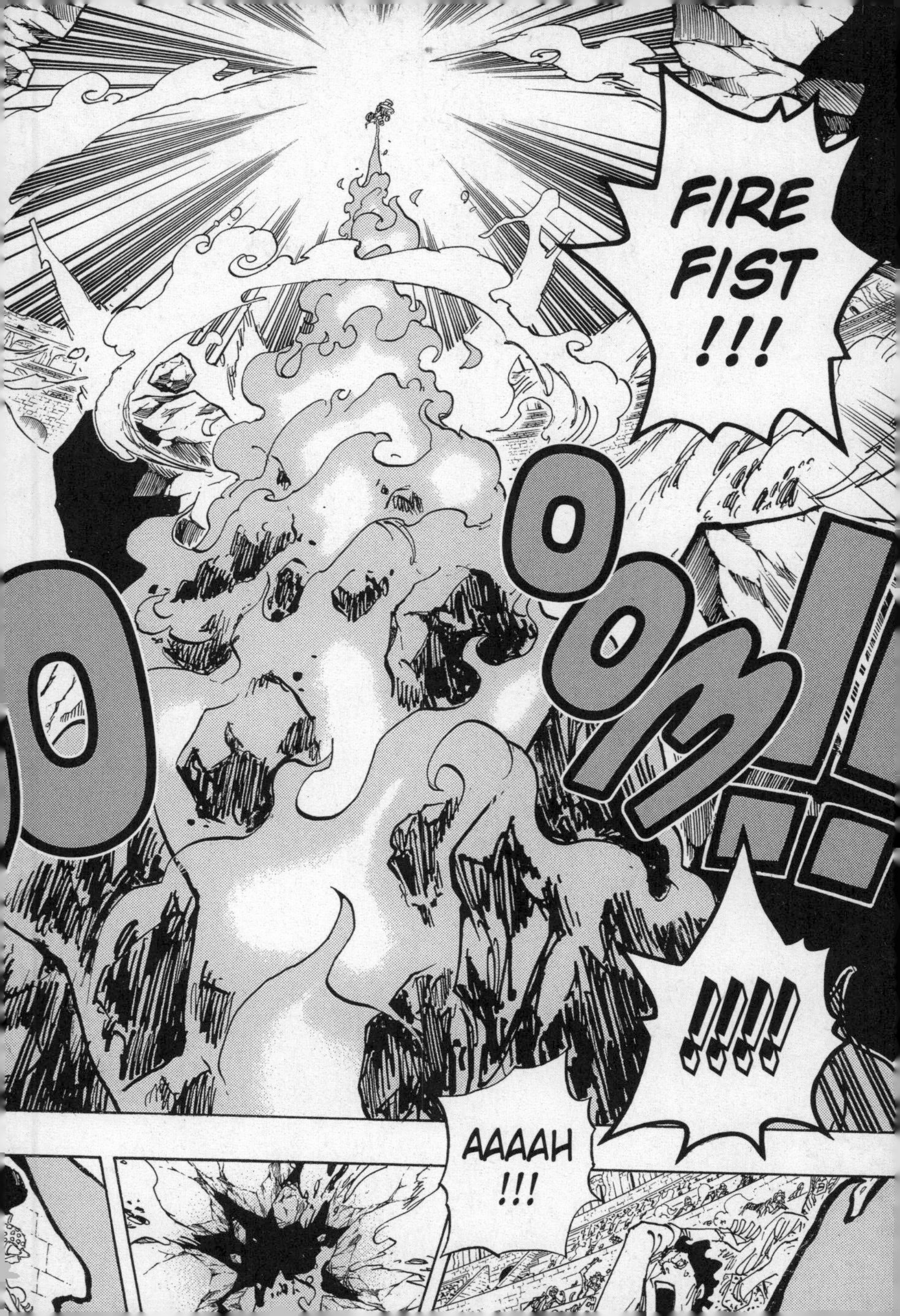
FIRE FIST !!!
!!!!
AAAAH !!!

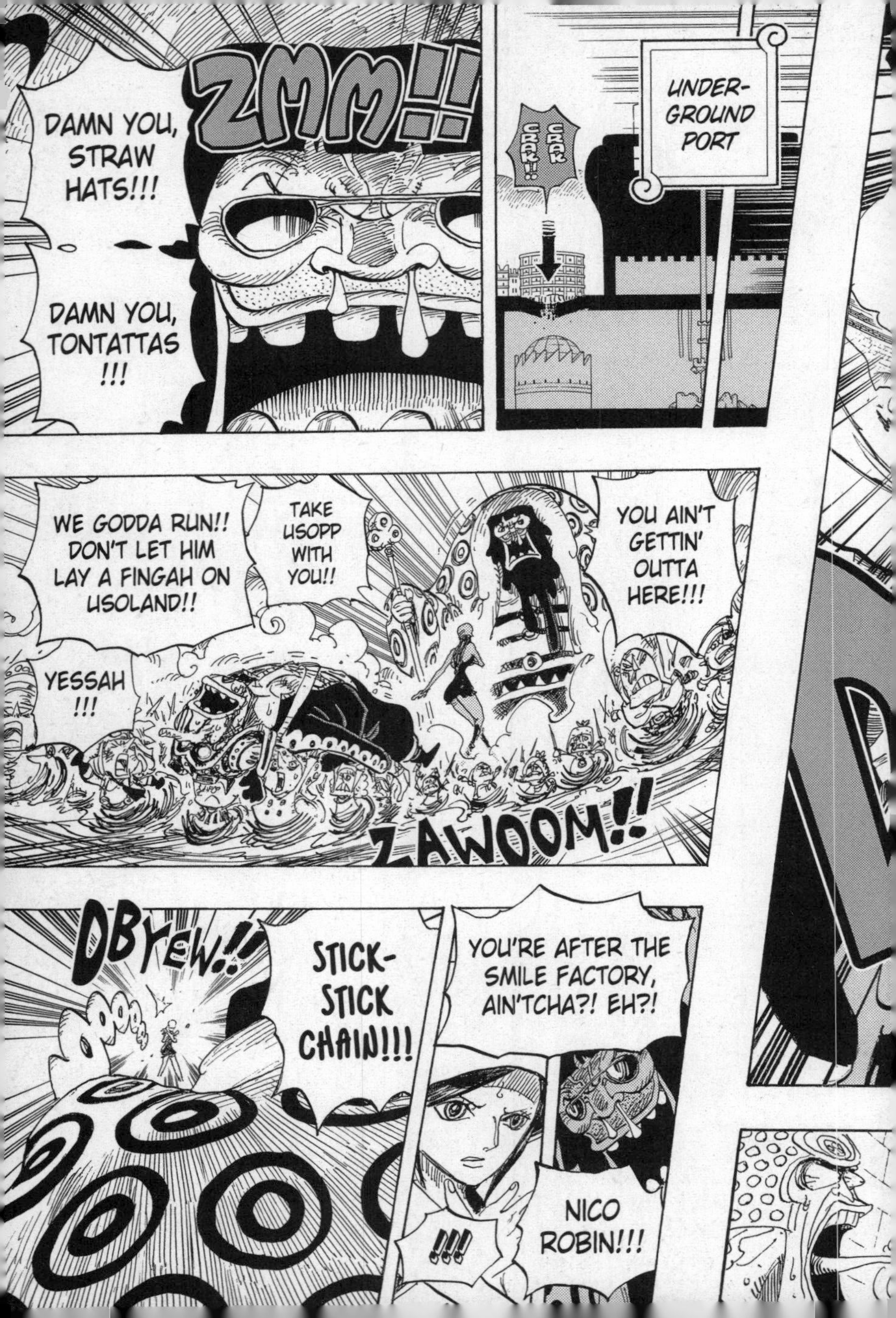
UNDER-GROUND PORT
CRAK CRAK!!
ZMM!!
DAMN YOU, STRAW HATS!!!
DAMN YOU, TONTATTAS !!!
YOU AIN'T GETTIN' OUTTA HERE!!!
TAKE USOPP WITH YOU!!
WE GODDA RUN!! DON'T LET HIM LAY A FINGAH ON USOLAND!!
YESSAH !!!
ZAWOOM!!
YOU'RE AFTER THE SMILE FACTORY, AIN'TCHA?! EH?!
NICO ROBIN!!!
!!!
STICK-STICK CHAIN!!!
DBYEW!!

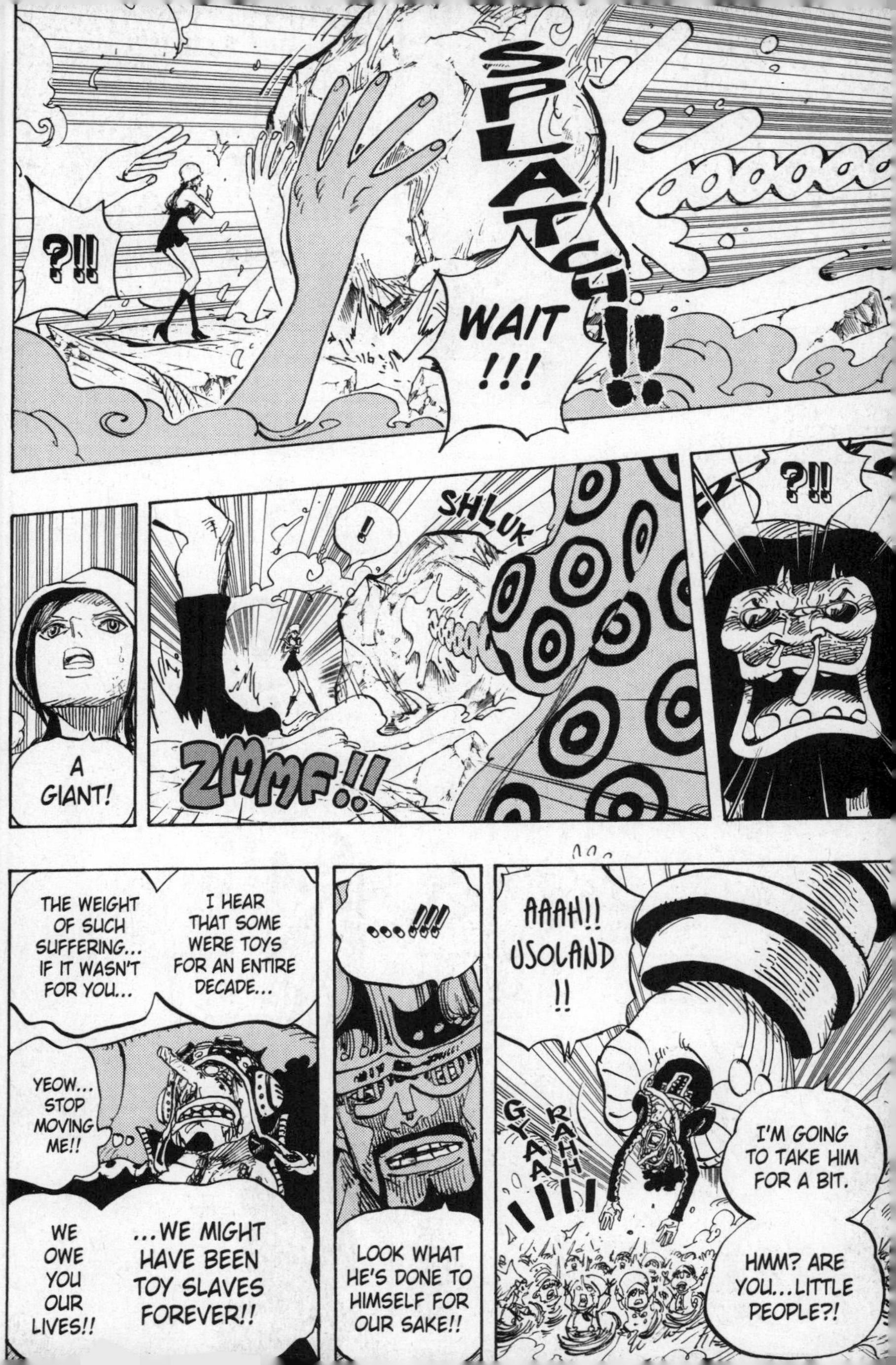
OOOOO
SPLATCH!!
WAIT !!!
?!!
?!!
SHLUK
!
ZMMF!!
A GIANT!
AAAH!! USOLAND !!
I'M GOING TO TAKE HIM FOR A BIT.
GYAAA RAHHH
HMM? ARE YOU...LITTLE PEOPLE?!
...!!!
LOOK WHAT HE'S DONE TO HIMSELF FOR OUR SAKE!!
I HEAR THAT SOME WERE TOYS FOR AN ENTIRE DECADE...
THE WEIGHT OF SUCH SUFFERING... IF IT WASN'T FOR YOU...
YEOW... STOP MOVING ME!!
...WE MIGHT HAVE BEEN TOY SLAVES FOREVER!!
WE OWE YOU OUR LIVES!!

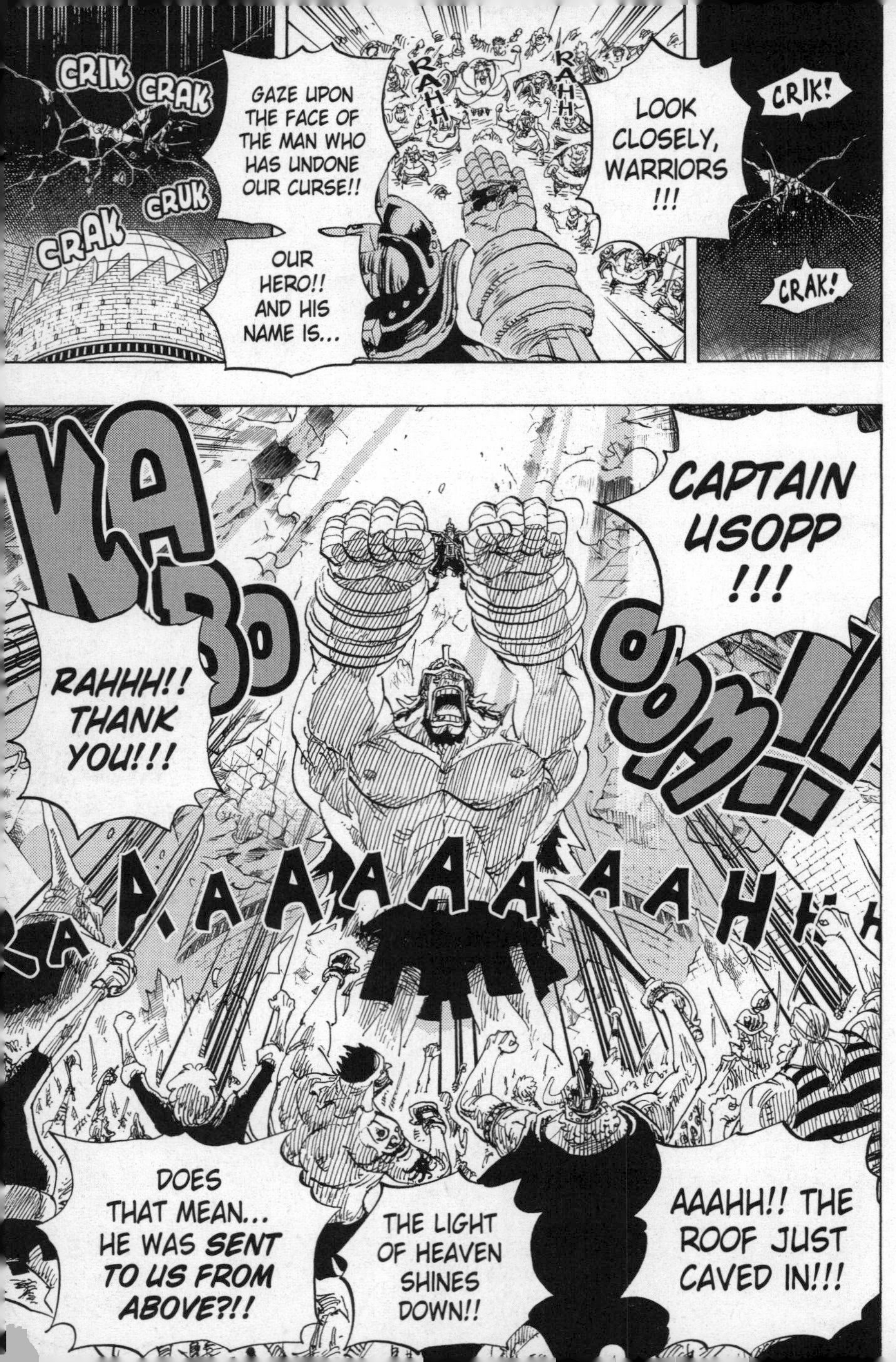
CRIK!
CRAK!
LOOK CLOSELY, WARRIORS!!!
RAHH
RAHH
GAZE UPON THE FACE OF THE MAN WHO HAS UNDONE OUR CURSE!!
OUR HERO!! AND HIS NAME IS...
CRIK CRAK
CRUK
CRAK
CAPTAIN USOPP!!!
KABOOOOM!!
RAHHH!! THANK YOU!!!
AAAAAAAAAAAH!!
AAAHH!! THE ROOF JUST CAVED IN!!!
THE LIGHT OF HEAVEN SHINES DOWN!!
DOES THAT MEAN... HE WAS SENT TO US FROM ABOVE?!!

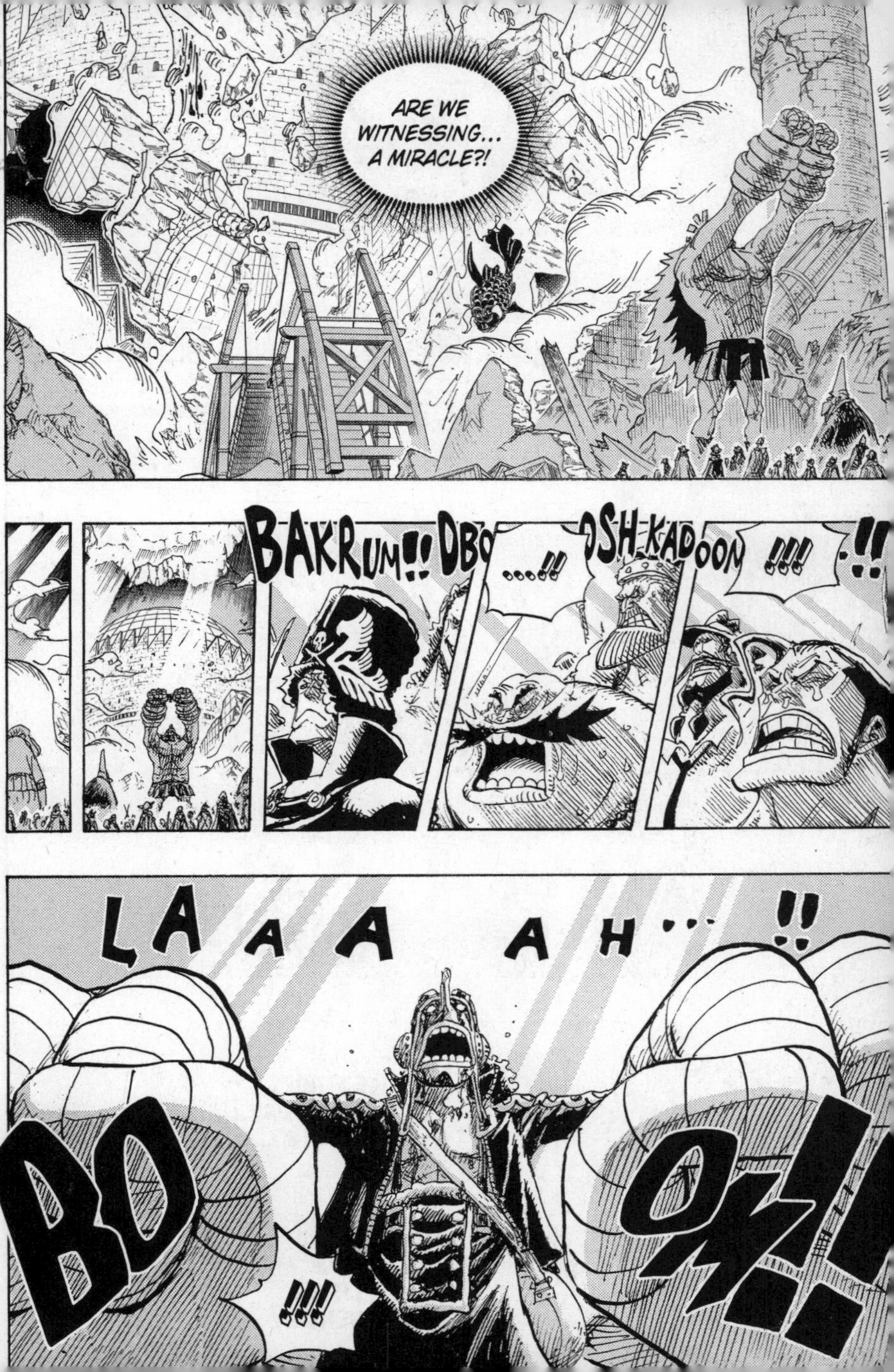

ARE WE WITNESSING... A MIRACLE?!
-!!
BAKRUM!! DBOOSH KADOON!!!
...!!
LAAAAH...!!
BO
OH!!
!!!

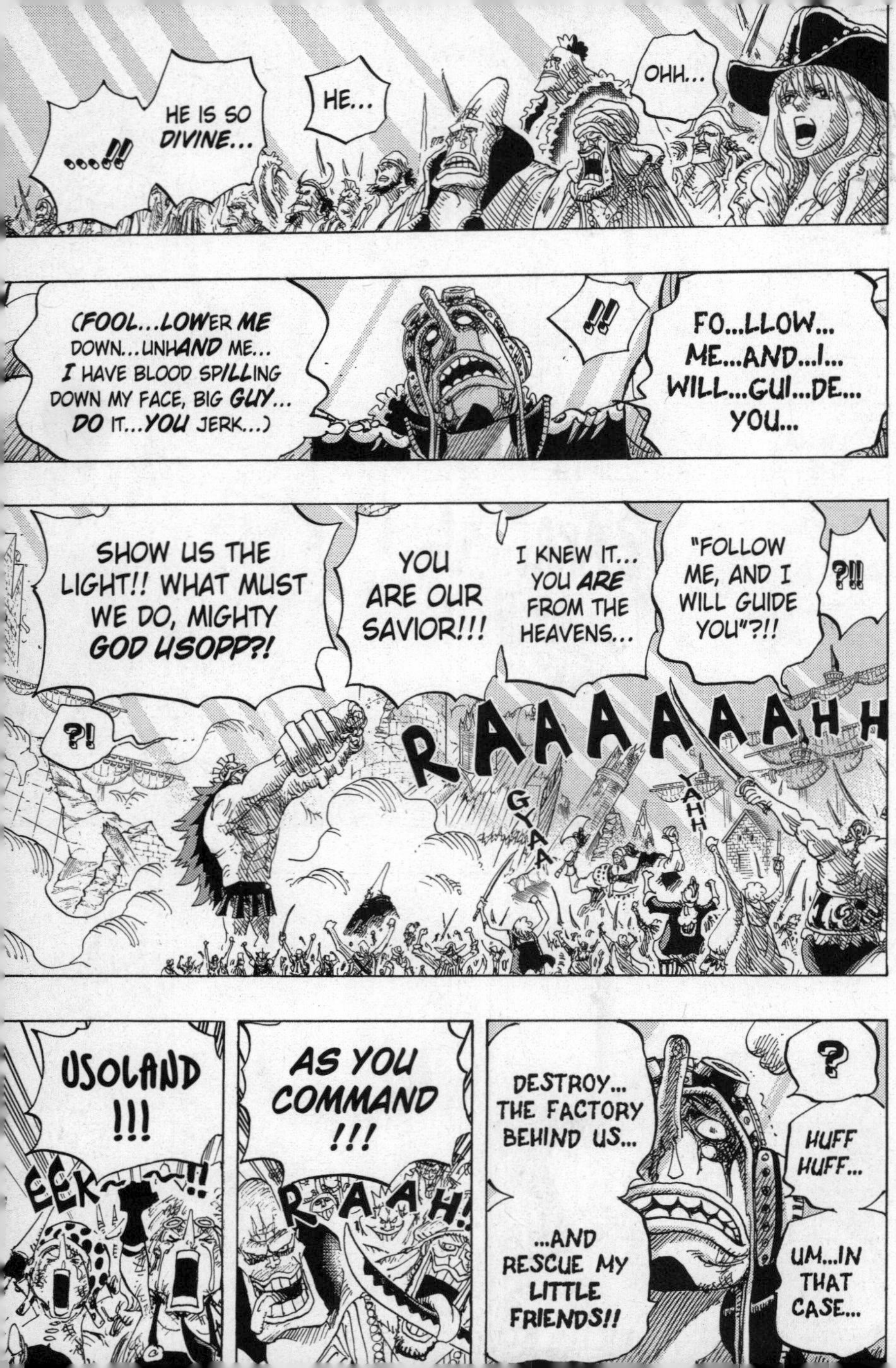
OHH...
HE...
HE IS SO DIVINE...
....!!
FO...LLOW... ME...AND...I... WILL...GUI...DE... YOU...
!!
(FOOL...LOWER ME DOWN...UNHAND ME... I HAVE BLOOD SPILLING DOWN MY FACE, BIG GUY... DO IT...YOU JERK...)
?!!
"FOLLOW ME, AND I WILL GUIDE YOU"?!!
I KNEW IT... YOU ARE FROM THE HEAVENS...
YOU ARE OUR SAVIOR!!!
SHOW US THE LIGHT!! WHAT MUST WE DO, MIGHTY GOD USOPP?!
?!
RAAAAAAHH
YAHH
GYAA
?
HUFF HUFF...
UM...IN THAT CASE...
DESTROY... THE FACTORY BEHIND US...
...AND RESCUE MY LITTLE FRIENDS!!
AS YOU COMMAND!!!
RAAH!!
USOLAND!!!
EEK~~~!!

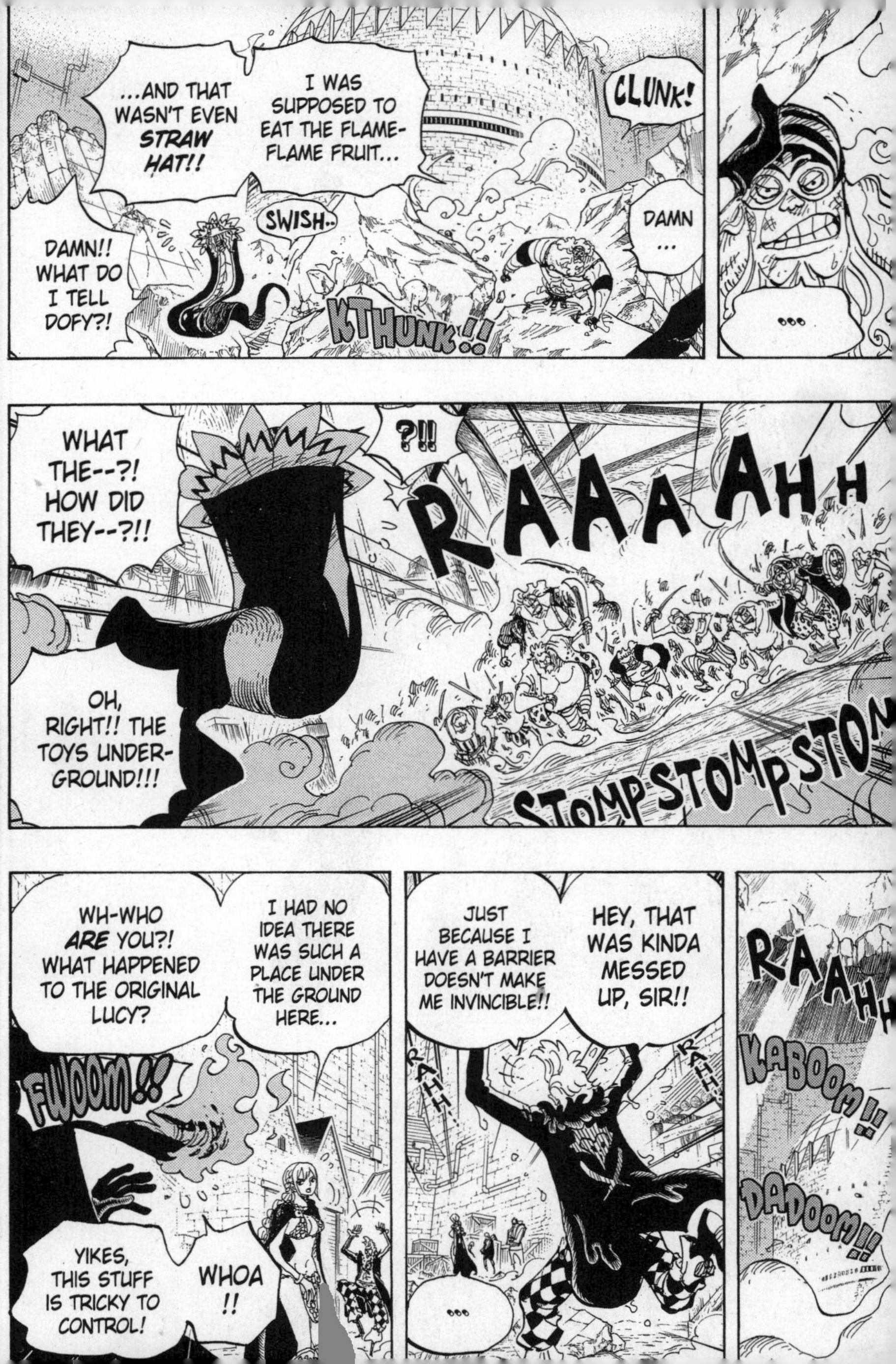
...
CLUNK!
DAMN ...
I WAS SUPPOSED TO EAT THE FLAME-FLAME FRUIT...
...AND THAT WASN'T EVEN STRAW HAT!!
SWISH..
DAMN!! WHAT DO I TELL DOFY?!
KTHUNK!!
?!!
RAAAAHH
WHAT THE--?! HOW DID THEY--?!!
STOMPSTOMPSTOM
OH, RIGHT!! THE TOYS UNDERGROUND!!!
RAAHH
KABOOM!!
DADOOM!!
HEY, THAT WAS KINDA MESSED UP, SIR!!
JUST BECAUSE I HAVE A BARRIER DOESN'T MAKE ME INVINCIBLE!!
RAHH
RAHH..
...
I HAD NO IDEA THERE WAS SUCH A PLACE UNDER THE GROUND HERE...
WH-WHO ARE YOU?! WHAT HAPPENED TO THE ORIGINAL LUCY?
FWOOM!!
WHOA !!
YIKES, THIS STUFF IS TRICKY TO CONTROL!

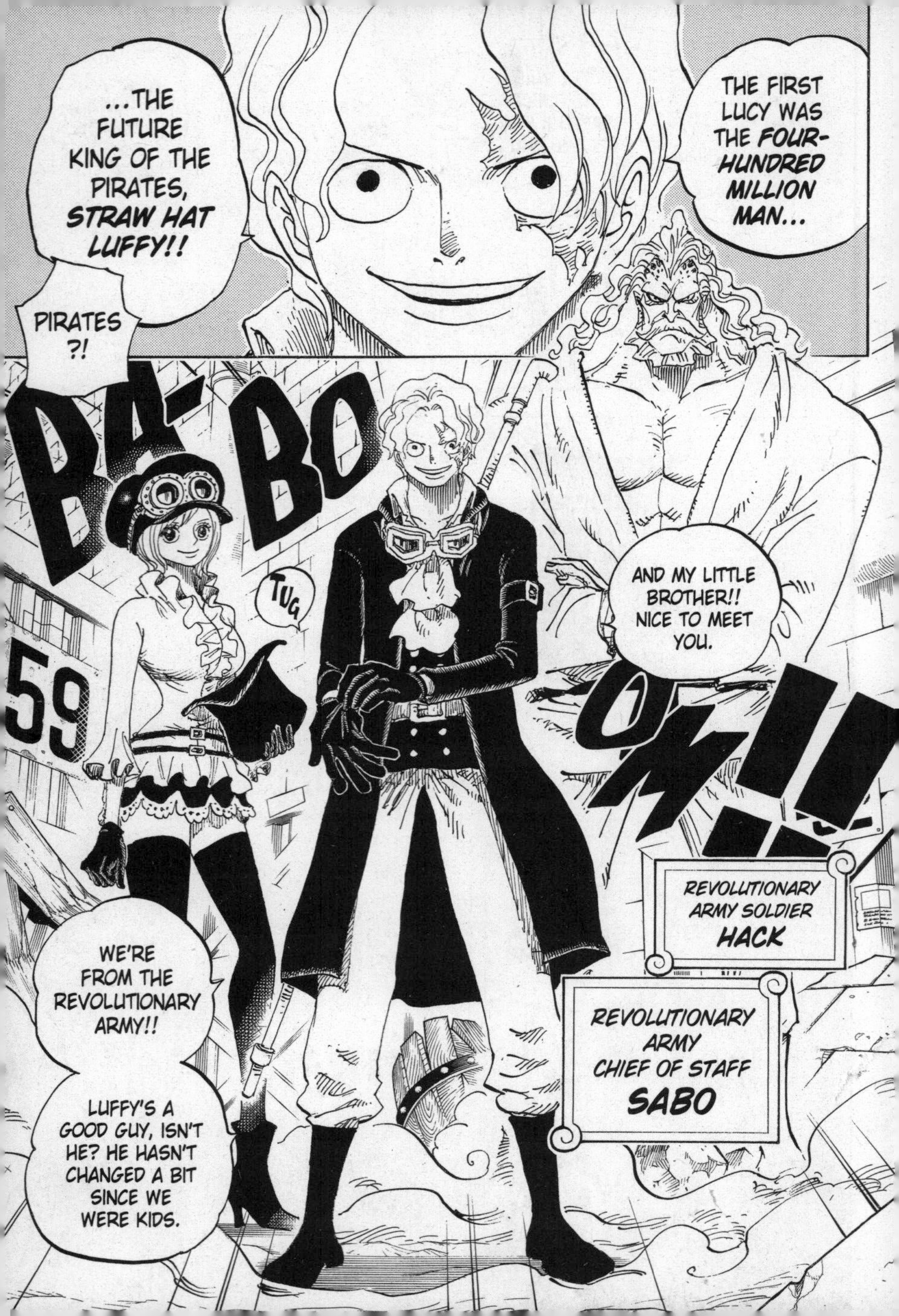
THE FIRST LUCY WAS THE FOUR-HUNDRED MILLION MAN...
...THE FUTURE KING OF THE PIRATES, STRAW HAT LUFFY!!
PIRATES ?!
BA-BO
OM!!
AND MY LITTLE BROTHER!! NICE TO MEET YOU.
REVOLUTIONARY ARMY SOLDIER HACK
REVOLUTIONARY ARMY CHIEF OF STAFF SABO
TUG
59
WE'RE FROM THE REVOLUTIONARY ARMY!!
LUFFY'S A GOOD GUY, ISN'T HE? HE HASN'T CHANGED A BIT SINCE WE WERE KIDS.

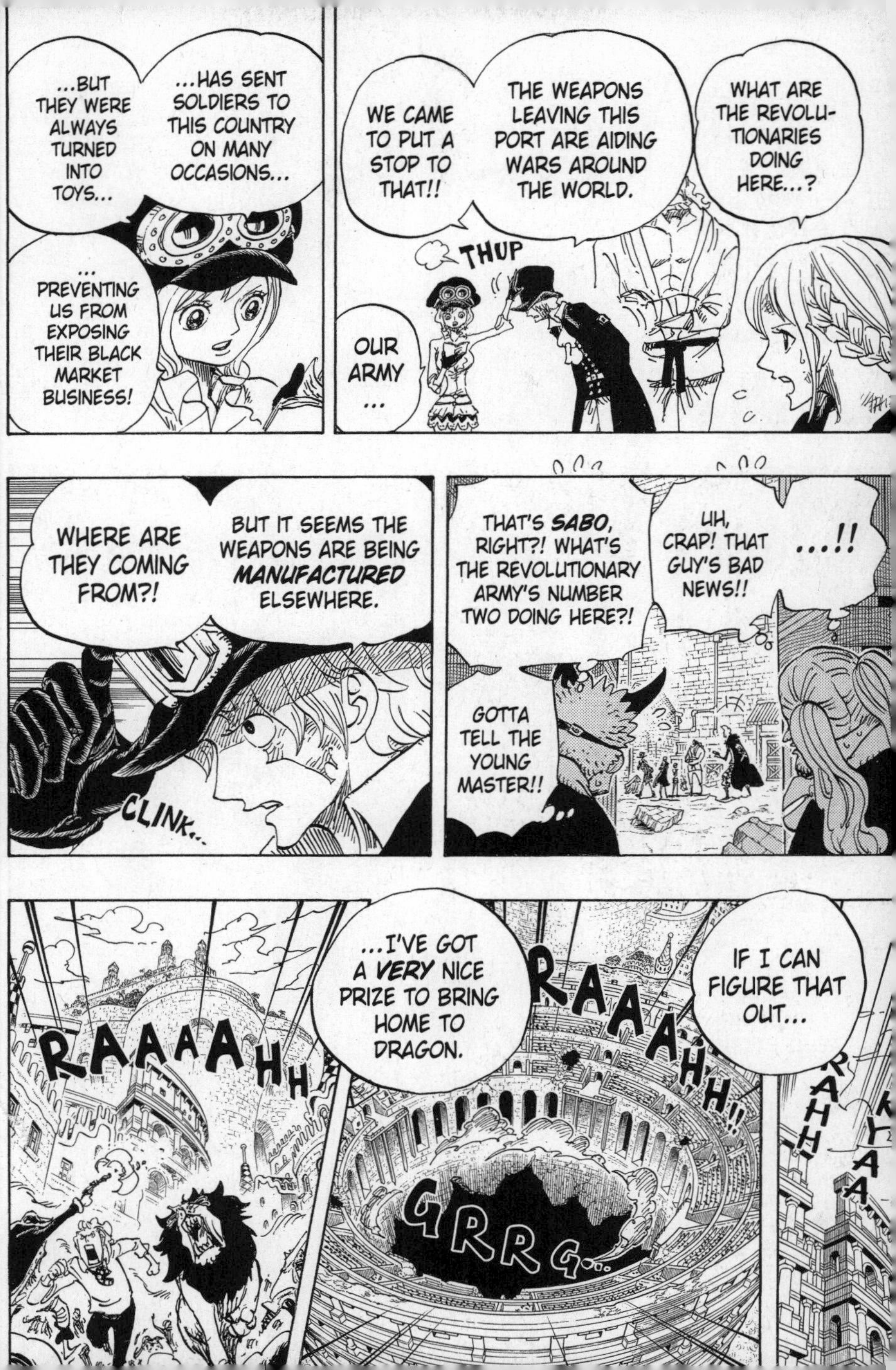
WHAT ARE THE REVOLUTIONARIES DOING HERE...?
THE WEAPONS LEAVING THIS PORT ARE AIDING WARS AROUND THE WORLD.
WE CAME TO PUT A STOP TO THAT!!
THUP
OUR ARMY ...
...HAS SENT SOLDIERS TO THIS COUNTRY ON MANY OCCASIONS...
...BUT THEY WERE ALWAYS TURNED INTO TOYS...
... PREVENTING US FROM EXPOSING THEIR BLACK MARKET BUSINESS!
...!!
UH, CRAP! THAT GUY'S BAD NEWS!!
THAT'S SABO, RIGHT?! WHAT'S THE REVOLUTIONARY ARMY'S NUMBER TWO DOING HERE?!
GOTTA TELL THE YOUNG MASTER!!
BUT IT SEEMS THE WEAPONS ARE BEING MANUFACTURED ELSEWHERE.
WHERE ARE THEY COMING FROM?!
CLINK...
IF I CAN FIGURE THAT OUT...
KYAAA
RAHHH
RAAAAHHH!!
...I'VE GOT A VERY NICE PRIZE TO BRING HOME TO DRAGON.
GRRG...
RAAAAHH

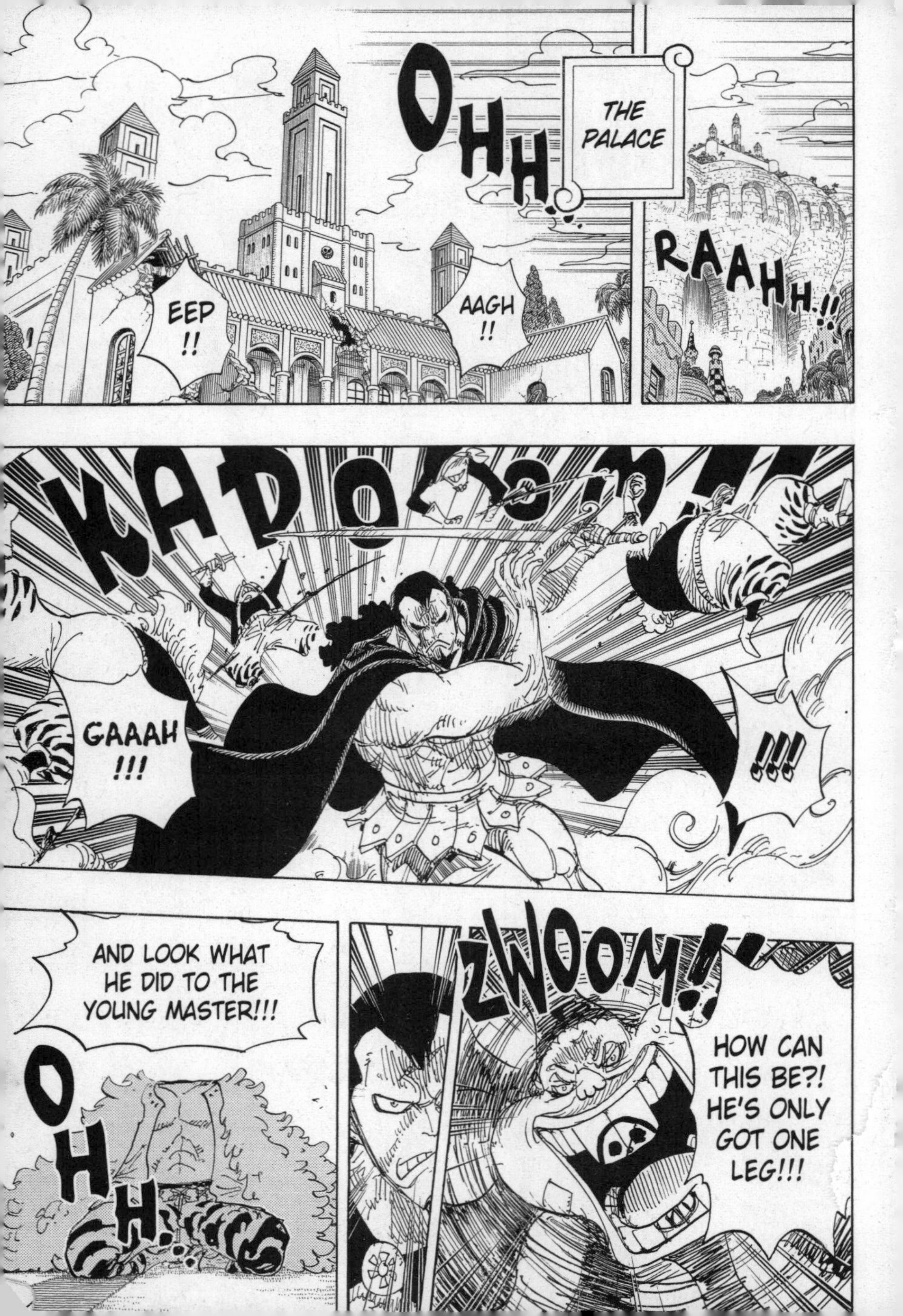
THE PALACE
RAAHH!!
OHH.
AAGH !!
EEP !!
KADO
!!!
GAAAH !!!
ZWOOM!!
HOW CAN THIS BE?! HE'S ONLY GOT ONE LEG!!!
AND LOOK WHAT HE DID TO THE YOUNG MASTER!!!
OHH.

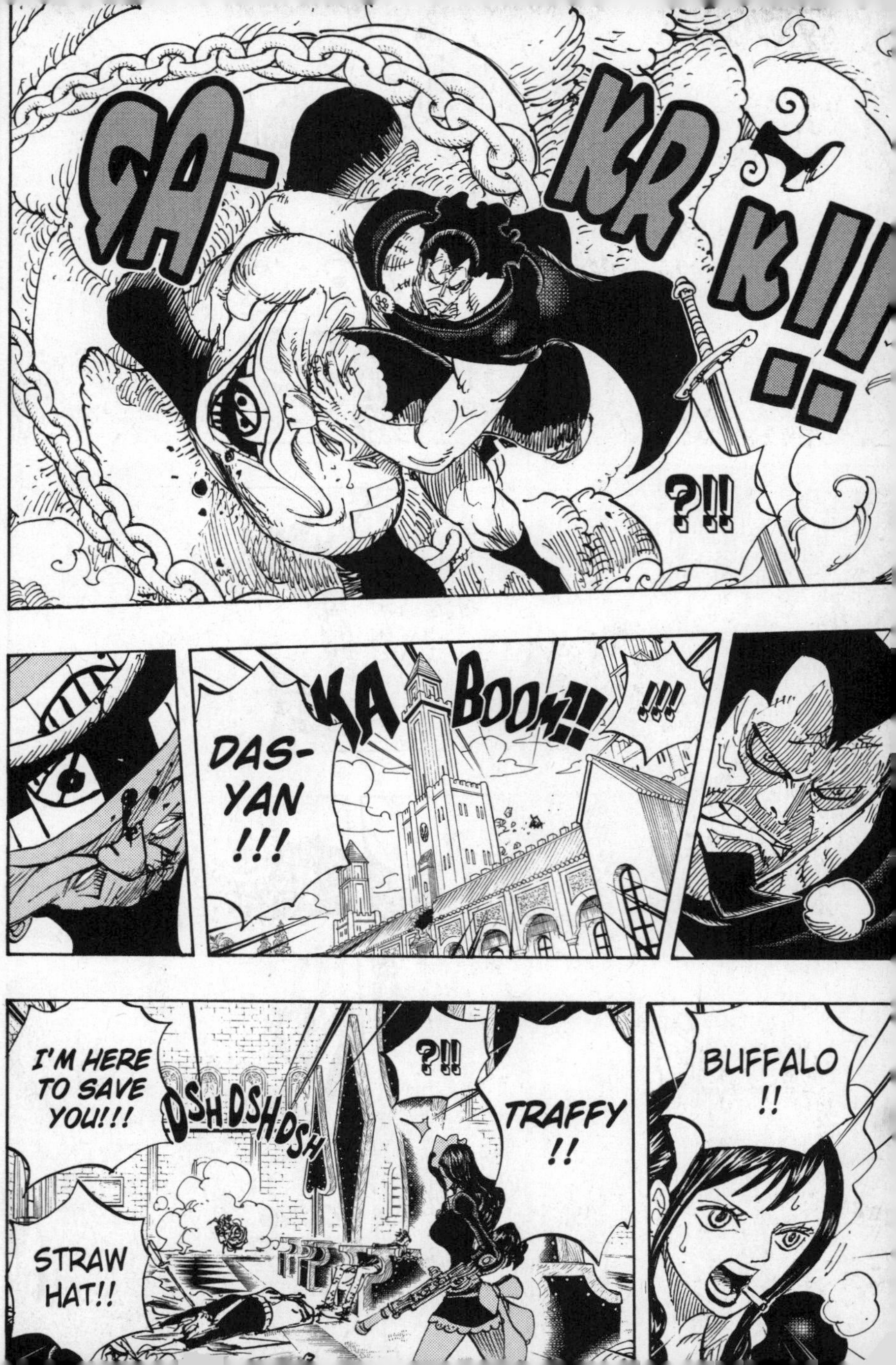
GA-KRAK!!
?!!
!!!
KA BOOM!!
DAS-YAN!!!
BUFFALO!!
?!!
TRAFFY!!
DSH DSH DSH
I'M HERE TO SAVE YOU!!!
STRAW HAT!!

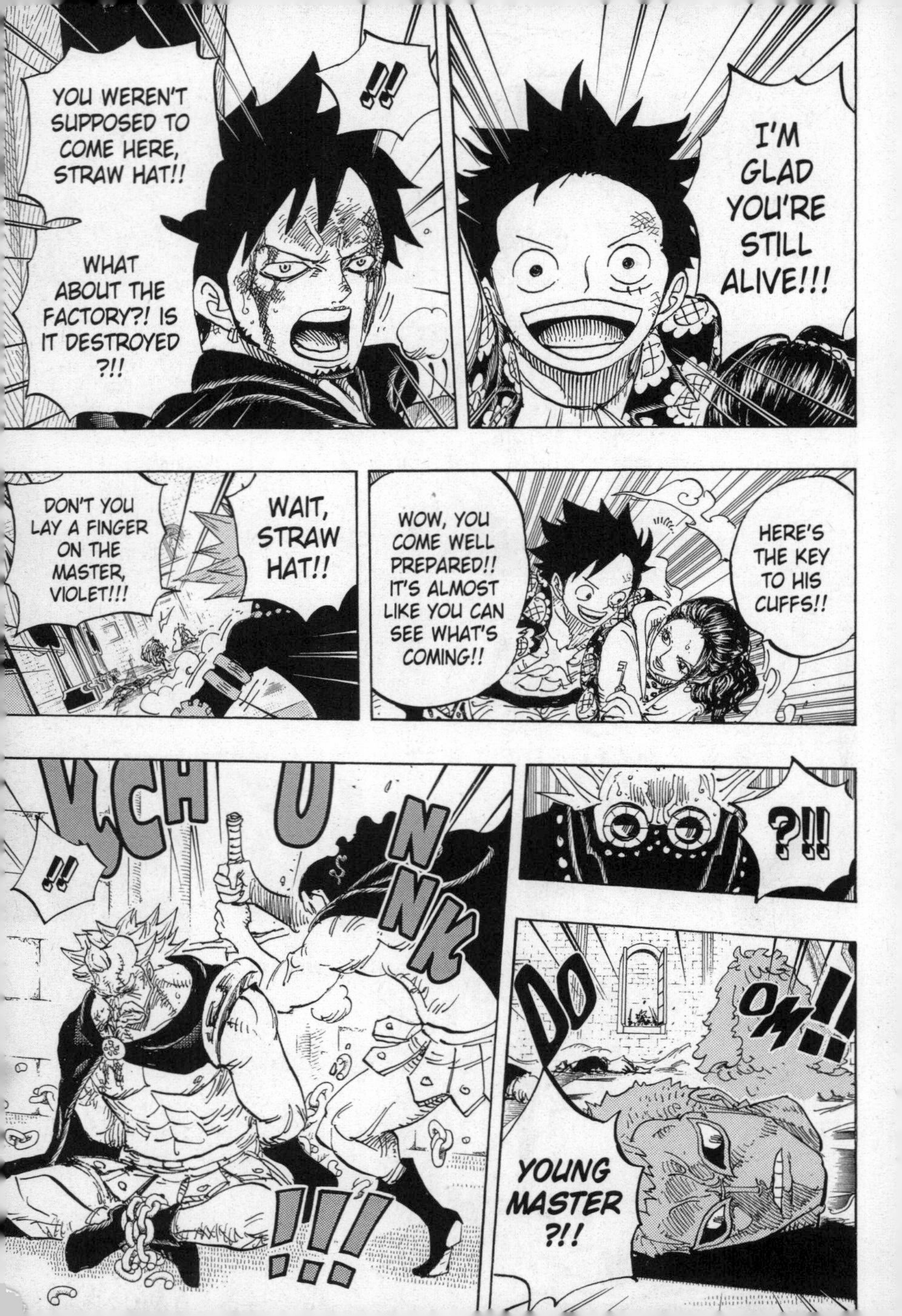
I'M GLAD YOU'RE STILL ALIVE!!!
!!
YOU WEREN'T SUPPOSED TO COME HERE, STRAW HAT!!
WHAT ABOUT THE FACTORY?! IS IT DESTROYED ?!!
HERE'S THE KEY TO HIS CUFFS!!
WOW, YOU COME WELL PREPARED!! IT'S ALMOST LIKE YOU CAN SEE WHAT'S COMING!!
WAIT, STRAW HAT!!
DON'T YOU LAY A FINGER ON THE MASTER, VIOLET!!!
?!!
DOOM!!
YOUNG MASTER ?!!
CH
U
NNK
!!
!!!

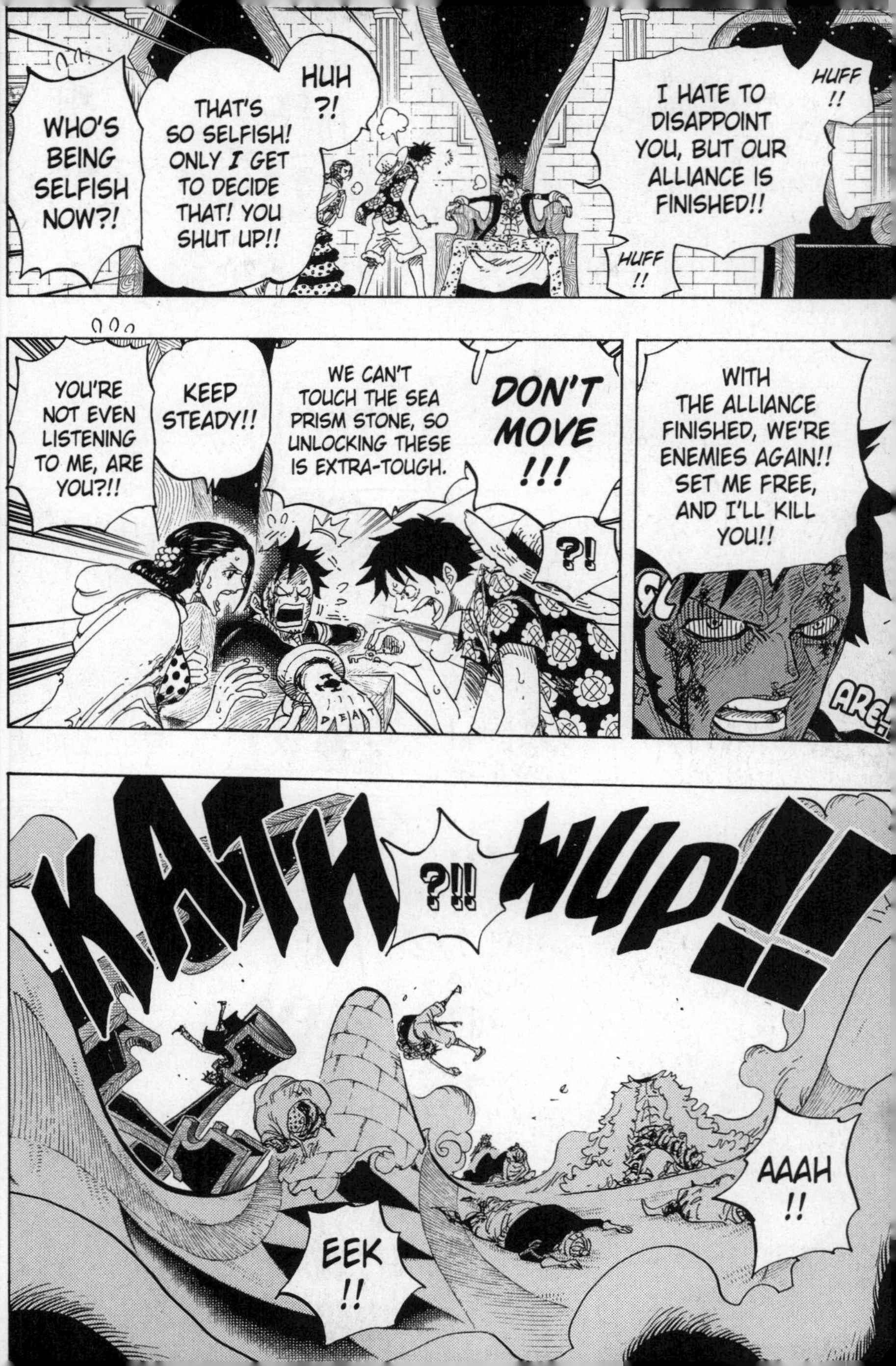
HUFF !!
I HATE TO DISAPPOINT YOU, BUT OUR ALLIANCE IS FINISHED!!
HUFF !!
HUH ?!
THAT'S SO SELFISH! ONLY I GET TO DECIDE THAT! YOU SHUT UP!!
WHO'S BEING SELFISH NOW?!
WITH THE ALLIANCE FINISHED, WE'RE ENEMIES AGAIN!! SET ME FREE, AND I'LL KILL YOU!!
GU
ARE-
DON'T MOVE !!!
?!
WE CAN'T TOUCH THE SEA PRISM STONE, SO UNLOCKING THESE IS EXTRA-TOUGH.
KEEP STEADY!!
YOU'RE NOT EVEN LISTENING TO ME, ARE YOU?!!
KATH WUP!!
?!!
AAAH !!
EEK !!

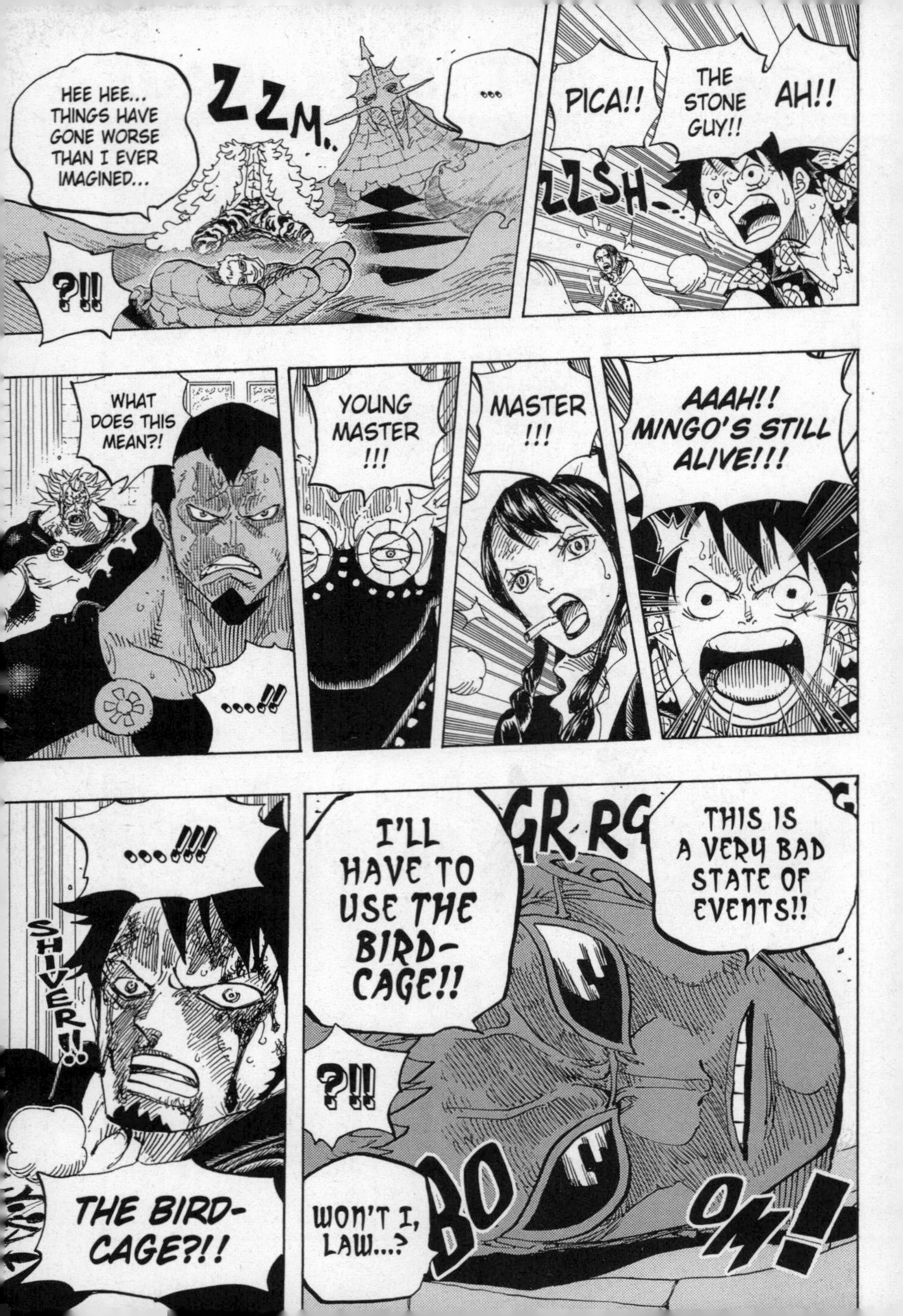
AH!!
THE STONE GUY!!
PICA!!
ZZSH
...
ZZM..
HEE HEE... THINGS HAVE GONE WORSE THAN I EVER IMAGINED...
?!!
AAAH!! MINGO'S STILL ALIVE!!!
MASTER !!!
YOUNG MASTER !!!
WHAT DOES THIS MEAN?!
...!!
THIS IS A VERY BAD STATE OF EVENTS!!
GR RG
I'LL HAVE TO USE THE BIRD-CAGE!!
?!!
BOOM!!
WON'T I, LAW...?
...!!!
SHIVER!!
THE BIRD-CAGE?!!

Chapter 745: THE BIRDCAGE

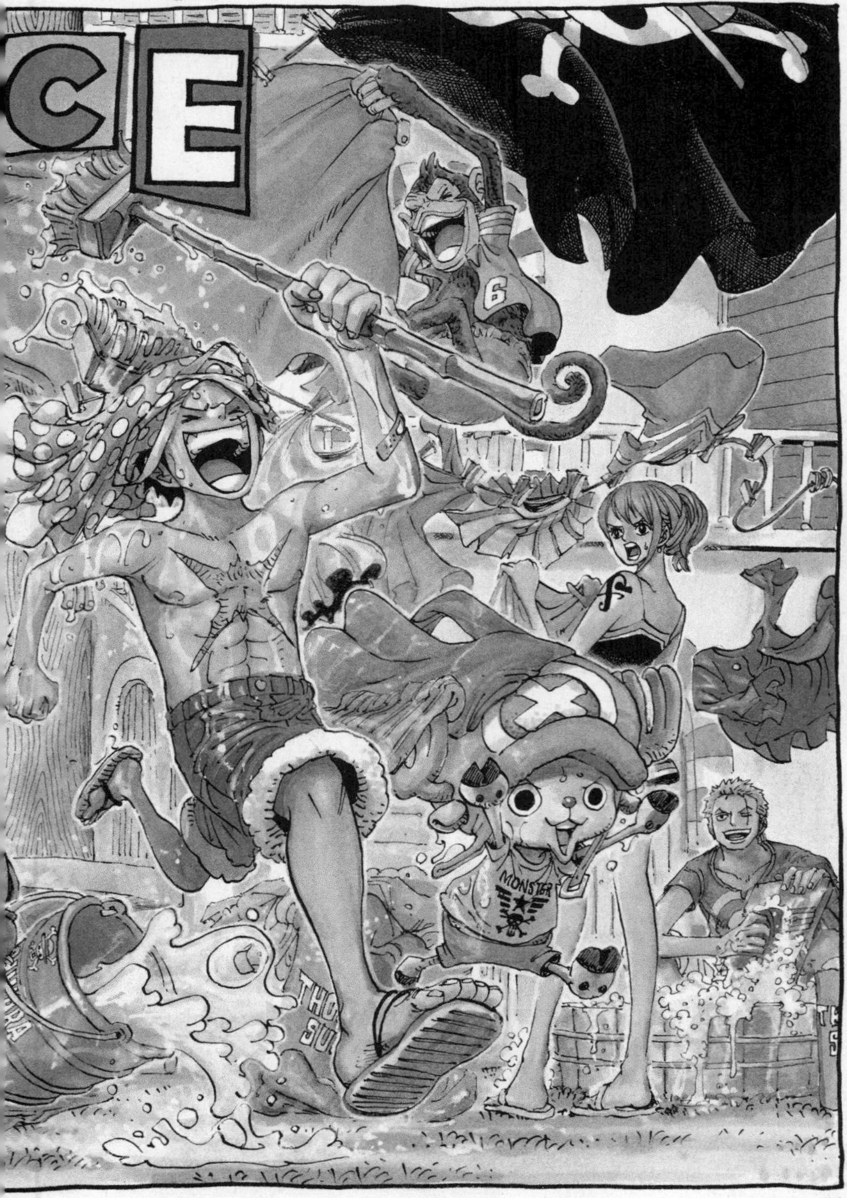
CE
MONSTER

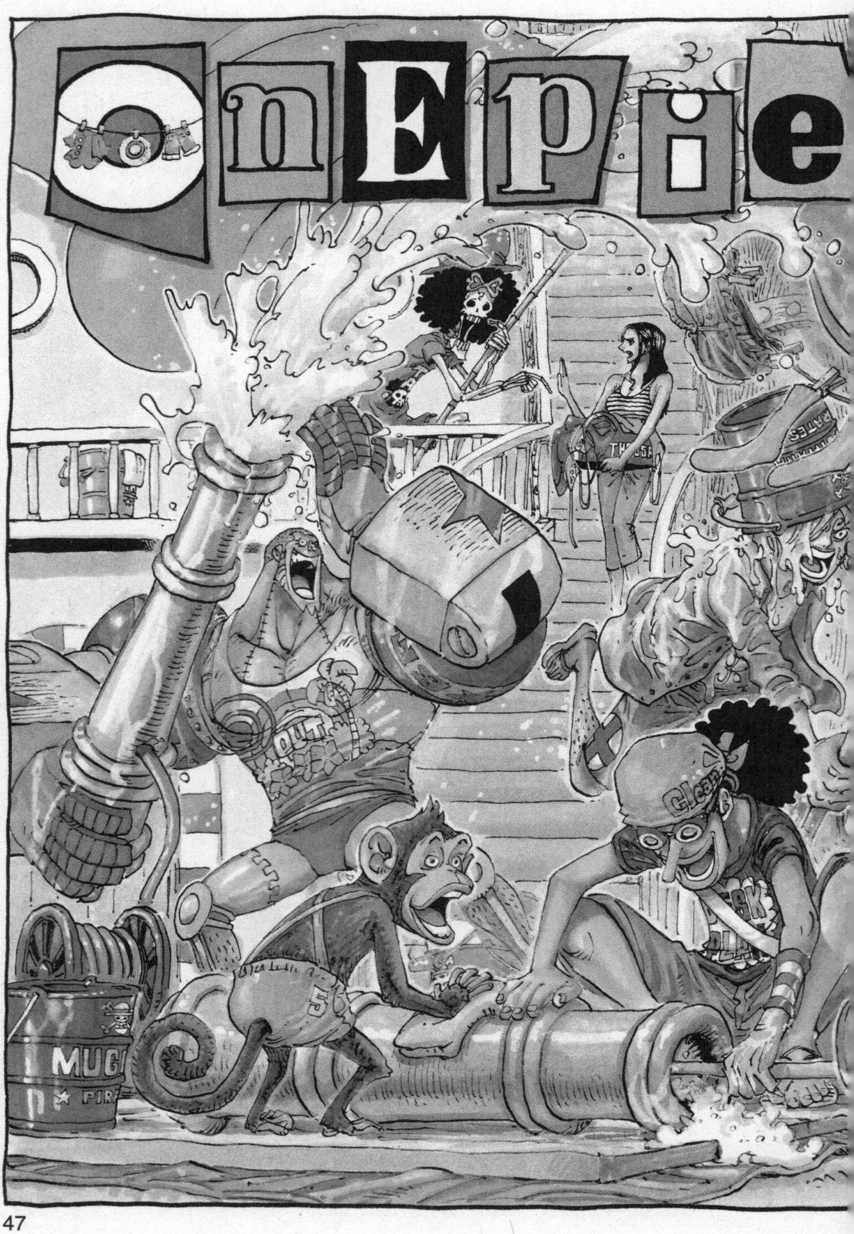
OnEPie
OUT
Clean
MUG
PIR

vol. 75

ONE PIECE

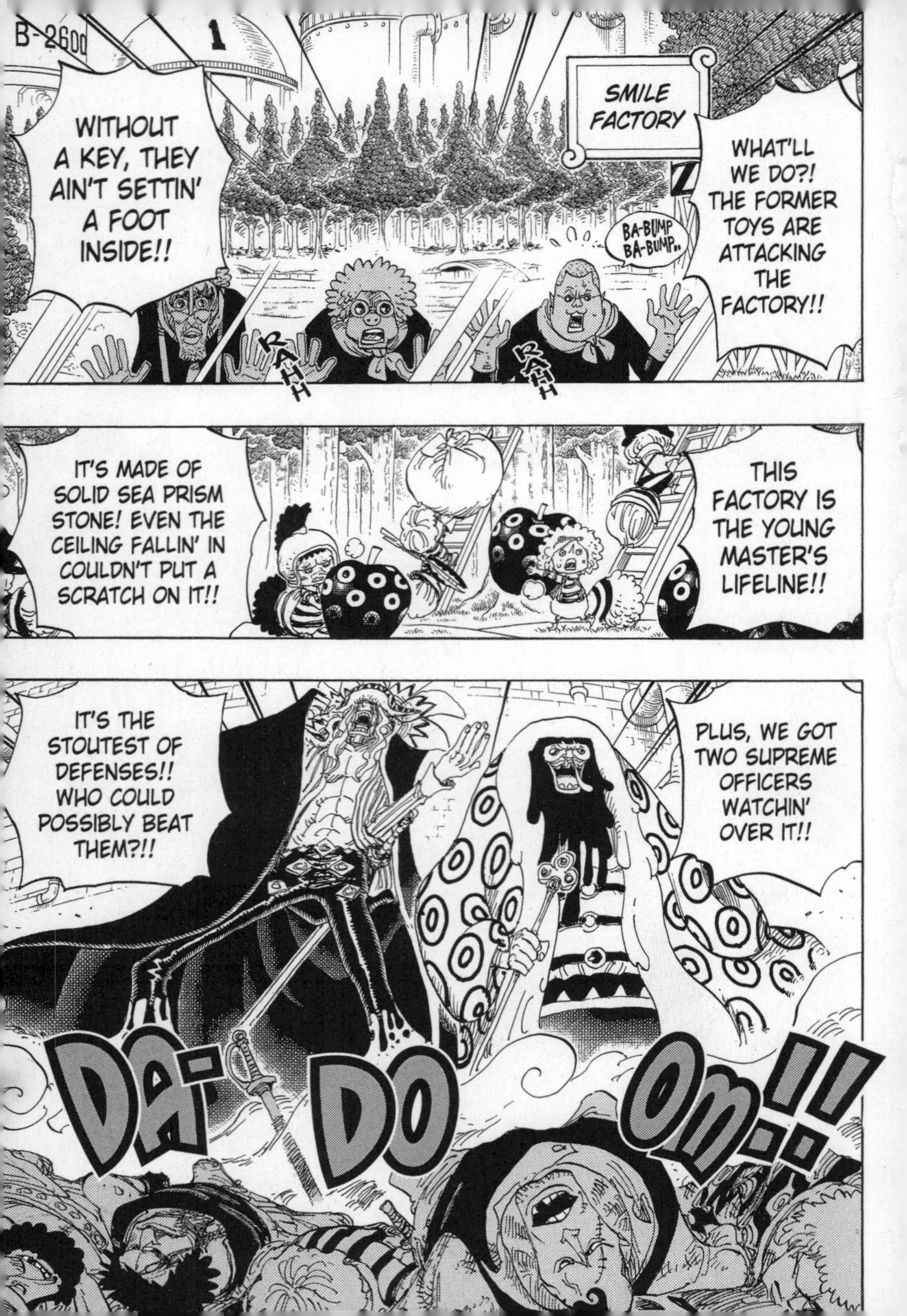
B-2600
1
SMILE FACTORY
WHAT'LL WE DO?! THE FORMER TOYS ARE ATTACKING THE FACTORY!!
BA-BUMP BA-BUMP..
WITHOUT A KEY, THEY AIN'T SETTIN' A FOOT INSIDE!!
RAHH
RAHH
THIS FACTORY IS THE YOUNG MASTER'S LIFELINE!!
IT'S MADE OF SOLID SEA PRISM STONE! EVEN THE CEILING FALLIN' IN COULDN'T PUT A SCRATCH ON IT!!
PLUS, WE GOT TWO SUPREME OFFICERS WATCHIN' OVER IT!!
IT'S THE STOUTEST OF DEFENSES!! WHO COULD POSSIBLY BEAT THEM?!!
DA-DOOM!!

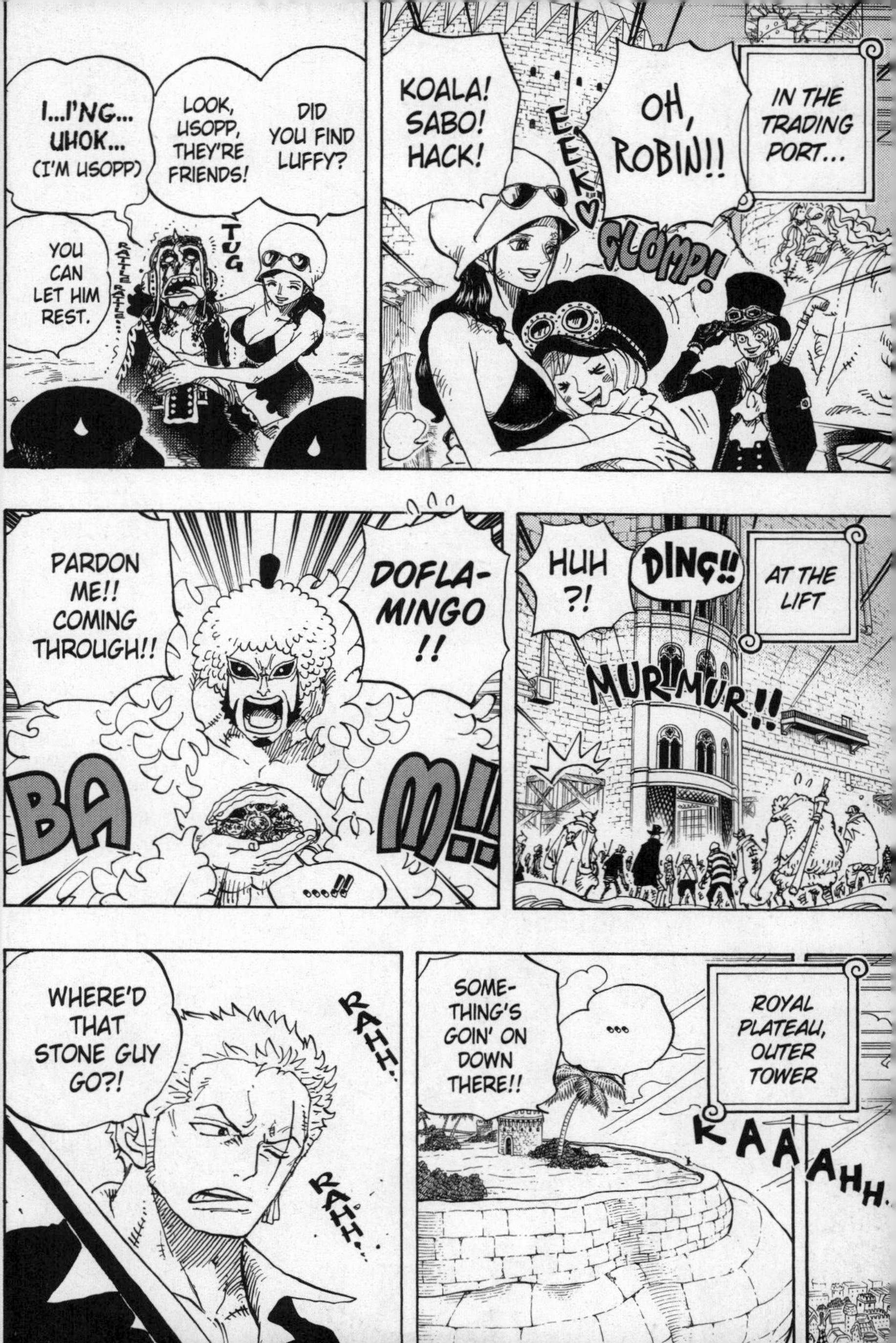
IN THE TRADING PORT...
OH, ROBIN!!
EEK♥
KOALA! SABO! HACK!
GLOMP!
DID YOU FIND LUFFY?
LOOK, USOPP, THEY'RE FRIENDS!
TUG
I...I'NG... UHOK... (I'M USOPP)
RATTLE RATTLE
YOU CAN LET HIM REST.
AT THE LIFT
DING!!
HUH ?!
MURMUR!!
DOFLA-MINGO !!
PARDON ME!! COMING THROUGH!!
BAM!!
...!!
ROYAL PLATEAU, OUTER TOWER
KAAAAHH..
...
SOME-THING'S GOIN' ON DOWN THERE!!
WHERE'D THAT STONE GUY GO?!
RAHH..
RAHH..

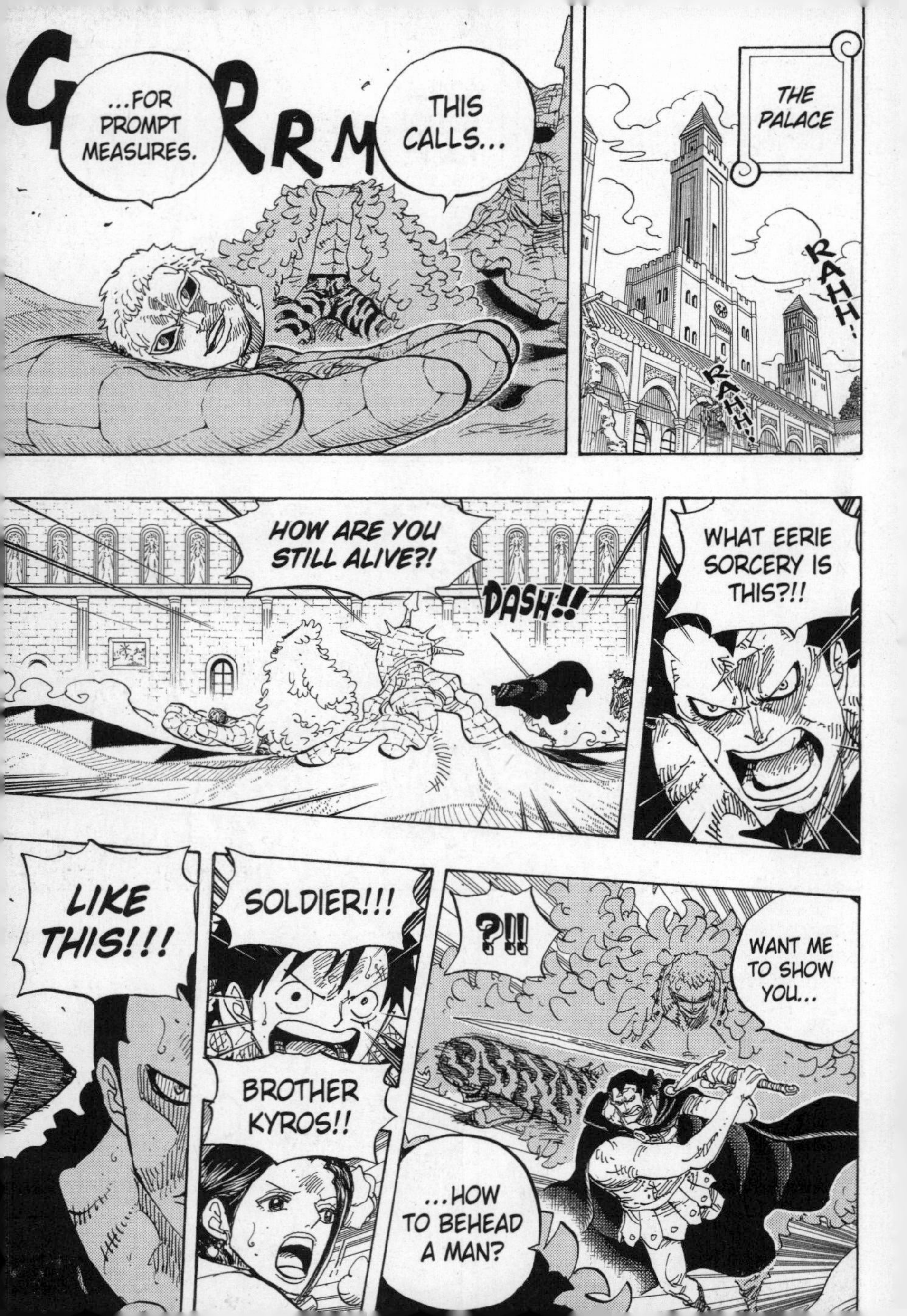
THE PALACE
RAHH!
RAHH!
THIS CALLS...
GRRM
...FOR PROMPT MEASURES.
WHAT EERIE SORCERY IS THIS?!!
HOW ARE YOU STILL ALIVE?!
DASH!!
WANT ME TO SHOW YOU...
?!!
...HOW TO BEHEAD A MAN?
SOLDIER!!!
BROTHER KYROS!!
LIKE THIS!!!

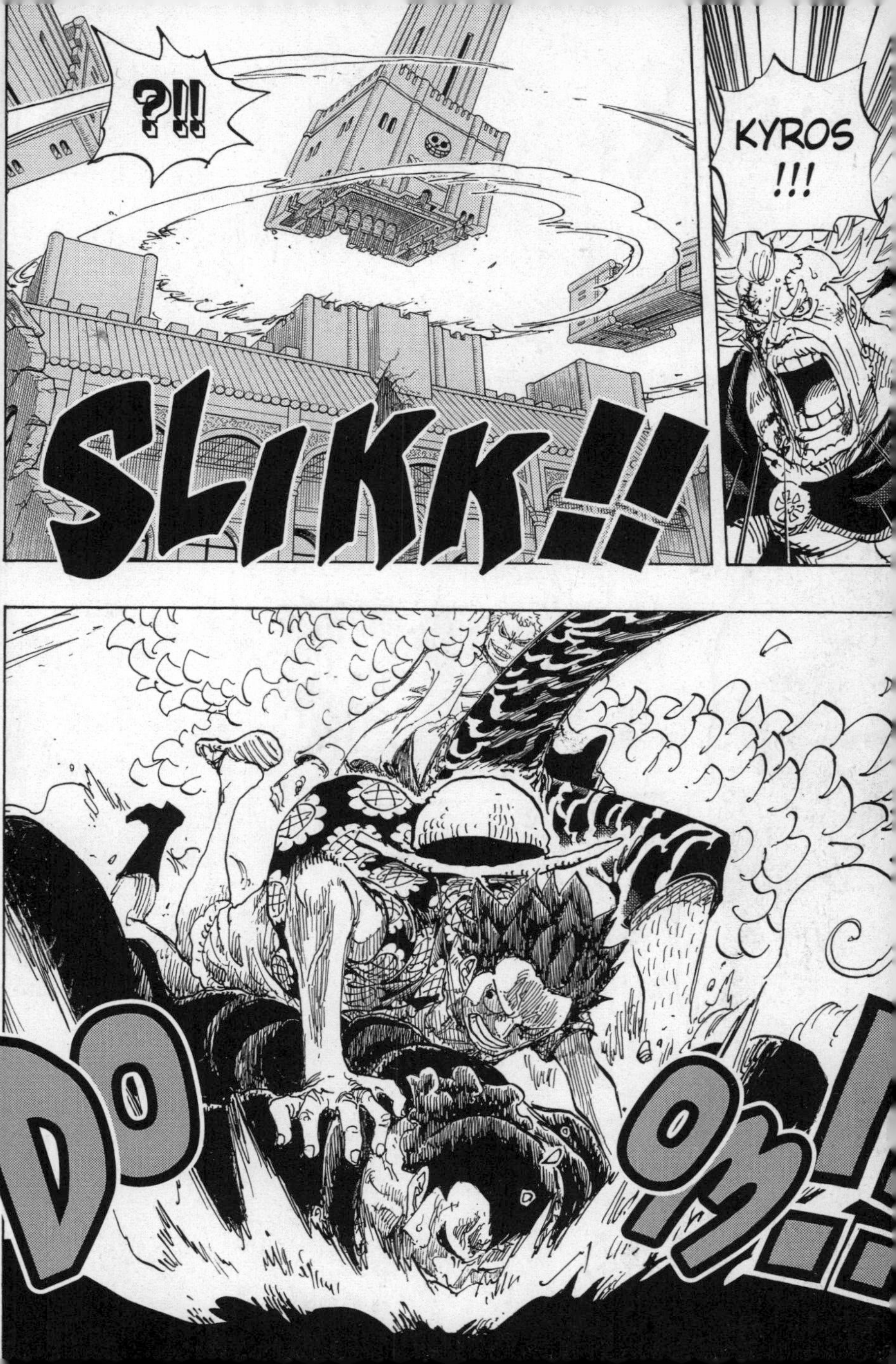
KYROS !!!
?!!
SLIKK!!
DOOOM!!

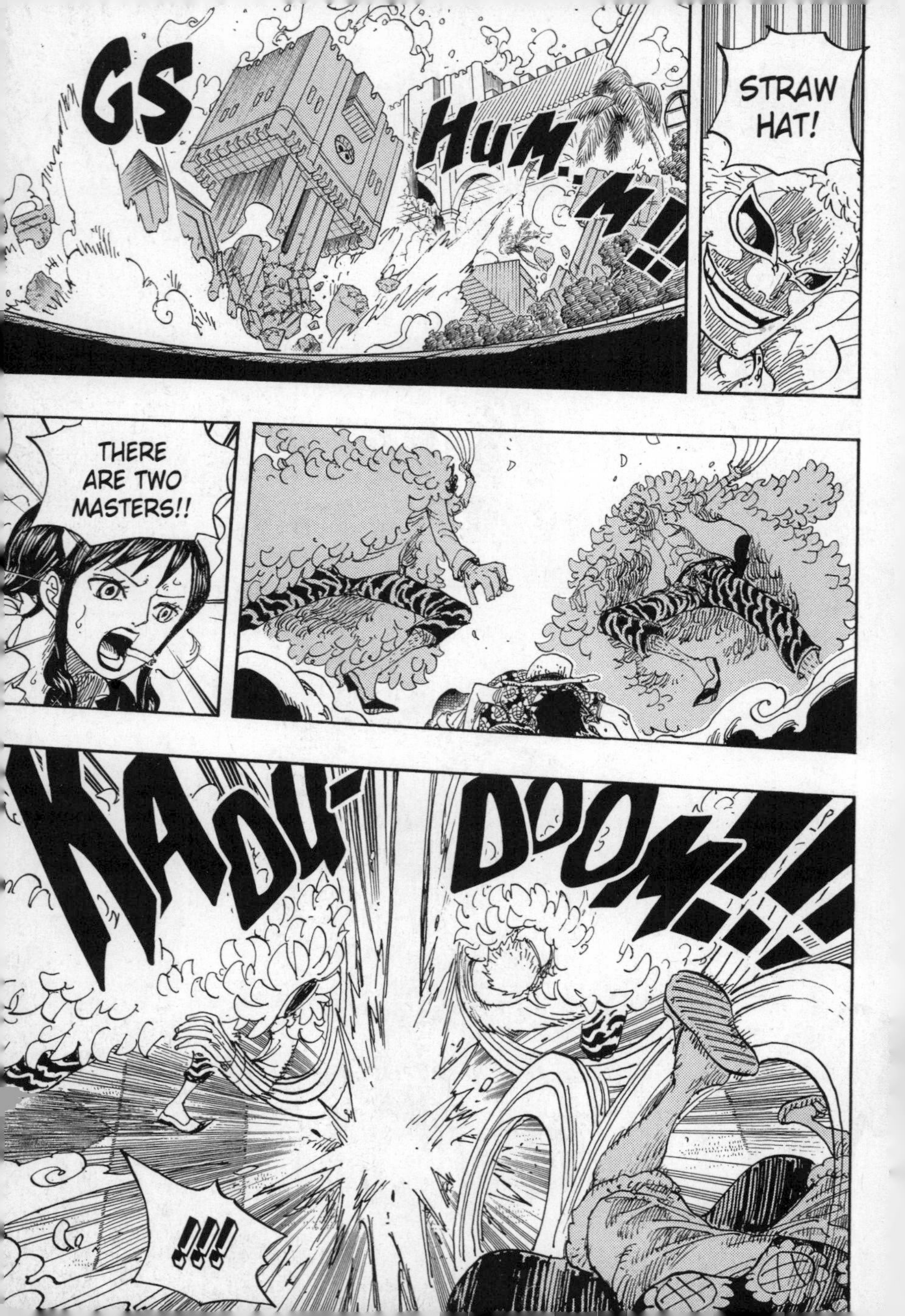
STRAW HAT!
GS
HUM..M!!
THERE ARE TWO MASTERS!!
KADU-DOOM!!
!!!

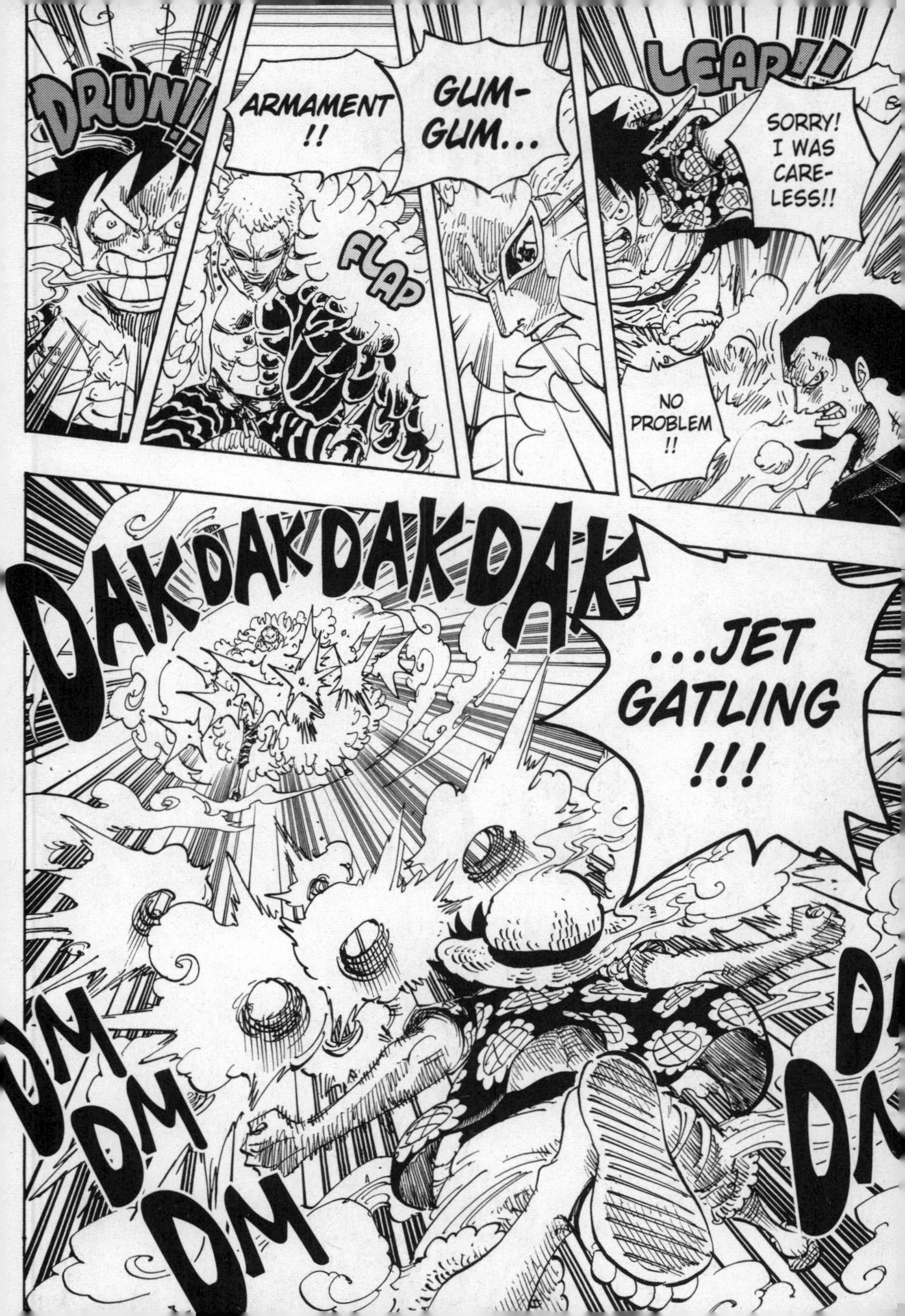
LEAP!!
SORRY! I WAS CARELESS!!
NO PROBLEM!!
GUM-GUM...
FLAP
ARMAMENT!!
DRUN!!
...JET GATLING!!!
DAK DAK DAK DAK DAK
DM DM DM

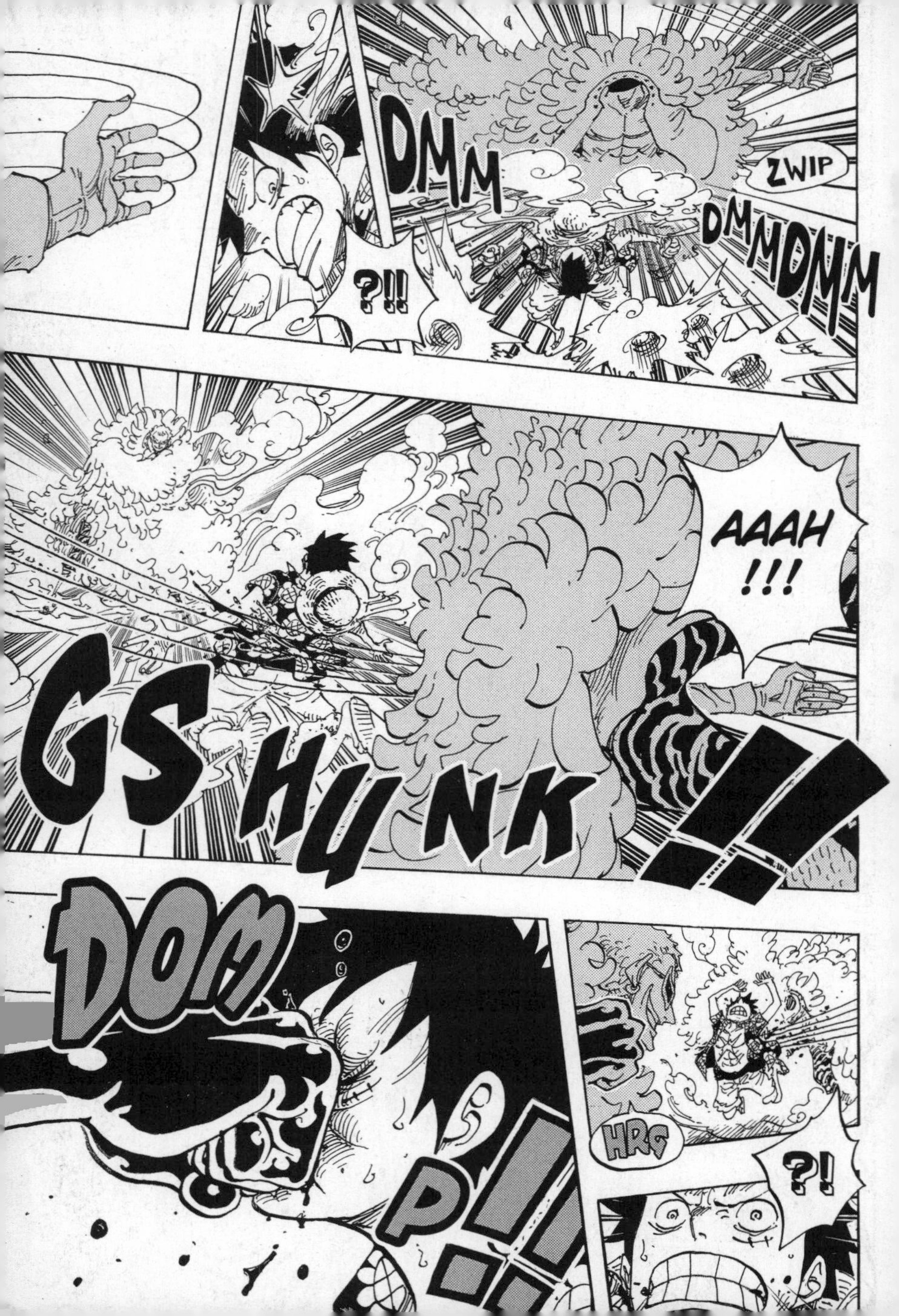
ZWIP
DMM
DMMDMM
?!!
AAAH
!!!
GSHUNK!!!
HRG
?!
DOM
P!!

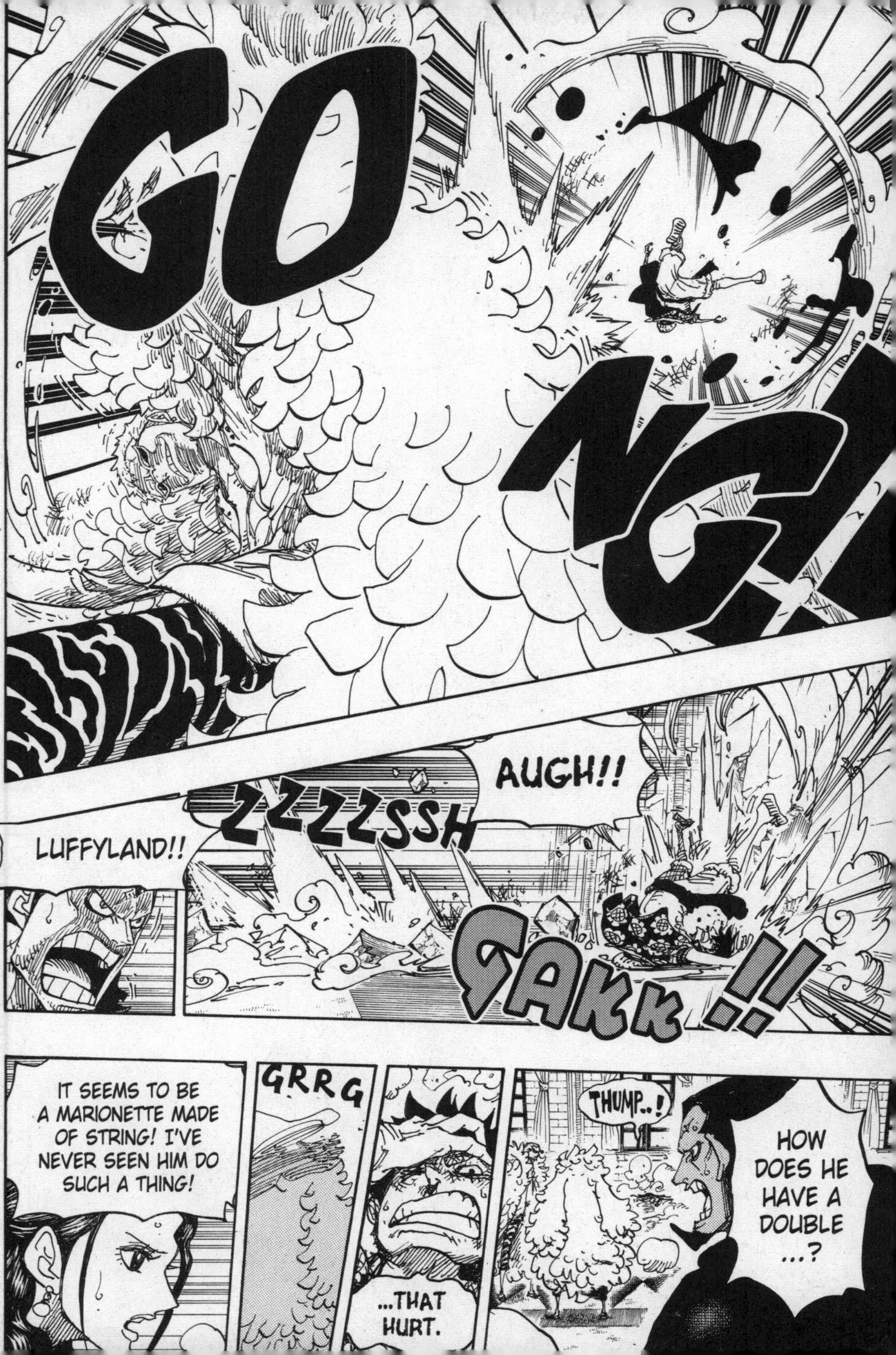
GO NG!
AUGH!!
ZZZZZSSH
GAKK!!
LUFFYLAND!!
THUMP..!
HOW DOES HE HAVE A DOUBLE ...?
GRRG
...THAT HURT.
IT SEEMS TO BE A MARIONETTE MADE OF STRING! I'VE NEVER SEEN HIM DO SUCH A THING!

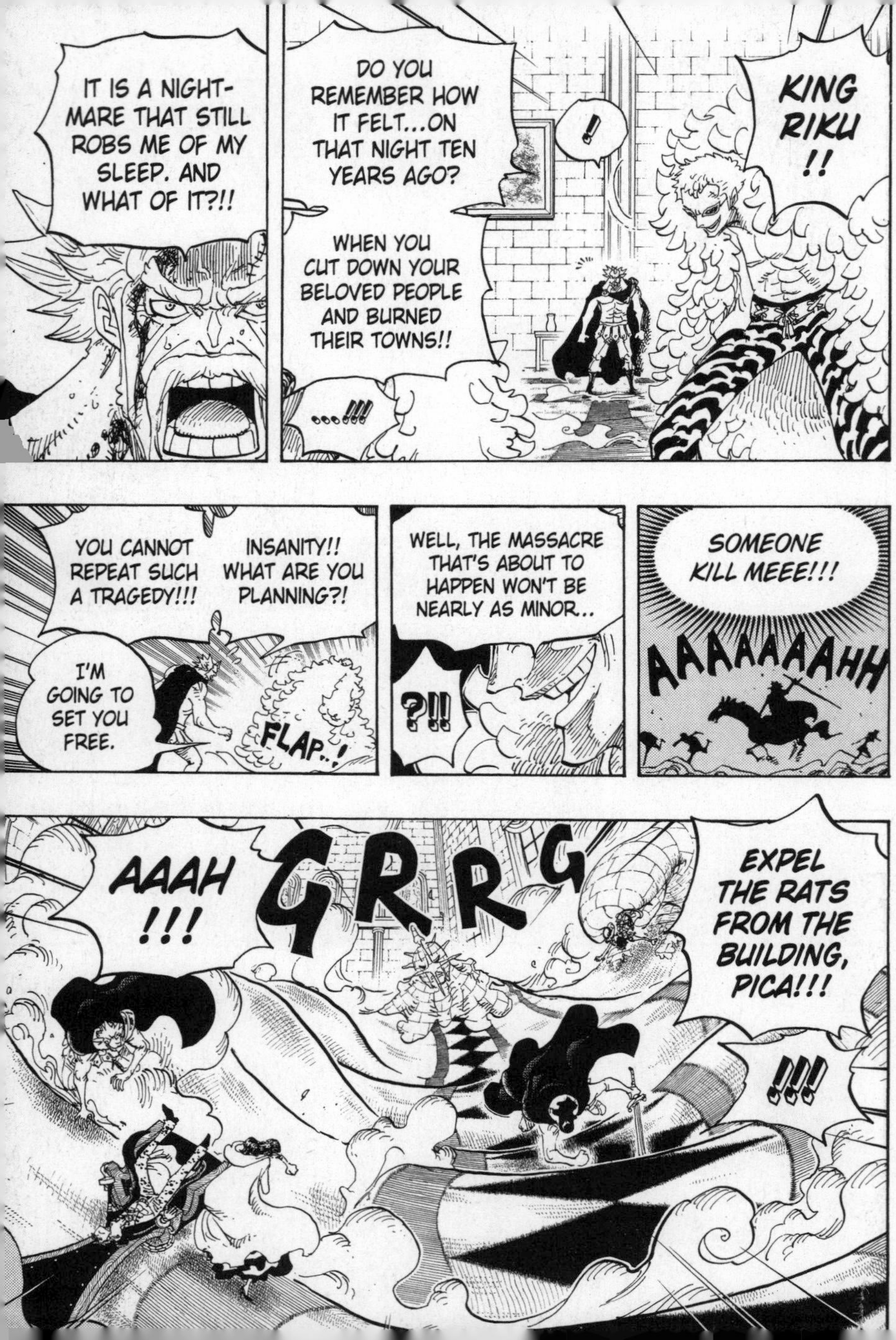
KING RIKU !!
!
DO YOU REMEMBER HOW IT FELT...ON THAT NIGHT TEN YEARS AGO?
WHEN YOU CUT DOWN YOUR BELOVED PEOPLE AND BURNED THEIR TOWNS!!
...!!!
IT IS A NIGHT-MARE THAT STILL ROBS ME OF MY SLEEP. AND WHAT OF IT?!!
SOMEONE KILL MEEE!!!
AAAAAAAHH
WELL, THE MASSACRE THAT'S ABOUT TO HAPPEN WON'T BE NEARLY AS MINOR...
?!!
INSANITY!! WHAT ARE YOU PLANNING?!
YOU CANNOT REPEAT SUCH A TRAGEDY!!!
FLAP..!
I'M GOING TO SET YOU FREE.
EXPEL THE RATS FROM THE BUILDING, PICA!!!
GRRG
AAAH !!!
!!!

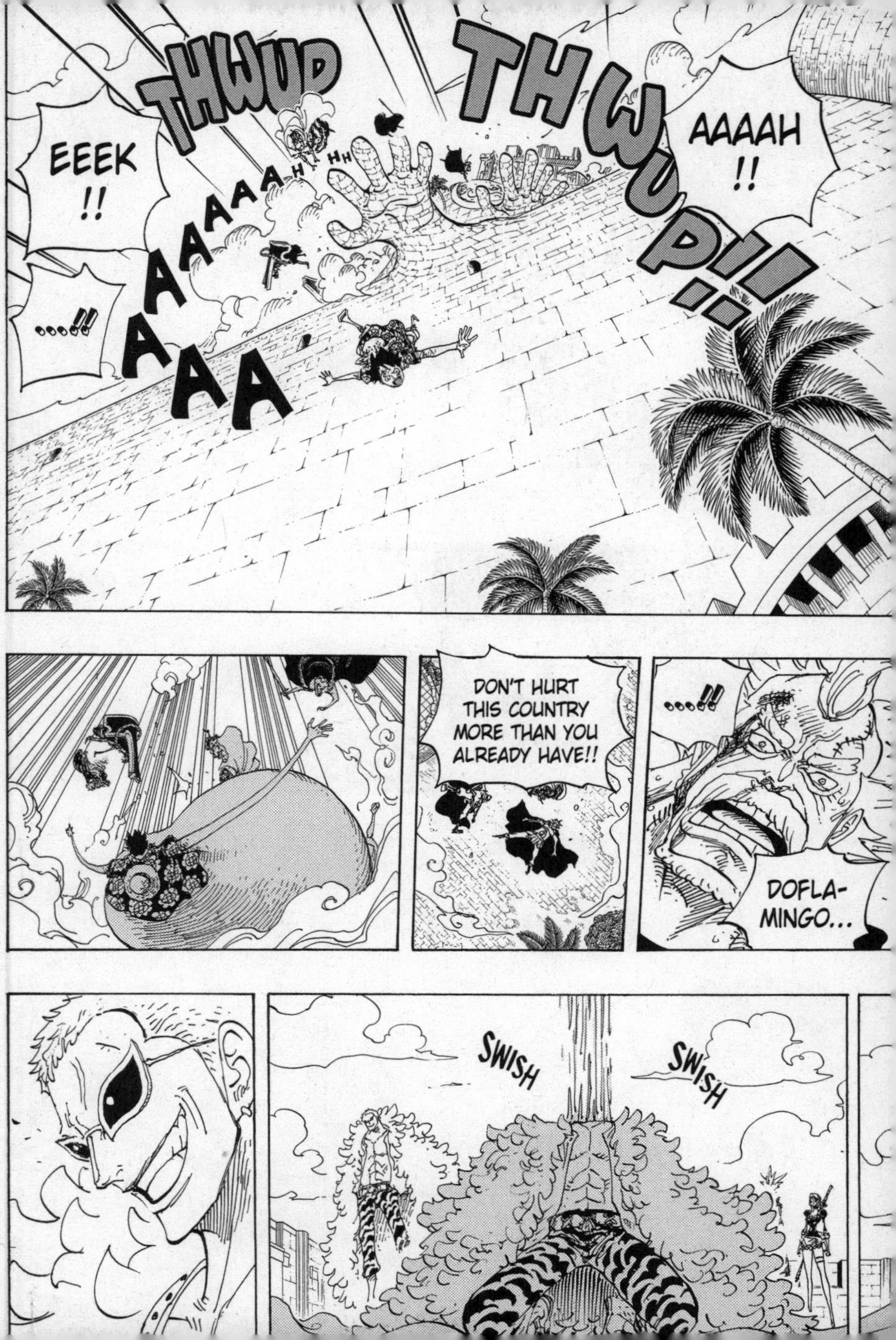
AAAAH !!
THWUP!!!
THWUD
EEEK !!
AAAAAAAAAHHH
...!!
...!!
DOFLA-MINGO...
DON'T HURT THIS COUNTRY MORE THAN YOU ALREADY HAVE!!
SWISH
SWISH

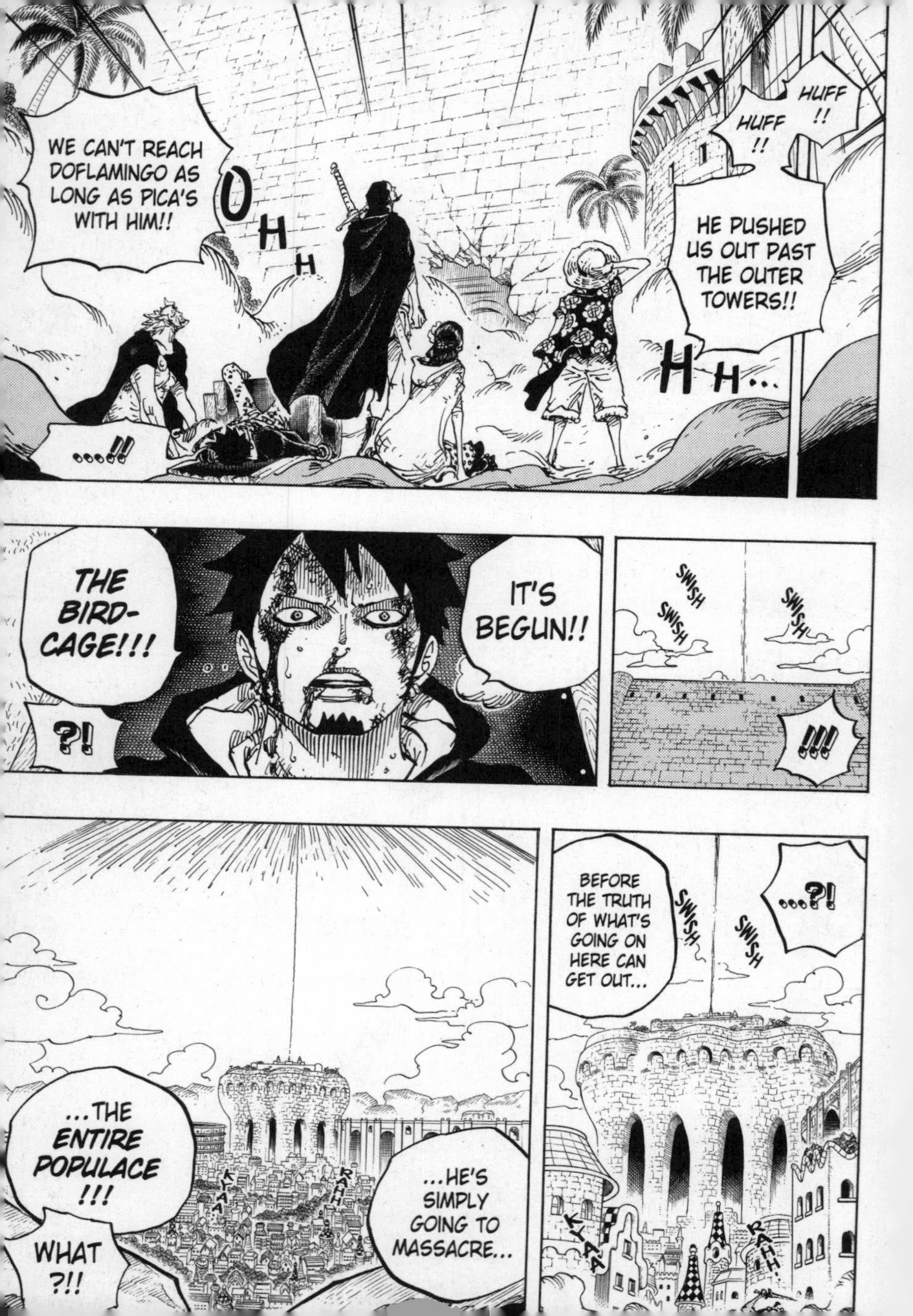
HUFF !!
HUFF !!
HE PUSHED US OUT PAST THE OUTER TOWERS!!
HH...
OHHH
WE CAN'T REACH DOFLAMINGO AS LONG AS PICA'S WITH HIM!!
...!!
SWISH
SWISH
SWISH
!!!
IT'S BEGUN!!
THE BIRD-CAGE!!!
?!
...?!
SWISH
SWISH
BEFORE THE TRUTH OF WHAT'S GOING ON HERE CAN GET OUT...
RAHH...
KYAA
...HE'S SIMPLY GOING TO MASSACRE...
...THE ENTIRE POPULACE !!!
WHAT ?!!
RAHH
KYAA

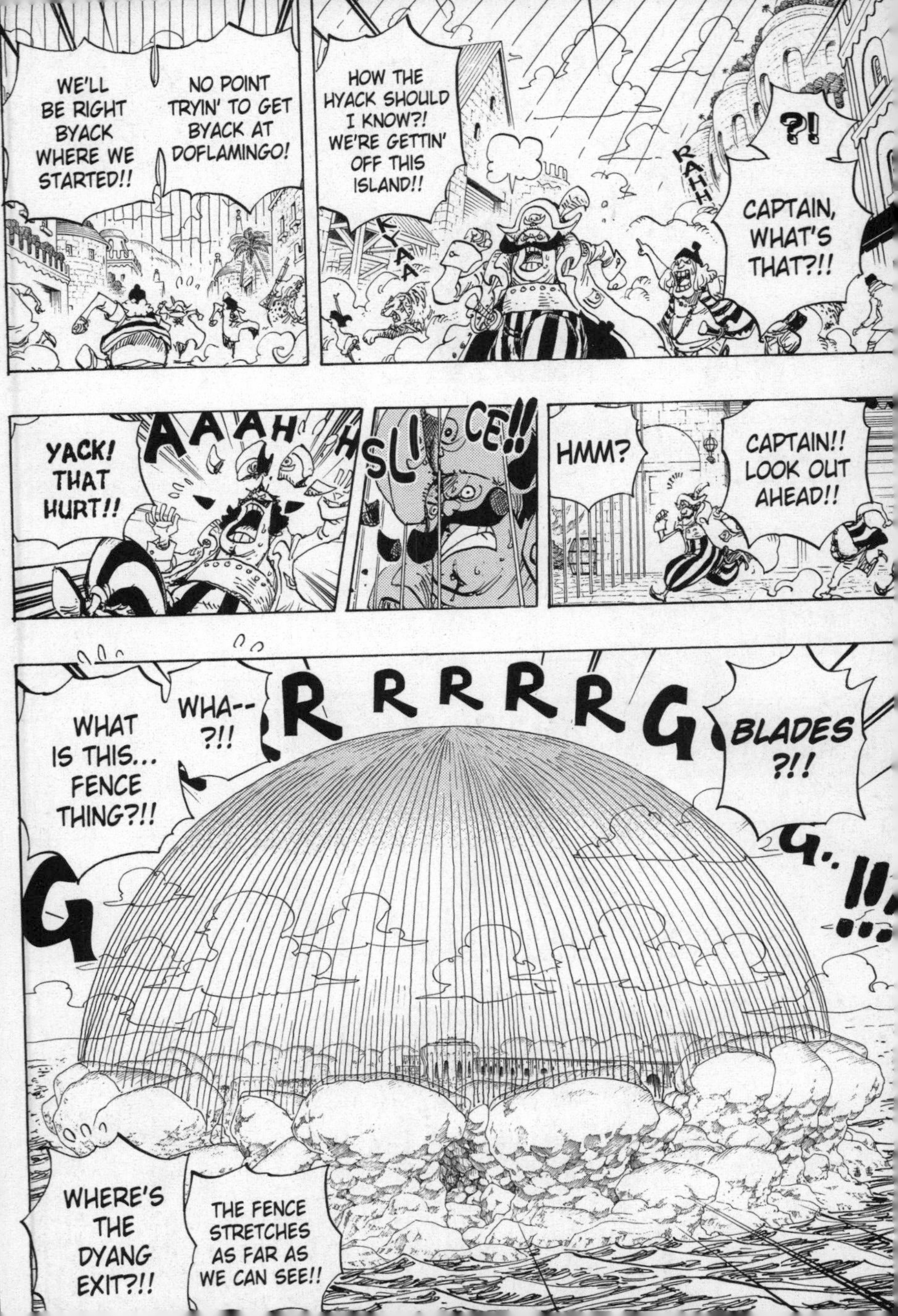
?!
RAHH
CAPTAIN, WHAT'S THAT?!!
HOW THE HYACK SHOULD I KNOW?! WE'RE GETTIN' OFF THIS ISLAND!!
KYAA
NO POINT TRYIN' TO GET BYACK AT DOFLAMINGO!
WE'LL BE RIGHT BYACK WHERE WE STARTED!!
CAPTAIN!! LOOK OUT AHEAD!!
HMM?
SLICE!!
AAAH
YACK! THAT HURT!!
BLADES?!!
G..!!
R R R R R G
WHA-- ?!!
WHAT IS THIS... FENCE THING?!!
G
THE FENCE STRETCHES AS FAR AS WE CAN SEE!!
WHERE'S THE DYANG EXIT?!!

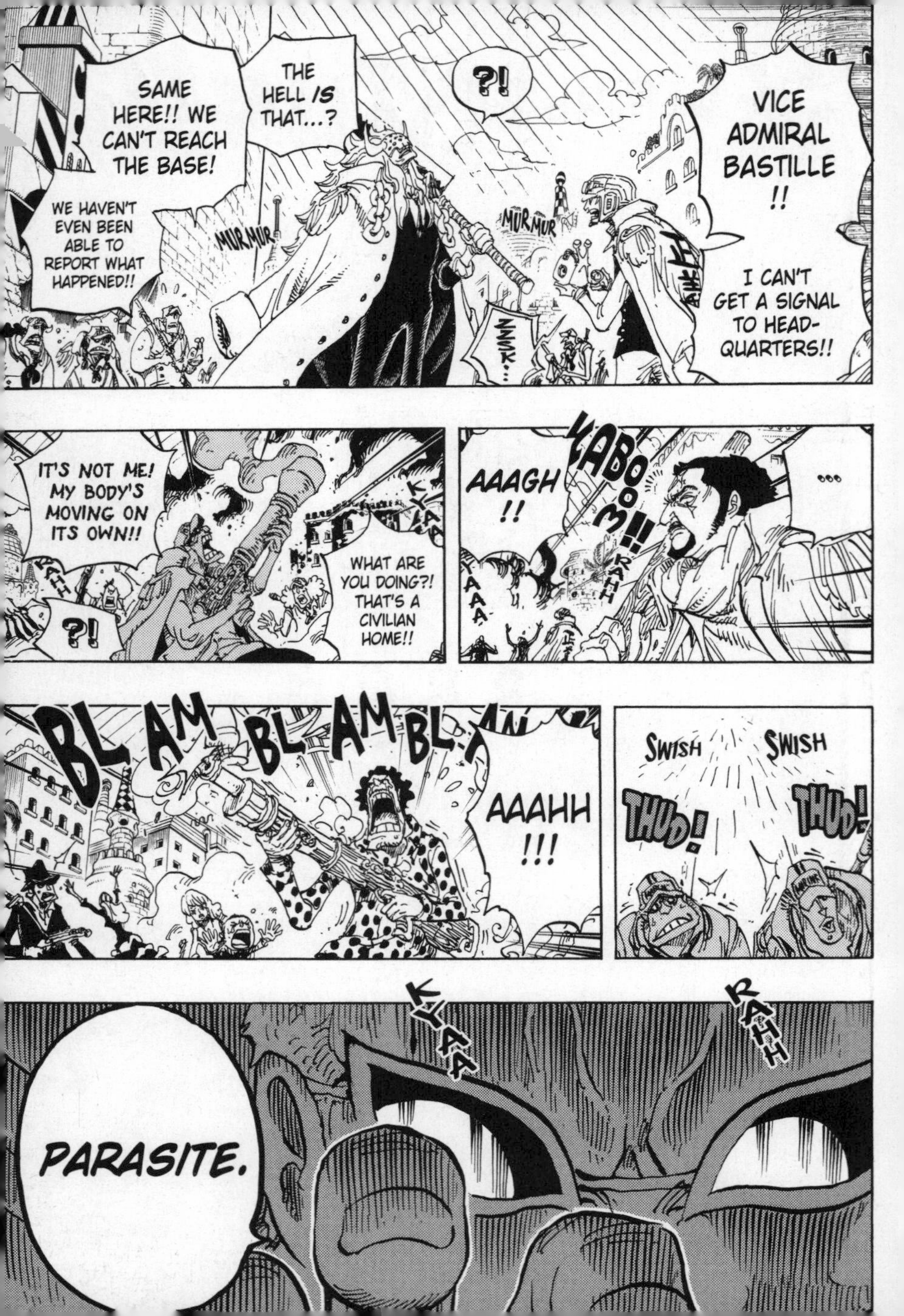

VICE ADMIRAL BASTILLE !!
I CAN'T GET A SIGNAL TO HEAD-QUARTERS!!
ZZSK...
MURMUR
?!
THE HELL *IS* THAT...?
MURMUR
SAME HERE!! WE CAN'T REACH THE BASE!
WE HAVEN'T EVEN BEEN ABLE TO REPORT WHAT HAPPENED!!
...
KABOOM!!
AAAGH !!
RAHH
AAA
KYAA
WHAT ARE YOU DOING?! THAT'S A CIVILIAN HOME!!
IT'S NOT ME! MY BODY'S MOVING ON ITS OWN!!
RAHH
?!
SWISH
SWISH
THUD!
THUD!
AAAHH !!!
BLAM BLAM BLAM
RAHH
KYAA
PARASITE.

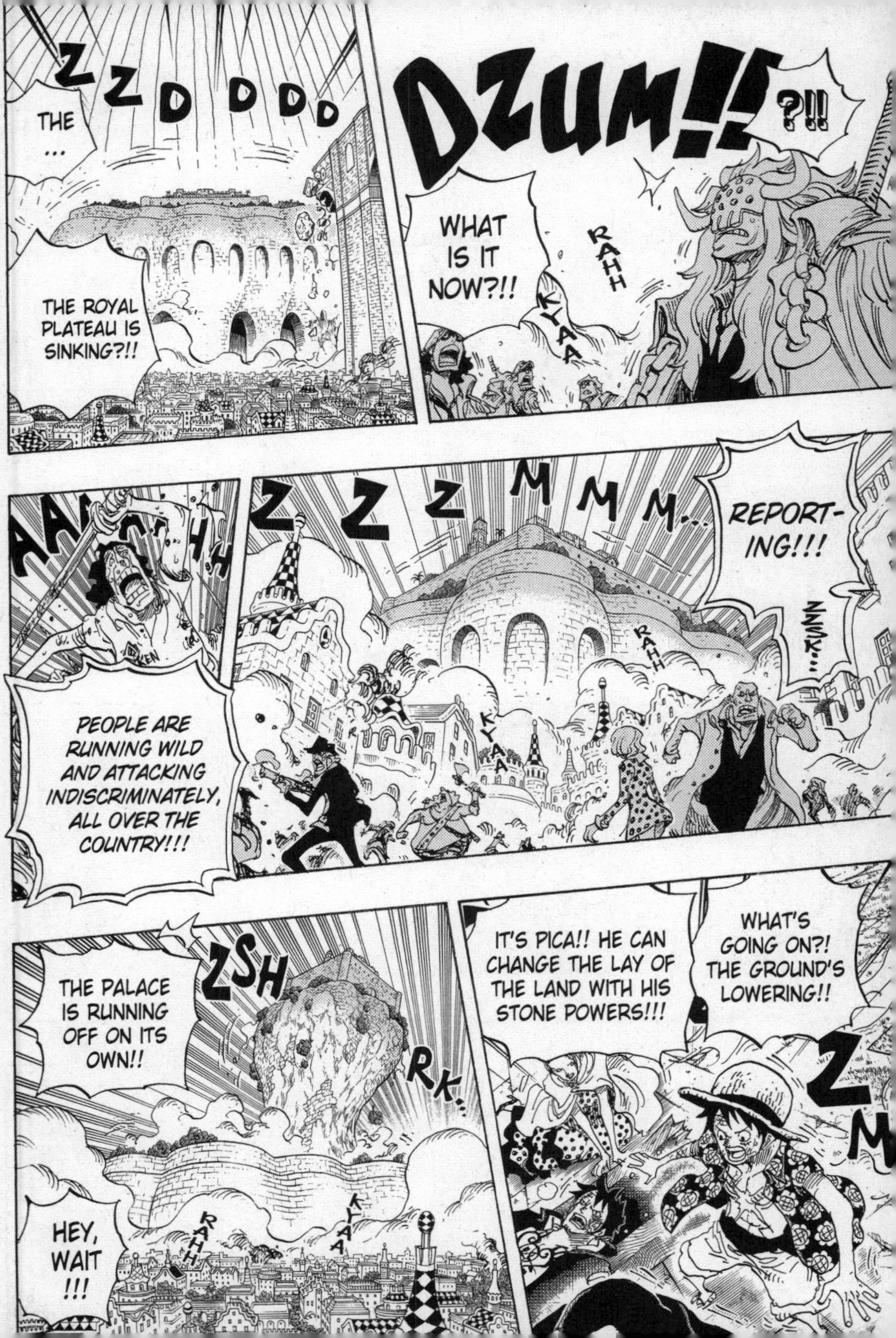
DZUM!!
?!!
WHAT IS IT NOW?!!
RAHH
KYAA
ZZD DDD
THE ...
THE ROYAL PLATEAU IS SINKING?!!
ZZZ MMM...
REPORTING!!!
ZZSK...
RAHH
KYAA
PEOPLE ARE RUNNING WILD AND ATTACKING INDISCRIMINATELY, ALL OVER THE COUNTRY!!!
WHAT'S GOING ON?! THE GROUND'S LOWERING!!
IT'S PICA!! HE CAN CHANGE THE LAY OF THE LAND WITH HIS STONE POWERS!!!
ZSH
THE PALACE IS RUNNING OFF ON ITS OWN!!
RK...
KYAA
RAHH
HEY, WAIT!!!

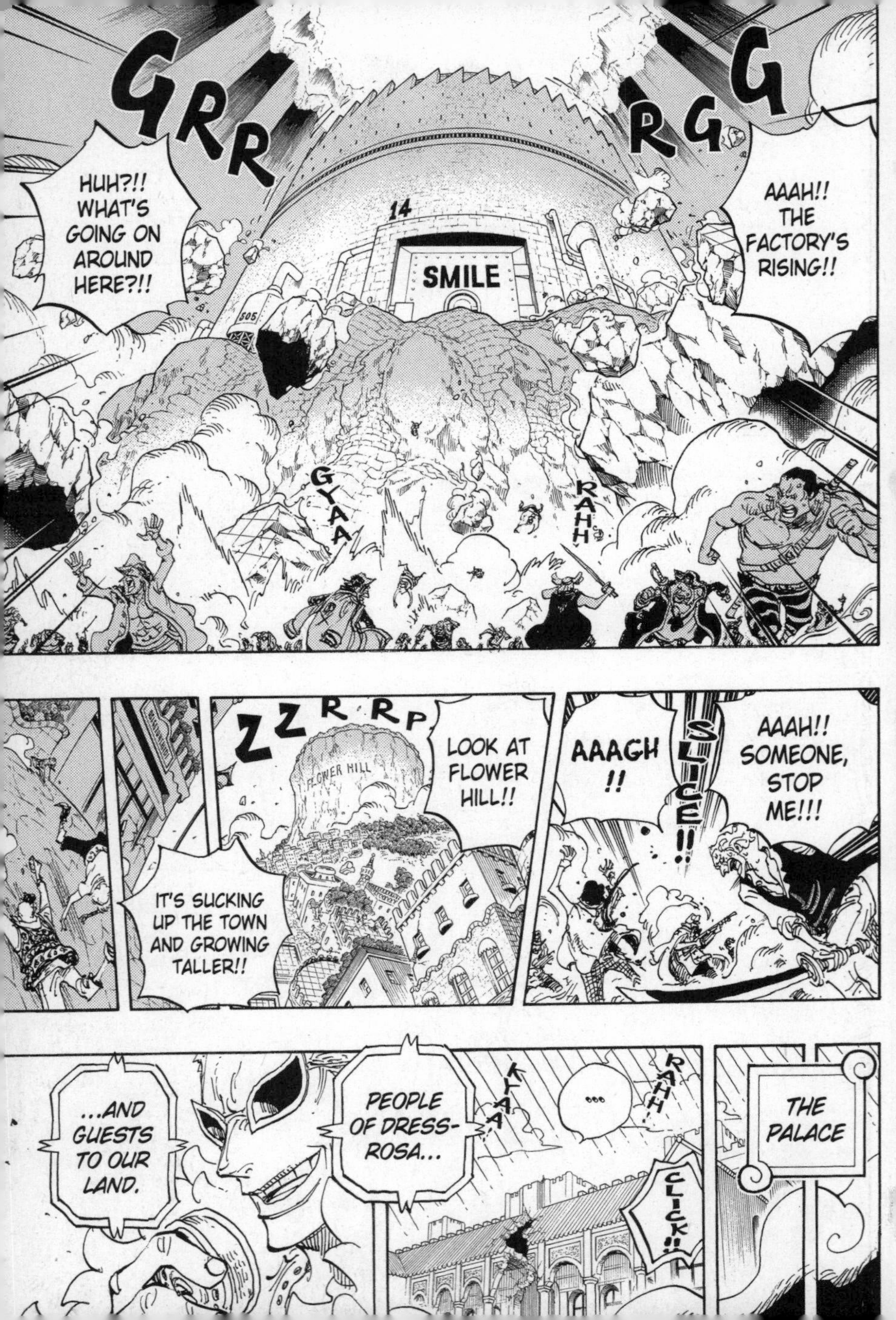
GRRRGG
AAAH!! THE FACTORY'S RISING!!
HUH?!! WHAT'S GOING ON AROUND HERE?!!
14
SMILE
505
RAHH
GYAA
AAAH!! SOMEONE, STOP ME!!!
SLICE!!
AAAGH!!
ZZZRRRP
LOOK AT FLOWER HILL!!
FLOWER HILL
IT'S SUCKING UP THE TOWN AND GROWING TALLER!!
THE PALACE
RAHH
...
KLAA
CLICK!!
PEOPLE OF DRESS-ROSA...
...AND GUESTS TO OUR LAND.

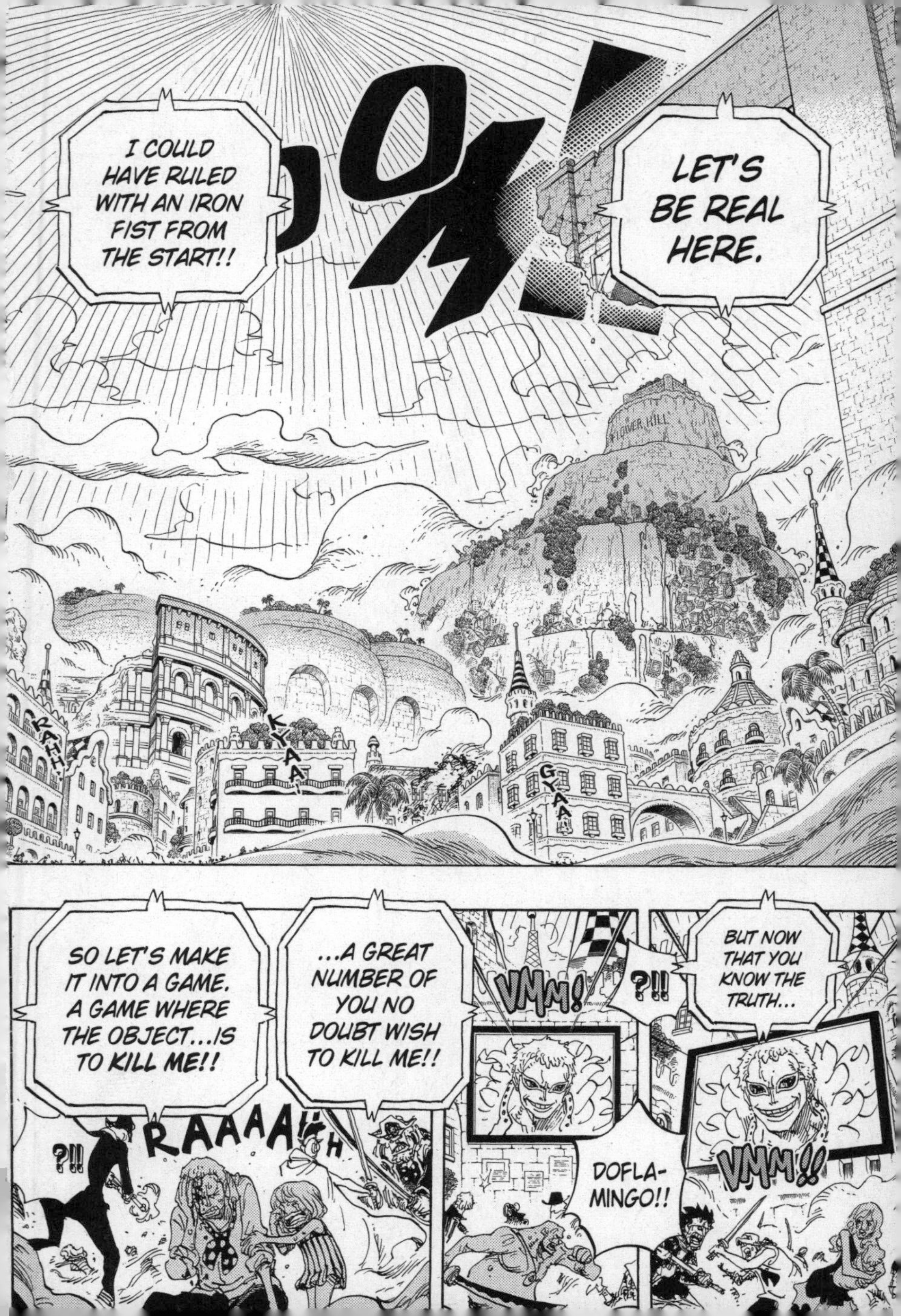
LET'S BE REAL HERE.
I COULD HAVE RULED WITH AN IRON FIST FROM THE START!!
GYAA!!
KYAA!
RAHH!
BUT NOW THAT YOU KNOW THE TRUTH...
VMM!!
DOFLA-MINGO!!
?!!
VMM!
...A GREAT NUMBER OF YOU NO DOUBT WISH TO KILL ME!!
SO LET'S MAKE IT INTO A GAME. A GAME WHERE THE OBJECT...IS TO KILL ME!!
RAAAAHH
?!!

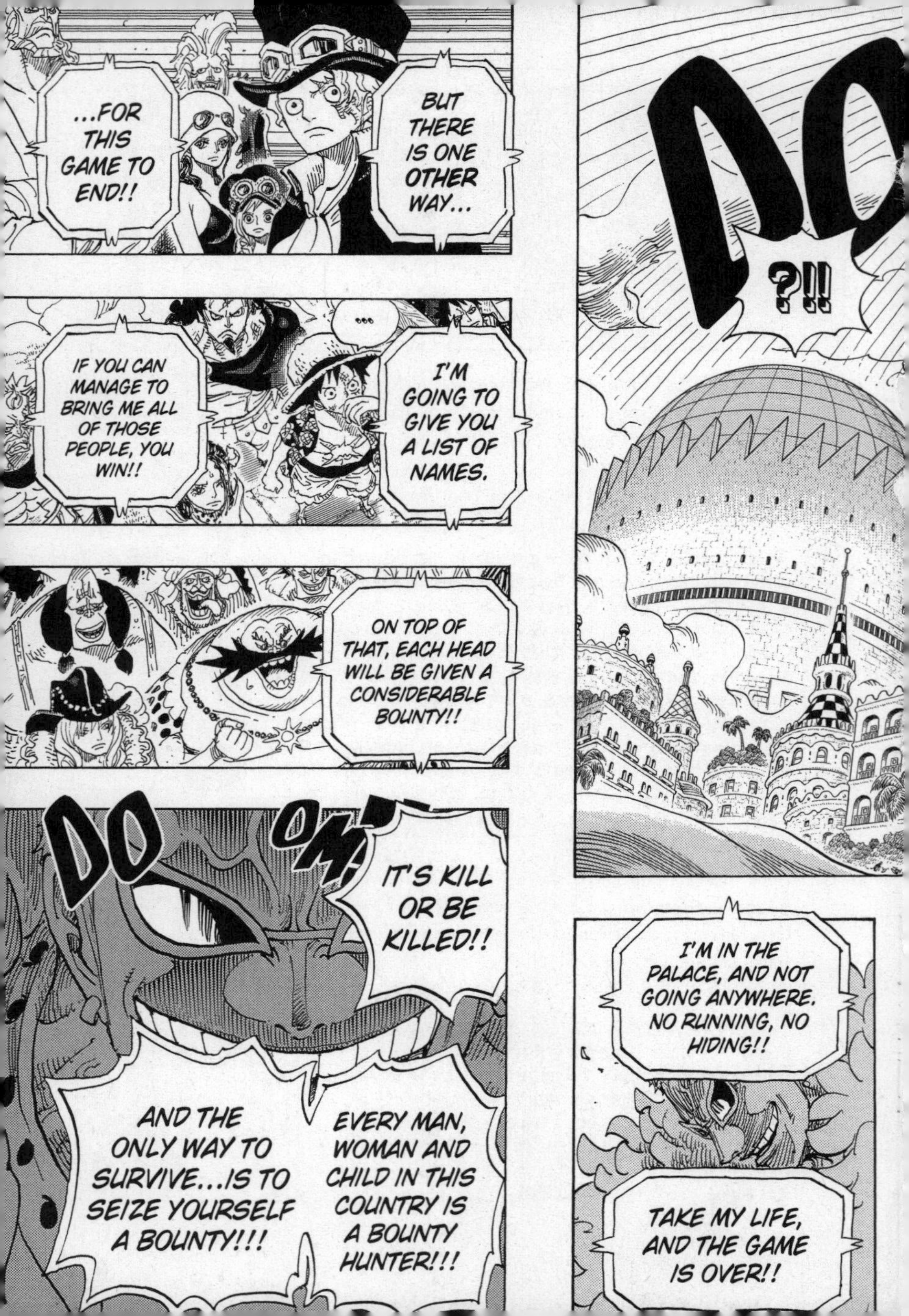
DOO
?!!
I'M IN THE PALACE, AND NOT GOING ANYWHERE. NO RUNNING, NO HIDING!!
TAKE MY LIFE, AND THE GAME IS OVER!!
BUT THERE IS ONE OTHER WAY...
...FOR THIS GAME TO END!!
...
I'M GOING TO GIVE YOU A LIST OF NAMES.
IF YOU CAN MANAGE TO BRING ME ALL OF THOSE PEOPLE, YOU WIN!!
ON TOP OF THAT, EACH HEAD WILL BE GIVEN A CONSIDERABLE BOUNTY!!
DO OM
IT'S KILL OR BE KILLED!!
EVERY MAN, WOMAN AND CHILD IN THIS COUNTRY IS A BOUNTY HUNTER!!!
AND THE ONLY WAY TO SURVIVE...IS TO SEIZE YOURSELF A BOUNTY!!!

SBS Question Corner

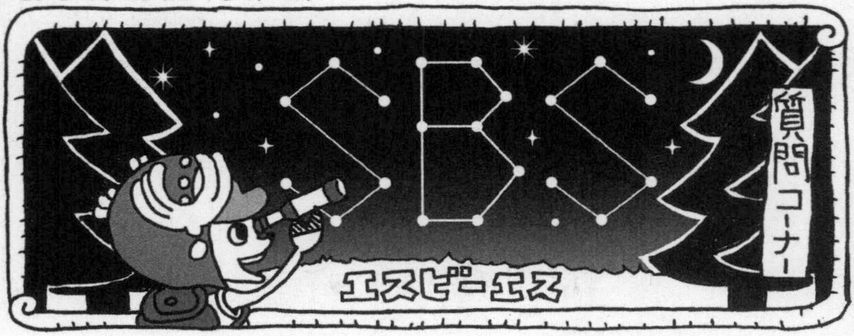
SBS
質問コーナー
エスピーエス

(Captain Y, Osaka)

Q: I was reading Volume 63 and stopping to look at how cute Shirahoshi was, and realized something. The former slave girl who Tiger brought home to her village was named Koala, right?? Right?!!!!
Well, why don't you explain it all, Mr. Oda?!!

--Grand Red Apple

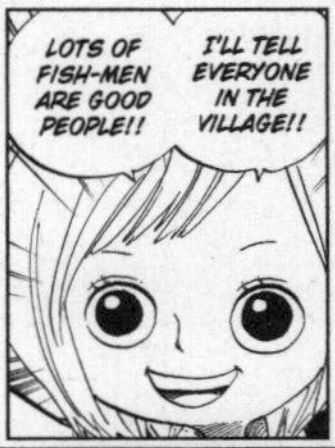
I'LL TELL EVERYONE IN THE VILLAGE!!
LOTS OF FISH-MEN ARE GOOD PEOPLE!!

A: That's right. If anyone didn't notice the connection, I'm perfectly happy with them treating her as a new character, but I was glad to see that many folks realized who she was. The people of the Revolutionary Army all have their own reasons for opposing the way the world works, but if you look at her title of "Assistant Fish-man Karate Master" and where she started, you can see what kind of life she's been through, and it brings a tear to your eye. To me, Koala's lived the exact opposite life of Hody, and that makes her very meaningful to me.

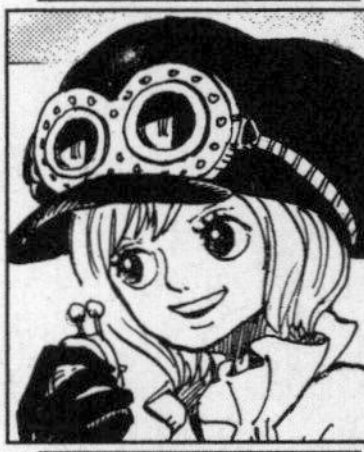

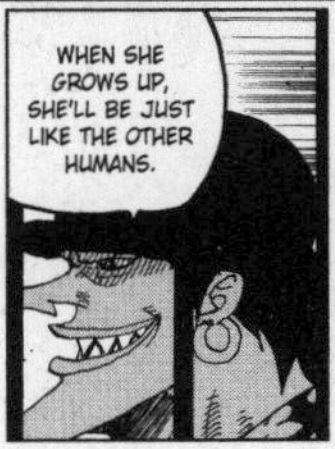
WHEN SHE GROWS UP, SHE'LL BE JUST LIKE THE OTHER HUMANS.

Q: Nice to meet you. I'm a shark-loving 24-year-old woman. Sharks are famous for having two penises. Does that mean that Hody has two penises too? How many penises do you have, Odacchi?

--I Want Shirahoshi for My Wife

A: They have two?! Sharks have two?!
I had no idea. That's a well-known fact?!
I've drawn a ton of sharks, but I never knew that. Thanks for the tip. In that case, Hody has two. I guess instead of a ding-dong, he's got a "ding-ding-dong-dong"!
I'm fine just having one.

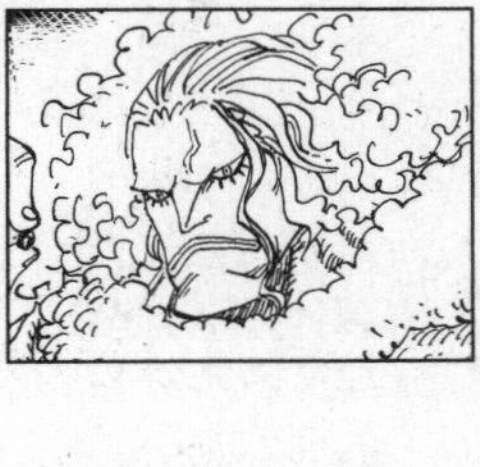

Chapter 746:
STARS

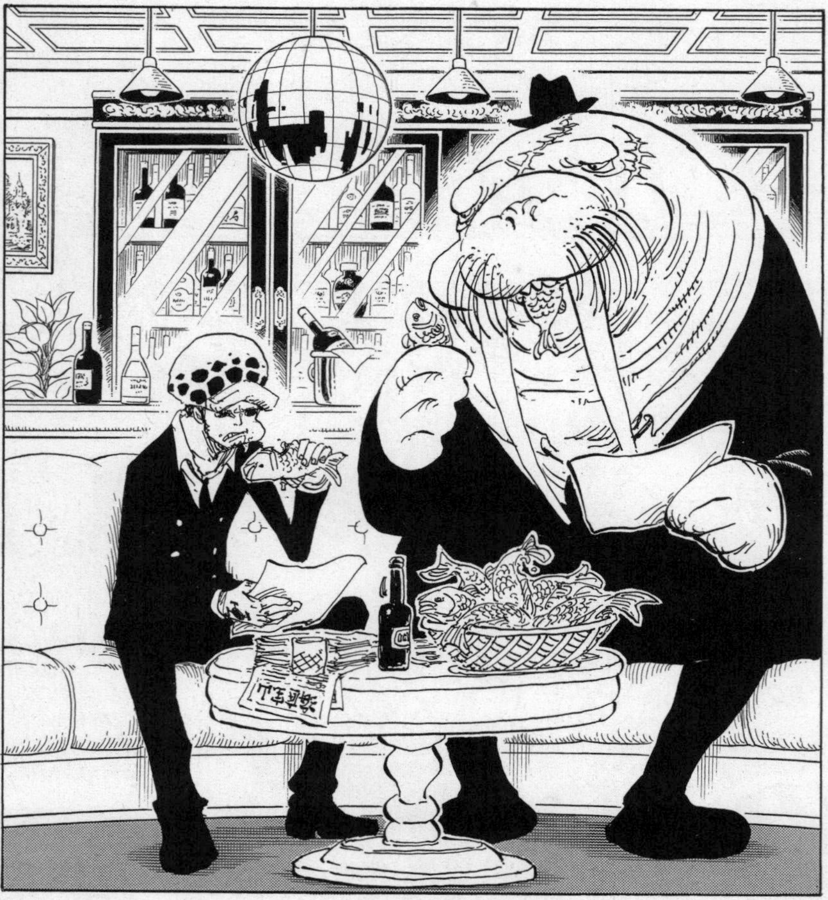

REQUEST: "LAW CONSPIRES WITH A BURLY WALRUS"
BY SLEEPING SAMURAI FROM TOKYO

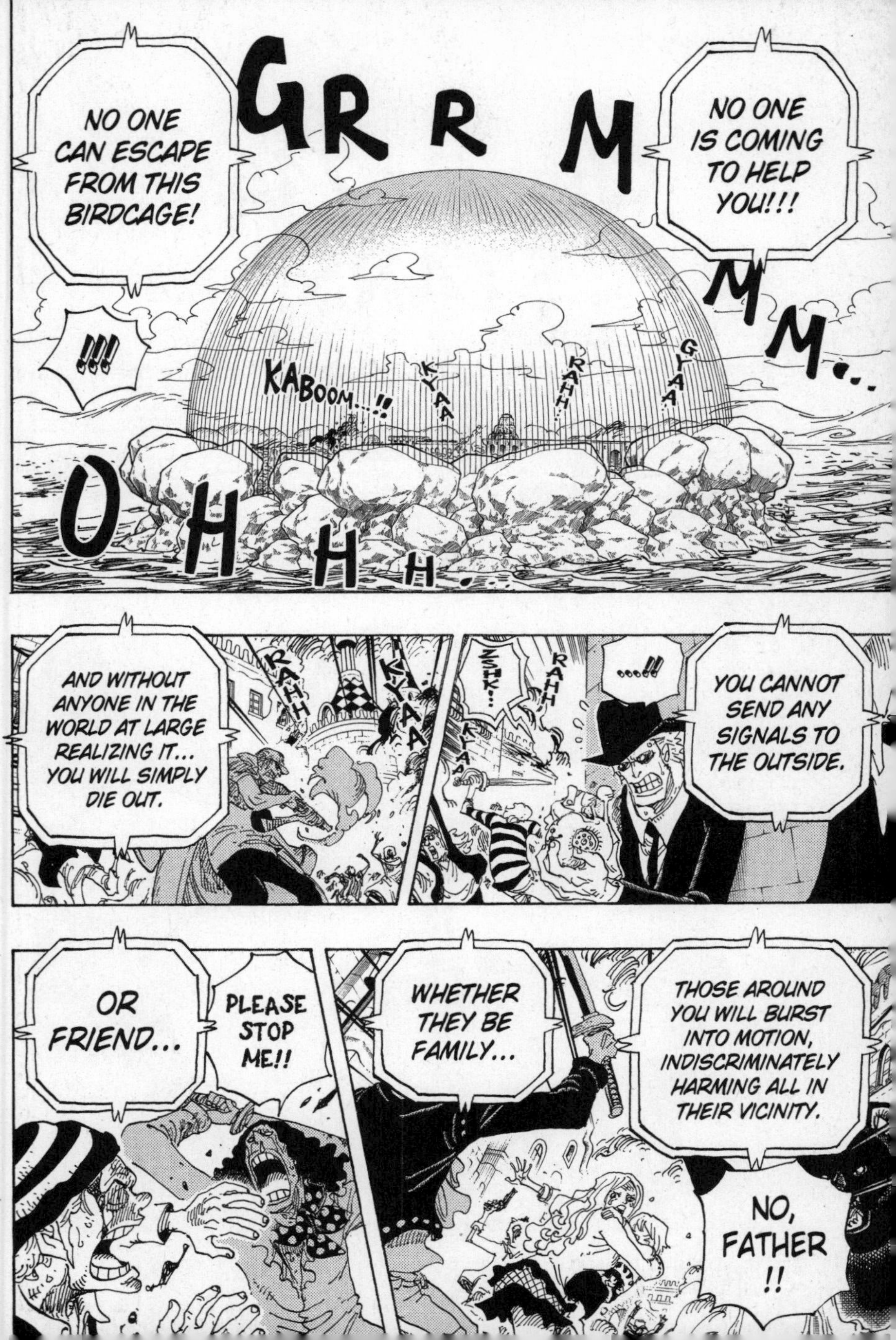
NO ONE IS COMING TO HELP YOU!!!
GRRRMMMM...
NO ONE CAN ESCAPE FROM THIS BIRDCAGE!
!!!
GYAA
RAHH...
KYAA
KABOOM...!!
OHHHH...
...!!
YOU CANNOT SEND ANY SIGNALS TO THE OUTSIDE.
RAHH
ZSHK!!
KYAA
KYAA
RAHH
AND WITHOUT ANYONE IN THE WORLD AT LARGE REALIZING IT... YOU WILL SIMPLY DIE OUT.
THOSE AROUND YOU WILL BURST INTO MOTION, INDISCRIMINATELY HARMING ALL IN THEIR VICINITY.
WHETHER THEY BE FAMILY...
NO, FATHER !!
PLEASE STOP ME!!
OR FRIEND...

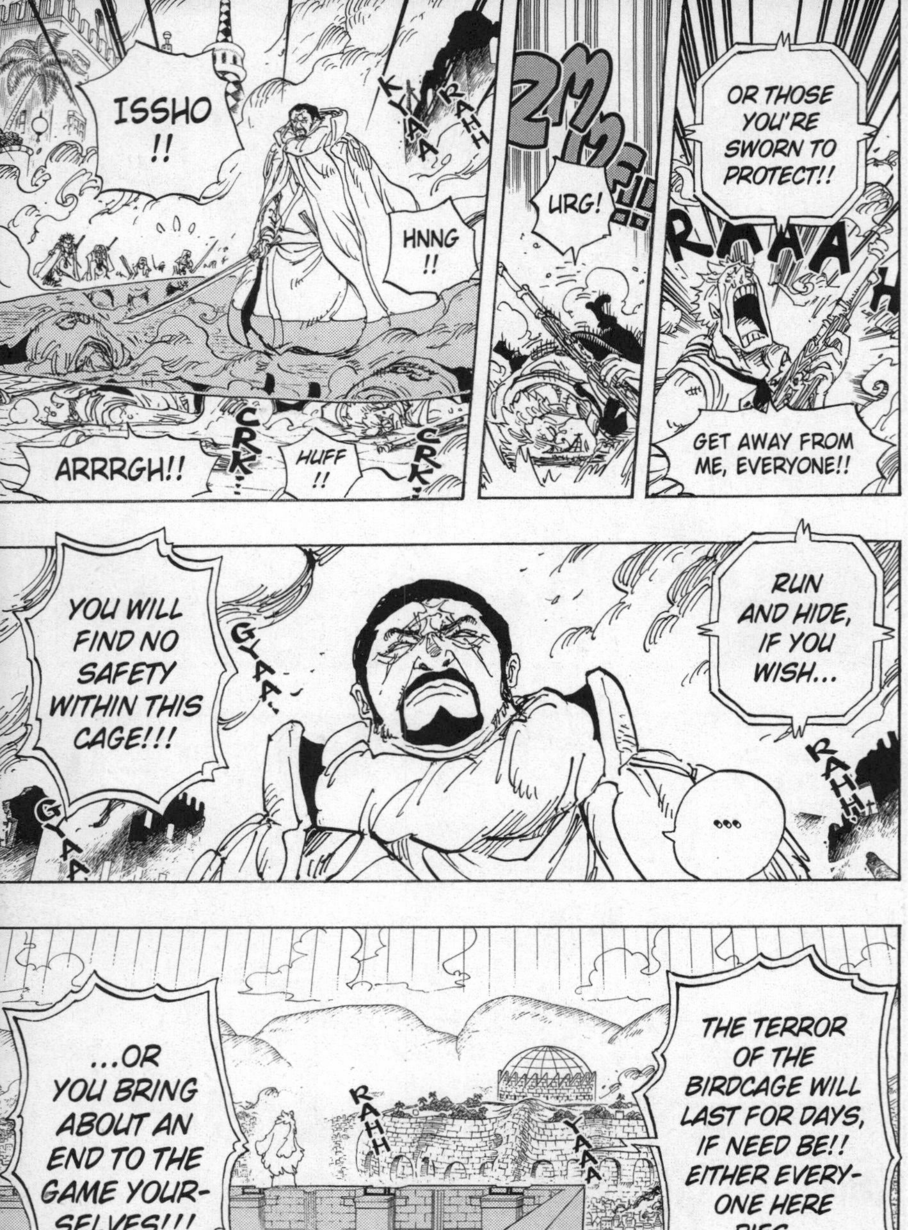
OR THOSE YOU'RE SWORN TO PROTECT!!
RAAAH
GET AWAY FROM ME, EVERYONE!!
URG!
ISSHO!!
KYAA
RAHH
HNNG!!
ARRRGH!!
CRK
HUFF!!
CRK
RUN AND HIDE, IF YOU WISH...
RAHH
...
YOU WILL FIND NO SAFETY WITHIN THIS CAGE!!!
GYAA
GYAA
THE TERROR OF THE BIRDCAGE WILL LAST FOR DAYS, IF NEED BE!! EITHER EVERY-ONE HERE DIES...
YAAA
RAHH
...OR YOU BRING ABOUT AN END TO THE GAME YOUR-SELVES!!!

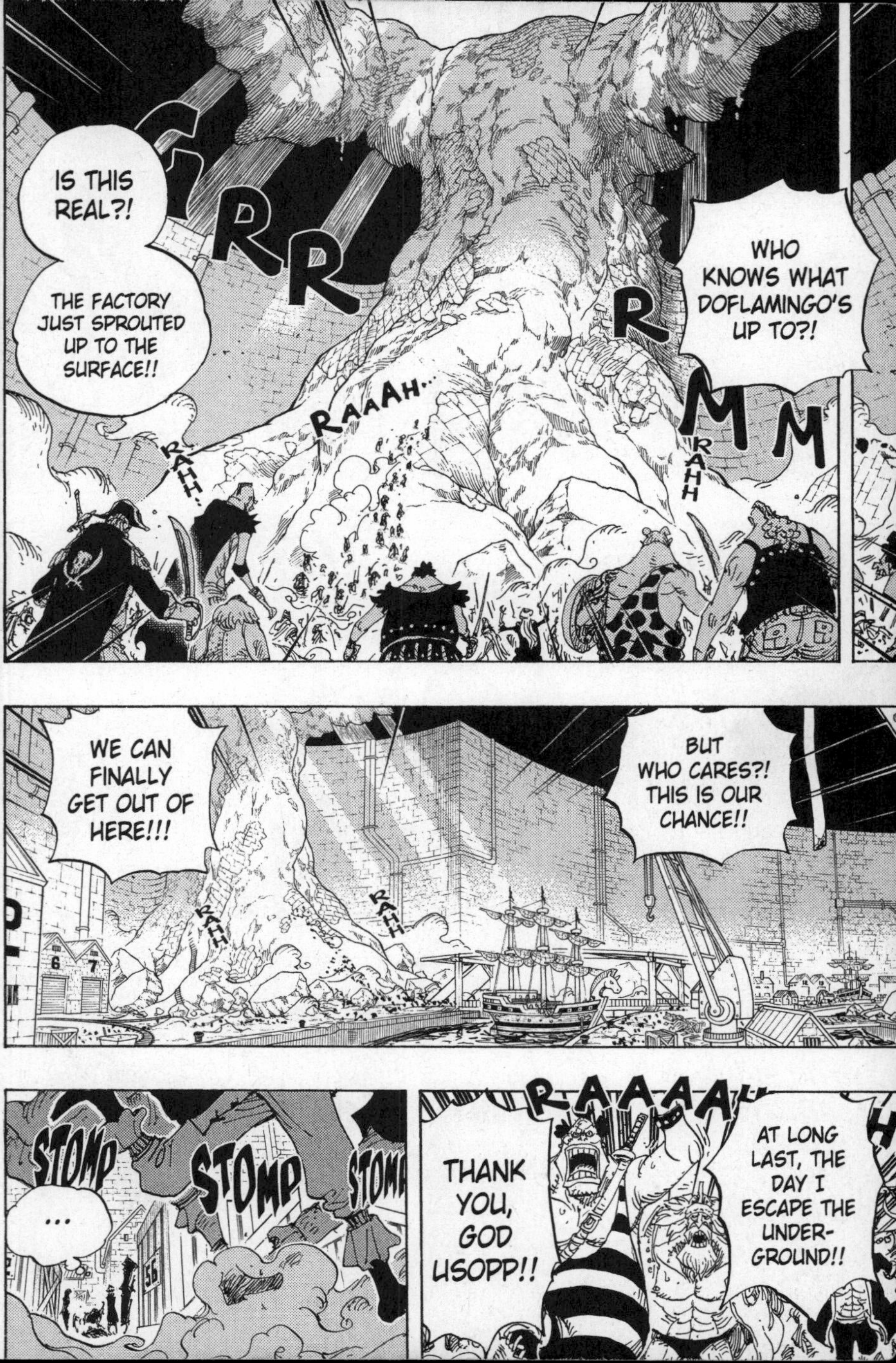
WHO KNOWS WHAT DOFLAMINGO'S UP TO?!
GRRRMMM
RAHH
RAAAH...
IS THIS REAL?!
THE FACTORY JUST SPROUTED UP TO THE SURFACE!!
RAHH
BUT WHO CARES?! THIS IS OUR CHANCE!!
RAHH
RAHH
WE CAN FINALLY GET OUT OF HERE!!!
AT LONG LAST, THE DAY I ESCAPE THE UNDER-GROUND!!
THANK YOU, GOD USOPP!!
STOMP
STOMP
STOMP
...

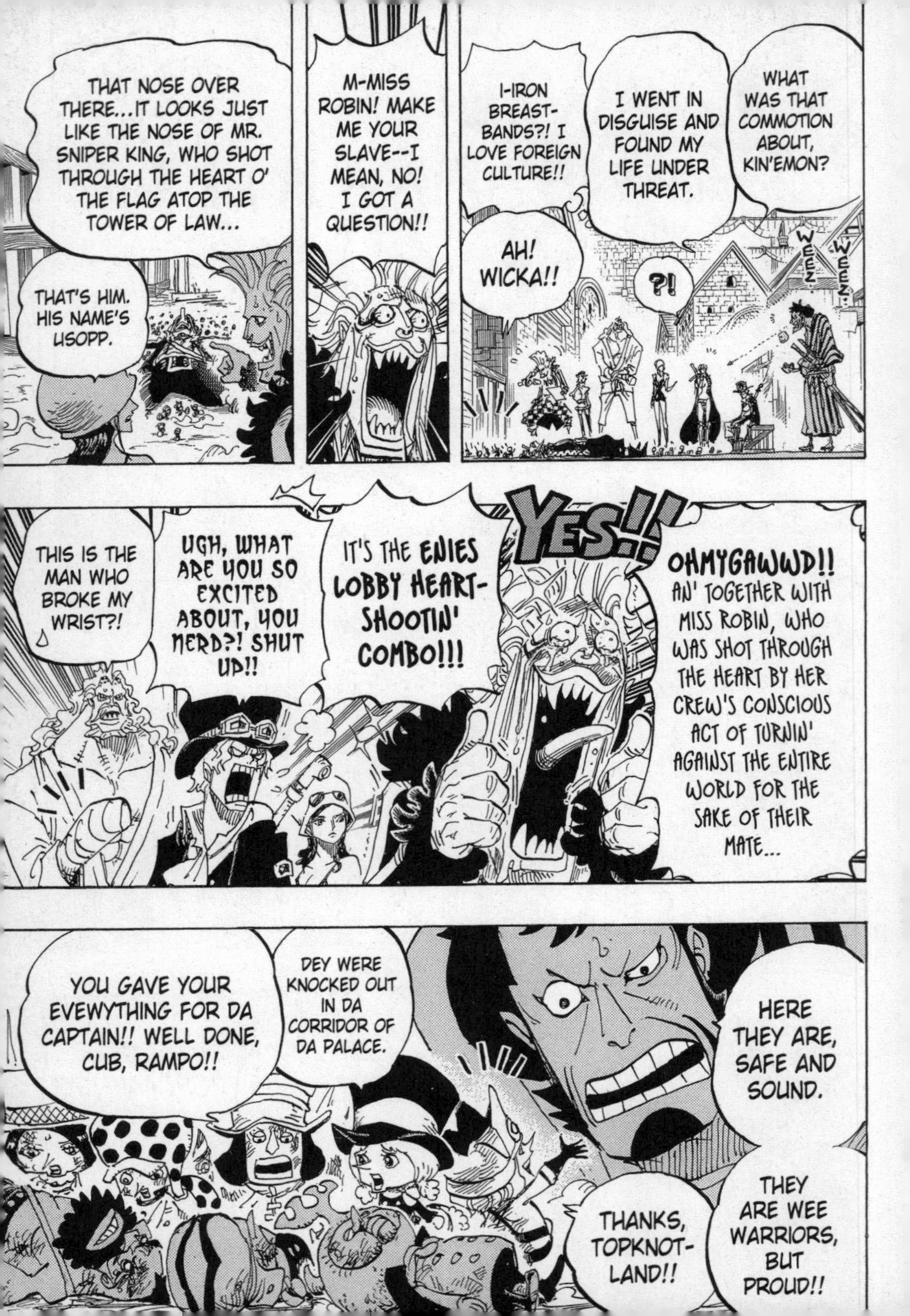
WHAT WAS THAT COMMOTION ABOUT, KIN'EMON?
I WENT IN DISGUISE AND FOUND MY LIFE UNDER THREAT.
I-IRON BREAST-BANDS?! I LOVE FOREIGN CULTURE!!
WEEZ
WEEZ
?!
AH! WICKA!!
M-MISS ROBIN! MAKE ME YOUR SLAVE--I MEAN, NO! I GOT A QUESTION!!
THAT NOSE OVER THERE...IT LOOKS JUST LIKE THE NOSE OF MR. SNIPER KING, WHO SHOT THROUGH THE HEART O' THE FLAG ATOP THE TOWER OF LAW...
THAT'S HIM. HIS NAME'S USOPP.
OHMYGAWWD!! AN' TOGETHER WITH MISS ROBIN, WHO WAS SHOT THROUGH THE HEART BY HER CREW'S CONSCIOUS ACT OF TURNIN' AGAINST THE ENTIRE WORLD FOR THE SAKE OF THEIR MATE...
YES!!
IT'S THE ENIES LOBBY HEART-SHOOTIN' COMBO!!!
UGH, WHAT ARE YOU SO EXCITED ABOUT, YOU NERD?! SHUT UP!!
THIS IS THE MAN WHO BROKE MY WRIST?!
HERE THEY ARE, SAFE AND SOUND.
THEY ARE WEE WARRIORS, BUT PROUD!!
THANKS, TOPKNOT-LAND!!
DEY WERE KNOCKED OUT IN DA CORRIDOR OF DA PALACE.
YOU GAVE YOUR EVEWYTHING FOR DA CAPTAIN!! WELL DONE, CUB, RAMPO!!

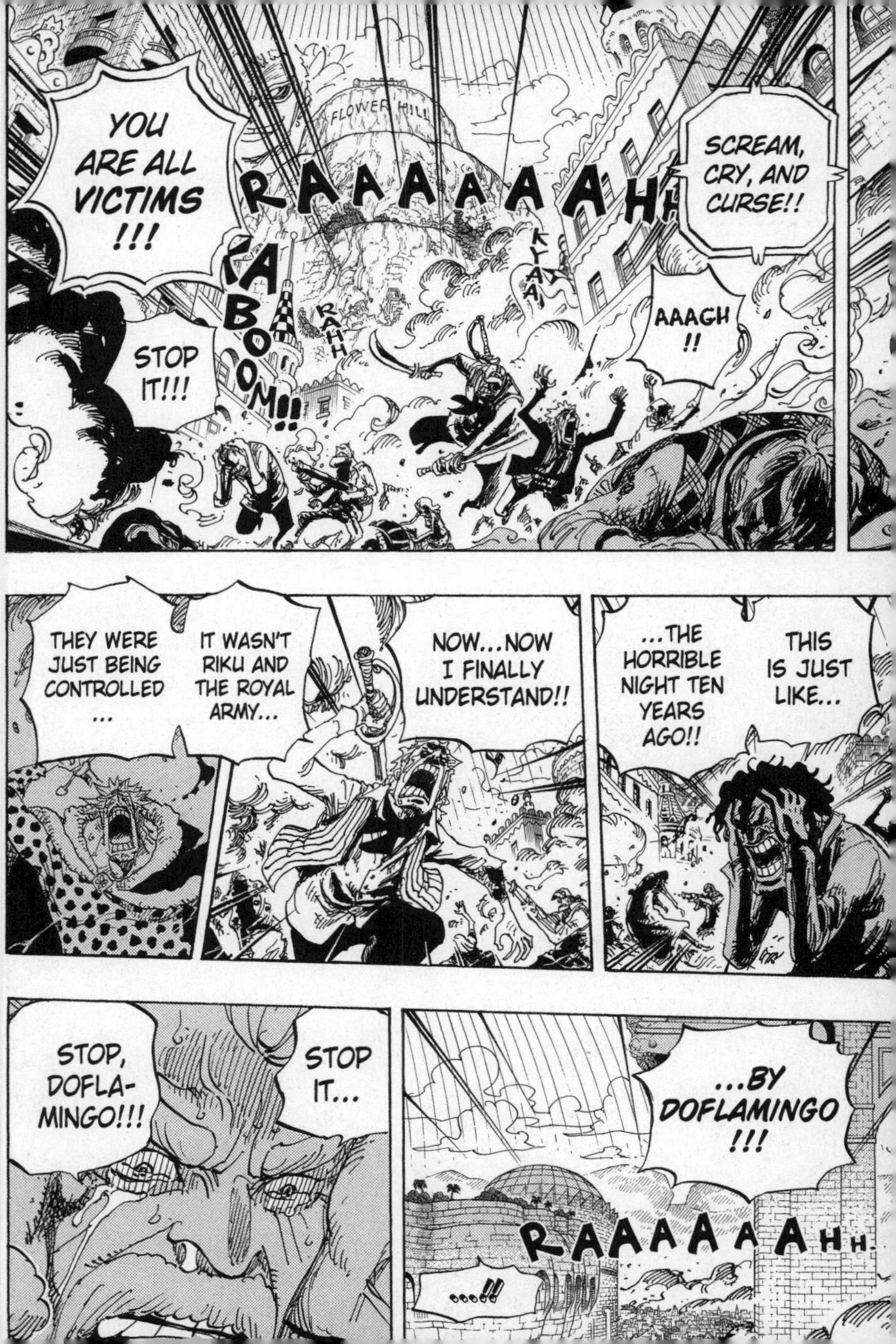
SCREAM, CRY, AND CURSE!!
RAAAAAAH
YOU ARE ALL VICTIMS!!!
KYAA
AAAGH!!
RAHH
KABOOM!!
STOP IT!!!
THIS IS JUST LIKE...
...THE HORRIBLE NIGHT TEN YEARS AGO!!
NOW...NOW I FINALLY UNDERSTAND!!
IT WASN'T RIKU AND THE ROYAL ARMY...
THEY WERE JUST BEING CONTROLLED...
...BY DOFLAMINGO!!!
RAAAAAAHH
......!!
STOP IT...
STOP, DOFLAMINGO!!!

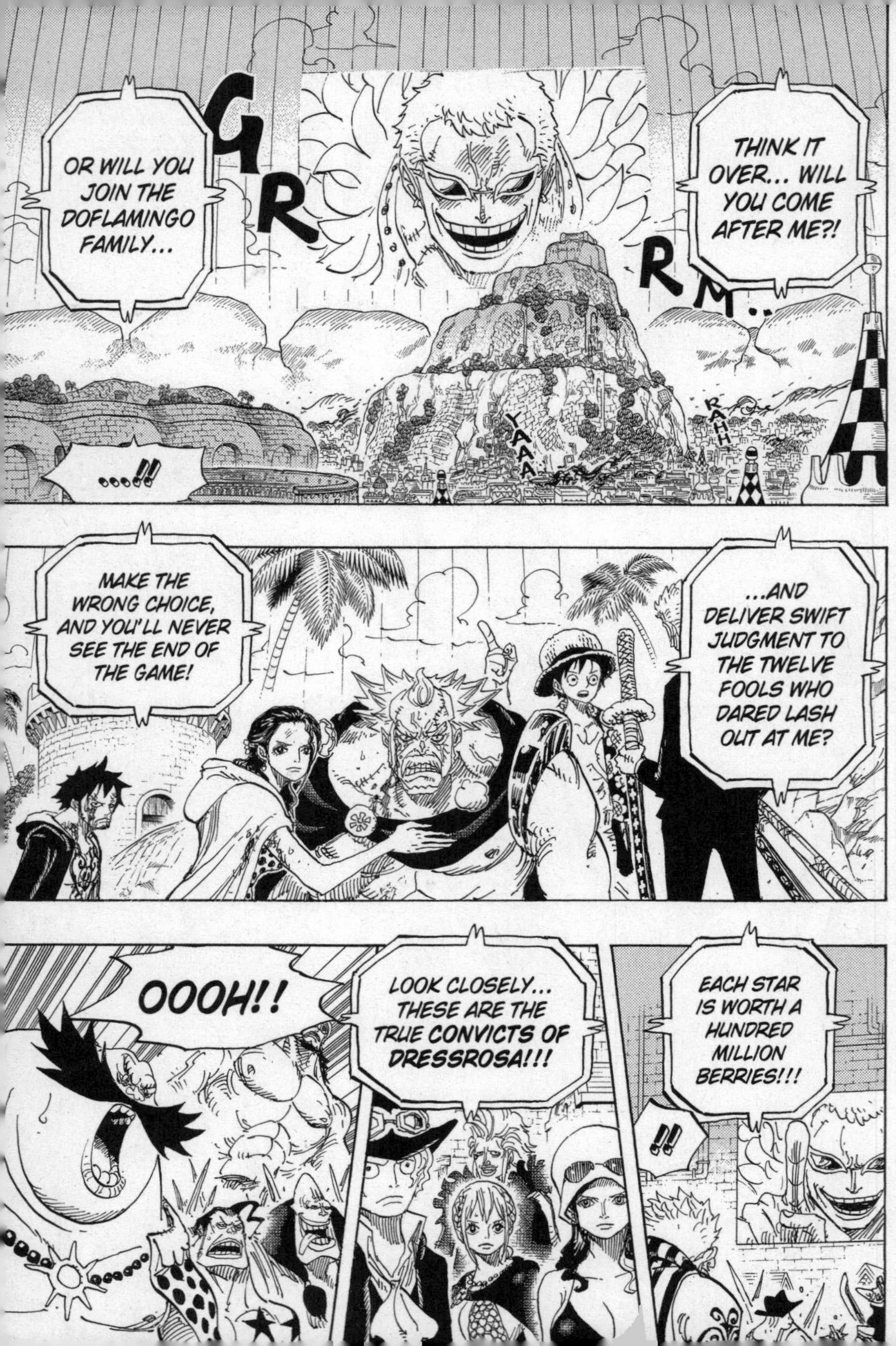
THINK IT OVER... WILL YOU COME AFTER ME?!
OR WILL YOU JOIN THE DOFLAMINGO FAMILY...
GRRM..
RAHH
YAAA
...!!
...AND DELIVER SWIFT JUDGMENT TO THE TWELVE FOOLS WHO DARED LASH OUT AT ME?
MAKE THE WRONG CHOICE, AND YOU'LL NEVER SEE THE END OF THE GAME!
EACH STAR IS WORTH A HUNDRED MILLION BERRIES!!!
!!
LOOK CLOSELY... THESE ARE THE TRUE CONVICTS OF DRESSROSA!!!
OOOH!!

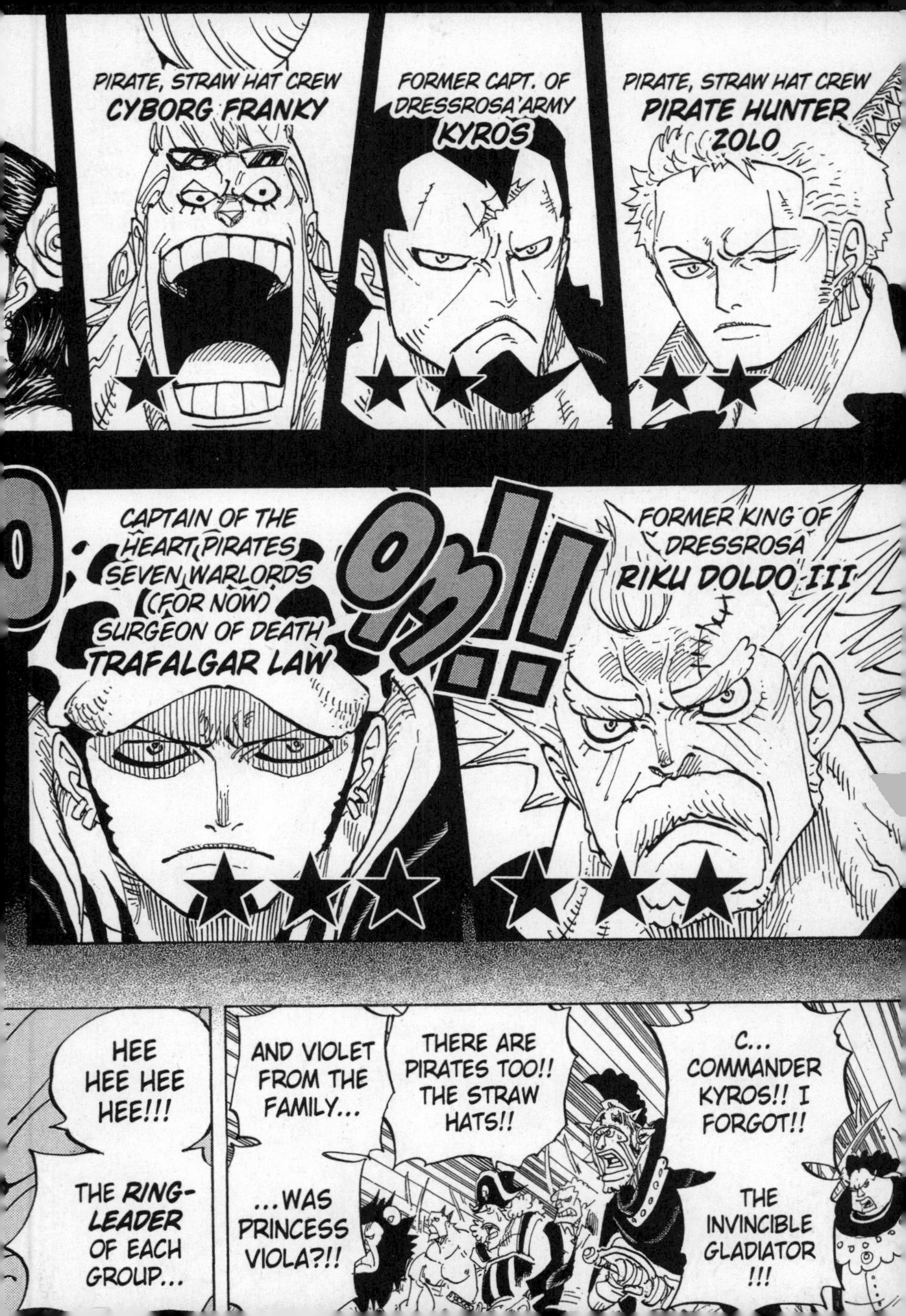
PIRATE, STRAW HAT CREW PIRATE HUNTER ZOLO
FORMER CAPT. OF DRESSROSA ARMY KYROS
PIRATE, STRAW HAT CREW CYBORG FRANKY
FORMER KING OF DRESSROSA RIKU DOLDO III
OM!!
CAPTAIN OF THE HEART PIRATES SEVEN WARLORDS (FOR NOW) SURGEON OF DEATH TRAFALGAR LAW
C... COMMANDER KYROS!! I FORGOT!!
THE INVINCIBLE GLADIATOR !!!
THERE ARE PIRATES TOO!! THE STRAW HATS!!
AND VIOLET FROM THE FAMILY...
...WAS PRINCESS VIOLA?!!
HEE HEE HEE HEE!!!
THE *RING-LEADER* OF EACH GROUP...

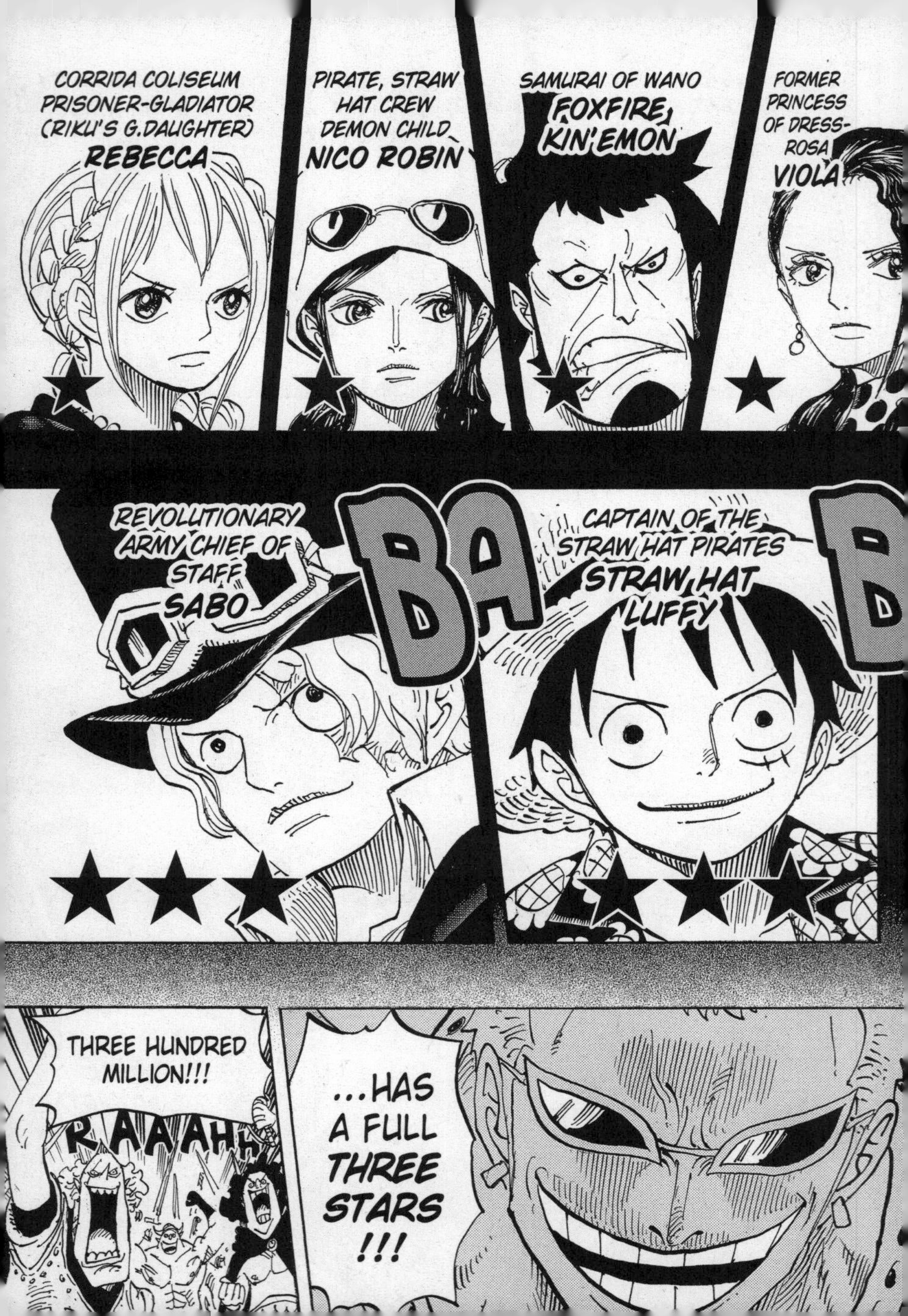
FORMER PRINCESS OF DRESS-ROSA
VIOLA
SAMURAI OF WANO
FOXFIRE KIN'EMON
PIRATE, STRAW HAT CREW
DEMON CHILD
NICO ROBIN
CORRIDA COLISEUM PRISONER-GLADIATOR (RIKU'S G.DAUGHTER)
REBECCA
CAPTAIN OF THE STRAW HAT PIRATES
STRAW HAT LUFFY
BA
REVOLUTIONARY ARMY CHIEF OF STAFF
SABO
...HAS A FULL THREE STARS!!!
THREE HUNDRED MILLION!!!
RAAAHH

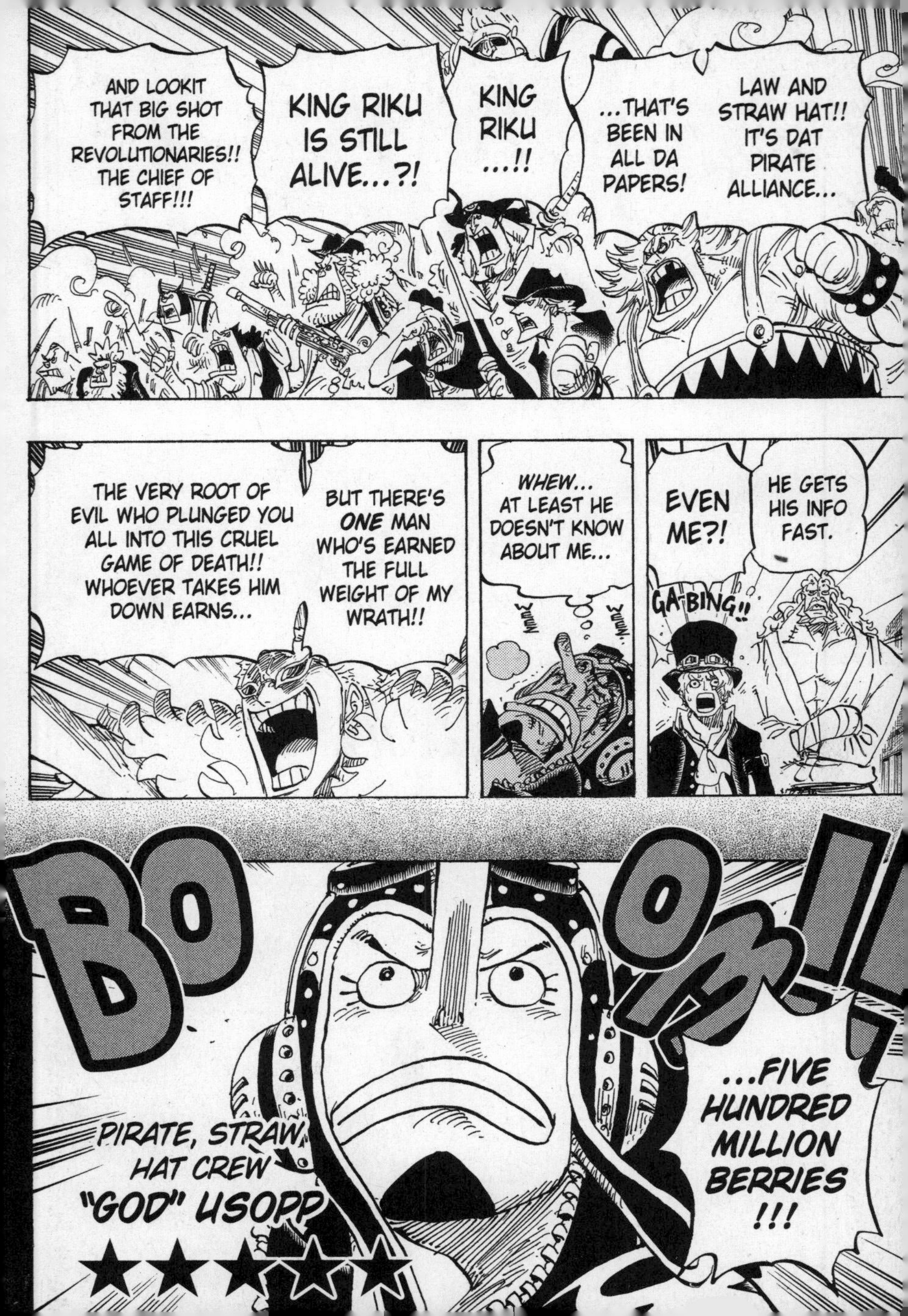
LAW AND STRAW HAT!! IT'S DAT PIRATE ALLIANCE...
...THAT'S BEEN IN ALL DA PAPERS!
KING RIKU ...!!
KING RIKU IS STILL ALIVE...?!
AND LOOKIT THAT BIG SHOT FROM THE REVOLUTIONARIES!! THE CHIEF OF STAFF!!!
HE GETS HIS INFO FAST.
EVEN ME?!
GA-BING!!
WHEW... AT LEAST HE DOESN'T KNOW ABOUT ME...
BUT THERE'S ONE MAN WHO'S EARNED THE FULL WEIGHT OF MY WRATH!!
THE VERY ROOT OF EVIL WHO PLUNGED YOU ALL INTO THIS CRUEL GAME OF DEATH!! WHOEVER TAKES HIM DOWN EARNS...
BOOM!!
...FIVE HUNDRED MILLION BERRIES !!!
PIRATE, STRAW HAT CREW "GOD" USOPP

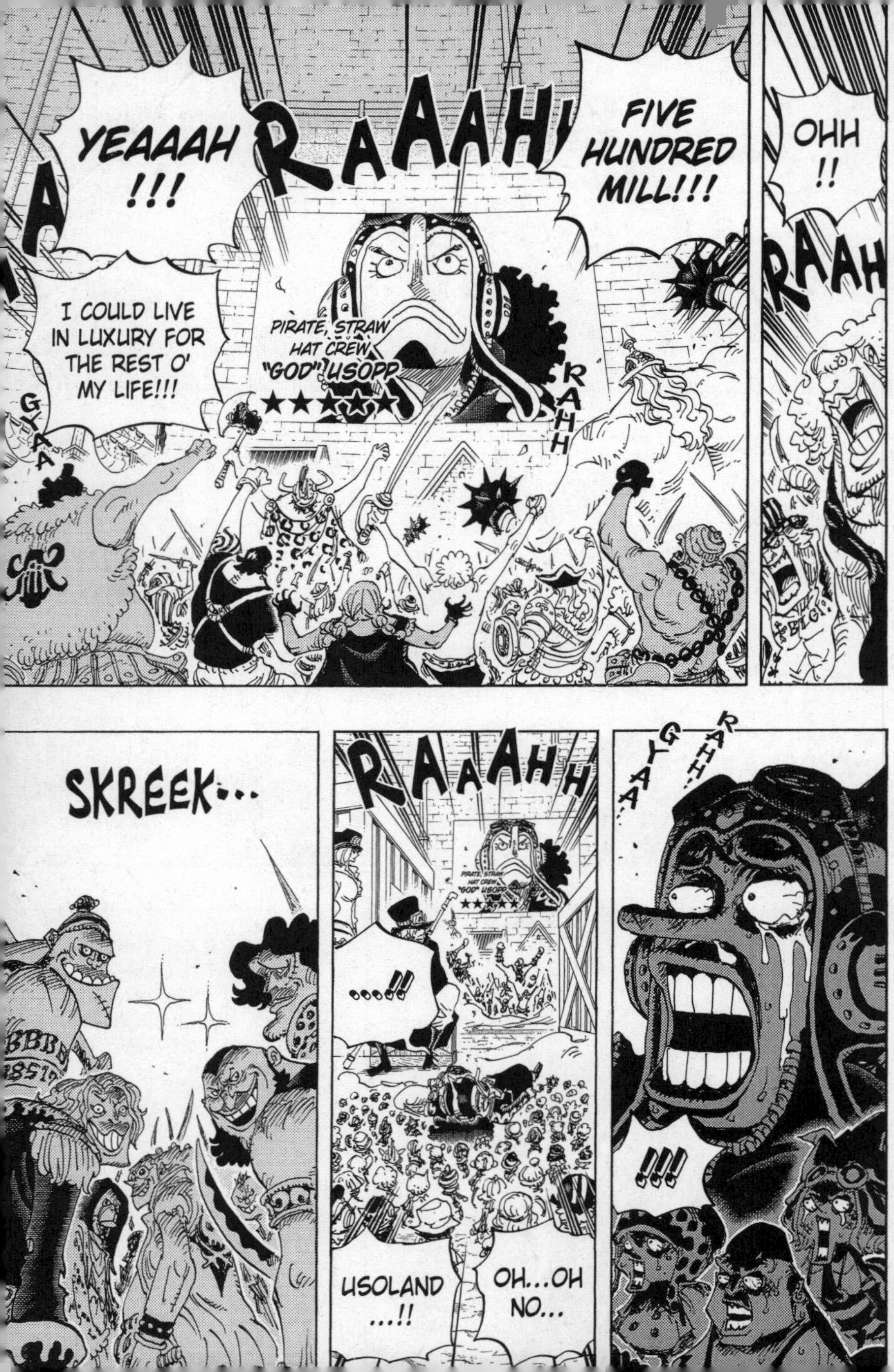
OHH !!
RAAH
FIVE HUNDRED MILL!!!
RAAAH!
YEAAAH !!!
A
I COULD LIVE IN LUXURY FOR THE REST O' MY LIFE!!!
PIRATE, STRAW HAT CREW "GOD" USOPP
RAHH
GYAA
RAHH!
GYAA...
!!!
RAAAHH
PIRATE, STRAW HAT CREW "GOD" USOPP
....!!
OH...OH NO...
USOLAND ...!!
SKREEK...

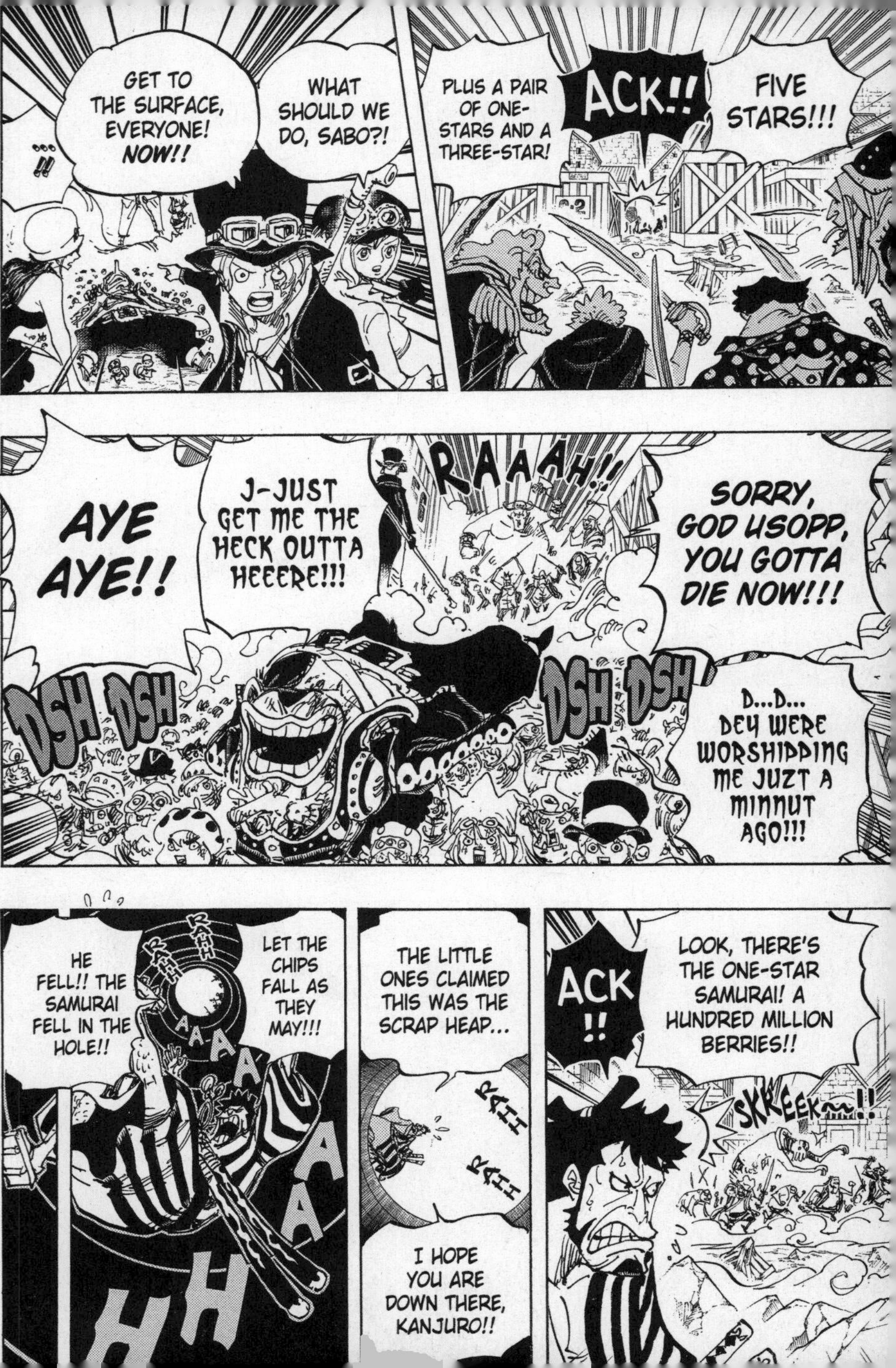
FIVE STARS!!!
ACK!!
PLUS A PAIR OF ONE-STARS AND A THREE-STAR!
WHAT SHOULD WE DO, SABO?!
GET TO THE SURFACE, EVERYONE! NOW!!
...!!
SORRY, GOD USOPP, YOU GOTTA DIE NOW!!!
RAAAH!!
J-JUST GET ME THE HECK OUTTA HEEERE!!!
AYE AYE!!
D...D... DEY WERE WORSHIPPING ME JUZT A MINNUT AGO!!!
DSH DSH
DSH DSH
LOOK, THERE'S THE ONE-STAR SAMURAI! A HUNDRED MILLION BERRIES!!
ACK !!
SKREEEK~!!
THE LITTLE ONES CLAIMED THIS WAS THE SCRAP HEAP...
RAHH
RAHH
I HOPE YOU ARE DOWN THERE, KANJURO!!
LET THE CHIPS FALL AS THEY MAY!!!
HE FELL!! THE SAMURAI FELL IN THE HOLE!!
RAHH
RAHH
AAAAAAAHH

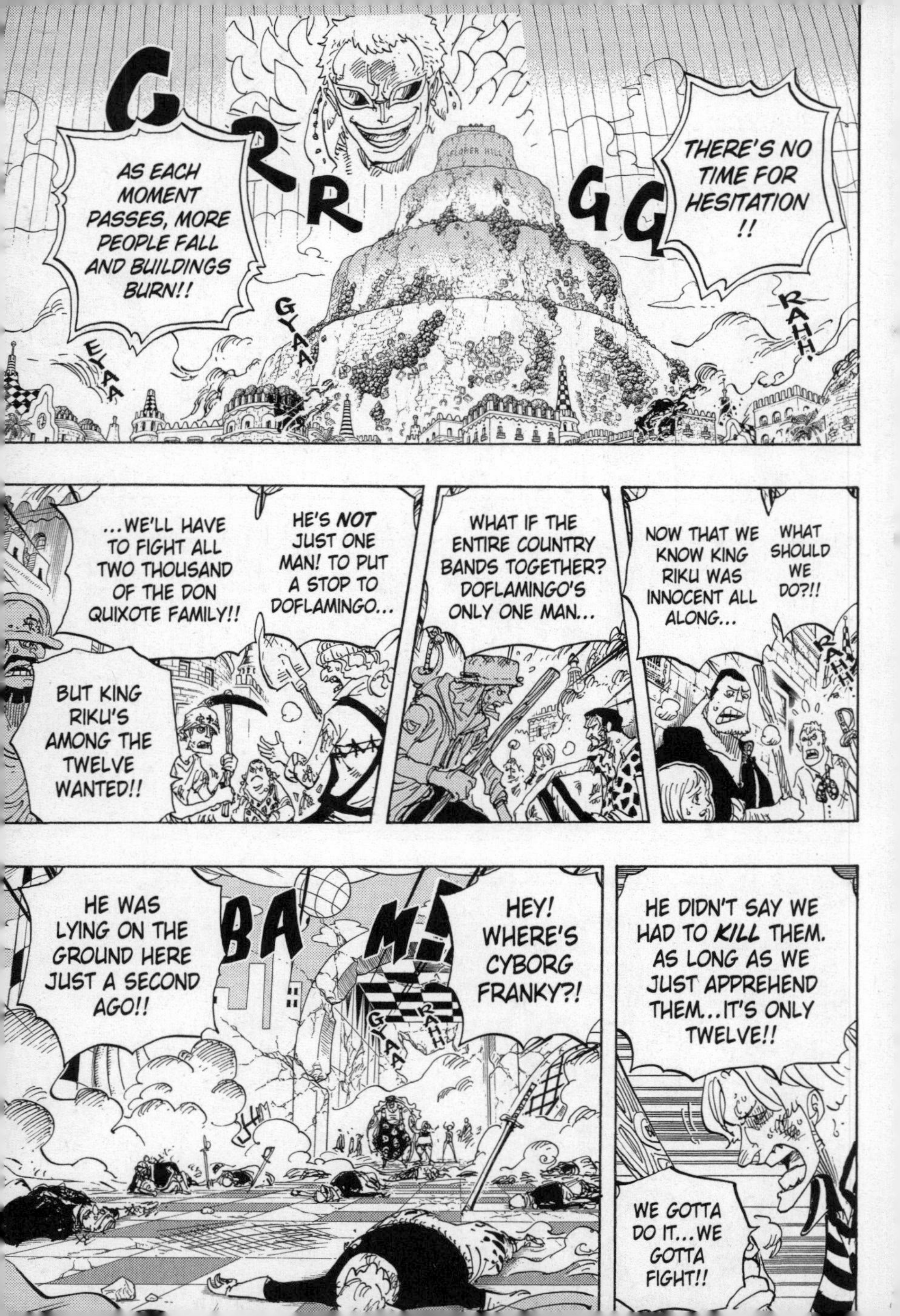
THERE'S NO TIME FOR HESITATION !!
GRRGG
AS EACH MOMENT PASSES, MORE PEOPLE FALL AND BUILDINGS BURN!!
RAHH!
GYAA
EYAA
WHAT SHOULD WE DO?!!
NOW THAT WE KNOW KING RIKU WAS INNOCENT ALL ALONG...
RAHH
WHAT IF THE ENTIRE COUNTRY BANDS TOGETHER? DOFLAMINGO'S ONLY ONE MAN...
HE'S NOT JUST ONE MAN! TO PUT A STOP TO DOFLAMINGO...
...WE'LL HAVE TO FIGHT ALL TWO THOUSAND OF THE DON QUIXOTE FAMILY!!
BUT KING RIKU'S AMONG THE TWELVE WANTED!!
HE DIDN'T SAY WE HAD TO KILL THEM. AS LONG AS WE JUST APPREHEND THEM...IT'S ONLY TWELVE!!
WE GOTTA DO IT...WE GOTTA FIGHT!!
HEY! WHERE'S CYBORG FRANKY?!
BAM
HE WAS LYING ON THE GROUND HERE JUST A SECOND AGO!!
RAHH
GYAA

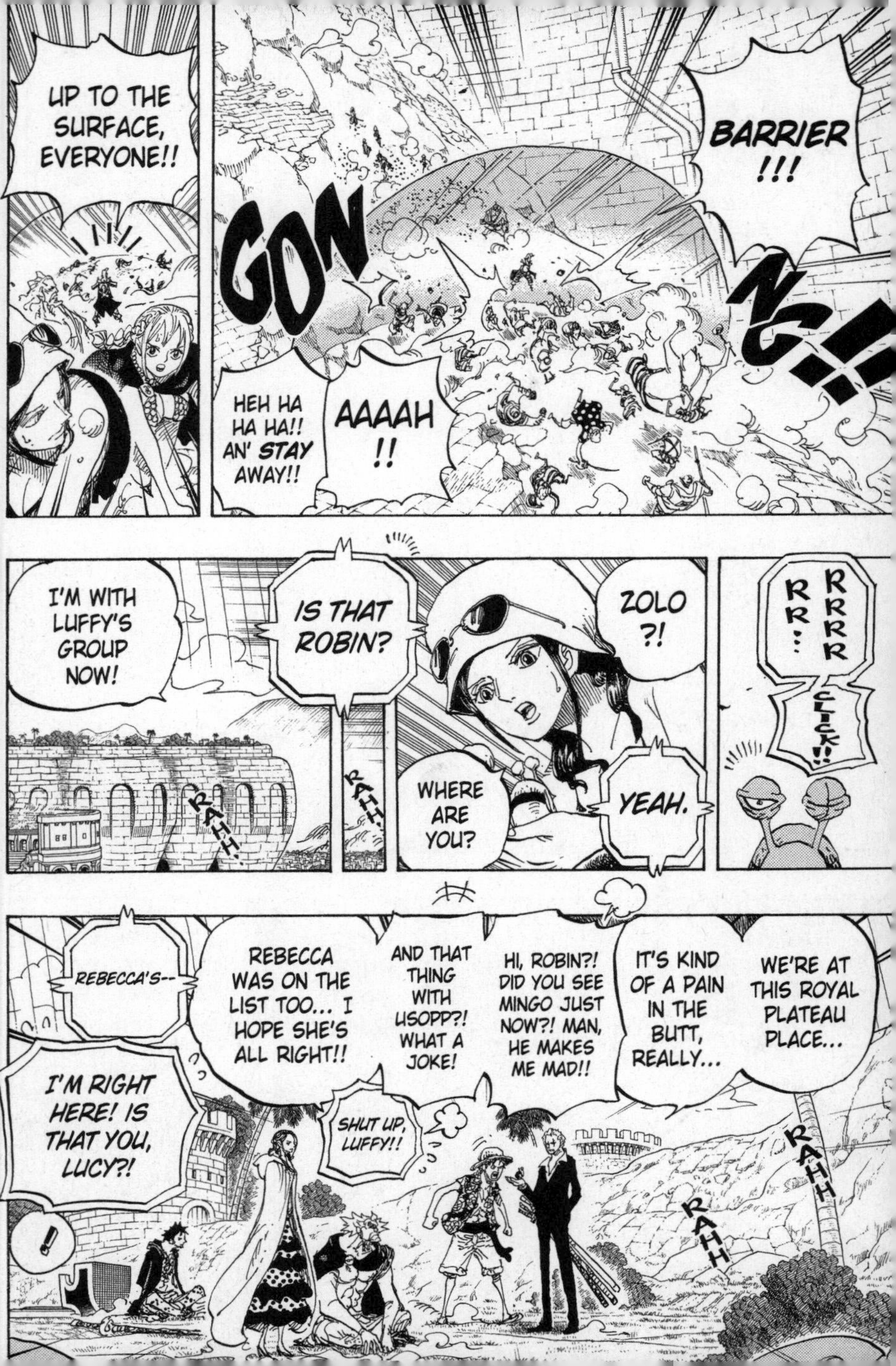
BARRIER!!!
GON
NG!!
AAAAH!!
HEH HA HA HA!! AN' STAY AWAY!!
UP TO THE SURFACE, EVERYONE!!
RR... RRRR
CLICK!!
ZOLO?!
YEAH.
WHERE ARE YOU?
IS THAT ROBIN?
RAHH.
I'M WITH LUFFY'S GROUP NOW!
RAHH.
WE'RE AT THIS ROYAL PLATEAU PLACE...
IT'S KIND OF A PAIN IN THE BUTT, REALLY...
HI, ROBIN?! DID YOU SEE MINGO JUST NOW?! MAN, HE MAKES ME MAD!!
AND THAT THING WITH USOPP?! WHAT A JOKE!
REBECCA WAS ON THE LIST TOO... I HOPE SHE'S ALL RIGHT!!
REBECCA'S--
RAHH
RAHH
SHUT UP, LUFFY!!
I'M RIGHT HERE! IS THAT YOU, LUCY?!
!

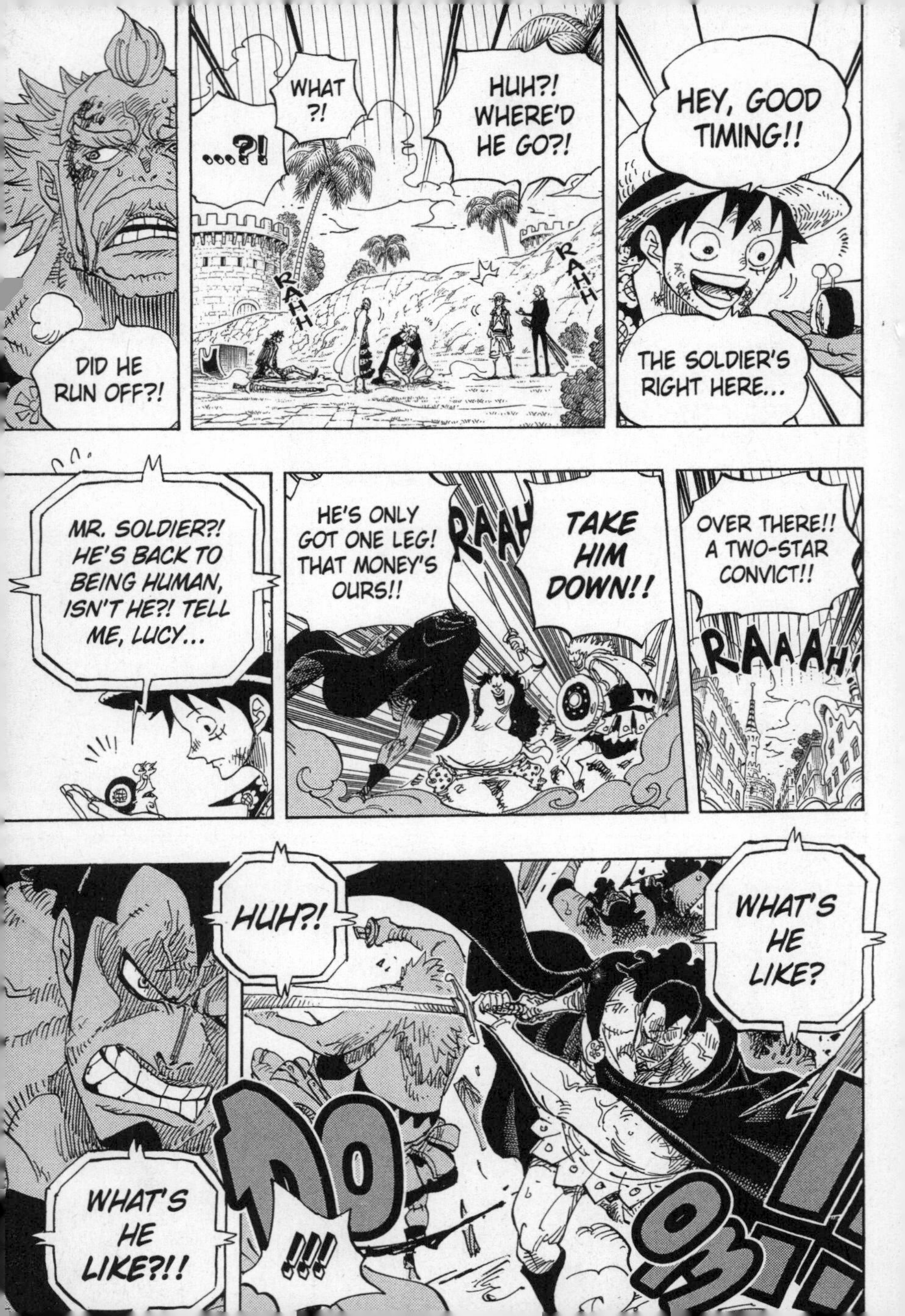
HEY, GOOD TIMING!!
THE SOLDIER'S RIGHT HERE...
HUH?! WHERE'D HE GO?!
WHAT ?!
...?!
RAHH
RAHH
DID HE RUN OFF?!
OVER THERE!! A TWO-STAR CONVICT!!
RAAAH
TAKE HIM DOWN!!
RAAH
HE'S ONLY GOT ONE LEG! THAT MONEY'S OURS!!
MR. SOLDIER?! HE'S BACK TO BEING HUMAN, ISN'T HE?! TELL ME, LUCY...
WHAT'S HE LIKE?
HUH?!
WHAT'S HE LIKE?!!
!!!

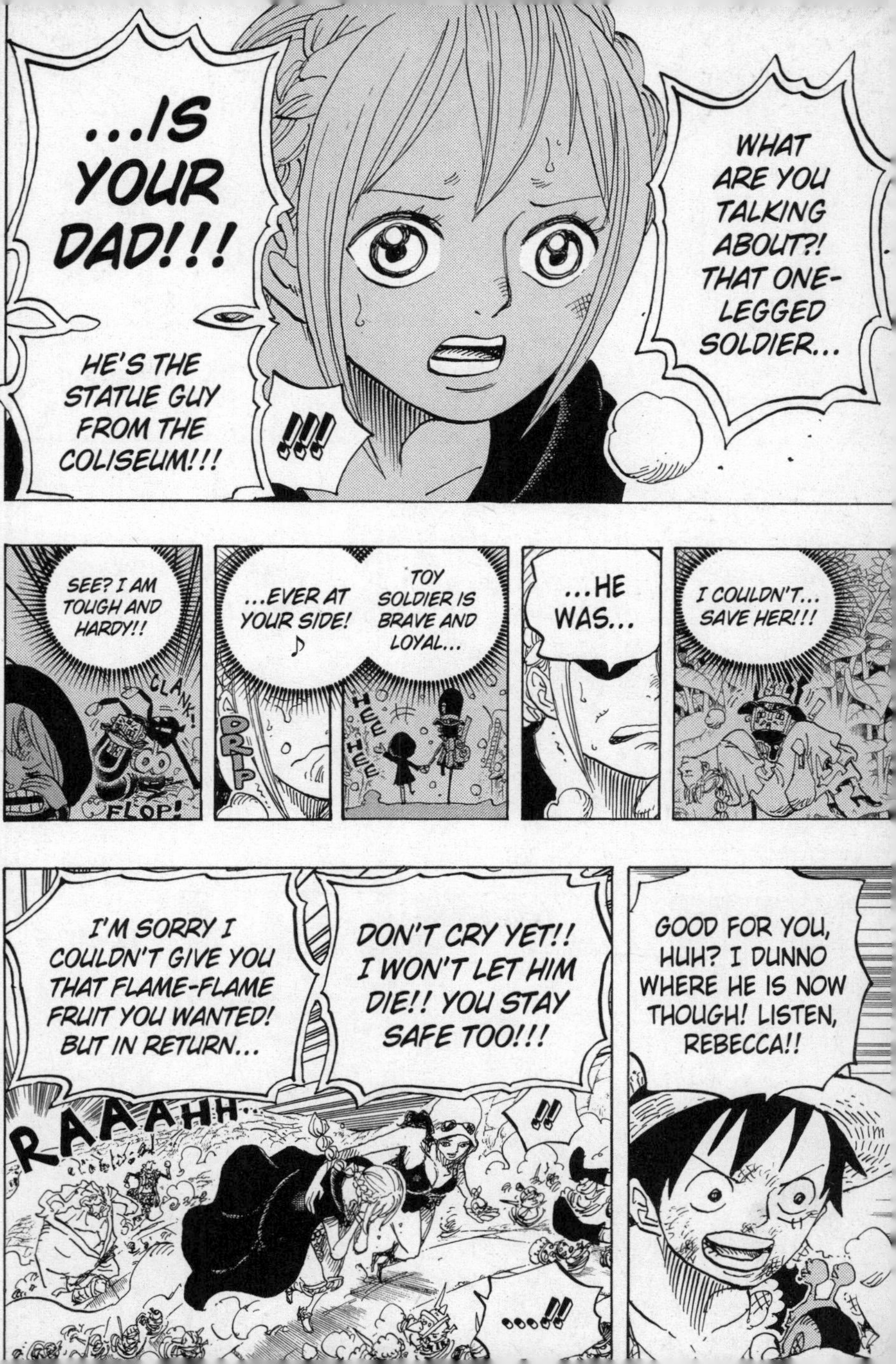
WHAT ARE YOU TALKING ABOUT?! THAT ONE-LEGGED SOLDIER...
...IS YOUR DAD!!!
HE'S THE STATUE GUY FROM THE COLISEUM!!!
!!!
I COULDN'T... SAVE HER!!!
...HE WAS...
TOY SOLDIER IS BRAVE AND LOYAL...
HEE HEE
...EVER AT YOUR SIDE! ♪
DRIP
SEE? I AM TOUGH AND HARDY!!
CLANK!
FLOP!
GOOD FOR YOU, HUH? I DUNNO WHERE HE IS NOW THOUGH! LISTEN, REBECCA!!
DON'T CRY YET!! I WON'T LET HIM DIE!! YOU STAY SAFE TOO!!!
I'M SORRY I COULDN'T GIVE YOU THAT FLAME-FLAME FRUIT YOU WANTED! BUT IN RETURN...
!!
RAAAHH...
...!!

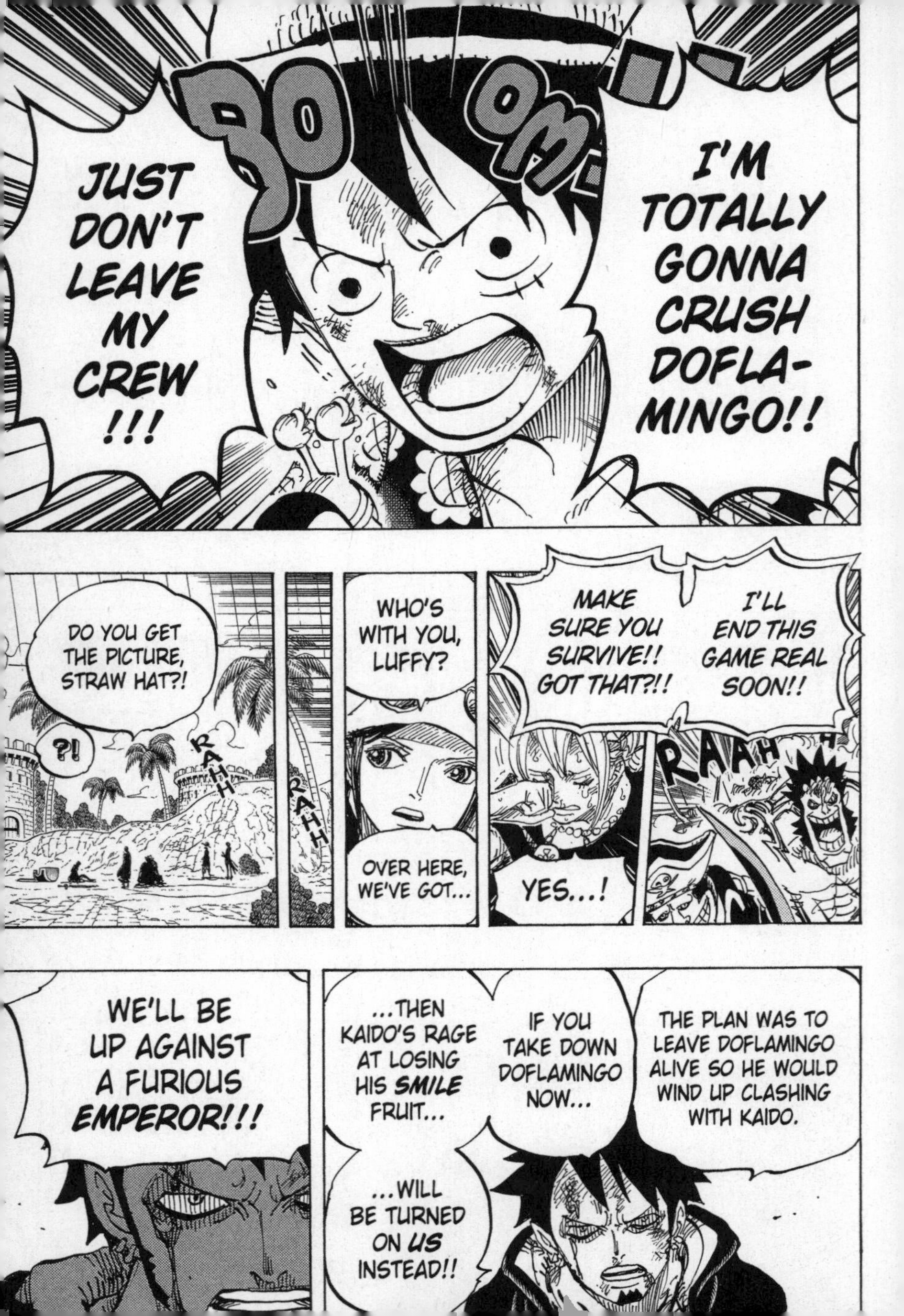

I'M TOTALLY GONNA CRUSH DOFLA-MINGO!!
BOOOM
JUST DON'T LEAVE MY CREW!!!
I'LL END THIS GAME REAL SOON!!
MAKE SURE YOU SURVIVE!! GOT THAT?!!
RAAHH
YES...!
WHO'S WITH YOU, LUFFY?
OVER HERE, WE'VE GOT...
RAHH
RAHH
DO YOU GET THE PICTURE, STRAW HAT?!
?!
THE PLAN WAS TO LEAVE DOFLAMINGO ALIVE SO HE WOULD WIND UP CLASHING WITH KAIDO.
IF YOU TAKE DOWN DOFLAMINGO NOW...
...THEN KAIDO'S RAGE AT LOSING HIS SMILE FRUIT...
...WILL BE TURNED ON US INSTEAD!!
WE'LL BE UP AGAINST A FURIOUS EMPEROR!!!

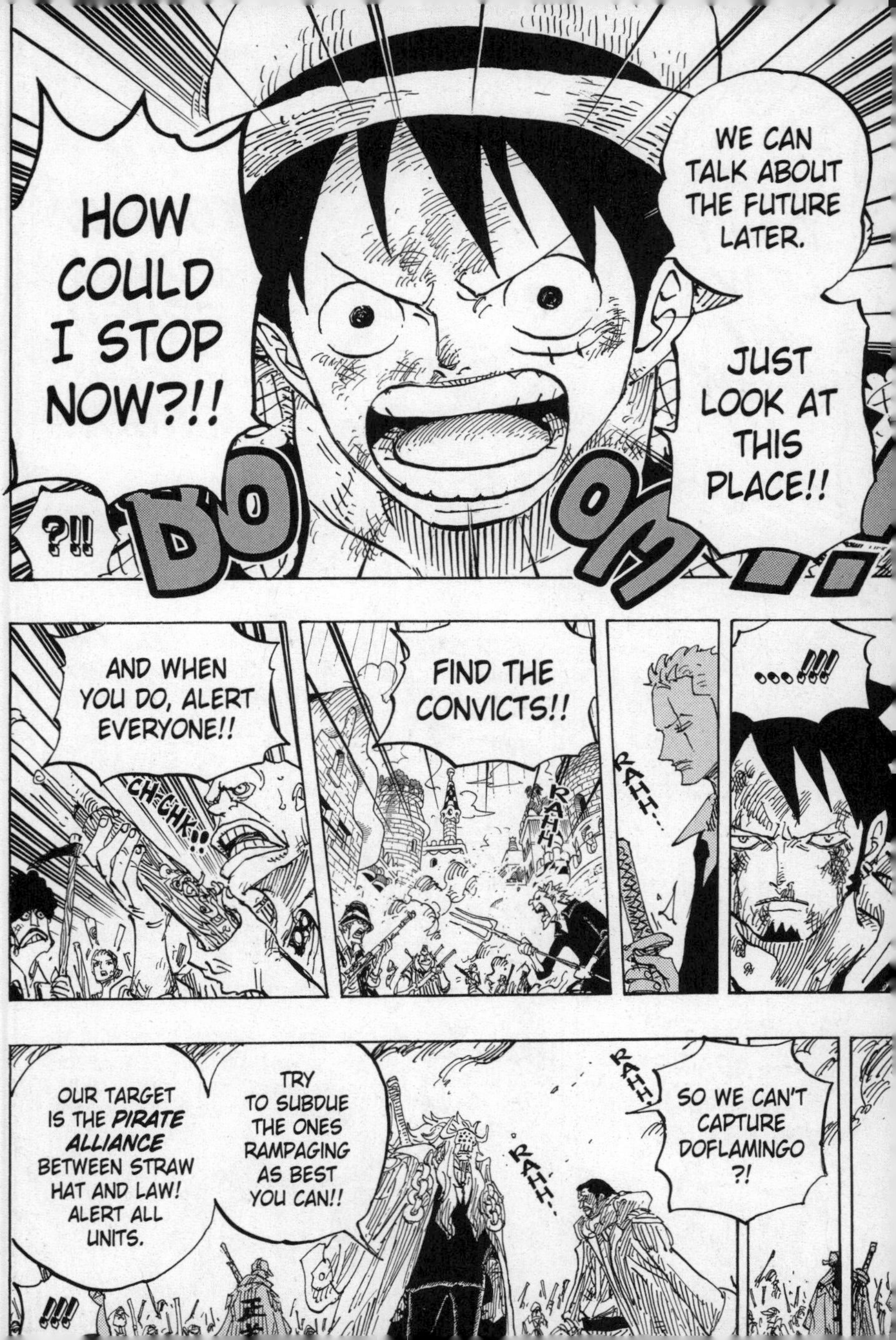
WE CAN TALK ABOUT THE FUTURE LATER.
JUST LOOK AT THIS PLACE!!
HOW COULD I STOP NOW?!!
?!!
DOOM...
...!!!
RAHH...
RAHH
FIND THE CONVICTS!!
AND WHEN YOU DO, ALERT EVERYONE!!
CH-CHK!!
SO WE CAN'T CAPTURE DOFLAMINGO ?!
RAHH
RAHH...
TRY TO SUBDUE THE ONES RAMPAGING AS BEST YOU CAN!!
OUR TARGET IS THE *PIRATE ALLIANCE* BETWEEN STRAW HAT AND LAW! ALERT ALL UNITS.
!!!

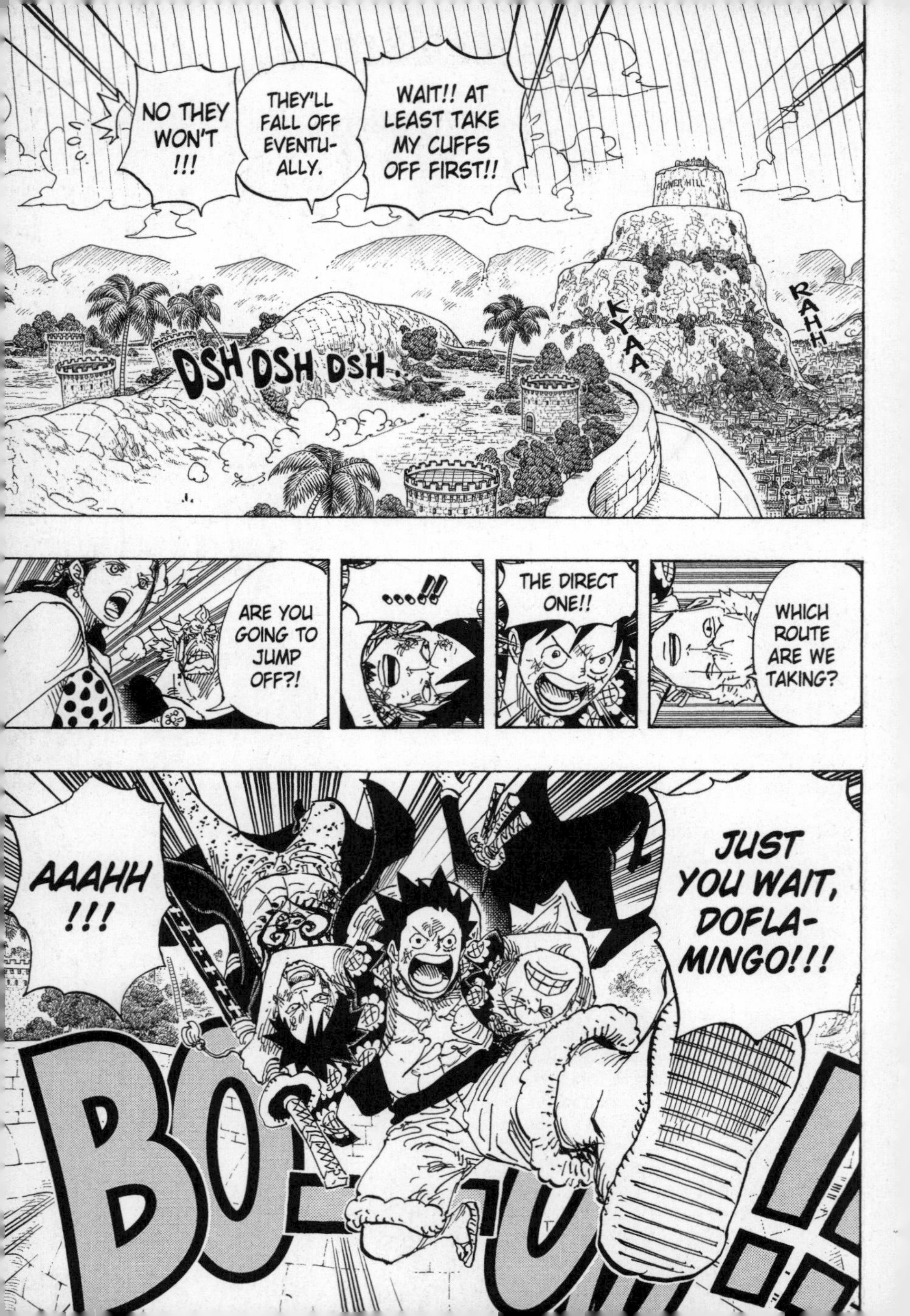
WAIT!! AT LEAST TAKE MY CUFFS OFF FIRST!!
THEY'LL FALL OFF EVENTU-ALLY.
NO THEY WON'T !!!
FLOWER HILL
RAHH
KYAA
DSH DSH DSH
WHICH ROUTE ARE WE TAKING?
THE DIRECT ONE!!
....!!
ARE YOU GOING TO JUMP OFF?!
JUST YOU WAIT, DOFLA-MINGO!!!
AAAHH !!!

SBS Question Corner

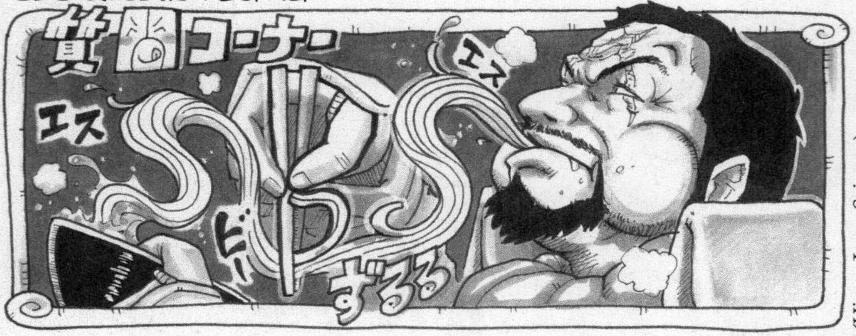

質問コーナー
エス
エス
ビー
ずるる

(Hippo Iron, Saitama)

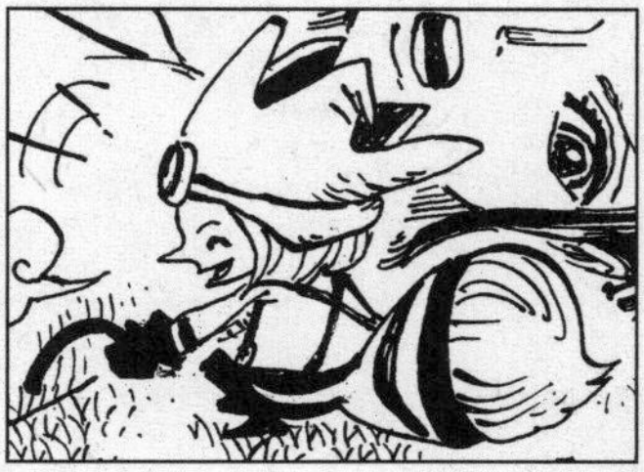

Q: What are those things that look like tails growing from the Tontattas' butts?

--Maa

A: Um, tails. They might seem to be fluffy at first glance, but they have firm bone and muscle underneath. The tails help them move swiftly, and serve as powerful bludgeons in combat.

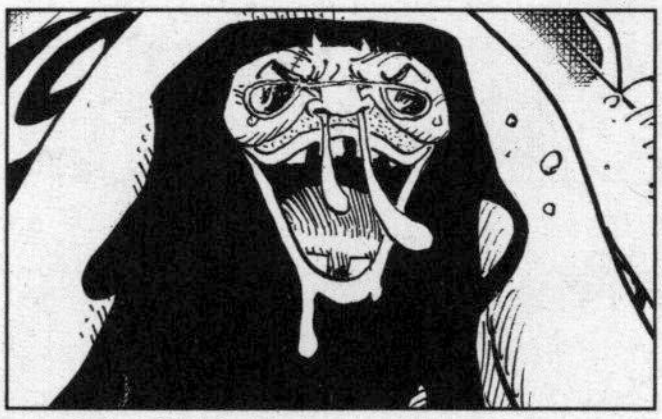

Q: I have a question. I always thought my husband had the Stick-Stick Fruit powers. His face and neck and armpits are always sticky. But if it turns out that Trebol had the Stick-Stick Fruit…then what powers does my husband have?

--Emukichi

A: He's just oily.

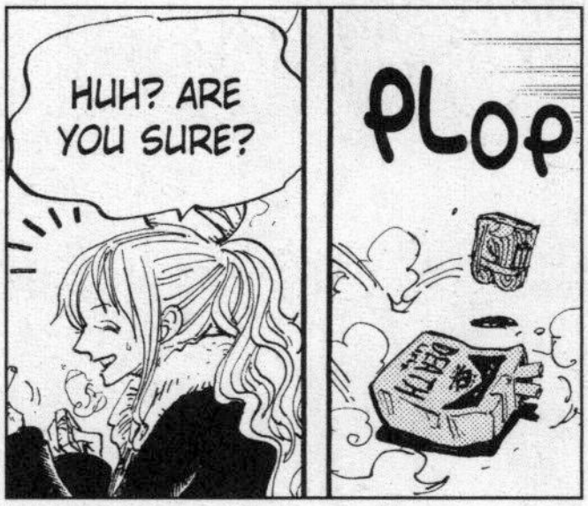

PLOP
HUH? ARE YOU SURE?

Q: Are the lighter that Sanji used in *One Piece Film Z* and the lighter from the opening theme song "Hands Up!" in the anime series actually the same thing?

--Cook-Obsessed A.K.

A: "Hands Up!" was the previous opening, right? I don't know if they used it there too, but when producing Film Z, I did a personal collaboration with the French company Dupont, and the lighter we designed went into the movie. As a matter of fact, it also showed up in Chapter 663 (Volume 67) of the manga. Did I mention this before? Whatever.
I bet you can see pictures if you just do an internet image search for "Dupont Oda." Sanji uses that lighter.

Chapter 747: SUPREME OFFICER PICA

REQUEST: "CUTE LITTLE CUBS LIKE MIHAWK WHILE PERONA IS JEALOUS" BY YONEMI FROM YOKOHAMA

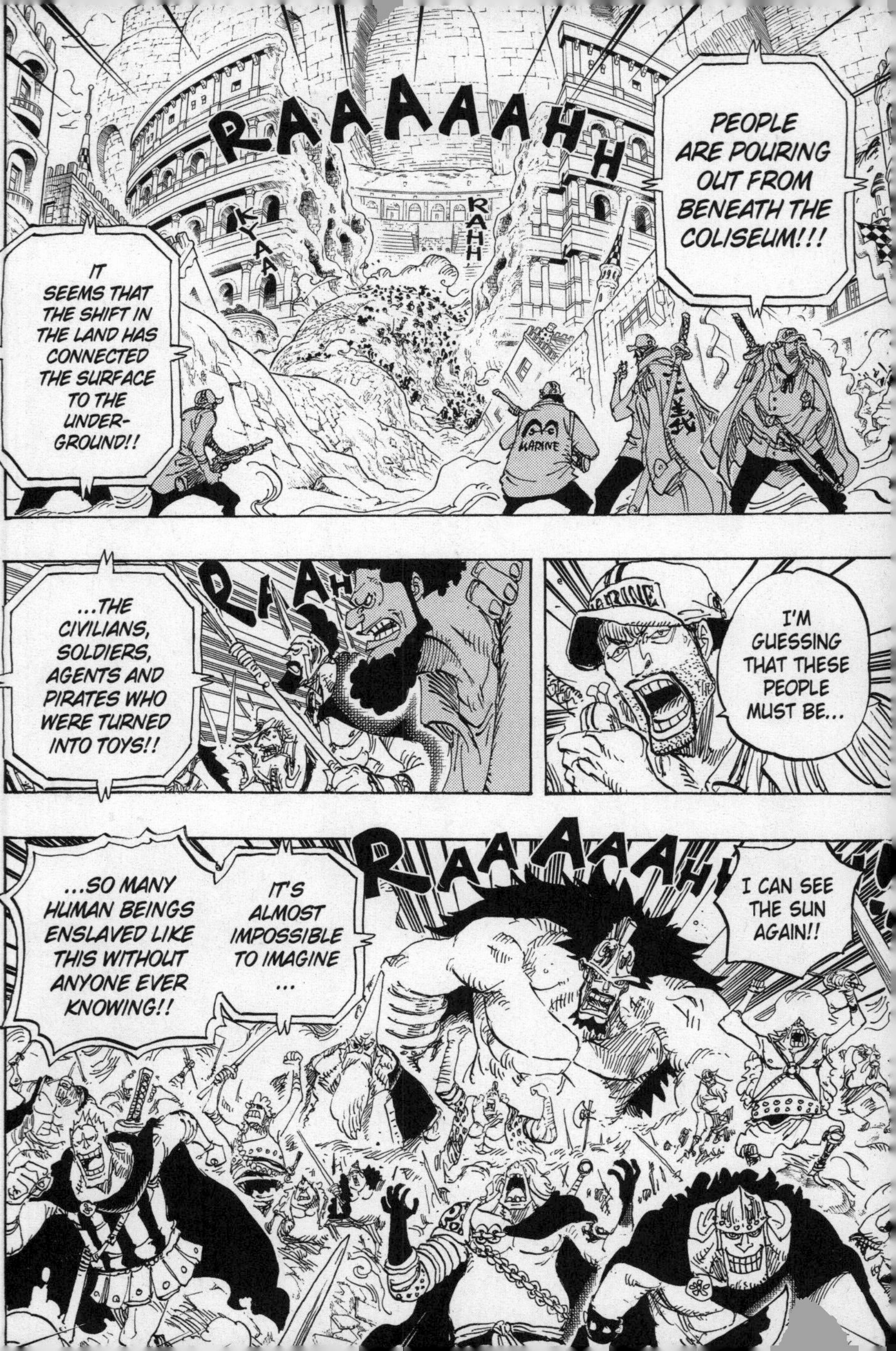
RAAAAAAHH
PEOPLE ARE POURING OUT FROM BENEATH THE COLISEUM!!!
KYAA
RAHH
IT SEEMS THAT THE SHIFT IN THE LAND HAS CONNECTED THE SURFACE TO THE UNDER-GROUND!!
I'M GUESSING THAT THESE PEOPLE MUST BE...
RAH
...THE CIVILIANS, SOLDIERS, AGENTS AND PIRATES WHO WERE TURNED INTO TOYS!!
I CAN SEE THE SUN AGAIN!!
RAAAAAAH
IT'S ALMOST IMPOSSIBLE TO IMAGINE ...
...SO MANY HUMAN BEINGS ENSLAVED LIKE THIS WITHOUT ANYONE EVER KNOWING!!

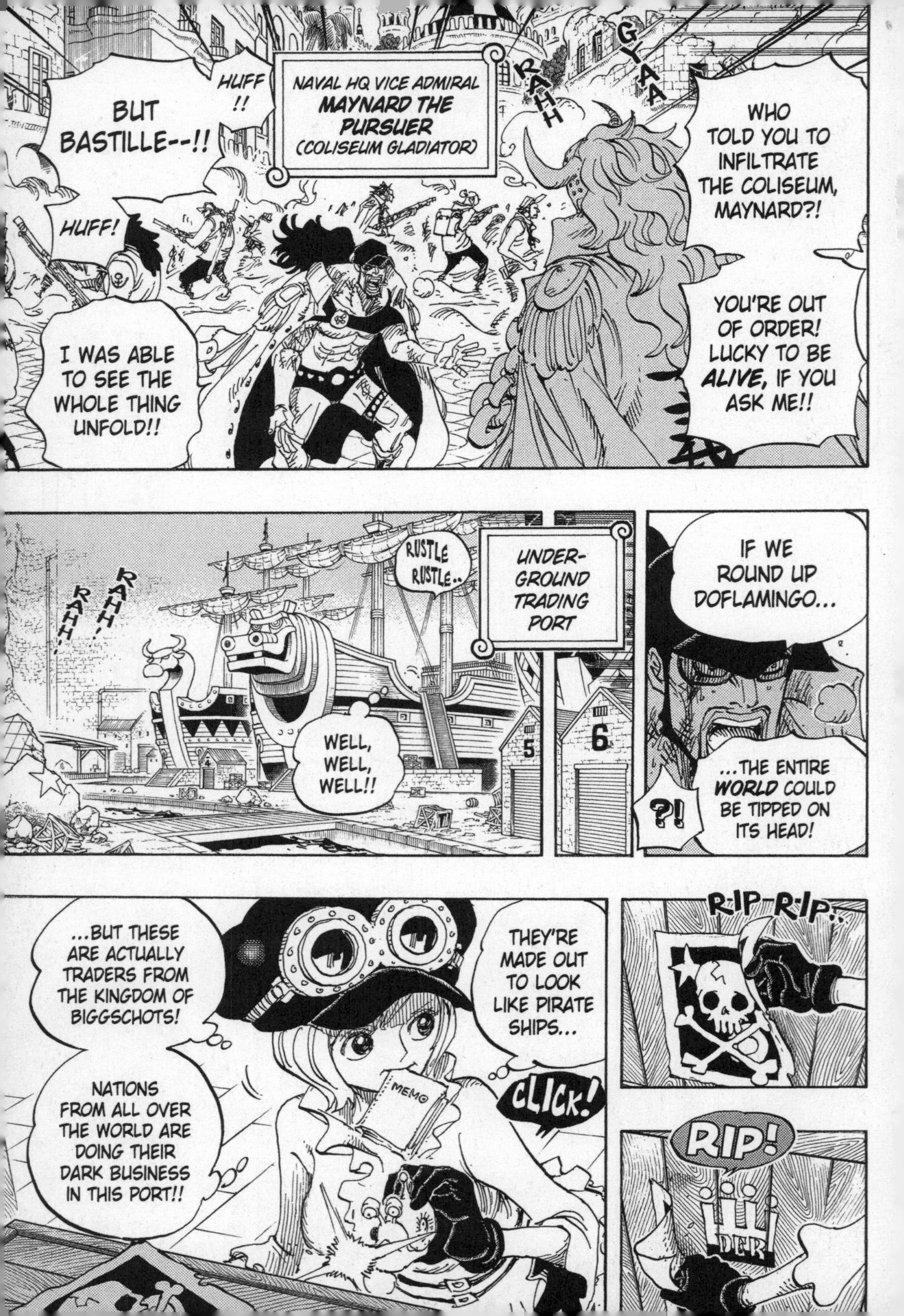
WHO TOLD YOU TO INFILTRATE THE COLISEUM, MAYNARD?!
GYAA
RAHH
YOU'RE OUT OF ORDER! LUCKY TO BE ALIVE, IF YOU ASK ME!!
NAVAL HQ VICE ADMIRAL MAYNARD THE PURSUER (COLISEUM GLADIATOR)
HUFF !!
BUT BASTILLE--!!
HUFF!
I WAS ABLE TO SEE THE WHOLE THING UNFOLD!!
IF WE ROUND UP DOFLAMINGO...
...THE ENTIRE WORLD COULD BE TIPPED ON ITS HEAD!
?!
UNDER-GROUND TRADING PORT
RUSTLE RUSTLE..
RAHH! RAHH!
6
5
WELL, WELL, WELL!!
RIP RIP..
RIP!
DER
THEY'RE MADE OUT TO LOOK LIKE PIRATE SHIPS...
...BUT THESE ARE ACTUALLY TRADERS FROM THE KINGDOM OF BIGGSCHOTS!
CLICK!
MEMO
NATIONS FROM ALL OVER THE WORLD ARE DOING THEIR DARK BUSINESS IN THIS PORT!!

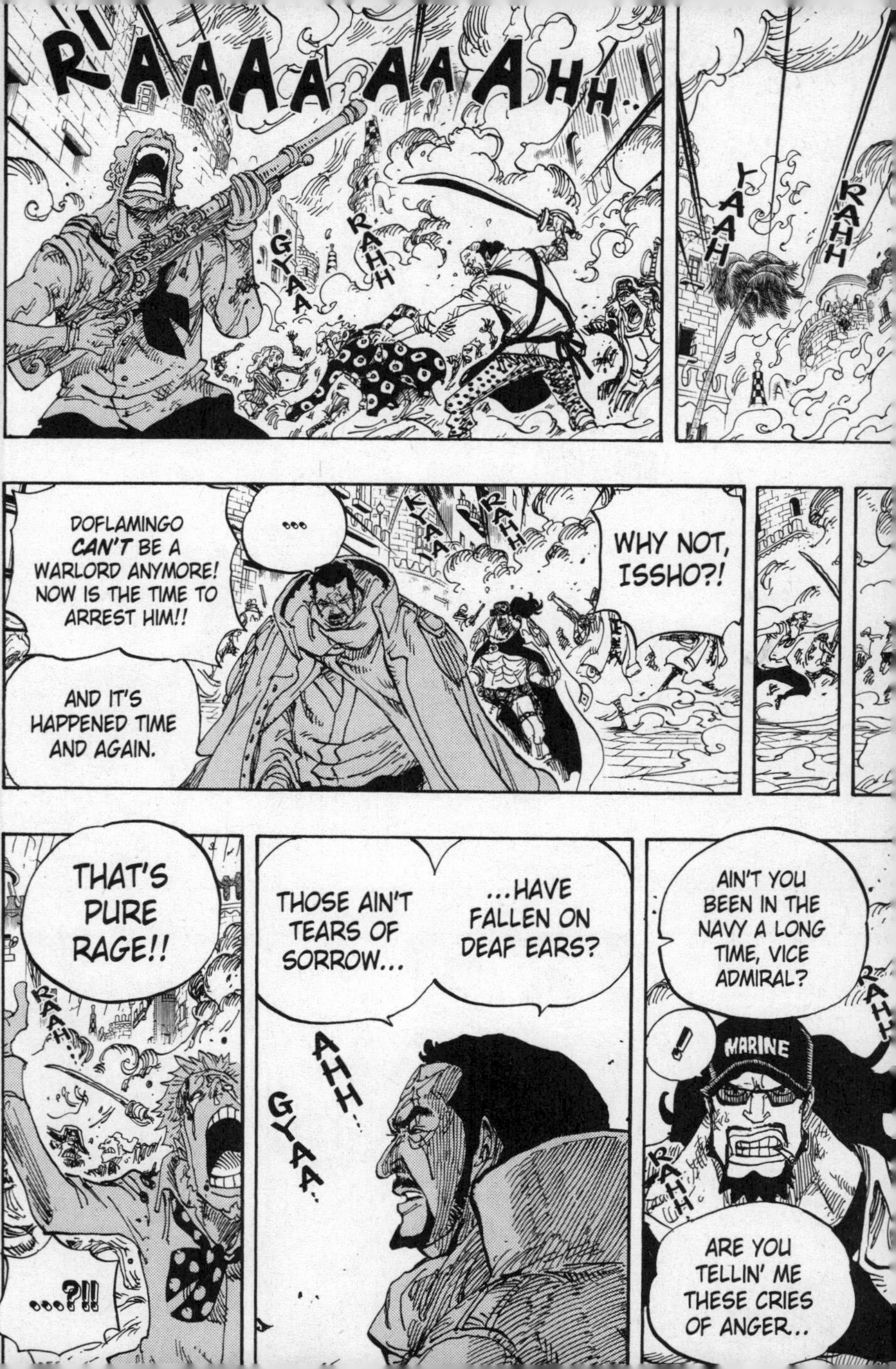
YAAAH
RAHH
RAAAAAAAHH
RAHH
GYAA
WHY NOT, ISSHO?!
RAHH
KYAA
...
DOFLAMINGO CAN'T BE A WARLORD ANYMORE! NOW IS THE TIME TO ARREST HIM!!
AND IT'S HAPPENED TIME AND AGAIN.
AIN'T YOU BEEN IN THE NAVY A LONG TIME, VICE ADMIRAL?
RAHH
!
RAHH
ARE YOU TELLIN' ME THESE CRIES OF ANGER...
...HAVE FALLEN ON DEAF EARS?
THOSE AIN'T TEARS OF SORROW...
AHH
GYAA
THAT'S PURE RAGE!!
RAHH
...?!!

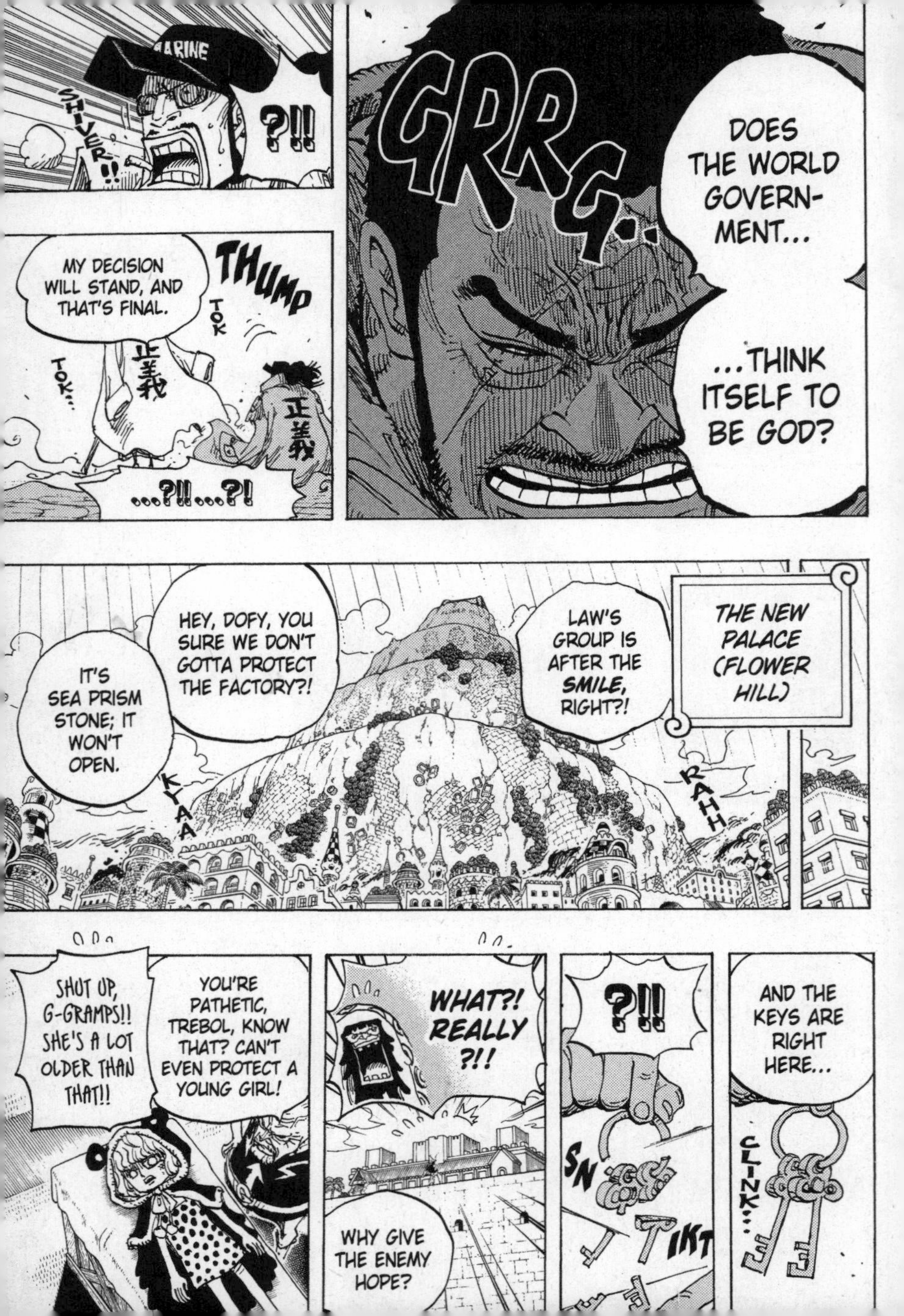
GRRG..
DOES THE WORLD GOVERNMENT...
...THINK ITSELF TO BE GOD?
SHIVER!!
?!!
MY DECISION WILL STAND, AND THAT'S FINAL.
THUMP
TOK
TOK...
正義
正義
...?!!...?!
THE NEW PALACE (FLOWER HILL)
LAW'S GROUP IS AFTER THE SMILE, RIGHT?!
RAHH
HEY, DOFY, YOU SURE WE DON'T GOTTA PROTECT THE FACTORY?!
IT'S SEA PRISM STONE; IT WON'T OPEN.
KYAA
AND THE KEYS ARE RIGHT HERE...
CLINK...
?!!
SNIKT
WHAT?! REALLY?!!
WHY GIVE THE ENEMY HOPE?
YOU'RE PATHETIC, TREBOL, KNOW THAT? CAN'T EVEN PROTECT A YOUNG GIRL!
SHUT UP, G-GRAMPS!! SHE'S A LOT OLDER THAN THAT!!

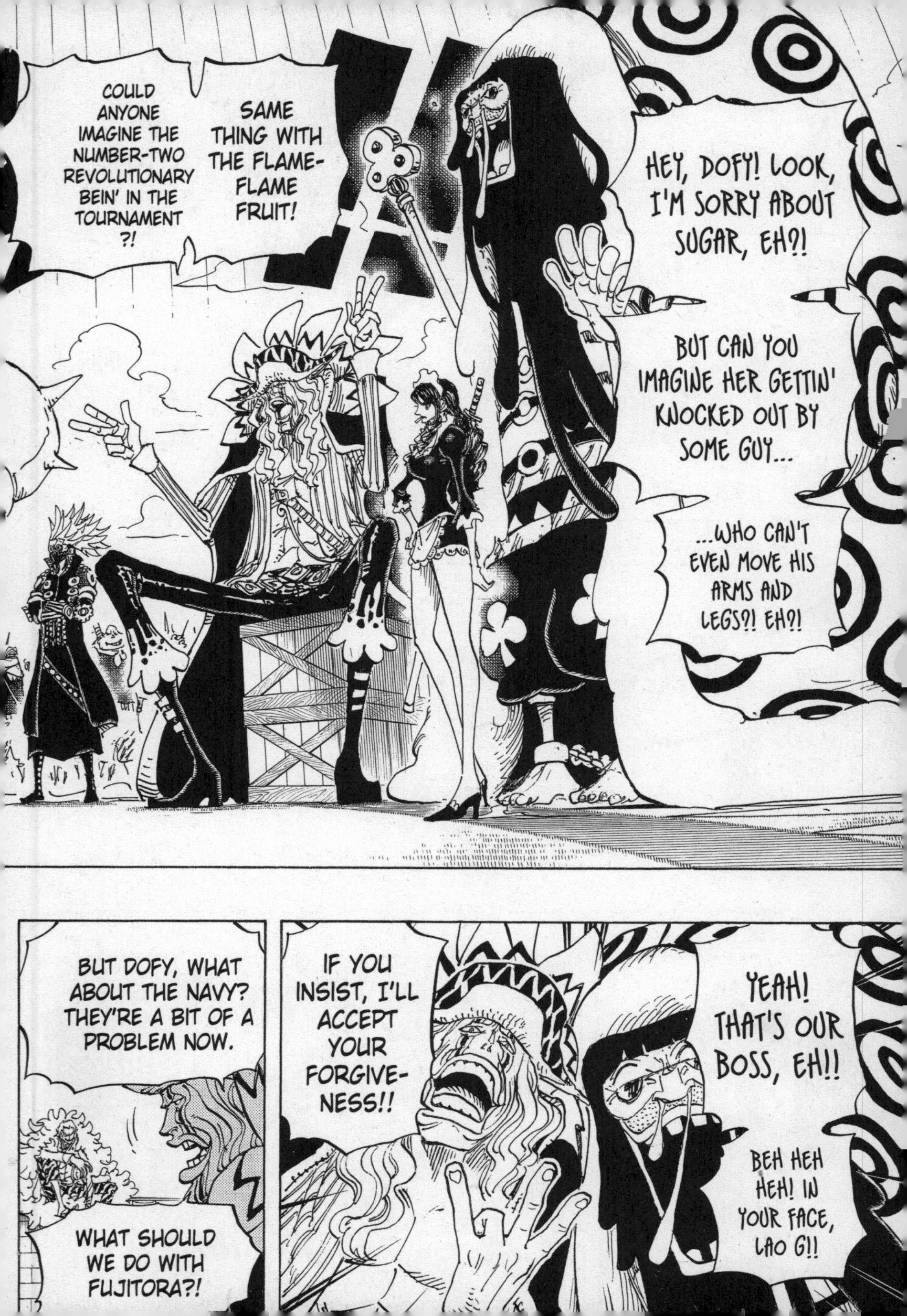
HEY, DOFY! LOOK, I'M SORRY ABOUT SUGAR, EH?!
BUT CAN YOU IMAGINE HER GETTIN' KNOCKED OUT BY SOME GUY...
...WHO CAN'T EVEN MOVE HIS ARMS AND LEGS?! EH?!
COULD ANYONE IMAGINE THE NUMBER-TWO REVOLUTIONARY BEIN' IN THE TOURNAMENT ?!
SAME THING WITH THE FLAME-FLAME FRUIT!
YEAH! THAT'S OUR BOSS, EH!!
IF YOU INSIST, I'LL ACCEPT YOUR FORGIVE-NESS!!
BEH HEH HEH! IN YOUR FACE, LAO G!!
BUT DOFY, WHAT ABOUT THE NAVY? THEY'RE A BIT OF A PROBLEM NOW.
WHAT SHOULD WE DO WITH FUJITORA?!

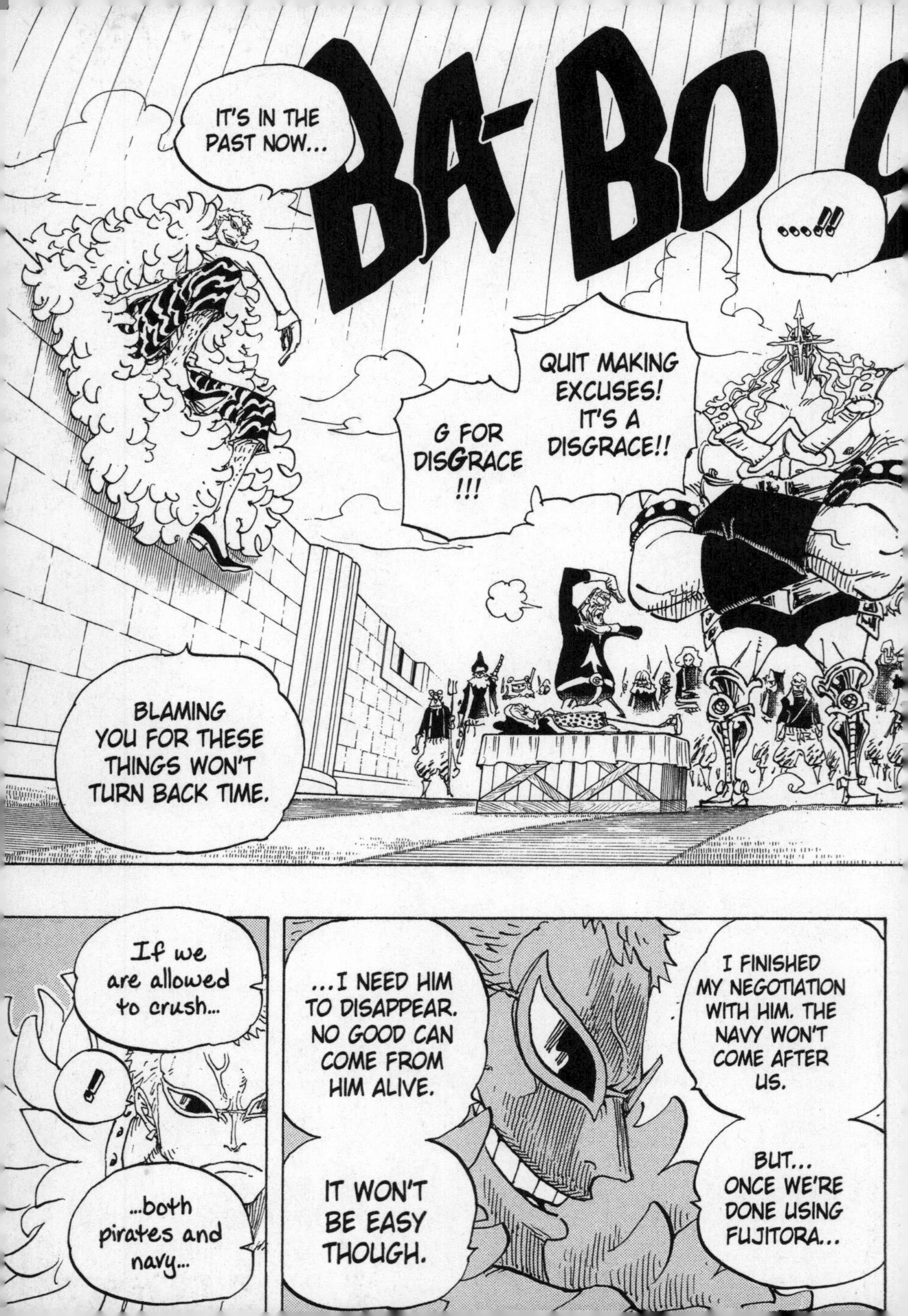
IT'S IN THE PAST NOW...
BA-BO
....!!
QUIT MAKING EXCUSES! IT'S A DISGRACE!!
G FOR DISGRACE!!!
BLAMING YOU FOR THESE THINGS WON'T TURN BACK TIME.
I FINISHED MY NEGOTIATION WITH HIM. THE NAVY WON'T COME AFTER US.
BUT... ONCE WE'RE DONE USING FUJITORA...
...I NEED HIM TO DISAPPEAR. NO GOOD CAN COME FROM HIM ALIVE.
IT WON'T BE EASY THOUGH.
If we are allowed to crush...
!
...both pirates and navy...

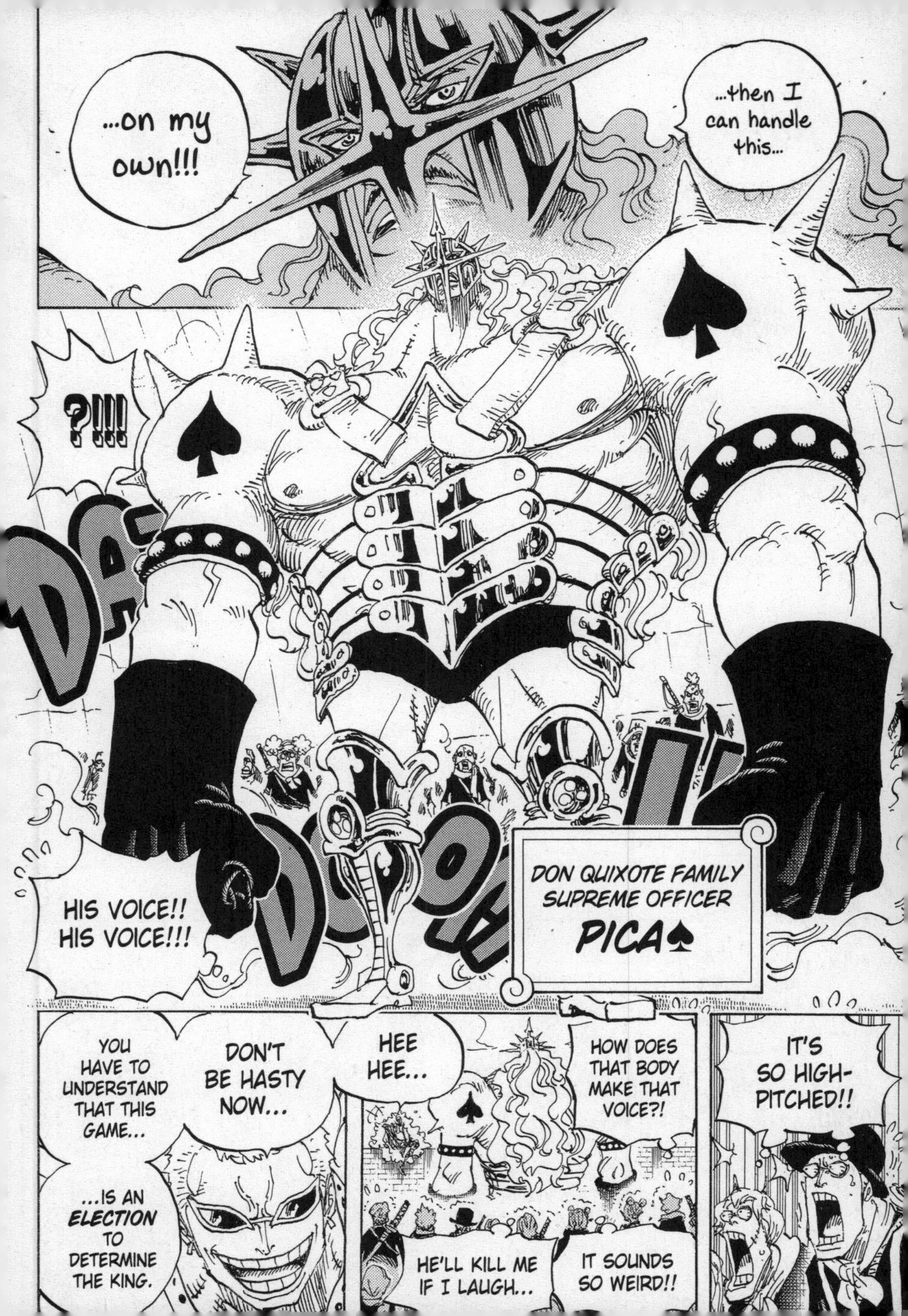

...then I can handle this...
...on my own!!!
DON QUIXOTE FAMILY SUPREME OFFICER PICA♠
?!!!
HIS VOICE!! HIS VOICE!!!
IT'S SO HIGH-PITCHED!!
HOW DOES THAT BODY MAKE THAT VOICE?!
HEE HEE...
IT SOUNDS SO WEIRD!!
HE'LL KILL ME IF I LAUGH...
DON'T BE HASTY NOW...
YOU HAVE TO UNDERSTAND THAT THIS GAME...
...IS AN ELECTION TO DETERMINE THE KING.

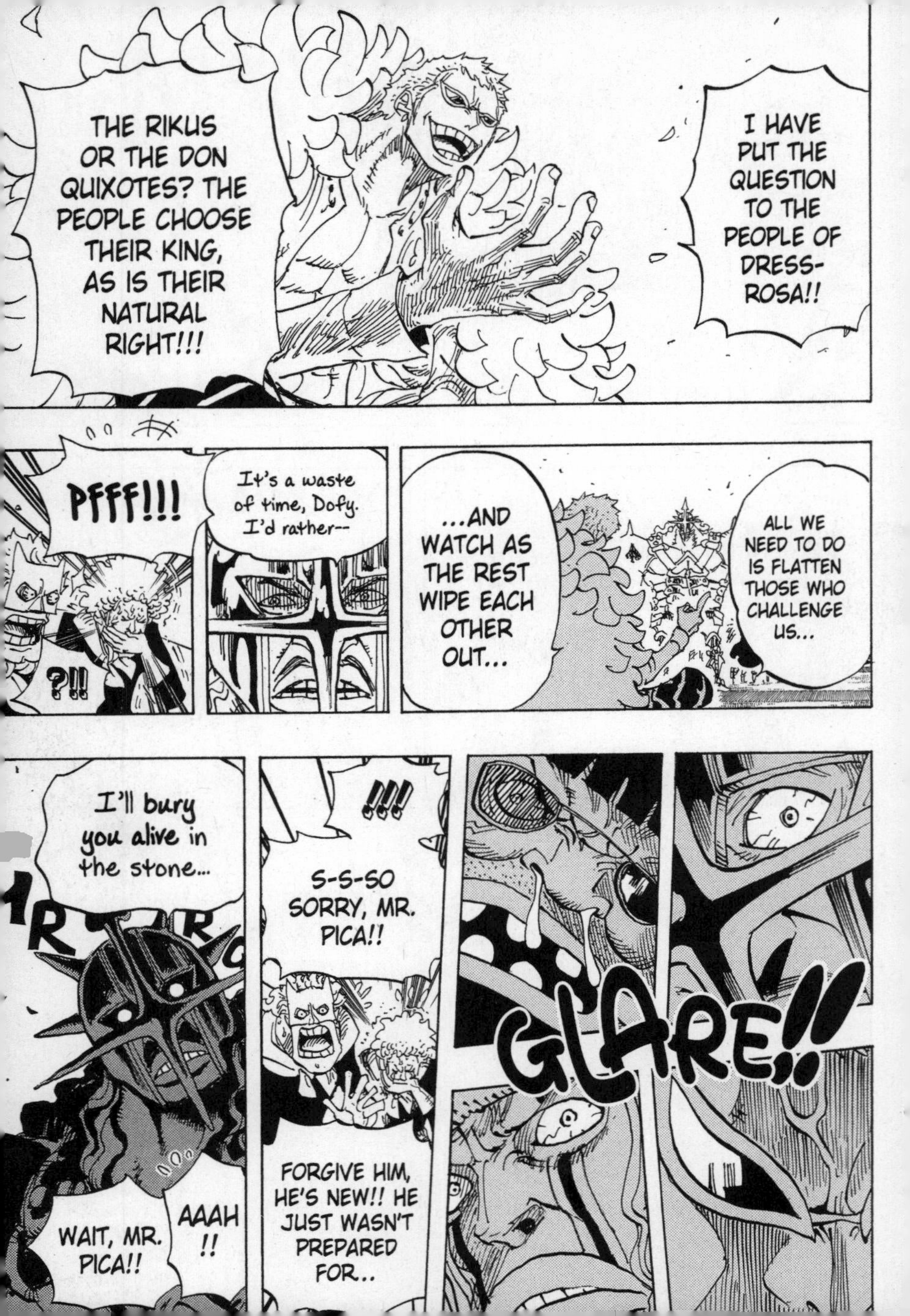
I HAVE PUT THE QUESTION TO THE PEOPLE OF DRESS-ROSA!!
THE RIKUS OR THE DON QUIXOTES? THE PEOPLE CHOOSE THEIR KING, AS IS THEIR NATURAL RIGHT!!!
ALL WE NEED TO DO IS FLATTEN THOSE WHO CHALLENGE US...
...AND WATCH AS THE REST WIPE EACH OTHER OUT...
It's a waste of time, Dofy. I'd rather--
PFFF!!!
?!!
GLARE!!
!!!
S-S-SO SORRY, MR. PICA!!
FORGIVE HIM, HE'S NEW!! HE JUST WASN'T PREPARED FOR..
I'll bury you alive in the stone...
AAAH!!
WAIT, MR. PICA!!

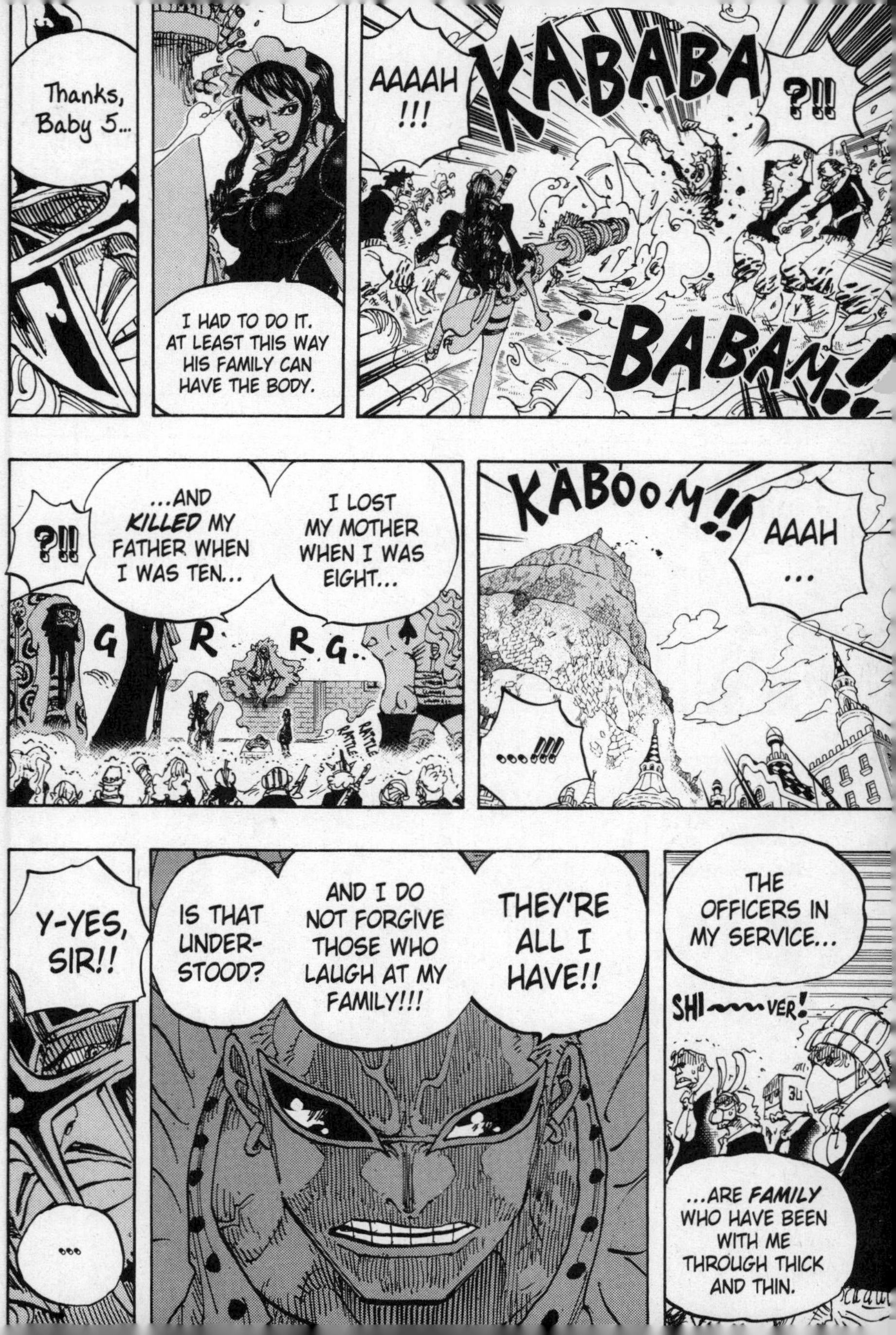
?!!
KABABA
AAAAH !!!
BABAM!!
I HAD TO DO IT. AT LEAST THIS WAY HIS FAMILY CAN HAVE THE BODY.
Thanks, Baby 5...
KABOOM!!
AAAH ...
...!!!
I LOST MY MOTHER WHEN I WAS EIGHT...
...AND *KILLED* MY FATHER WHEN I WAS TEN...
?!!
G R R G..
RATTLE RATTLE
THE OFFICERS IN MY SERVICE...
SHI~~VER!
...ARE *FAMILY* WHO HAVE BEEN WITH ME THROUGH THICK AND THIN.
THEY'RE ALL I HAVE!!
AND I DO NOT FORGIVE THOSE WHO LAUGH AT MY FAMILY!!!
IS THAT UNDER-STOOD?
Y-YES, SIR!!
...

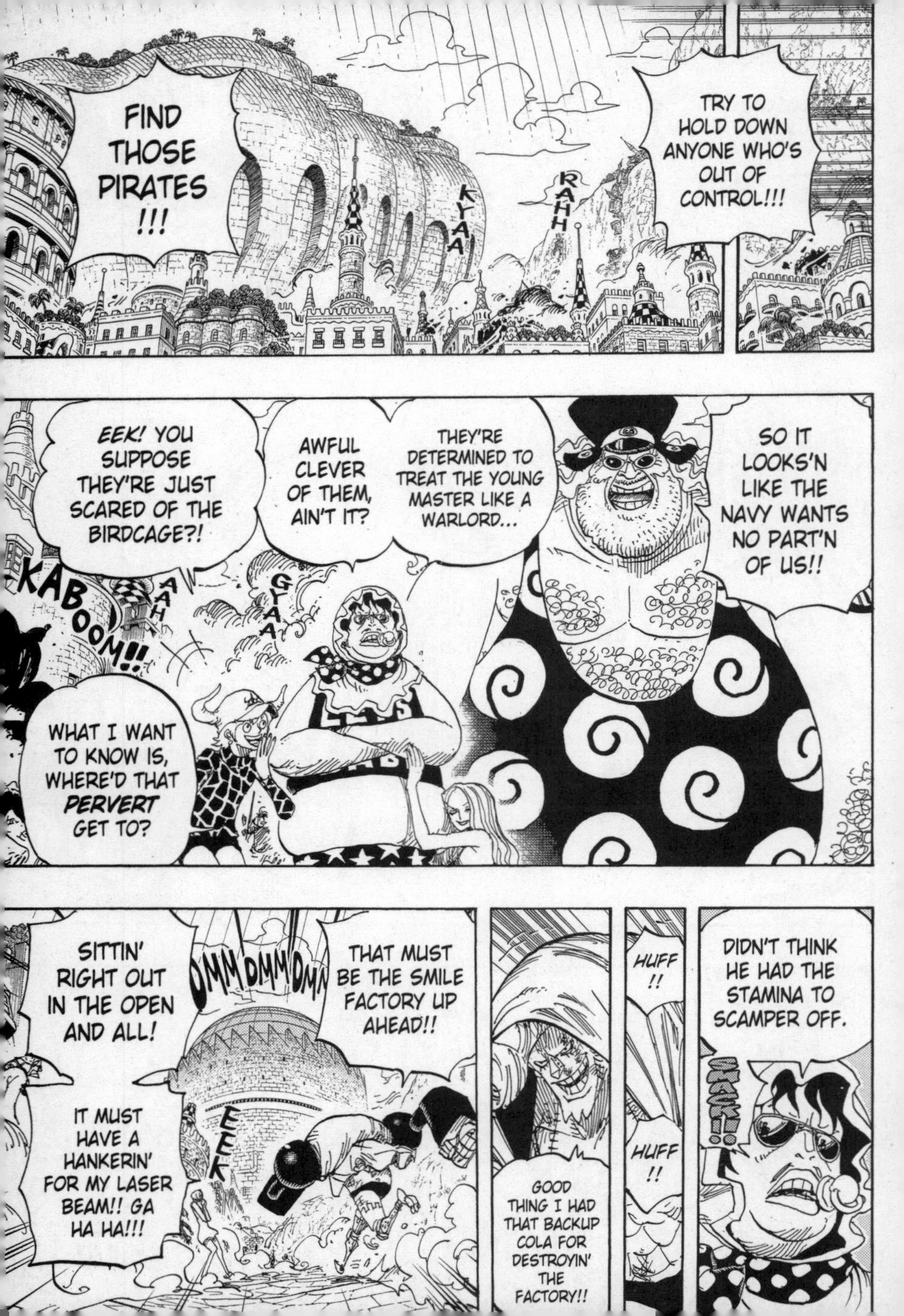
TRY TO HOLD DOWN ANYONE WHO'S OUT OF CONTROL!!!
RAHH
KYAA
FIND THOSE PIRATES!!!
SO IT LOOKS'N LIKE THE NAVY WANTS NO PART'N OF US!!
THEY'RE DETERMINED TO TREAT THE YOUNG MASTER LIKE A WARLORD...
AWFUL CLEVER OF THEM, AIN'T IT?
EEK! YOU SUPPOSE THEY'RE JUST SCARED OF THE BIRDCAGE?!
GYAA
AAH
KABOOM!!
WHAT I WANT TO KNOW IS, WHERE'D THAT PERVERT GET TO?
DIDN'T THINK HE HAD THE STAMINA TO SCAMPER OFF.
SMACK!!
HUFF!!
HUFF!!
GOOD THING I HAD THAT BACKUP COLA FOR DESTROYIN' THE FACTORY!!
THAT MUST BE THE SMILE FACTORY UP AHEAD!!
SITTIN' RIGHT OUT IN THE OPEN AND ALL!
DMM DMM DMM
EEK
IT MUST HAVE A HANKERIN' FOR MY LASER BEAM!! GA HA HA!!!

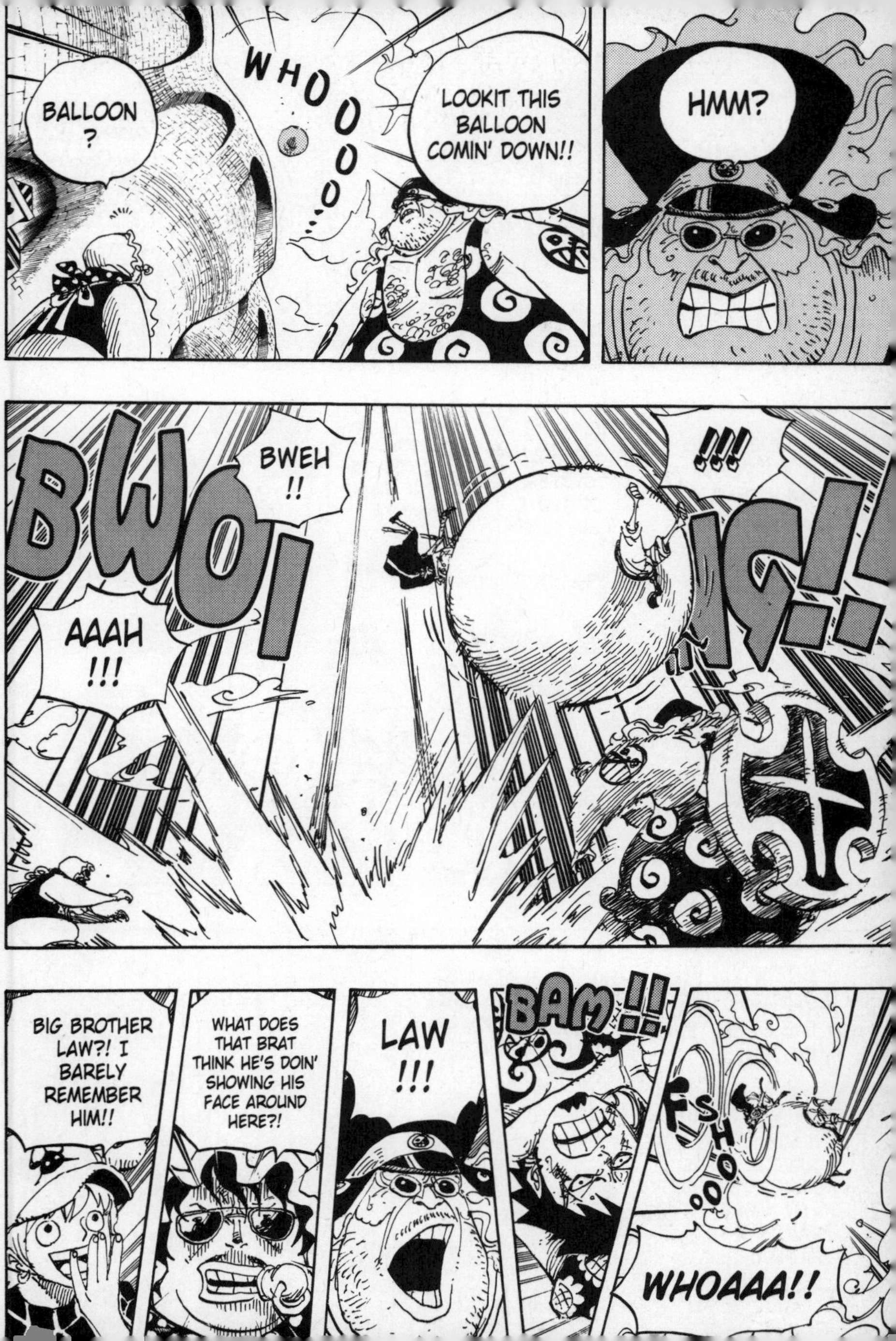
HMM?
LOOKIT THIS BALLOON COMIN' DOWN!!
WHOOOOOO...
BALLOON ?
!!!
BWOING!!
BWEH !!
AAAH !!!
WHOAAA!!
FSHOOO
BAM!!
LAW !!!
WHAT DOES THAT BRAT THINK HE'S DOIN' SHOWING HIS FACE AROUND HERE?!
BIG BROTHER LAW?! I BARELY REMEMBER HIM!!

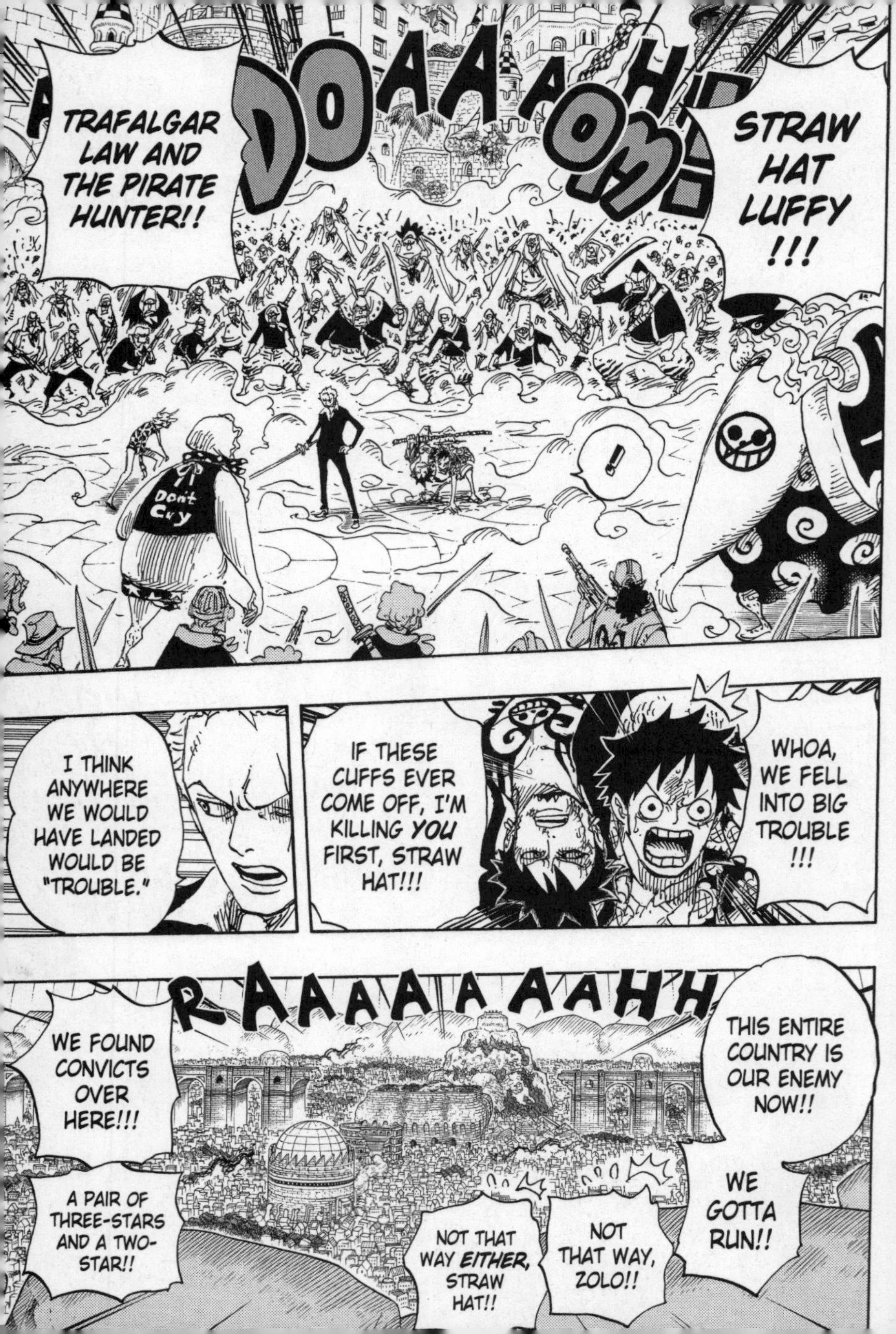
DOAAAOM
STRAW HAT LUFFY!!!
TRAFALGAR LAW AND THE PIRATE HUNTER!!
!
Don't Cry
WHOA, WE FELL INTO BIG TROUBLE!!!
IF THESE CUFFS EVER COME OFF, I'M KILLING *YOU* FIRST, STRAW HAT!!!
I THINK ANYWHERE WE WOULD HAVE LANDED WOULD BE "TROUBLE."
RAAAAAAAHH
THIS ENTIRE COUNTRY IS OUR ENEMY NOW!!
WE GOTTA RUN!!
NOT THAT WAY, ZOLO!!
NOT THAT WAY *EITHER*, STRAW HAT!!
WE FOUND CONVICTS OVER HERE!!!
A PAIR OF THREE-STARS AND A TWO-STAR!!

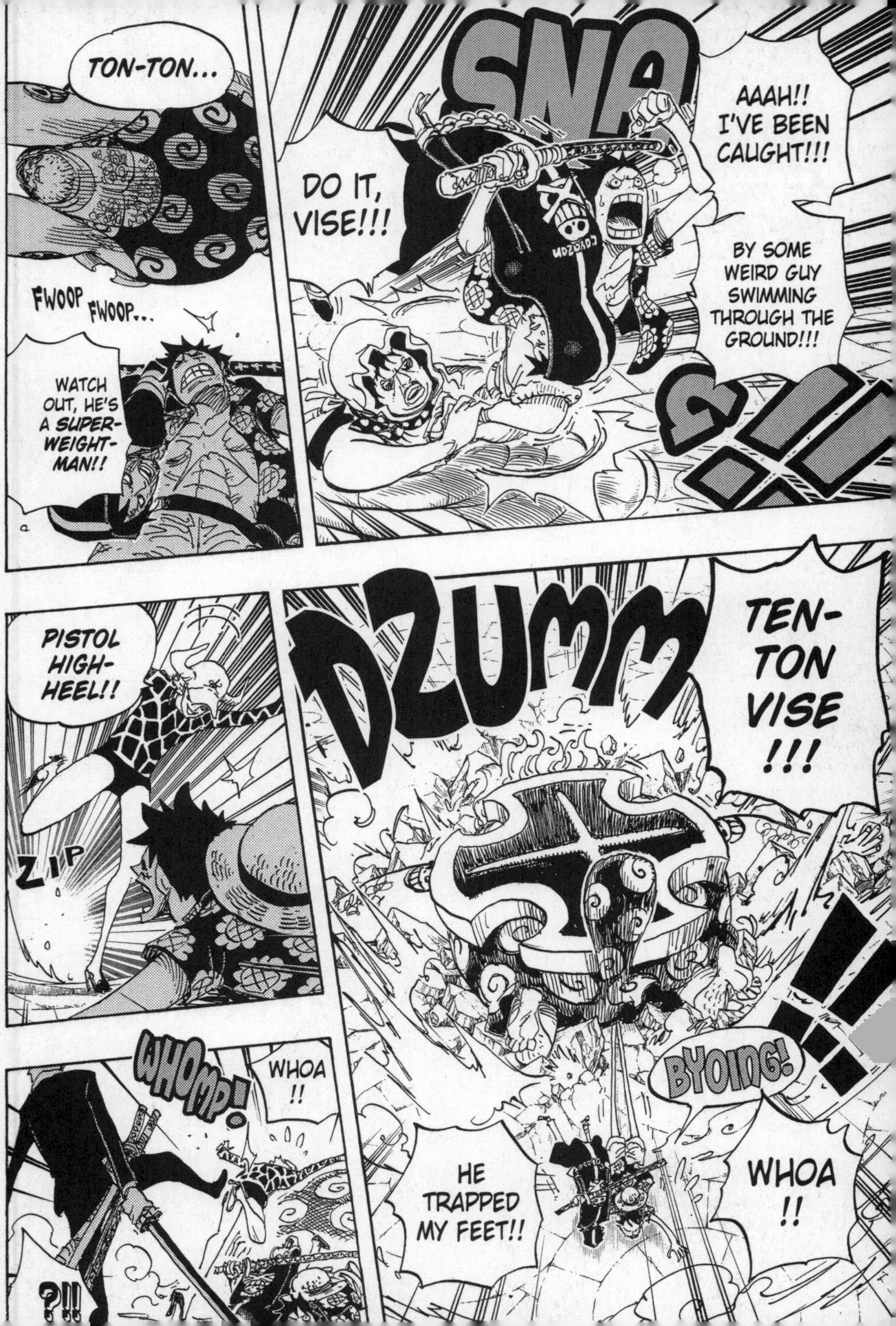
SNA
AAAH!! I'VE BEEN CAUGHT!!!
DO IT, VISE!!!
BY SOME WEIRD GUY SWIMMING THROUGH THE GROUND!!!
G!!
TON-TON...
FWOOP FWOOP...
WATCH OUT, HE'S A SUPER-WEIGHT-MAN!!
DZUMM
TEN-TON VISE!!!
BYOING!
WHOA!!
HE TRAPPED MY FEET!!
PISTOL HIGH-HEEL!!
ZIP
WHOMP!
WHOA!!
?!!

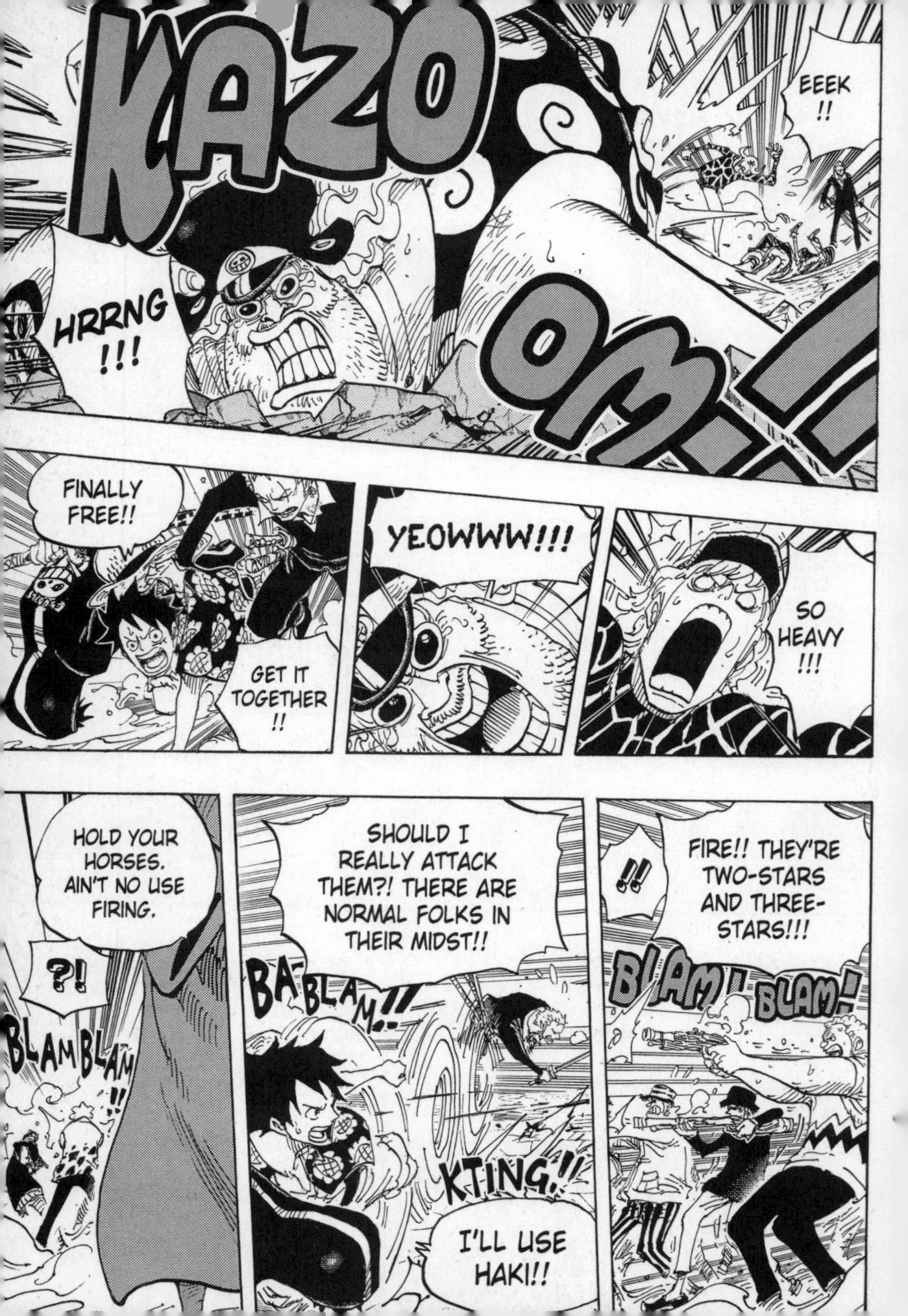
EEEK !!
KAZO
OM!!
HRRNG !!!
SO HEAVY !!!
YEOWWW!!!
FINALLY FREE!!
GET IT TOGETHER !!
FIRE!! THEY'RE TWO-STARS AND THREE-STARS!!!
!!
BLAM! BLAM!
SHOULD I REALLY ATTACK THEM?! THERE ARE NORMAL FOLKS IN THEIR MIDST!!
BA-BLAM!!
KTING!!
I'LL USE HAKI!!
HOLD YOUR HORSES. AIN'T NO USE FIRING.
?!
BLAM BLAM!!

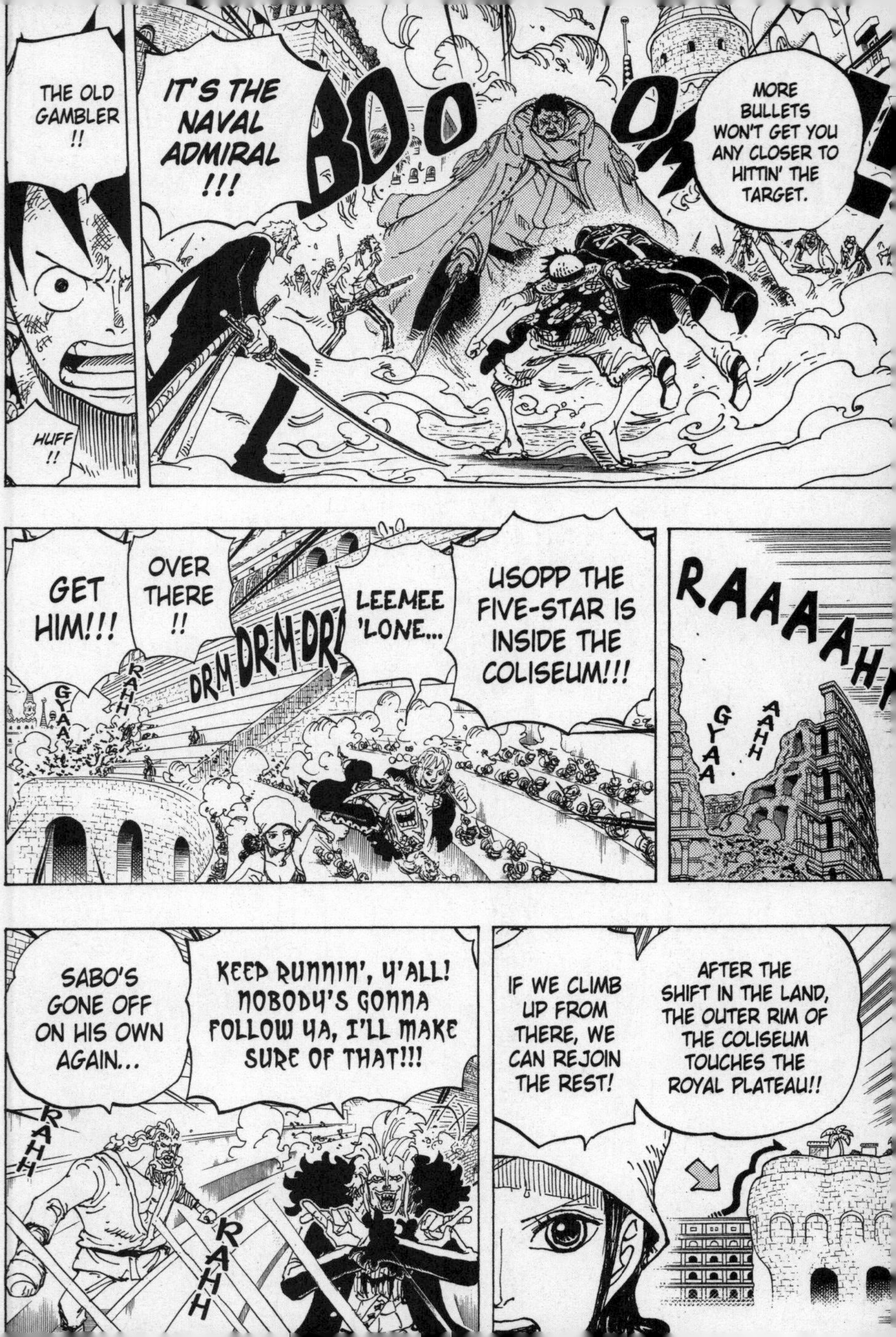

MORE BULLETS WON'T GET YOU ANY CLOSER TO HITTIN' THE TARGET.
BOOOM
IT'S THE NAVAL ADMIRAL!!!
THE OLD GAMBLER!!
HUFF!!
RAAAAAH
AAHH
GYAA
USOPP THE FIVE-STAR IS INSIDE THE COLISEUM!!!
LEEMEE 'LONE...
OVER THERE!!
GET HIM!!!
DRM DRM DRM
RAHH
GYAA
AFTER THE SHIFT IN THE LAND, THE OUTER RIM OF THE COLISEUM TOUCHES THE ROYAL PLATEAU!!
IF WE CLIMB UP FROM THERE, WE CAN REJOIN THE REST!
KEEP RUNNIN', Y'ALL! NOBODY'S GONNA FOLLOW YA, I'LL MAKE SURE OF THAT!!!
SABO'S GONE OFF ON HIS OWN AGAIN...
RAHH
RAHH

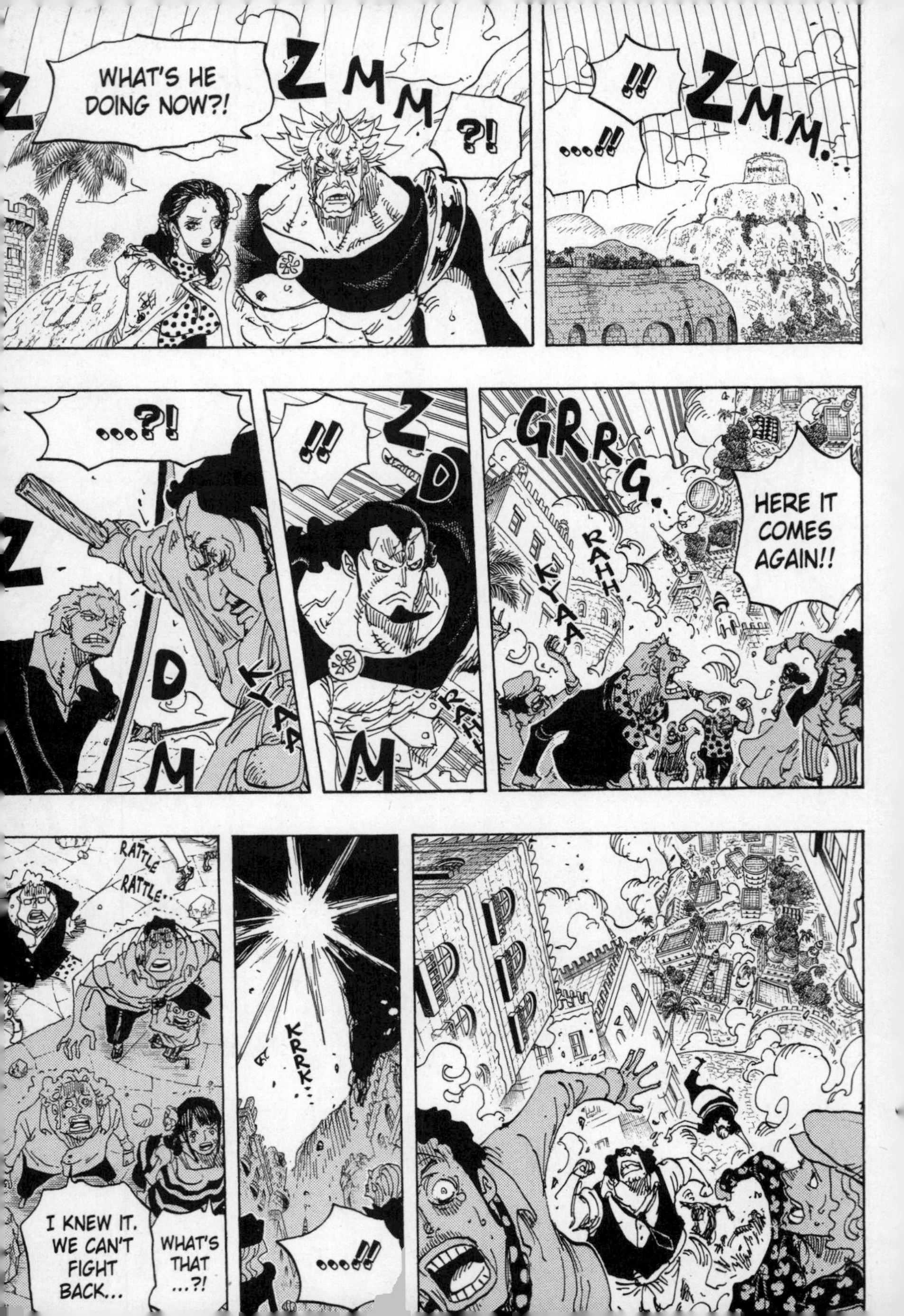

!!
ZMM.
...!!
?!
ZMM
WHAT'S HE DOING NOW?!
Z
HERE IT COMES AGAIN!!
GRRRG.
RAHH
KYAA
!!
ZDM
RAH
KYAA
...?!
ZDM
KRRK...
...!!
RATTLE
RATTLE...
WHAT'S THAT ...?!
I KNEW IT. WE CAN'T FIGHT BACK...

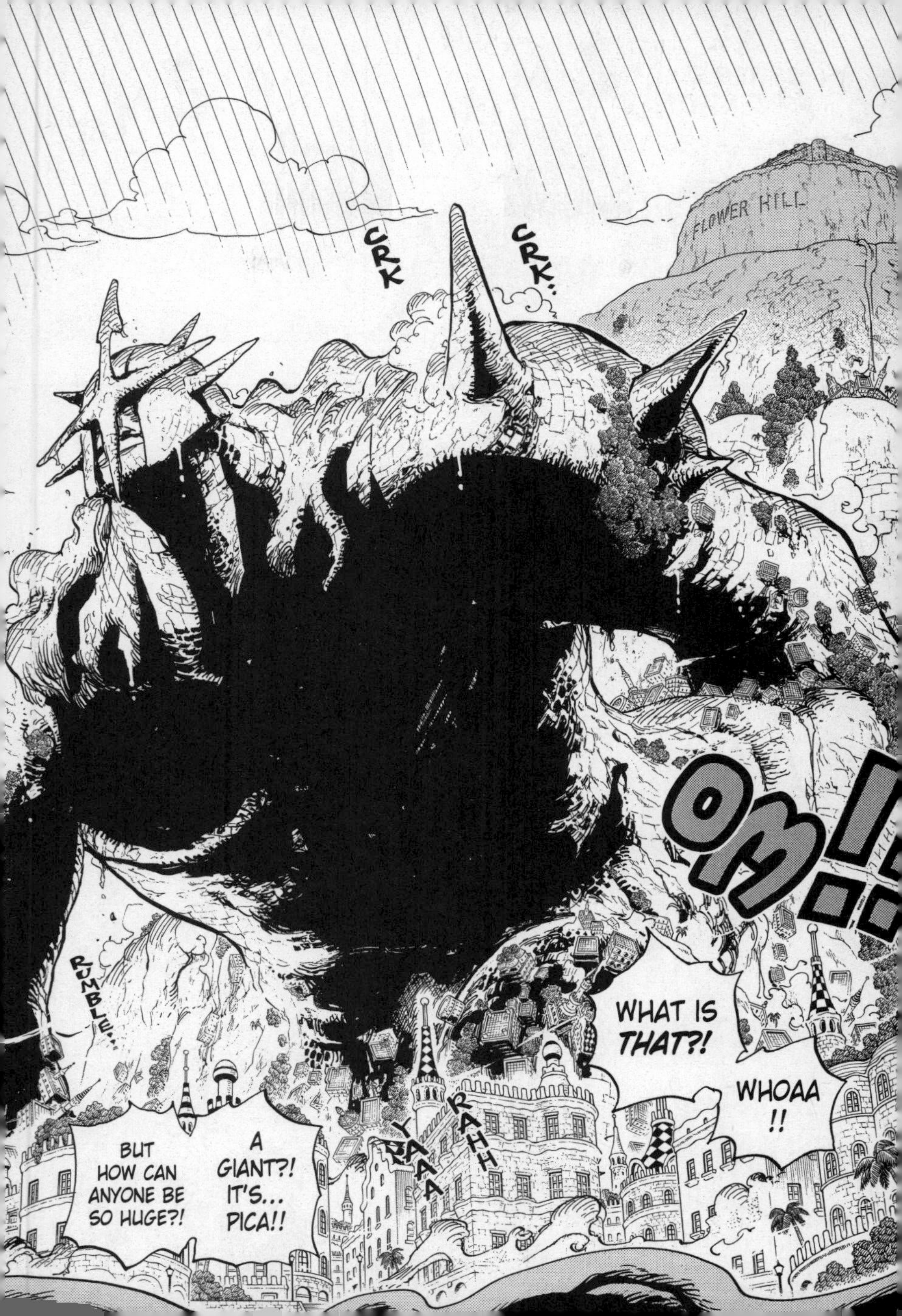
FLOWER HILL
CRK..
CRK
OM!!
WHAT IS THAT?!
WHOAA !!
RUMBLE...
RAHH
YAAAA
A GIANT?! IT'S... PICA!!
BUT HOW CAN ANYONE BE SO HUGE?!

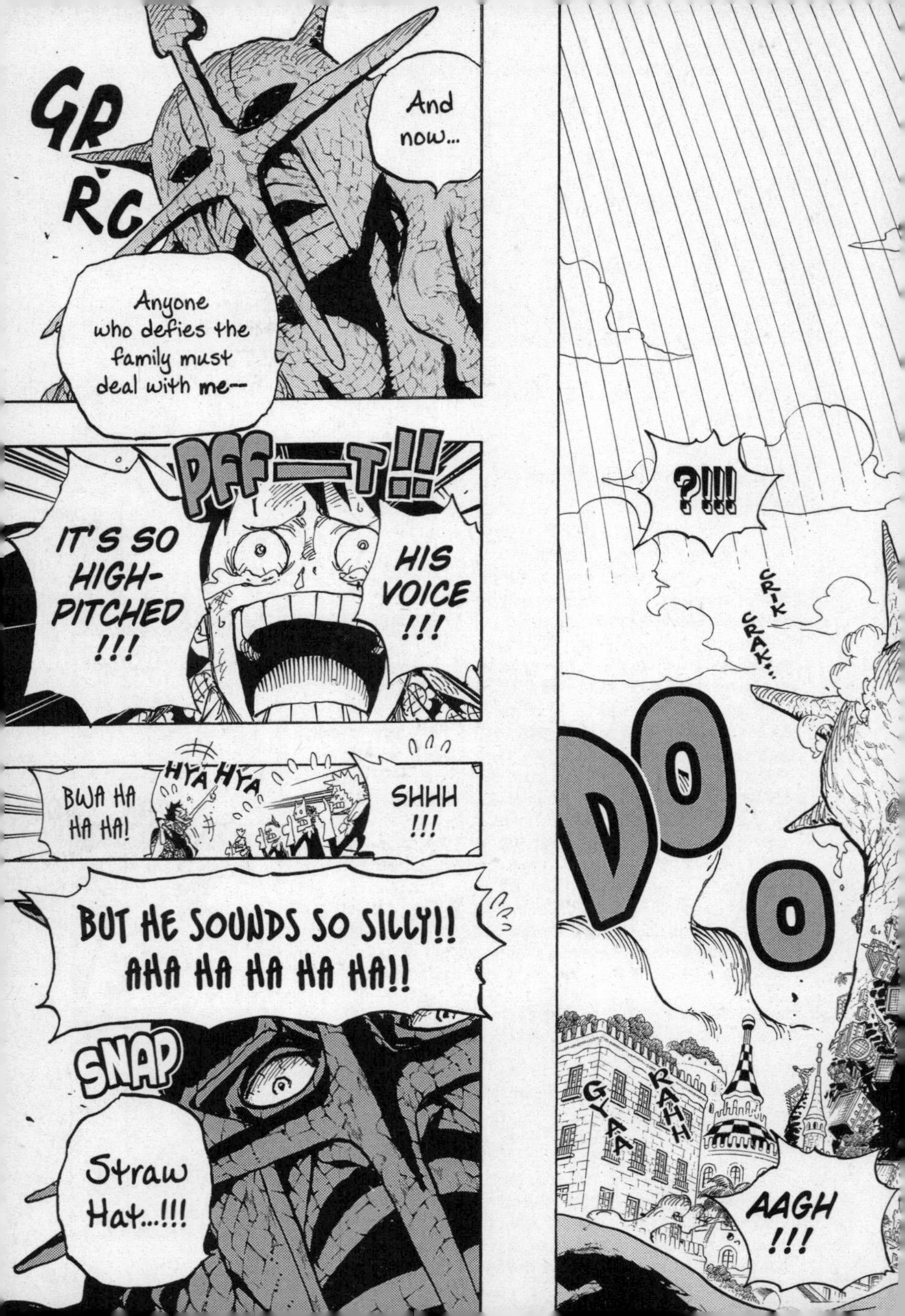
?!!!
CRIK CRAK...
DOOO
RAHH
GYAA
AAGH!!!
And now...
GRRC
Anyone who defies the family must deal with me--
PFF—T!!
HIS VOICE!!!
IT'S SO HIGH-PITCHED!!!
SHHH!!!
HYA HYA
BWA HA HA HA!
BUT HE SOUNDS SO SILLY!! AHA HA HA HA HA!!
SNAP
Straw Hat...!!!

SBS Question Corner

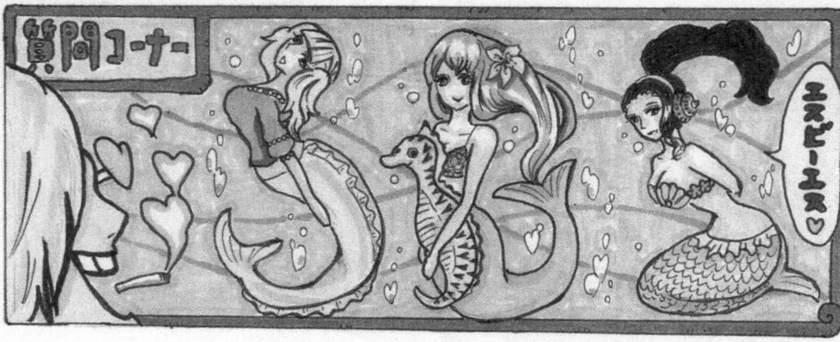

質問コーナー
エスピーエス♡

(Rio, Iwate)

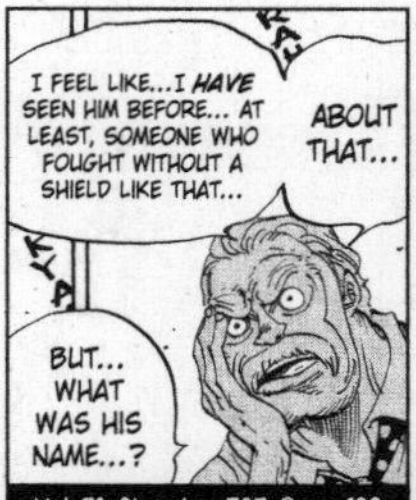

ABOUT THAT...
I FEEL LIKE...I *HAVE* SEEN HIM BEFORE... AT LEAST, SOMEONE WHO FOUGHT WITHOUT A SHIELD LIKE THAT...
BUT... WHAT WAS HIS NAME...?

Vol. 71, Chapter 707, Page 133

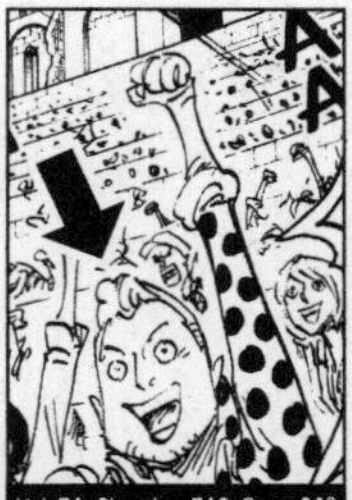

Vol. 74, Chapter 742, Page 208

Q: I have a question, Mr. Oda. These two fellows who love polka dots have to be the same person, right? I guess he really did see Ricky fight as a young man.

--Park Taguchi

A: You're referring to the scene in the present where the guy says he's seen the masked gladiator Ricky (secretly King Riku) fight before. In the past, there was indeed a masked fighter named Ricky. This person writing in wonders if this fellow in the stands was the same coliseum fan years ago. So close!! But you're on the right track. As a matter of fact, you can see him in a **different** flashback scene. See this fellow in Chapter 741? Doesn't he look exactly the same? Now look at the panel you originally pointed out, but look over his shoulder instead. That's him!! (ha ha)
So who is this connoisseur of the gladitorial arts? He is Sawyer Wayback, age 56. He loves watching sword combat so much, his wife and kids left him, but he's doing all right!

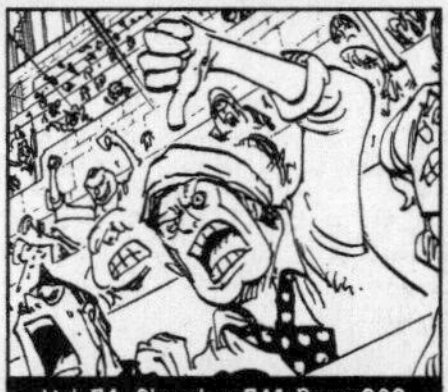

Vol. 74, Chapter 741, Page 202

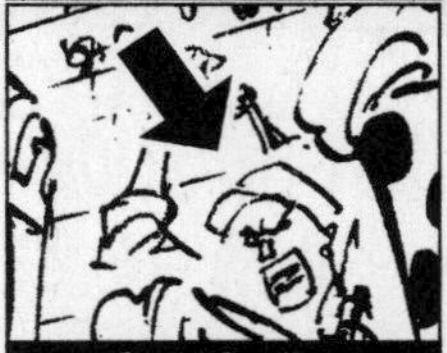

Panel in Question

Q: Good morning (at 3:00 AM). Look at Chapter 560 in Volume 57! When Luffy gave Hancock a bear hug, the Navy sailors called it a "sabaori" in Japanese, or a "mackerel snap." I've never heard this term before. Where does it come from?

--[T.T]

A: Sabaori is a sumo term, actually. It's a move where you leap onto the opponent with all your weight to push them over. The sailors must have assumed that's what he was doing when Hancock fainted away after that.

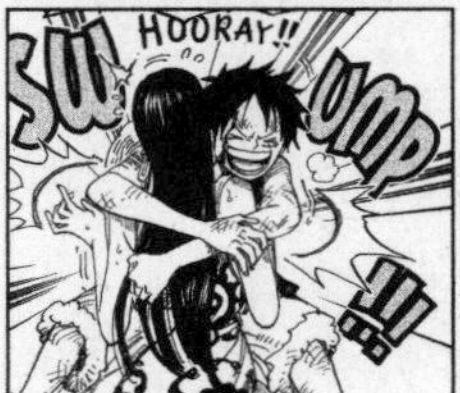

HOORAY!!

Chapter 748: REPAYING THE DEBT

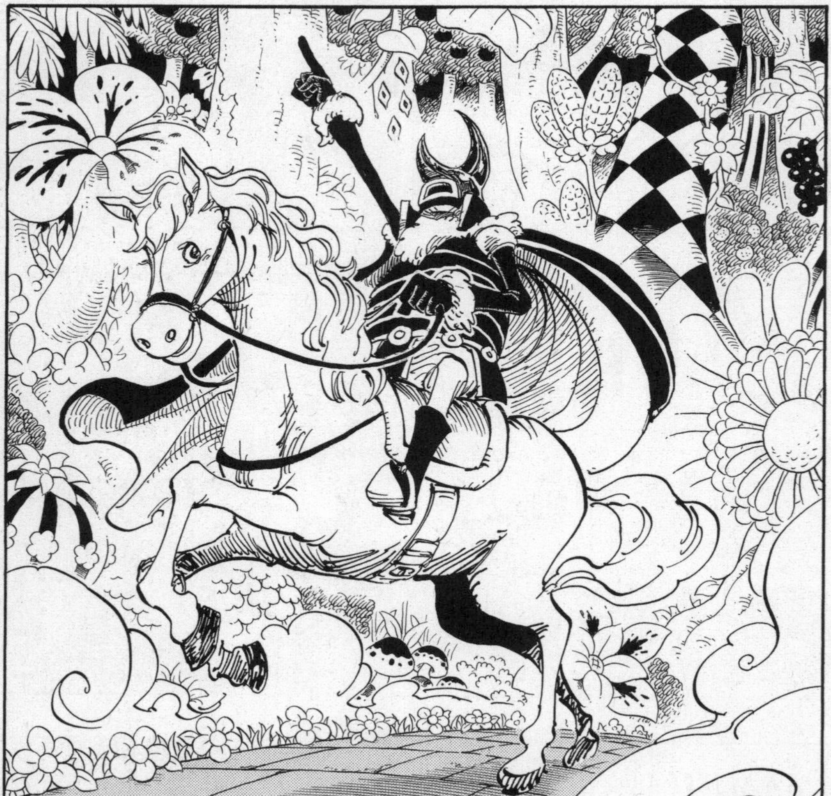

REQUEST: "HERACLESUN ACTING ALL COOL ON A HORSE"
BY NODA SKYWALKER

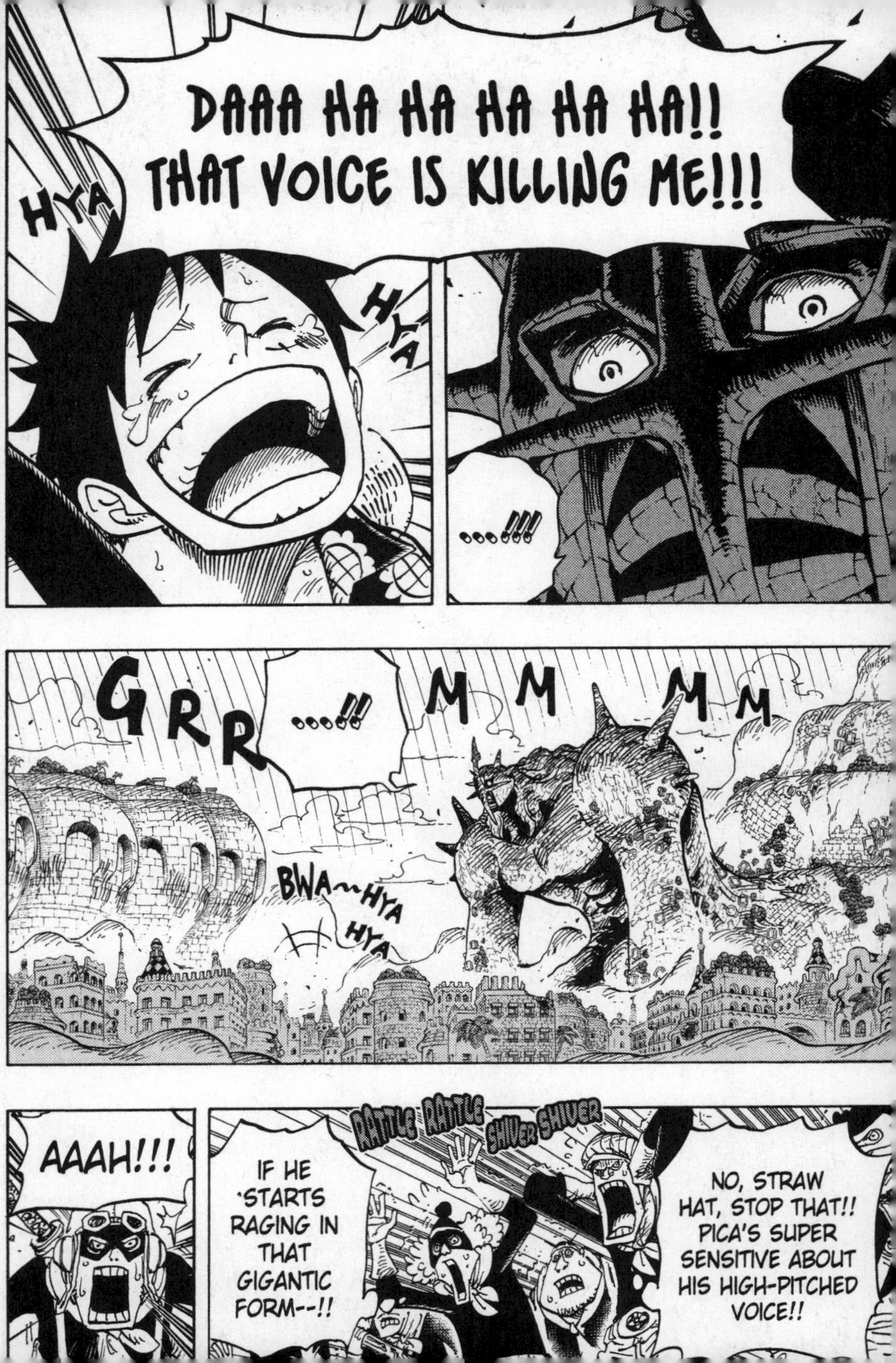
DAAA HA HA HA HA HA!!
THAT VOICE IS KILLING ME!!!!
...!!!
HYA
HYA
HYA
GRRR MMMMM
...!!
BWA~HYA HYA HYA
RATTLE RATTLE SHIVER SHIVER
NO, STRAW HAT, STOP THAT!! PICA'S SUPER SENSITIVE ABOUT HIS HIGH-PITCHED VOICE!!
IF HE STARTS RAGING IN THAT GIGANTIC FORM--!!
AAAH!!!

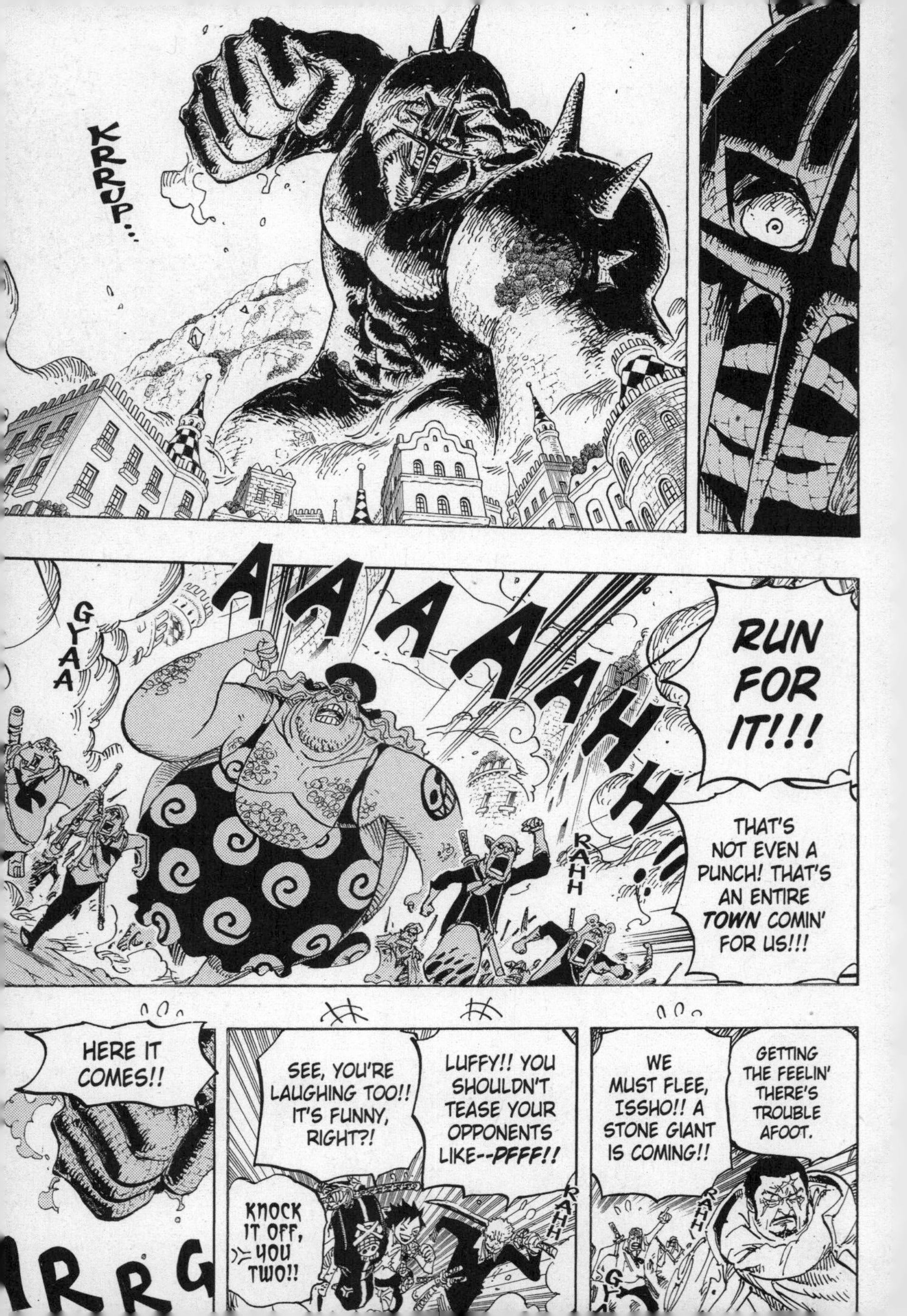
KRRRUP...
RUN FOR IT!!!
THAT'S NOT EVEN A PUNCH! THAT'S AN ENTIRE TOWN COMIN' FOR US!!!
AAAAAAH!!
RAHH
GYAA
GETTING THE FEELIN' THERE'S TROUBLE AFOOT.
WE MUST FLEE, ISSHO!! A STONE GIANT IS COMING!!
RAHH
LUFFY!! YOU SHOULDN'T TEASE YOUR OPPONENTS LIKE--PFFF!!
SEE, YOU'RE LAUGHING TOO!! IT'S FUNNY, RIGHT?!
KNOCK IT OFF, YOU TWO!!
RAHH
HERE IT COMES!!
IRRG

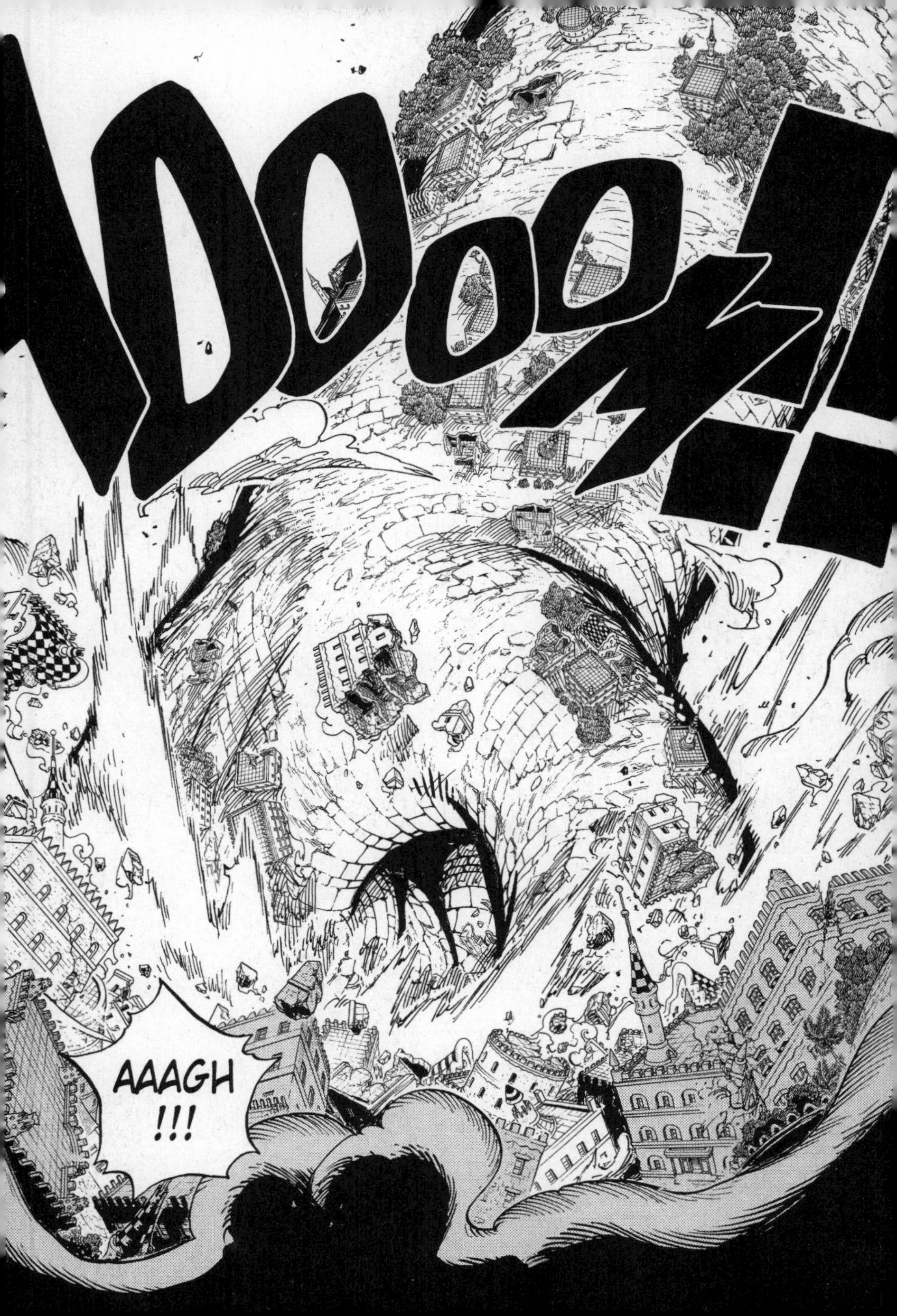
DOOON!!
AAAGH
!!!

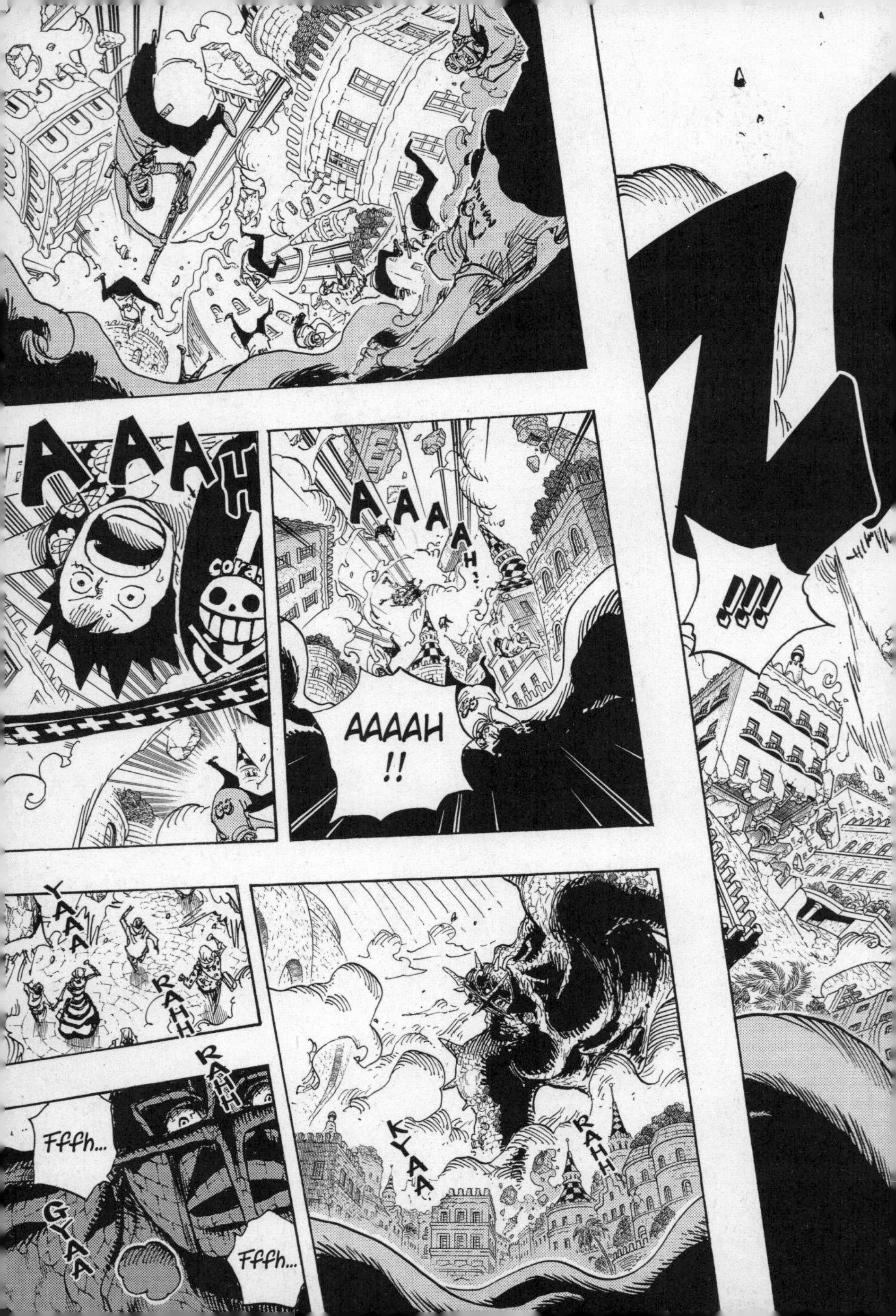
!!!
AAAAH!
AAAAH !!
AAAH
KYAA
RAHH
YAAA
RAHH
RAHH
Ffffh...
GYAA
Ffffh...

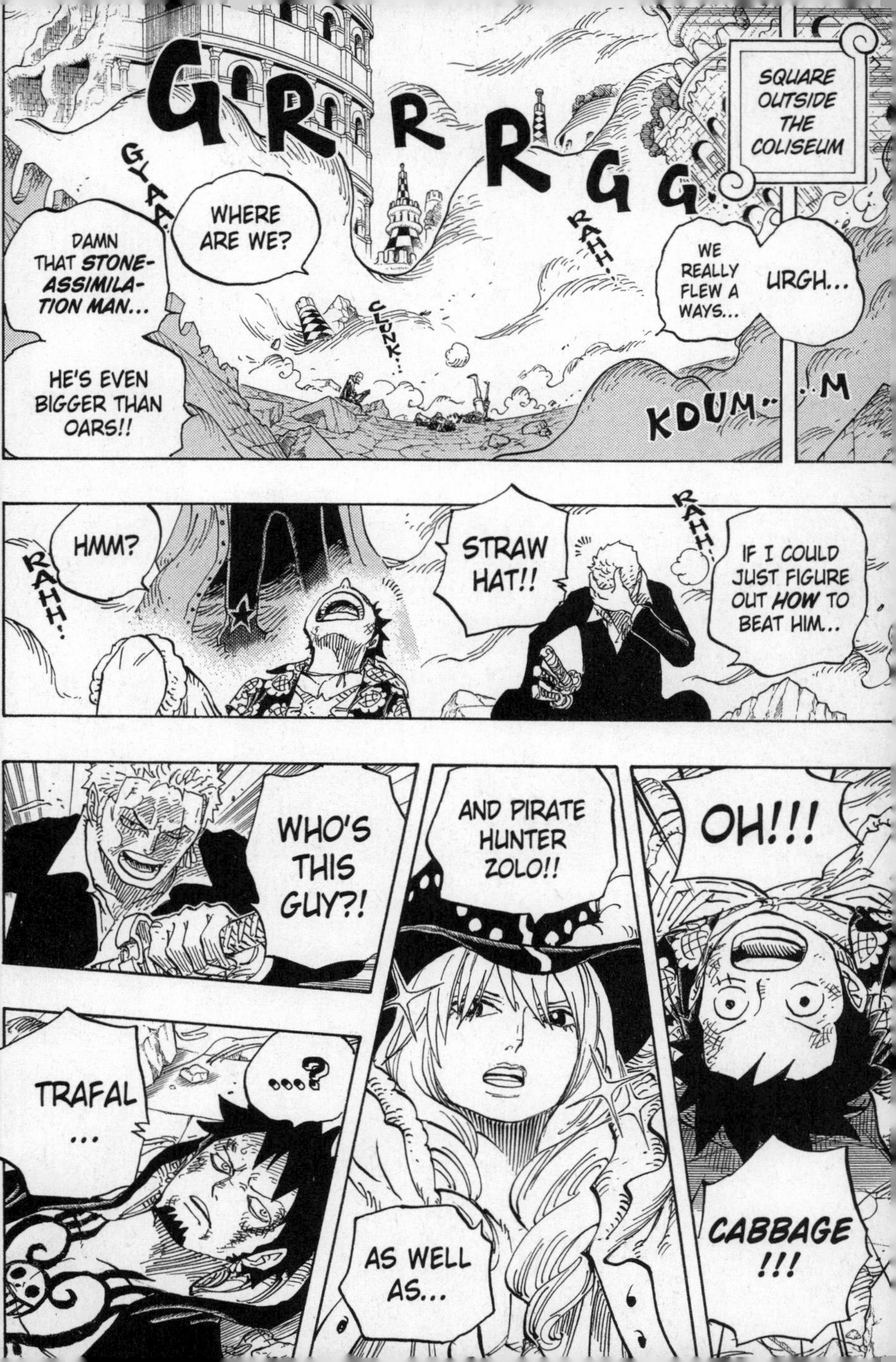
SQUARE OUTSIDE THE COLISEUM
GRRRRGG
URGH...
WE REALLY FLEW A WAYS...
KDUM...M
RAHH...
CLUNK...
WHERE ARE WE?
GYAA...
DAMN THAT STONE-ASSIMILATION MAN...
HE'S EVEN BIGGER THAN OARS!!
RAHH!
IF I COULD JUST FIGURE OUT HOW TO BEAT HIM..
STRAW HAT!!
HMM?
RAHH!
OH!!!
CABBAGE!!!
AND PIRATE HUNTER ZOLO!!
AS WELL AS...
WHO'S THIS GUY?!
...?
TRAFAL...

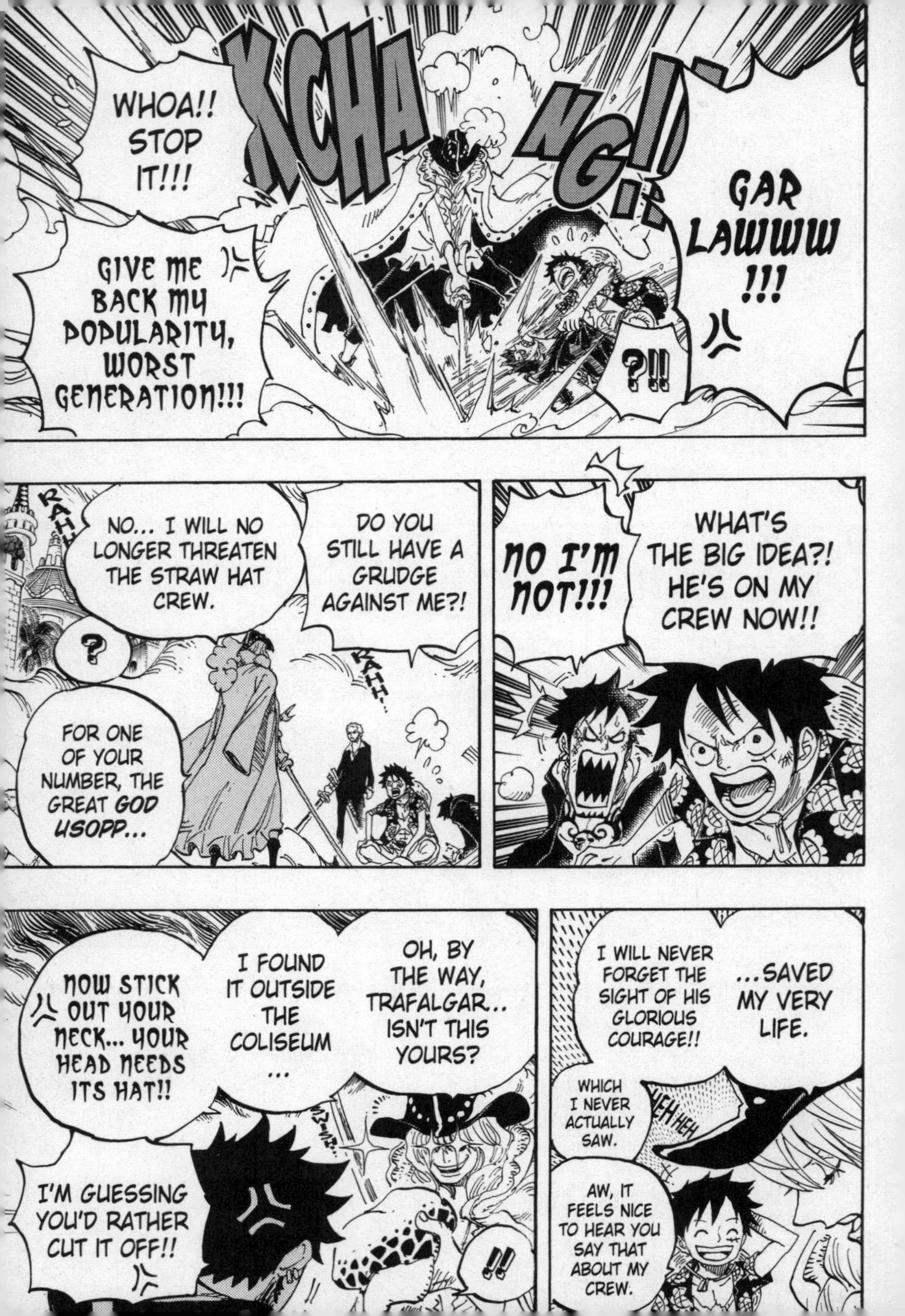
XCHANG!!
GAR LAWWW !!!
?!!
WHOA!! STOP IT!!!
GIVE ME BACK MY POPULARITY, WORST GENERATION!!!
WHAT'S THE BIG IDEA?! HE'S ON MY CREW NOW!!
NO I'M NOT!!!
DO YOU STILL HAVE A GRUDGE AGAINST ME?!
NO... I WILL NO LONGER THREATEN THE STRAW HAT CREW.
?
FOR ONE OF YOUR NUMBER, THE GREAT GOD USOPP...
...SAVED MY VERY LIFE.
I WILL NEVER FORGET THE SIGHT OF HIS GLORIOUS COURAGE!!
HEH HEH
WHICH I NEVER ACTUALLY SAW.
AW, IT FEELS NICE TO HEAR YOU SAY THAT ABOUT MY CREW.
OH, BY THE WAY, TRAFALGAR... ISN'T THIS YOURS?
I FOUND IT OUTSIDE THE COLISEUM...
NOW STICK OUT YOUR NECK... YOUR HEAD NEEDS ITS HAT!!
!!
I'M GUESSING YOU'D RATHER CUT IT OFF!!

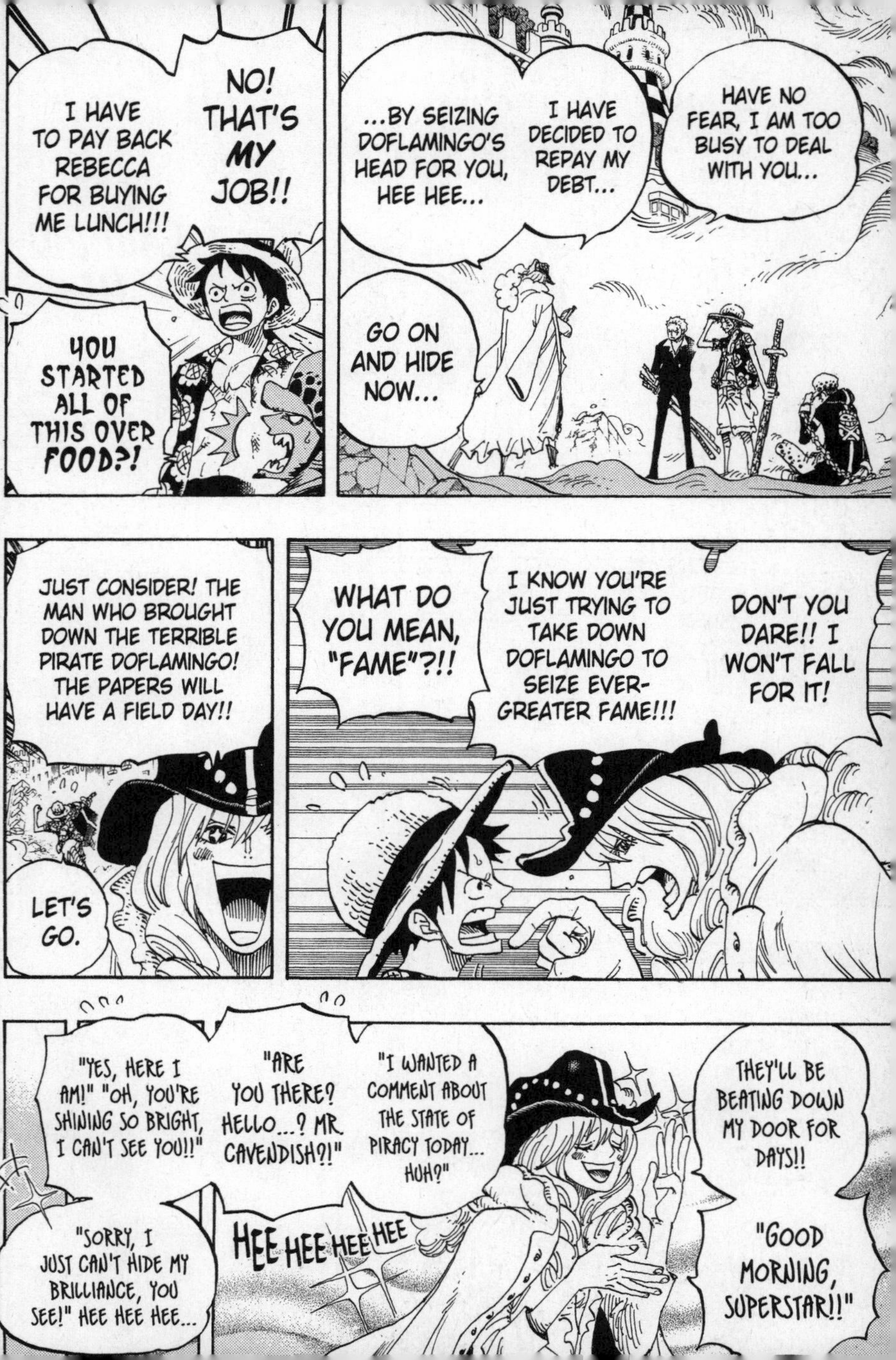
HAVE NO FEAR, I AM TOO BUSY TO DEAL WITH YOU...
I HAVE DECIDED TO REPAY MY DEBT...
...BY SEIZING DOFLAMINGO'S HEAD FOR YOU, HEE HEE...
GO ON AND HIDE NOW...
NO! THAT'S MY JOB!!
I HAVE TO PAY BACK REBECCA FOR BUYING ME LUNCH!!!
YOU STARTED ALL OF THIS OVER FOOD?!
DON'T YOU DARE!! I WON'T FALL FOR IT!
I KNOW YOU'RE JUST TRYING TO TAKE DOWN DOFLAMINGO TO SEIZE EVER-GREATER FAME!!!
WHAT DO YOU MEAN, "FAME"?!!
JUST CONSIDER! THE MAN WHO BROUGHT DOWN THE TERRIBLE PIRATE DOFLAMINGO! THE PAPERS WILL HAVE A FIELD DAY!!
LET'S GO.
THEY'LL BE BEATING DOWN MY DOOR FOR DAYS!!
"GOOD MORNING, SUPERSTAR!!"
"I WANTED A COMMENT ABOUT THE STATE OF PIRACY TODAY... HUH?"
"ARE YOU THERE? HELLO...? MR. CAVENDISH?!"
"YES, HERE I AM!" "OH, YOU'RE SHINING SO BRIGHT, I CAN'T SEE YOU!!"
"SORRY, I JUST CAN'T HIDE MY BRILLIANCE, YOU SEE!" HEE HEE HEE...
HEE HEE HEE HEE

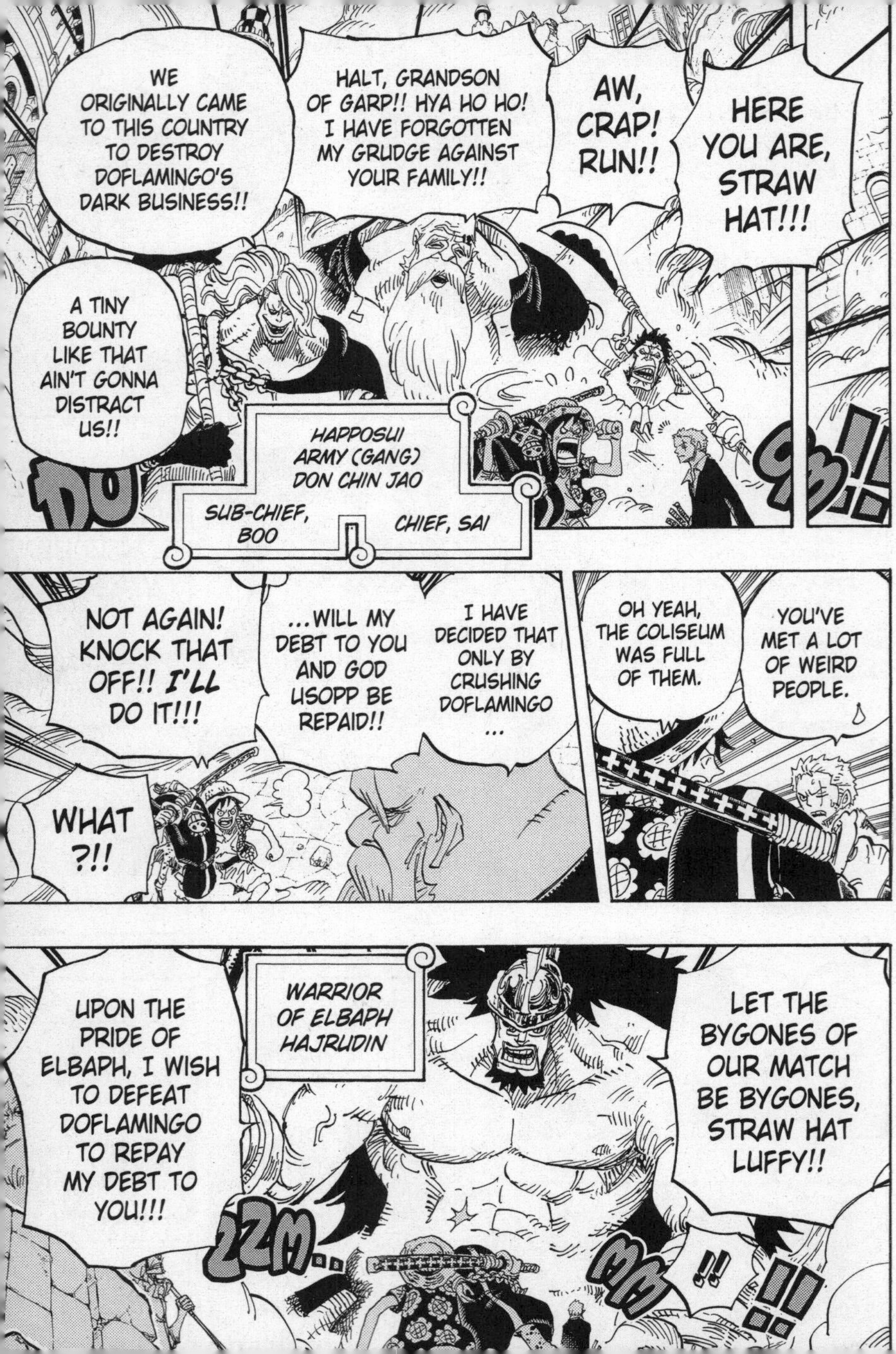
HERE YOU ARE, STRAW HAT!!!
AW, CRAP! RUN!!
HALT, GRANDSON OF GARP!! HYA HO HO! I HAVE FORGOTTEN MY GRUDGE AGAINST YOUR FAMILY!!
WE ORIGINALLY CAME TO THIS COUNTRY TO DESTROY DOFLAMINGO'S DARK BUSINESS!!
A TINY BOUNTY LIKE THAT AIN'T GONNA DISTRACT US!!
HAPPOSUI ARMY (GANG) DON CHIN JAO
CHIEF, SAI
SUB-CHIEF, BOO
OM!!
DO
YOU'VE MET A LOT OF WEIRD PEOPLE.
OH YEAH, THE COLISEUM WAS FULL OF THEM.
I HAVE DECIDED THAT ONLY BY CRUSHING DOFLAMINGO ...
...WILL MY DEBT TO YOU AND GOD USOPP BE REPAID!!
NOT AGAIN! KNOCK THAT OFF!! I'LL DO IT!!!
WHAT ?!!
LET THE BYGONES OF OUR MATCH BE BYGONES, STRAW HAT LUFFY!!
WARRIOR OF ELBAPH HAJRUDIN
UPON THE PRIDE OF ELBAPH, I WISH TO DEFEAT DOFLAMINGO TO REPAY MY DEBT TO YOU!!!
!!
MM
ZZM..

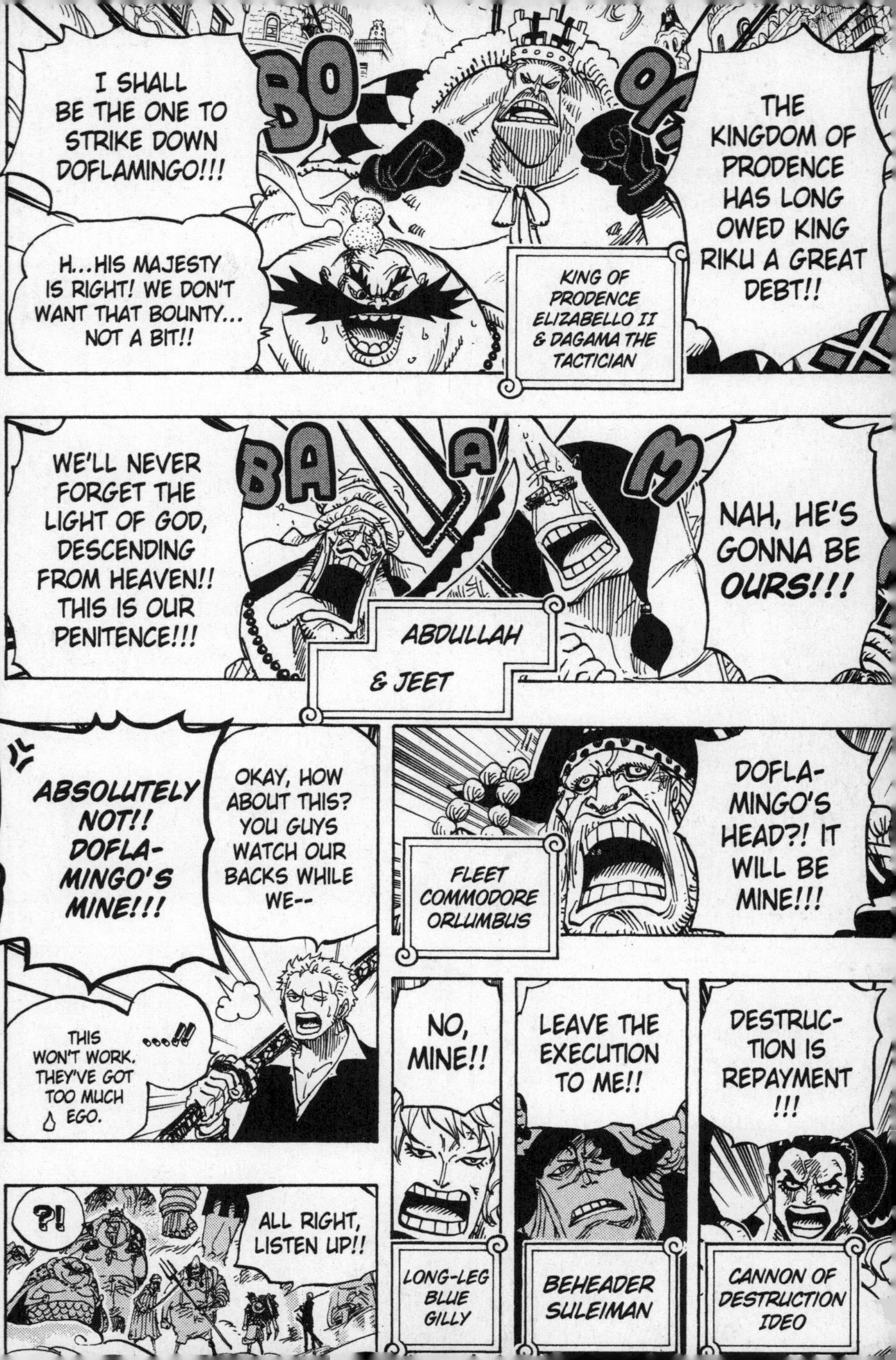
BOOM
THE KINGDOM OF PRODENCE HAS LONG OWED KING RIKU A GREAT DEBT!!
KING OF PRODENCE ELIZABELLO II & DAGAMA THE TACTICIAN
I SHALL BE THE ONE TO STRIKE DOWN DOFLAMINGO!!!
H...HIS MAJESTY IS RIGHT! WE DON'T WANT THAT BOUNTY... NOT A BIT!!
BAAM
NAH, HE'S GONNA BE OURS!!!
WE'LL NEVER FORGET THE LIGHT OF GOD, DESCENDING FROM HEAVEN!! THIS IS OUR PENITENCE!!!
ABDULLAH & JEET
DOFLA-MINGO'S HEAD?! IT WILL BE MINE!!!
FLEET COMMODORE ORLUMBUS
OKAY, HOW ABOUT THIS? YOU GUYS WATCH OUR BACKS WHILE WE--
ABSOLUTELY NOT!! DOFLA-MINGO'S MINE!!!
...!!
THIS WON'T WORK. THEY'VE GOT TOO MUCH EGO.
DESTRUC-TION IS REPAYMENT!!!
CANNON OF DESTRUCTION IDEO
LEAVE THE EXECUTION TO ME!!
BEHEADER SULEIMAN
NO, MINE!!
LONG-LEG BLUE GILLY
ALL RIGHT, LISTEN UP!!
?!

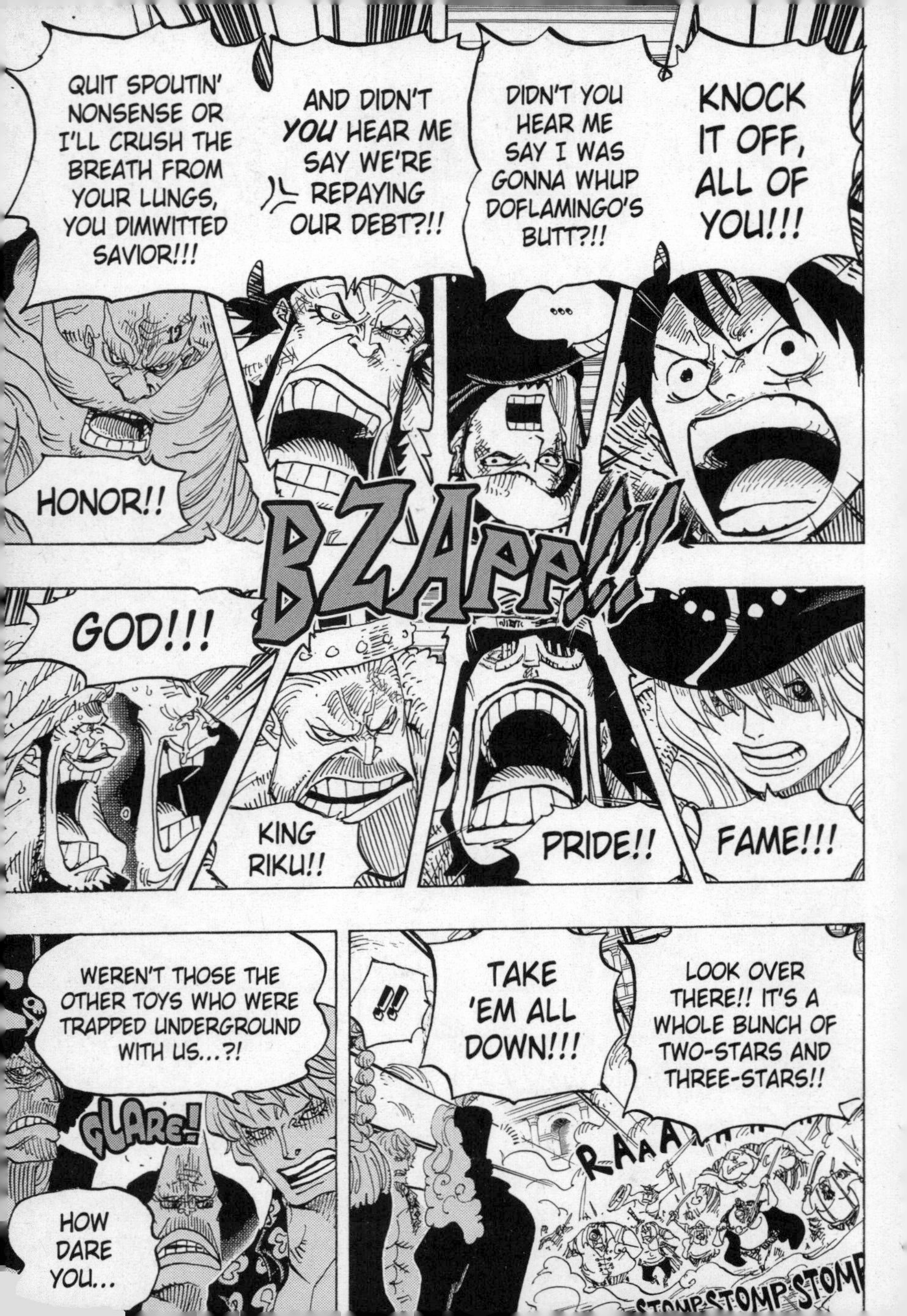
KNOCK IT OFF, ALL OF YOU!!!
DIDN'T YOU HEAR ME SAY I WAS GONNA WHUP DOFLAMINGO'S BUTT?!!
AND DIDN'T YOU HEAR ME SAY WE'RE REPAYING OUR DEBT?!!
QUIT SPOUTIN' NONSENSE OR I'LL CRUSH THE BREATH FROM YOUR LUNGS, YOU DIMWITTED SAVIOR!!!
...
HONOR!!
BZAPP!!
FAME!!!
PRIDE!!
KING RIKU!!
GOD!!!
LOOK OVER THERE!! IT'S A WHOLE BUNCH OF TWO-STARS AND THREE-STARS!!
TAKE 'EM ALL DOWN!!!
!!
RAAAA
STOMP STOMP STOMP
WEREN'T THOSE THE OTHER TOYS WHO WERE TRAPPED UNDERGROUND WITH US...?!
GLARE!
HOW DARE YOU...

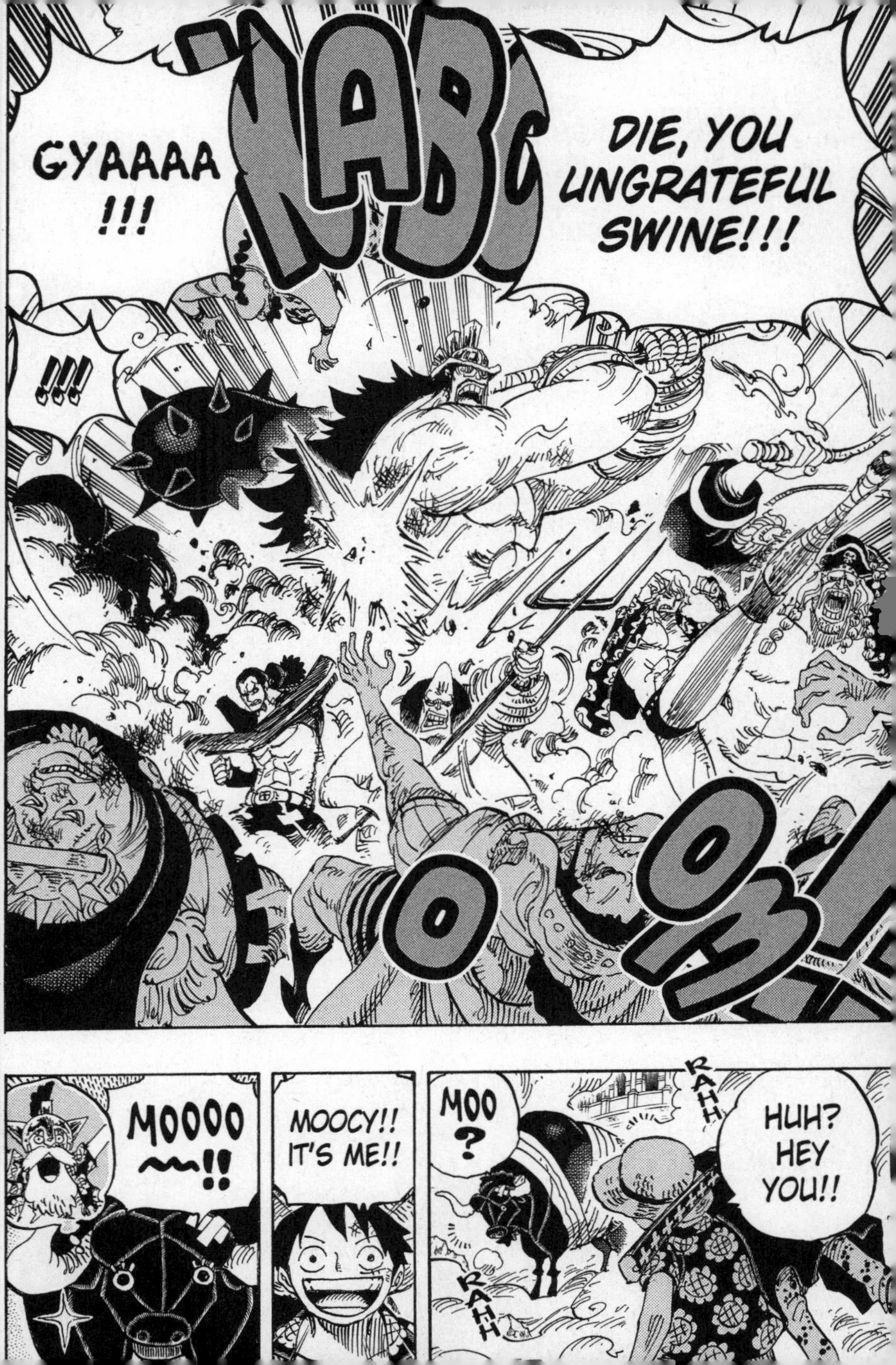
DIE, YOU UNGRATEFUL SWINE!!!
GYAAAA !!!
!!!
RAHH
HUH? HEY YOU!!
MOO ?
RAHH
MOOCY!! IT'S ME!!
MOOOO ~~!!

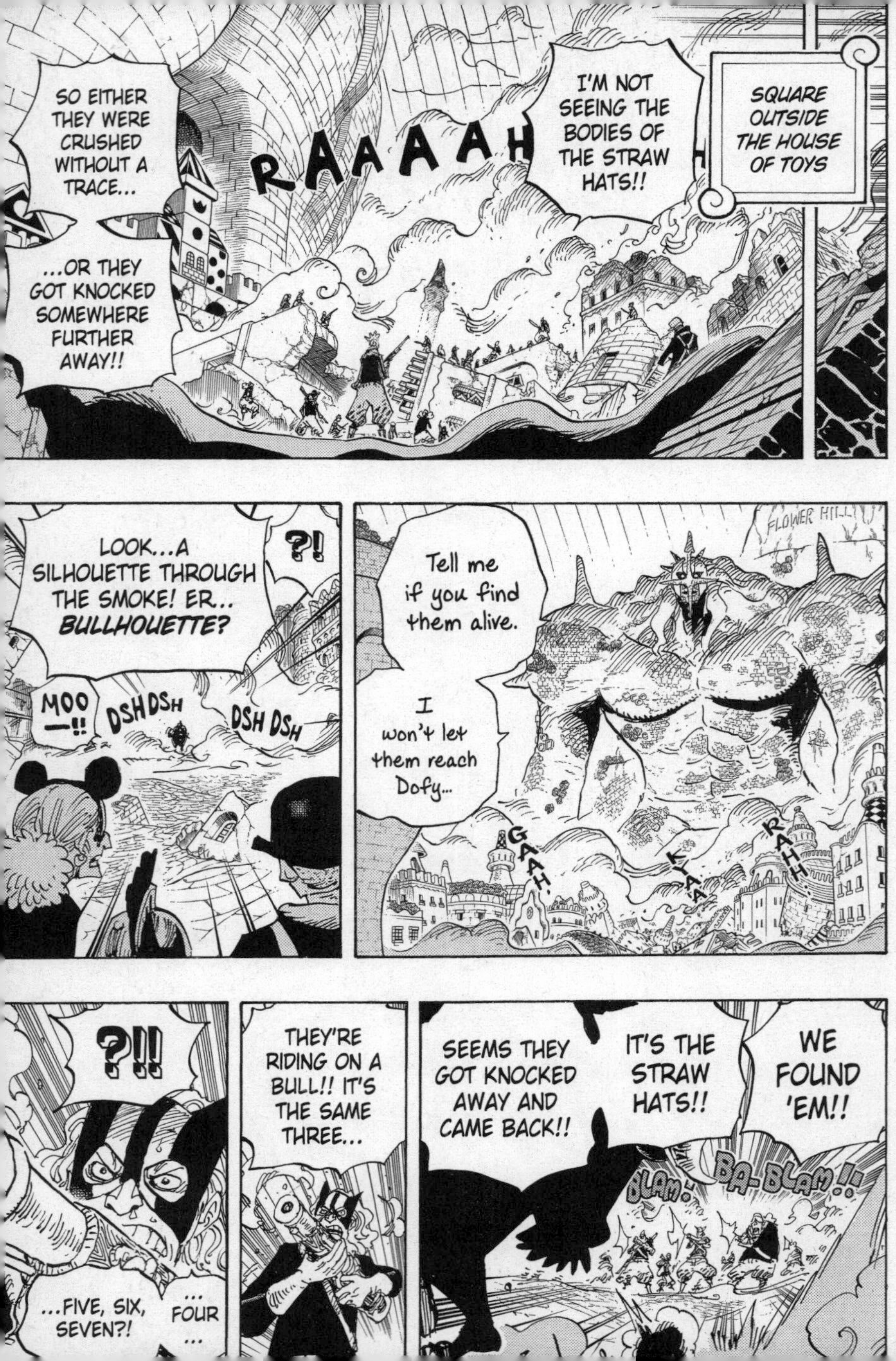
SQUARE OUTSIDE THE HOUSE OF TOYS
I'M NOT SEEING THE BODIES OF THE STRAW HATS!!
RAAAAHH
SO EITHER THEY WERE CRUSHED WITHOUT A TRACE...
...OR THEY GOT KNOCKED SOMEWHERE FURTHER AWAY!!
FLOWER HILL
Tell me if you find them alive.
I won't let them reach Dofy...
GAAAH
KYAA
RAHH
?!
LOOK...A SILHOUETTE THROUGH THE SMOKE! ER... *BULLHOUETTE?*
DSH DSH
DSHDSH
MOO—!!
WE FOUND 'EM!!
IT'S THE STRAW HATS!!
SEEMS THEY GOT KNOCKED AWAY AND CAME BACK!!
BA-BLAM!!
BLAM
THEY'RE RIDING ON A BULL!! IT'S THE SAME THREE...
?!!
...FOUR...
...FIVE, SIX, SEVEN?!

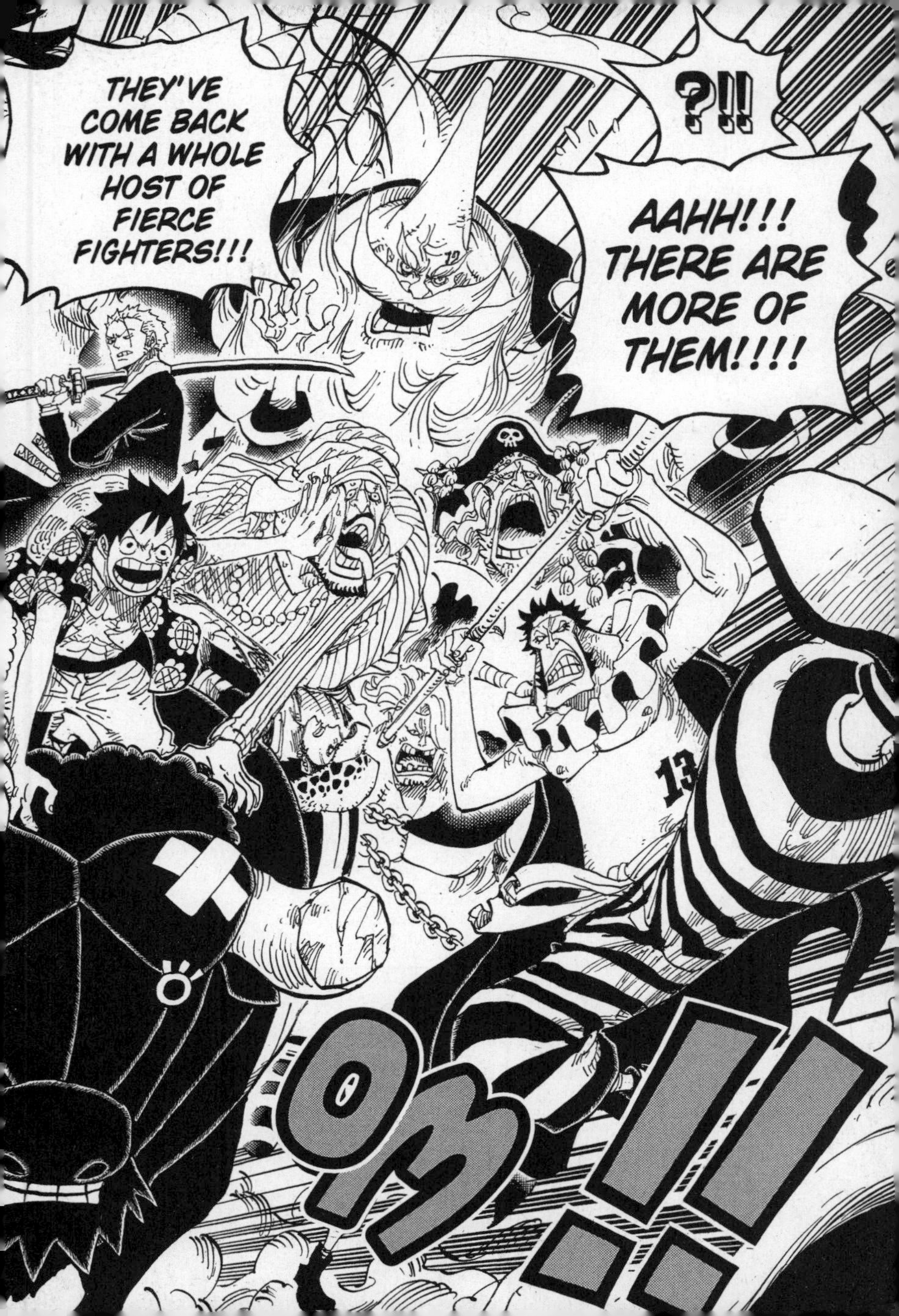
?!!
AAHH!!! THERE ARE MORE OF THEM!!!!
THEY'VE COME BACK WITH A WHOLE HOST OF FIERCE FIGHTERS!!!

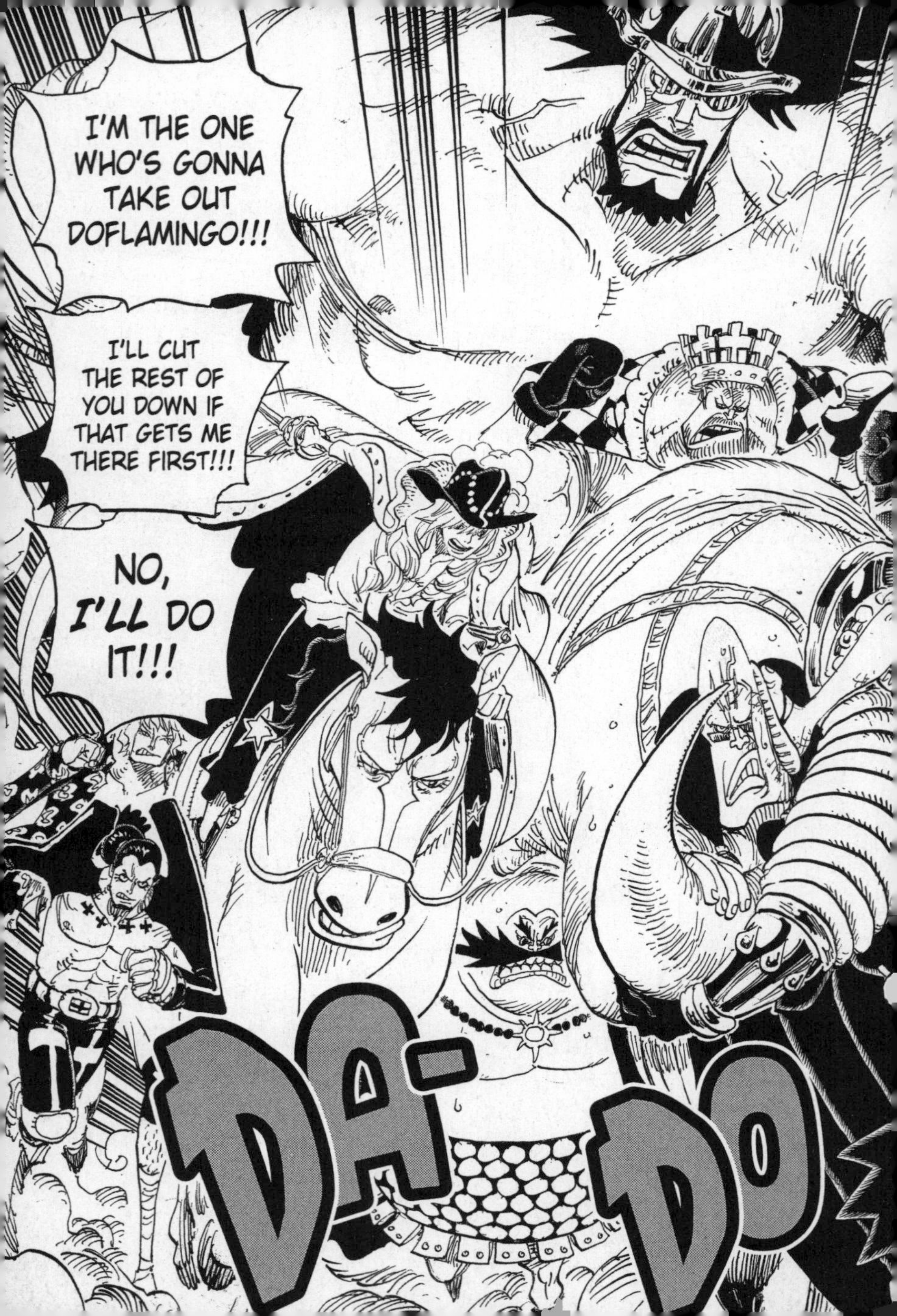
I'M THE ONE WHO'S GONNA TAKE OUT DOFLAMINGO!!!
I'LL CUT THE REST OF YOU DOWN IF THAT GETS ME THERE FIRST!!!
NO, *I'LL* DO IT!!!
DA-DOM

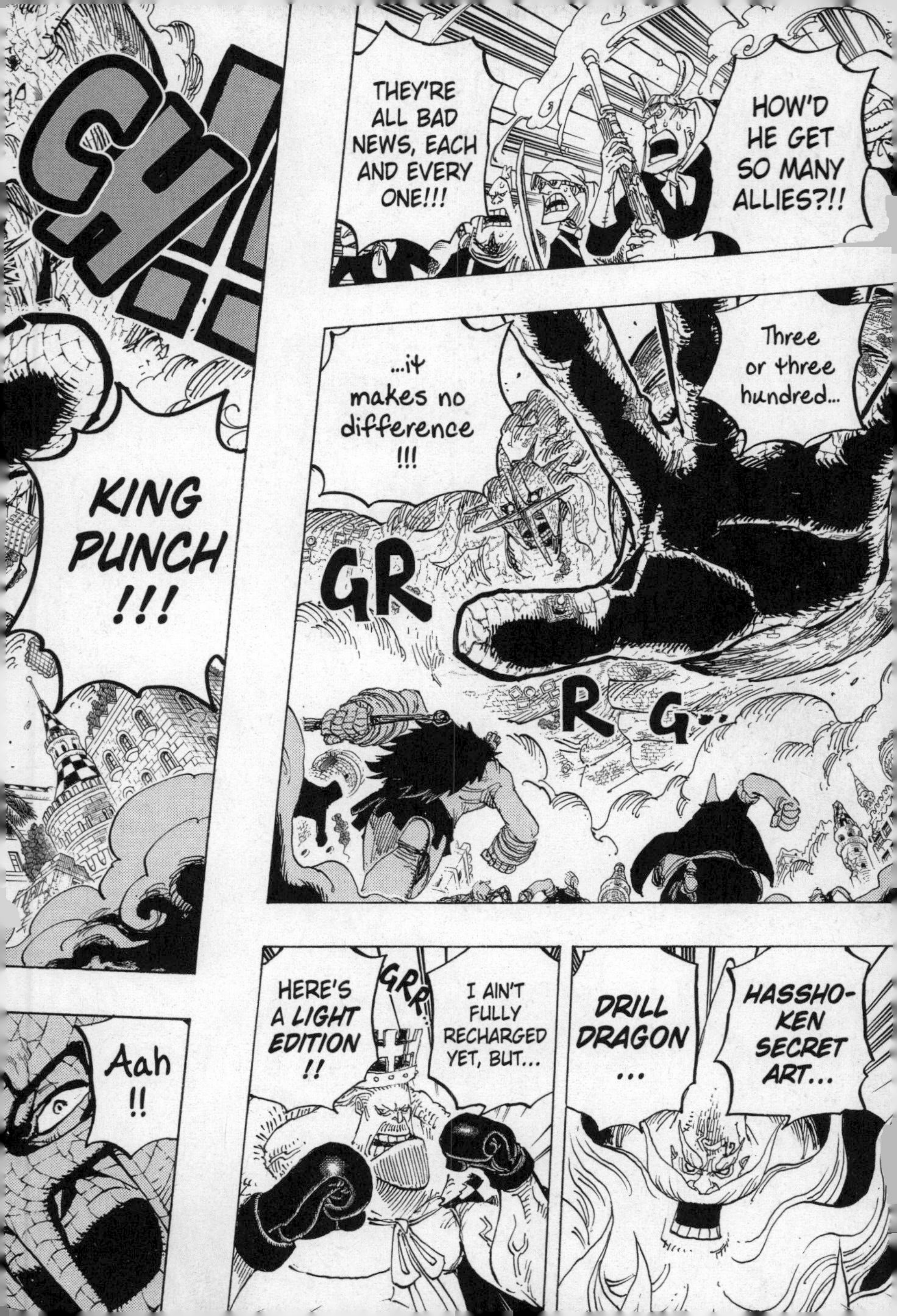
HOW'D HE GET SO MANY ALLIES?!!
THEY'RE ALL BAD NEWS, EACH AND EVERY ONE!!!
Three or three hundred...
...it makes no difference!!!
GR
R
G...
CH!
KING PUNCH!!!
HASSHO-KEN SECRET ART...
DRILL DRAGON...
I AIN'T FULLY RECHARGED YET, BUT...
GRR
HERE'S A LIGHT EDITION!!
Aah!!

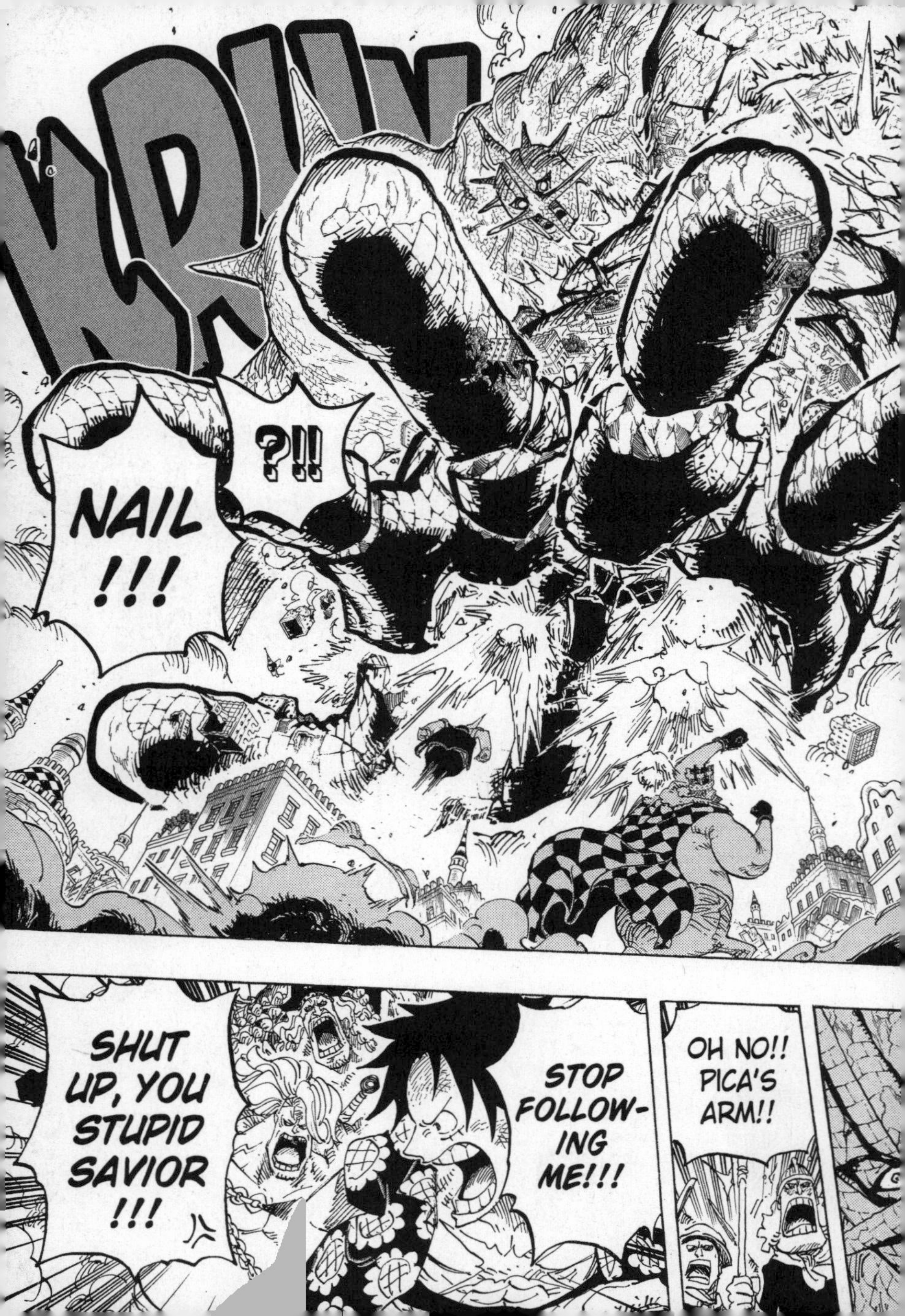
?!!
NAIL !!!
OH NO!! PICA'S ARM!!
STOP FOLLOW-ING ME!!!
SHUT UP, YOU STUPID SAVIOR !!!

SBS Question Corner

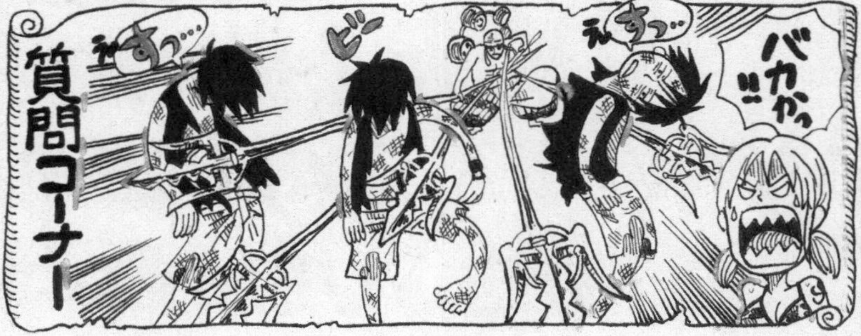
質問コーナー
バカかっ!!

(Nekosuke, Saitama)

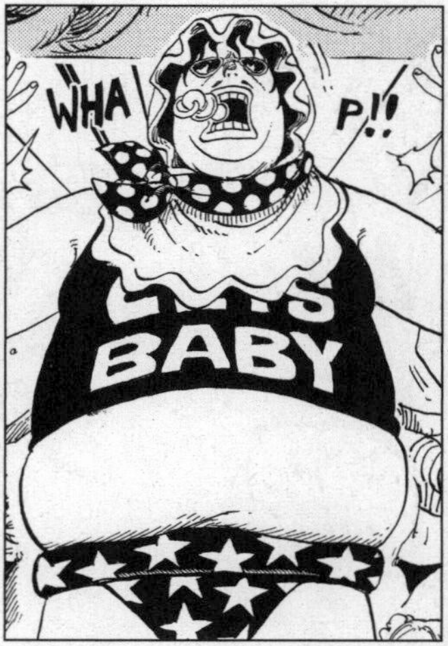
WHA
P!!
BABY

Q: As the representative of all young women, I have a statement for you.

No to Señor Pink! Just no!!

Odacchi, is that…what you're into…?

--Matsumokkuri, Girls' Rep

A: Yes!!! Yes all the way!!

Don't underestimate Señor, missy. It says here that you're seventeen years old. Well, young people have a tendency to judge others on their looks, but you'll see very soon. You'll see what a real man is like! You'll understand what it means to be hardboiled!! Just you wait!

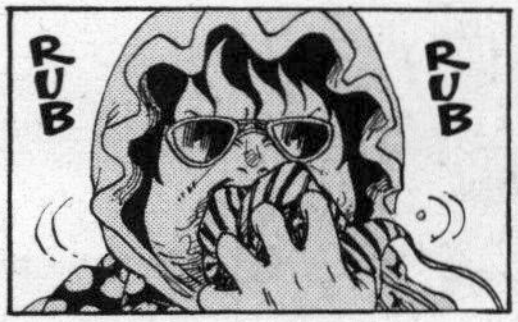
RUB
RUB

Q: Here's a question. If I was chowing down on a tomato next to a pool, and I used a nearby babe's swimsuit to wipe my mouth, what would happen?

……I know, right? She'll totally fall in love with me?! Okay, let's hit the pool! *Woo-hoo!!*

⬇

Odacchi… I got arrested… Why?!

--Chagero Kiyomizu's Wannabe Apprentice

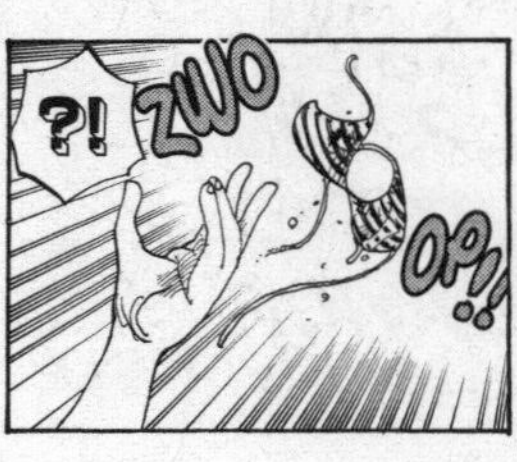
?!
ZWO
OP!!

A: Whoa... So you tried it too! Yeah, it's easy to look up to Señor. It says here you're thirteen now. First live another three decades, then just ooze coolness. I'm gonna draw how great Señor is, and that will be your guide!

Also, that's a bad pen name. Don't turn out like him!

Chapter 749: ONWARD, GALLERY OF ROGUES!!

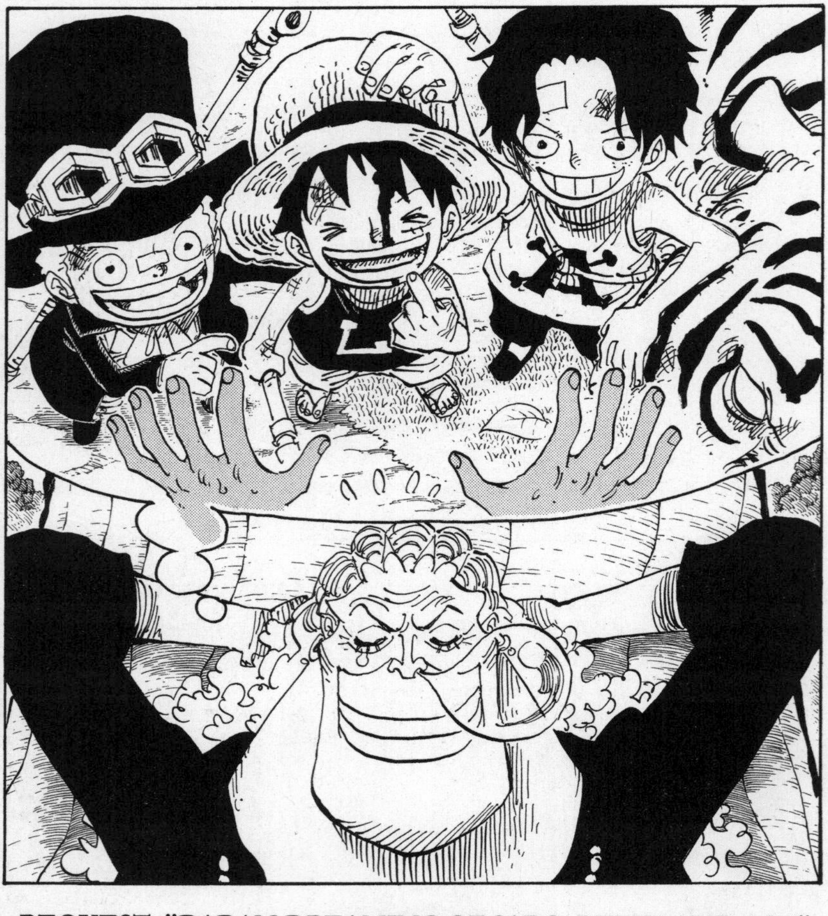

REQUEST: "DADAN DREAMING OF SABO, LUFFY AND ACE"
BY MARU X KAZU FROM MIYAGI

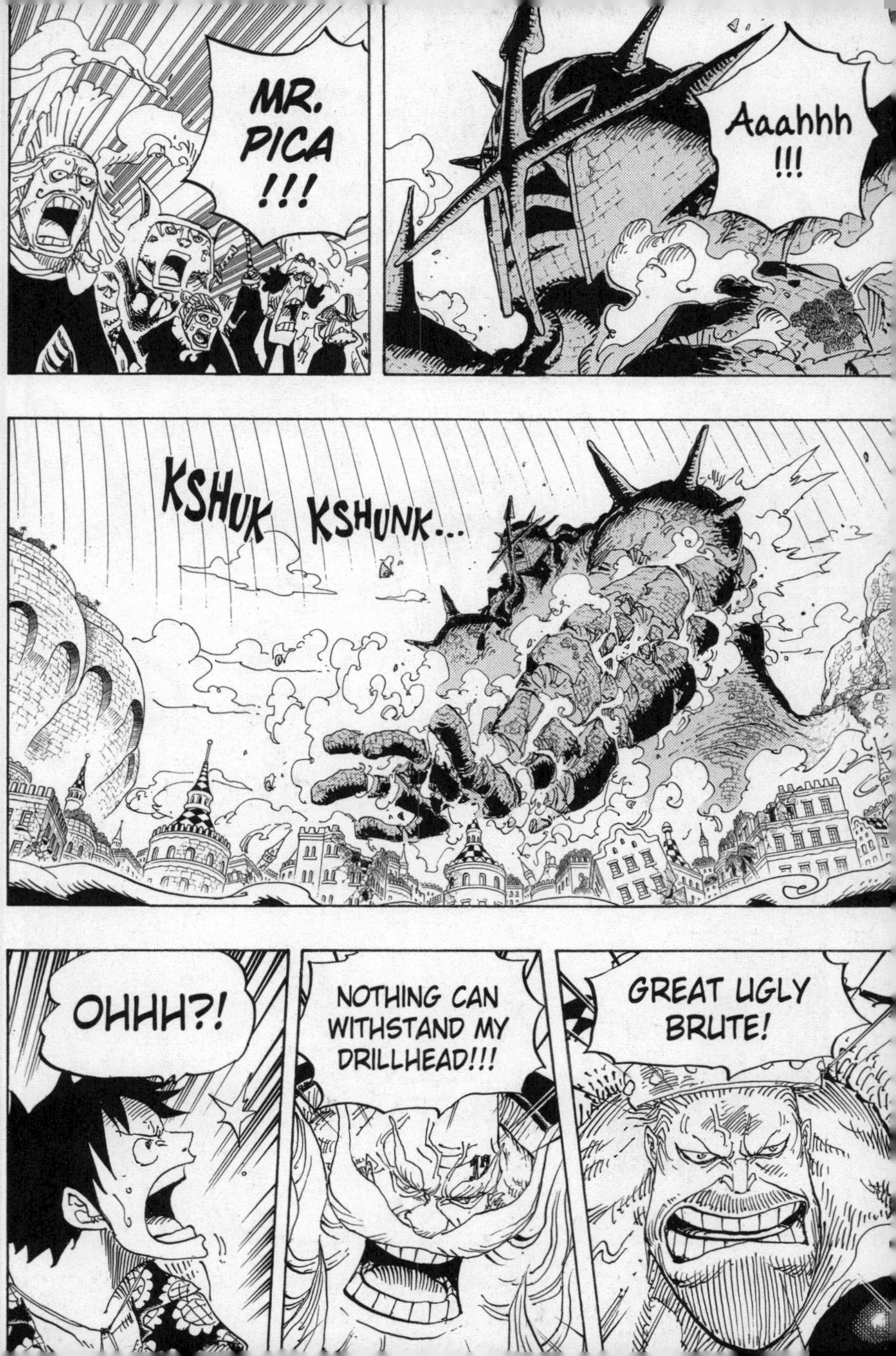
Aaahhh !!!
MR. PICA !!!
KSHUK KSHUNK...
GREAT UGLY BRUTE!
NOTHING CAN WITHSTAND MY DRILLHEAD!!!
OHHH?!

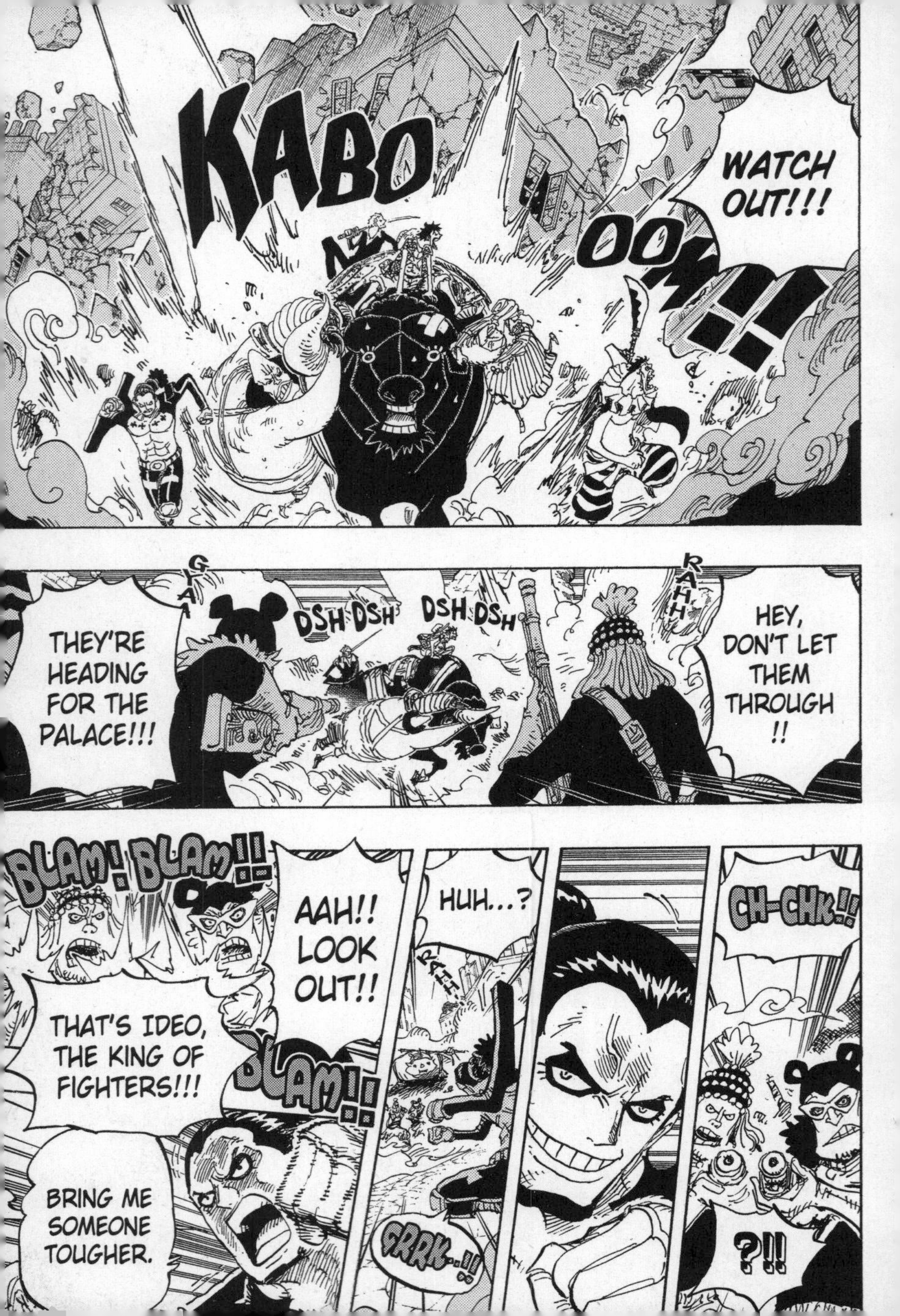
WATCH OUT!!!
KABOOOM!!
RAHH
HEY, DON'T LET THEM THROUGH !!
DSH DSH DSH DSH
GYAA
THEY'RE HEADING FOR THE PALACE!!!
CH-CHK!!
?!!
HUH...?
RAHH
GRRK..!!
AAH!! LOOK OUT!!
BLAM!!
BLAM! BLAM!!
THAT'S IDEO, THE KING OF FIGHTERS!!!
BRING ME SOMEONE TOUGHER.

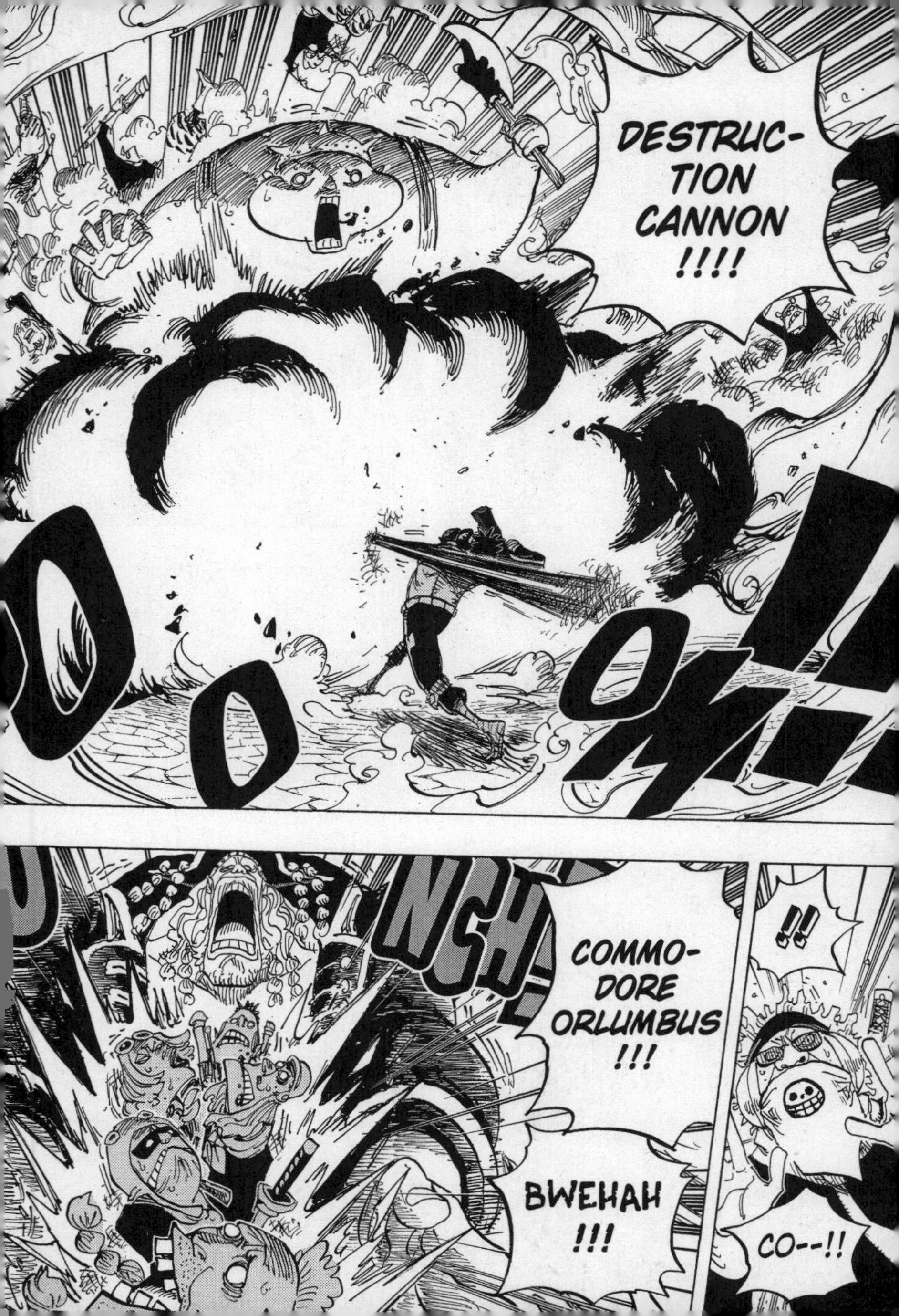
DESTRUCTION CANNON !!!!
!!
CO--!!
COMMODORE ORLUMBUS !!!
BWEHAH !!!

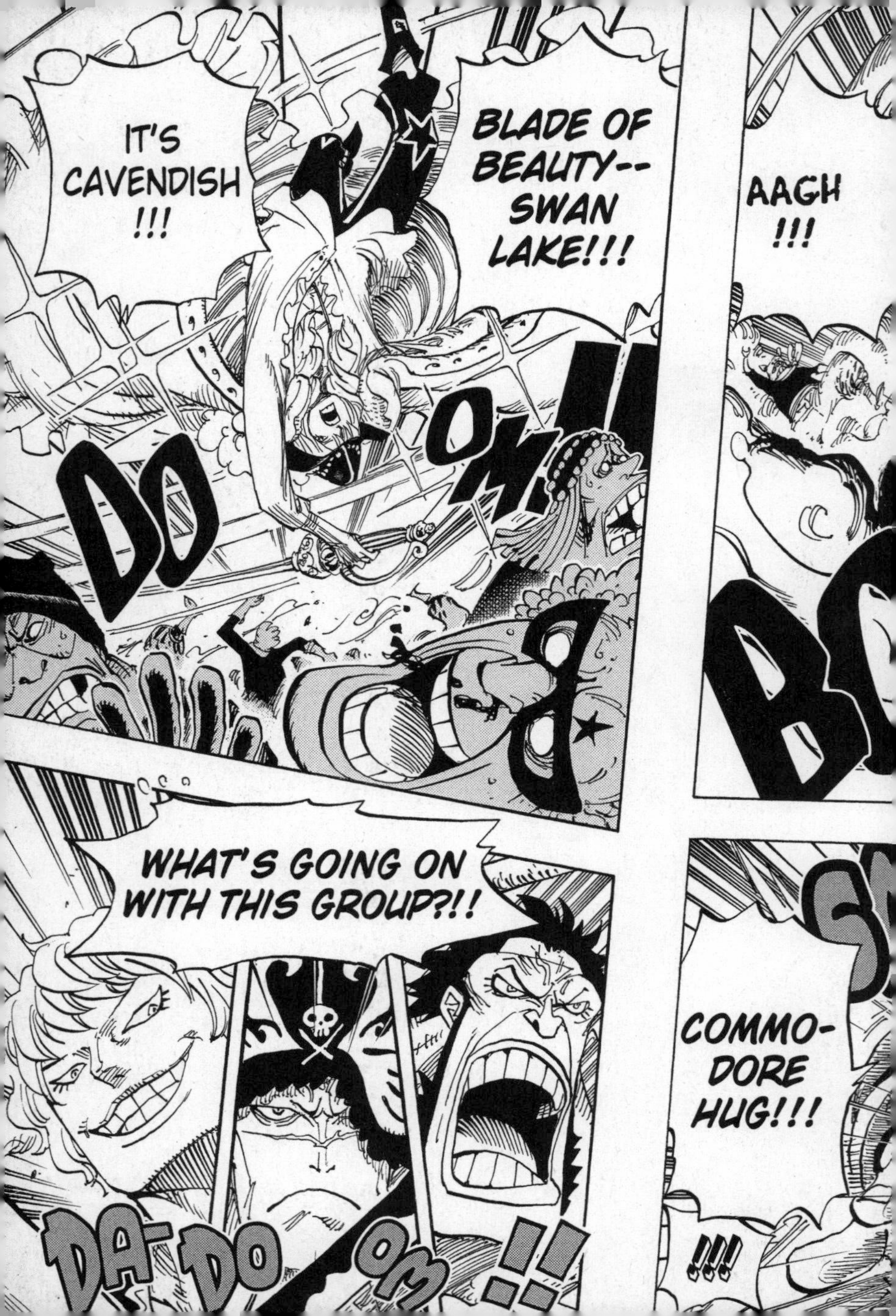
AAGH!!!
BLADE OF BEAUTY-- SWAN LAKE!!!
IT'S CAVENDISH!!!
DOOOM!!
COMMO-DORE HUG!!!
!!!
WHAT'S GOING ON WITH THIS GROUP?!!
DA-DOOM!!

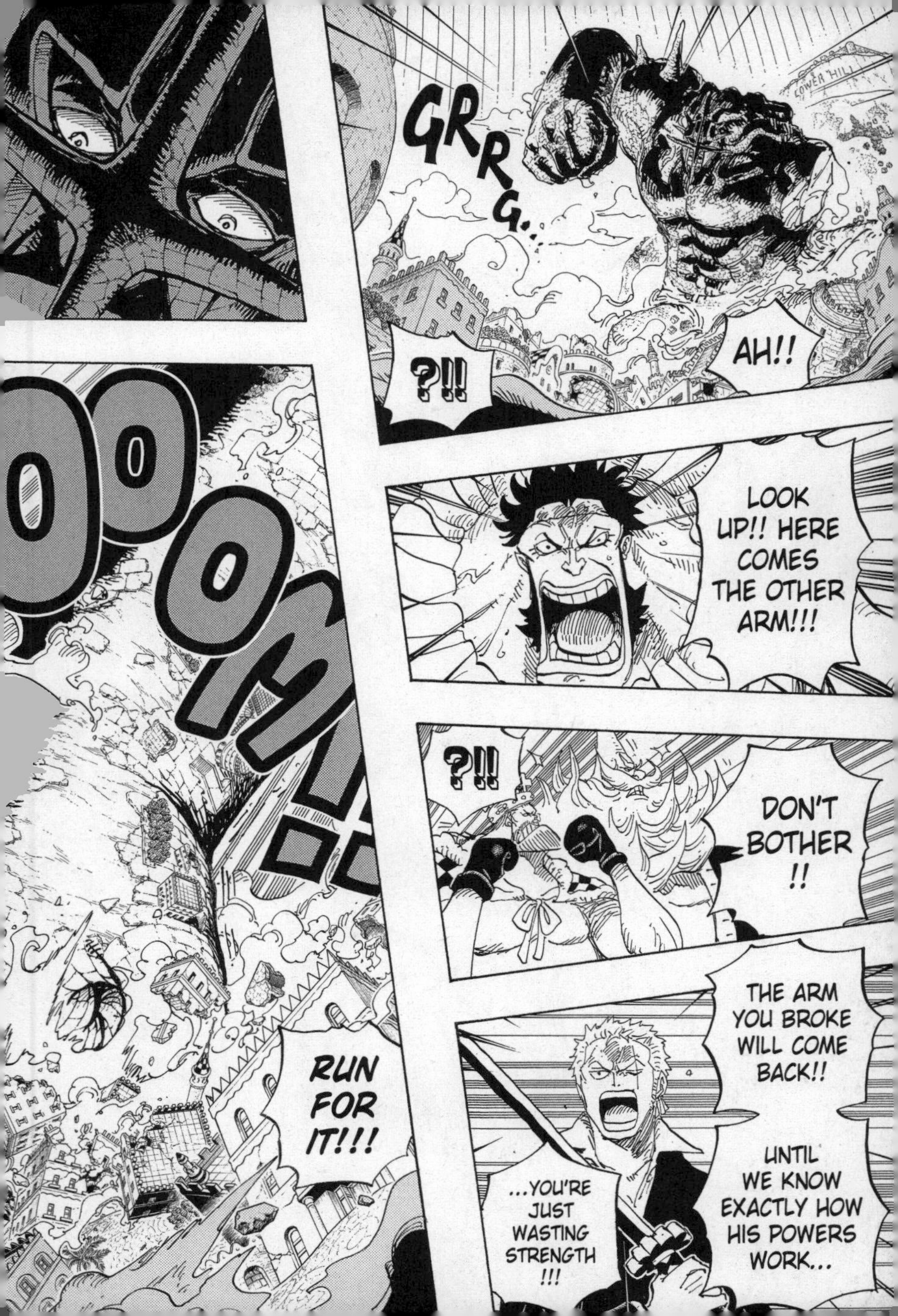
GRRG...
AH!!
?!!
LOOK UP!! HERE COMES THE OTHER ARM!!!
?!!
DON'T BOTHER!!
THE ARM YOU BROKE WILL COME BACK!!
UNTIL WE KNOW EXACTLY HOW HIS POWERS WORK...
...YOU'RE JUST WASTING STRENGTH!!!
OOOM!!
RUN FOR IT!!!

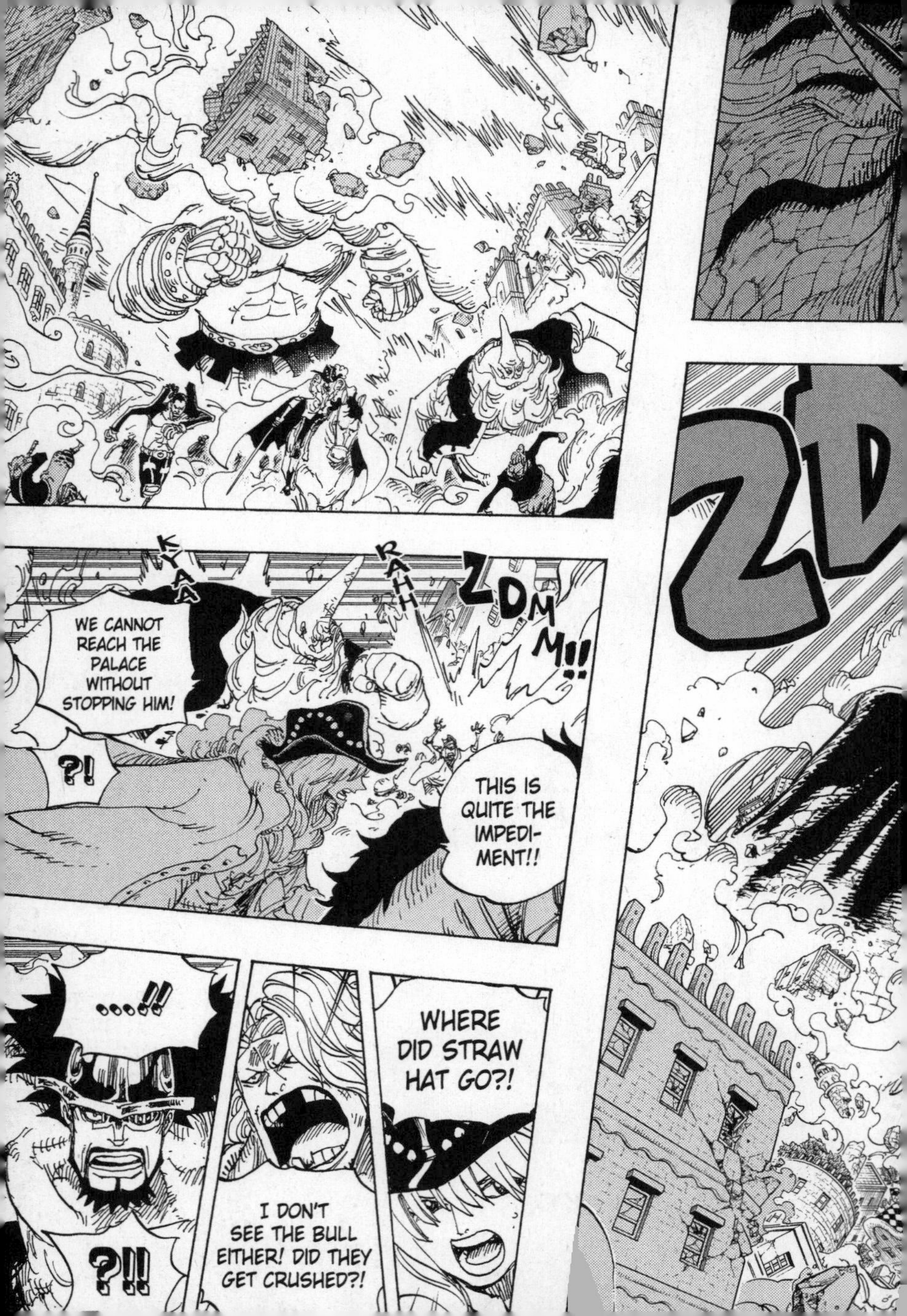
ZD
ZDMMM!!
RAHH
KYAA
WE CANNOT REACH THE PALACE WITHOUT STOPPING HIM!
THIS IS QUITE THE IMPEDI-MENT!!
?!
WHERE DID STRAW HAT GO?!
I DON'T SEE THE BULL EITHER! DID THEY GET CRUSHED?!
...!!
?!!

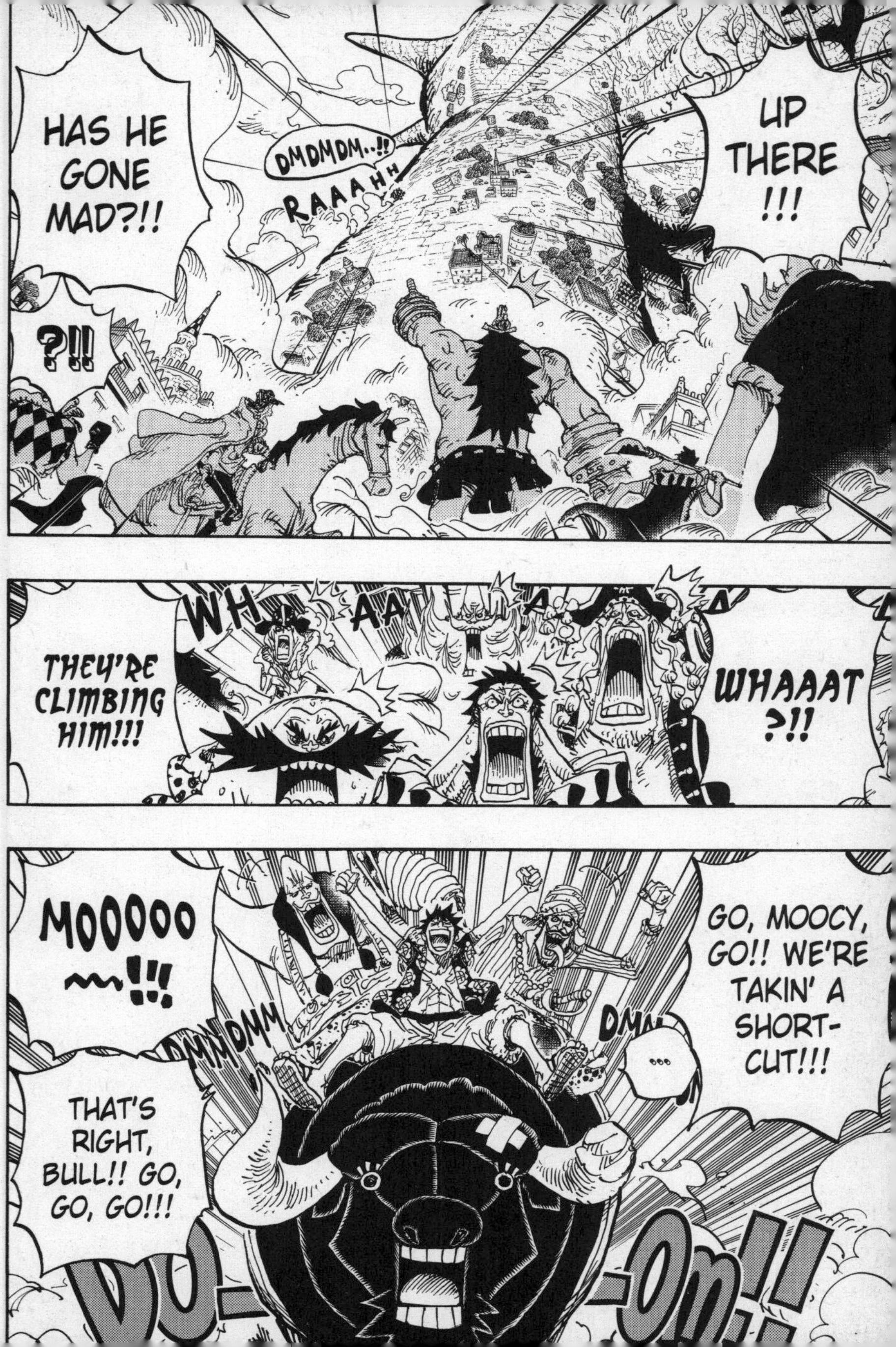
UP THERE !!!
DMDMDM..!!
RAAAHH
HAS HE GONE MAD?!!
?!!
WHAAAT ?!!
WH AA A A
THEY'RE CLIMBING HIM!!!
GO, MOOCY, GO!! WE'RE TAKIN' A SHORT-CUT!!!
...
DM
MOOOOO ~!!!
DMMDMM
THAT'S RIGHT, BULL!! GO, GO, GO!!!
VU- -OM!!

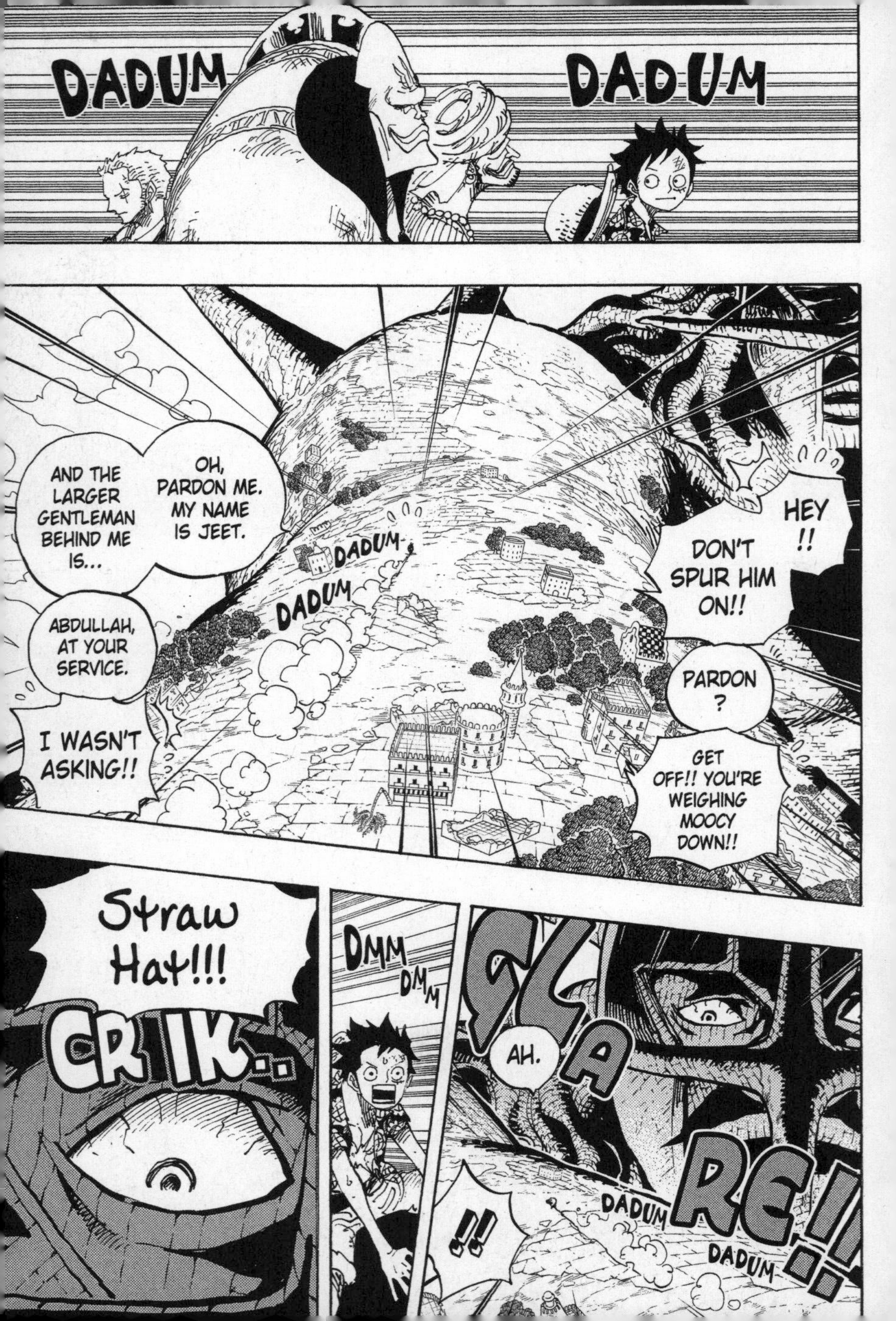
DADUM
DADUM
HEY!!
DON'T SPUR HIM ON!!
OH, PARDON ME. MY NAME IS JEET.
AND THE LARGER GENTLEMAN BEHIND ME IS...
DADUM
DADUM
PARDON?
ABDULLAH, AT YOUR SERVICE.
GET OFF!! YOU'RE WEIGHING MOOCY DOWN!!
I WASN'T ASKING!!
CL
A
AH.
RE!!
DADUM
DADUM
DMM
DMM
!!
Straw Hat!!!
CRIK..

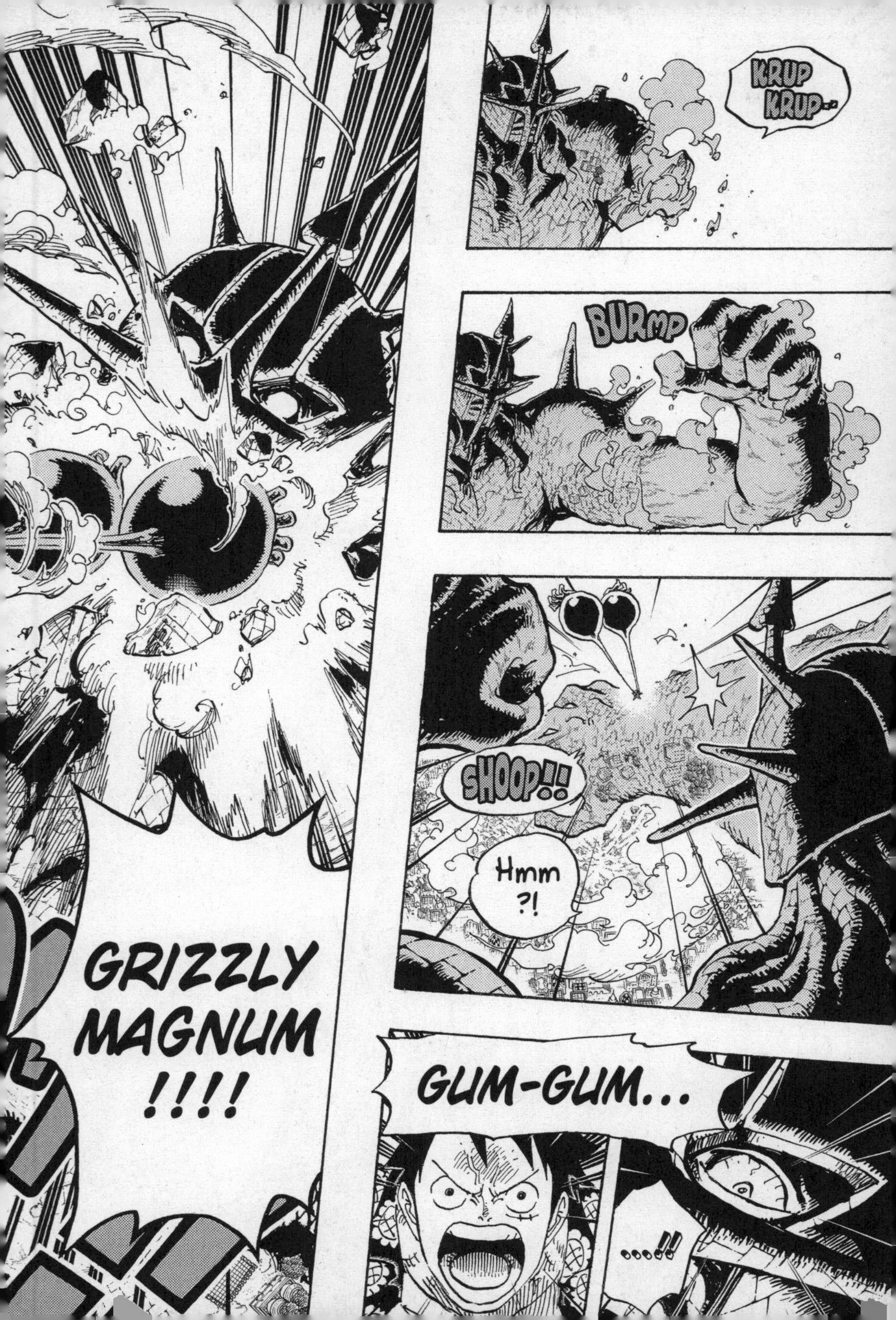
KRUP KRUP...
BURMP
SHOOP!!
Hmm ?!
GUM-GUM...
...!!
GRIZZLY MAGNUM !!!!

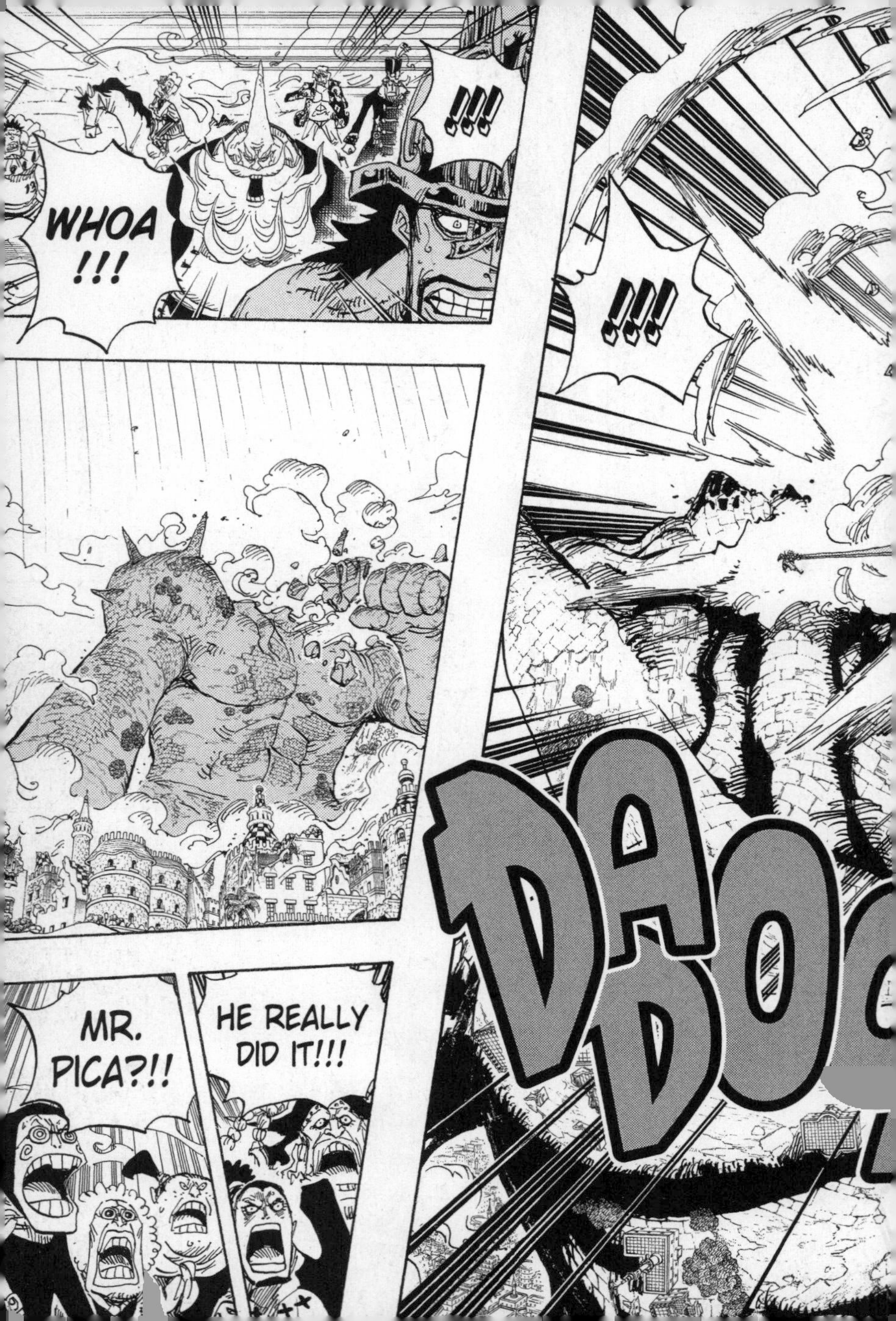
!!!
DADOO
!!!
WHOA !!!
HE REALLY DID IT!!!
MR. PICA?!!

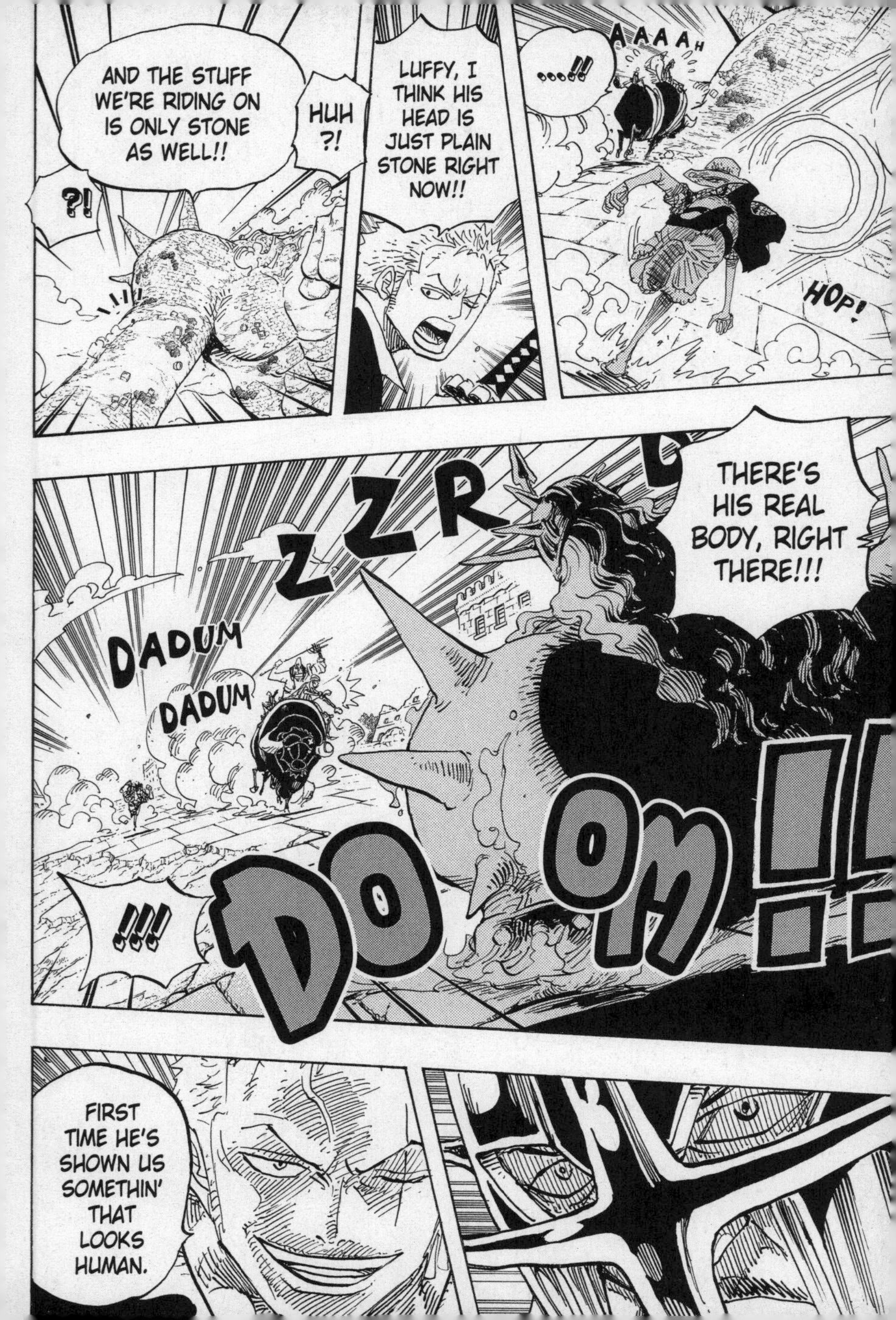

....!!
AAAAH
HOP!
LUFFY, I THINK HIS HEAD IS JUST PLAIN STONE RIGHT NOW!!
HUH ?!
AND THE STUFF WE'RE RIDING ON IS ONLY STONE AS WELL!!
?!
THERE'S HIS REAL BODY, RIGHT THERE!!!
ZZR
DADUM
DADUM
DOOM!!
!!!
FIRST TIME HE'S SHOWN US SOMETHIN' THAT LOOKS HUMAN.

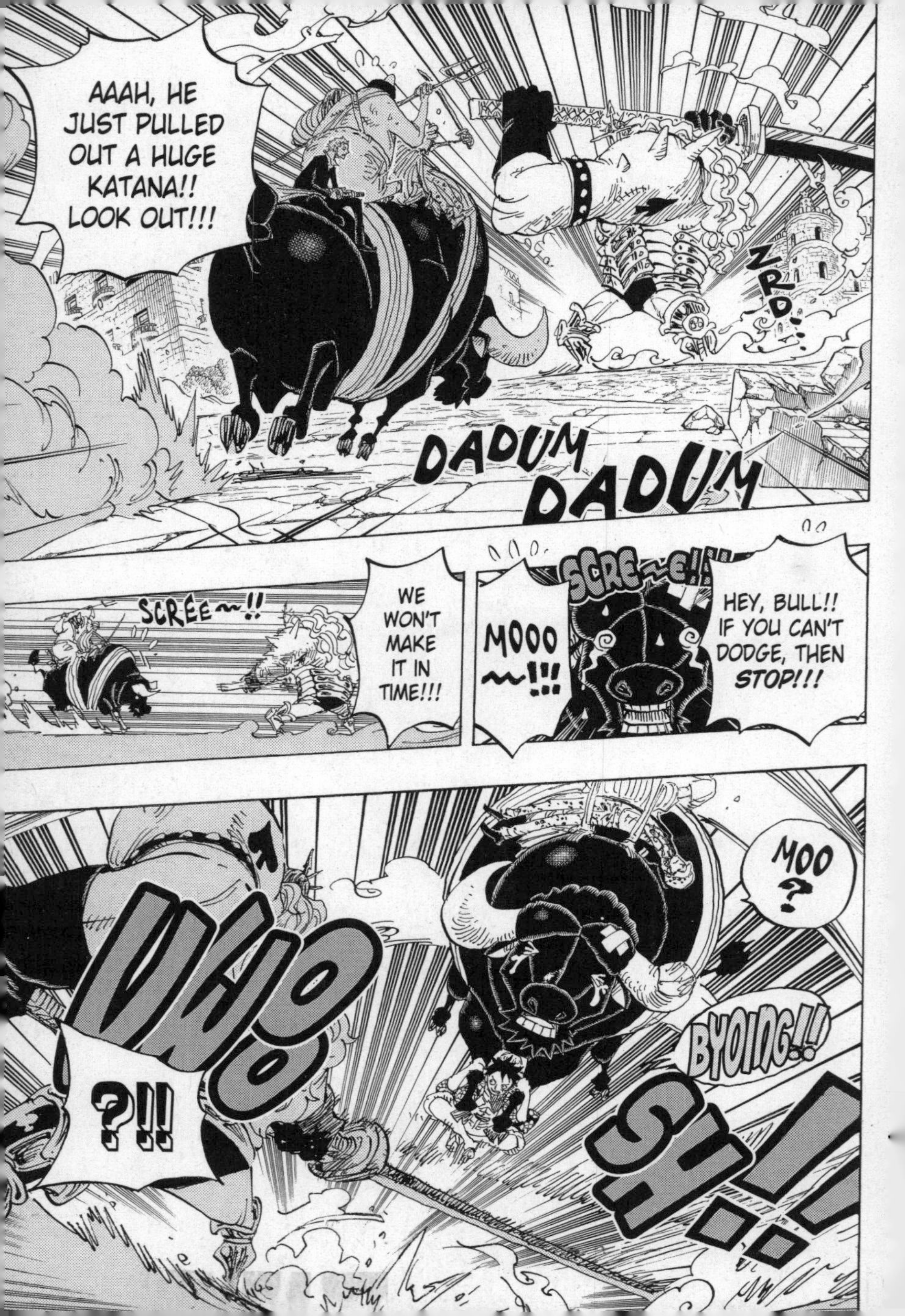
AAAH, HE JUST PULLED OUT A HUGE KATANA!! LOOK OUT!!!
ZRD
DADUM
DADUM
HEY, BULL!! IF YOU CAN'T DODGE, THEN STOP!!!
SCRE~E!!
MOOO ~~!!!
WE WON'T MAKE IT IN TIME!!!
SCREE~~!!
MOO ?
BYOING!!
?!!

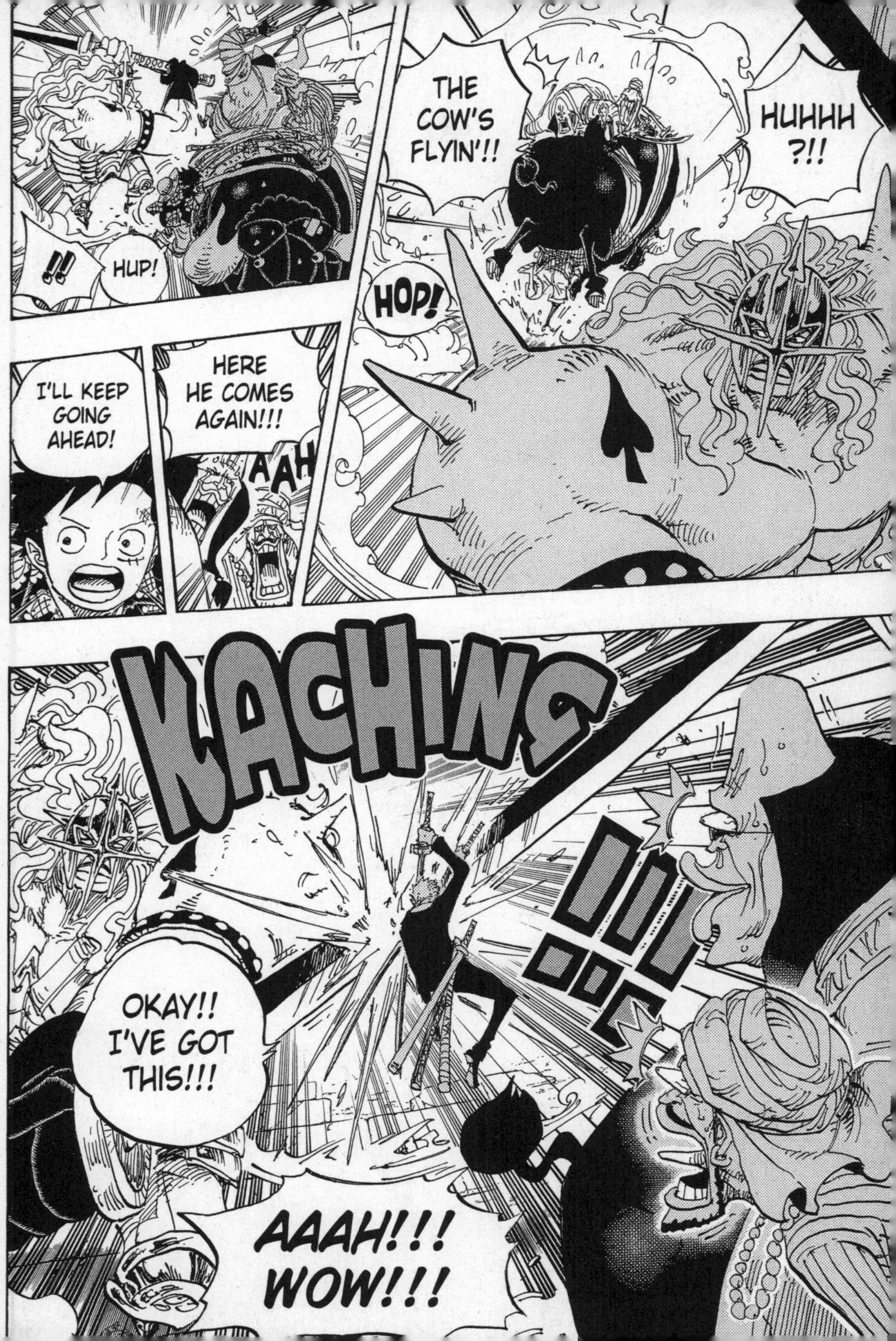
HUHHH ?!!
THE COW'S FLYIN'!!
HOP!
HUP!
!!
HERE HE COMES AGAIN!!!
AAH
I'LL KEEP GOING AHEAD!
KACHING
!!!
OKAY!! I'VE GOT THIS!!!
AAAH!!! WOW!!!

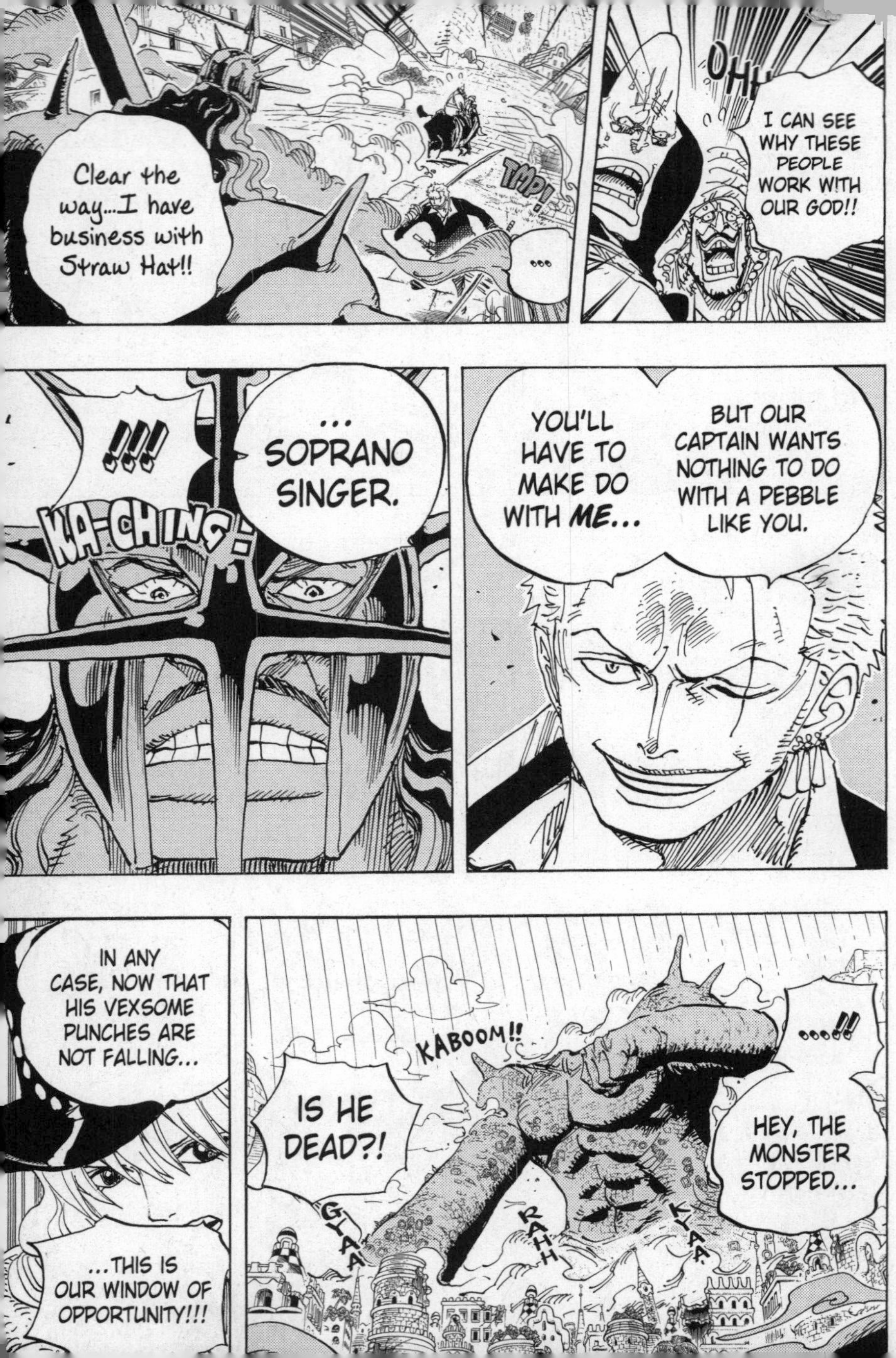
OHH
I CAN SEE WHY THESE PEOPLE WORK WITH OUR GOD!!
TMP!
...
Clear the way...I have business with Straw Hat!!
BUT OUR CAPTAIN WANTS NOTHING TO DO WITH A PEBBLE LIKE YOU.
YOU'LL HAVE TO MAKE DO WITH **ME**...
... SOPRANO SINGER.
!!!
KA-CHING!!
...!!
HEY, THE MONSTER STOPPED...
KABOOM!!
IS HE DEAD?!
KYAA
RAHH
GYAA
IN ANY CASE, NOW THAT HIS VEXSOME PUNCHES ARE NOT FALLING...
...THIS IS OUR WINDOW OF OPPORTUNITY!!!

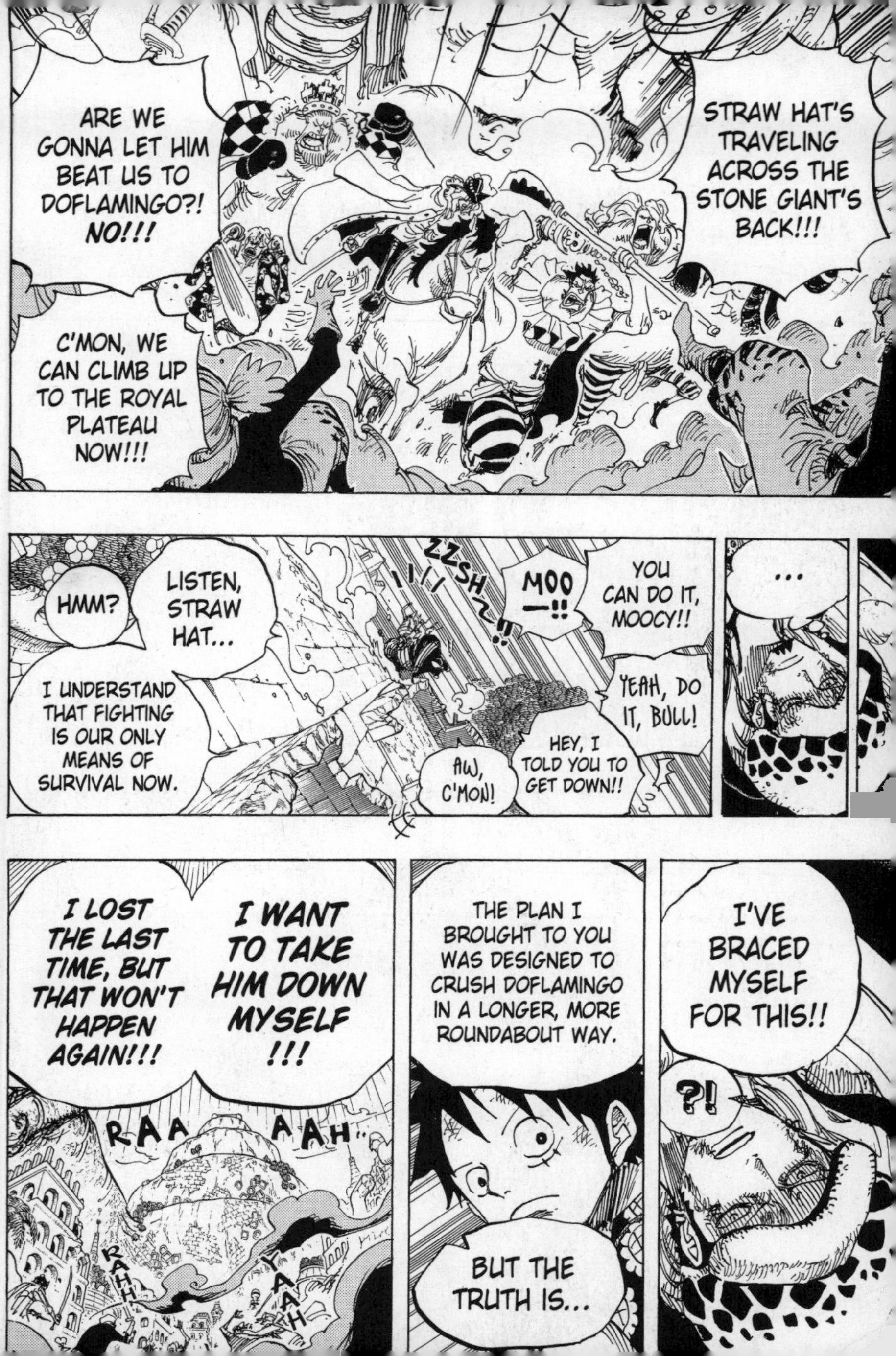
STRAW HAT'S TRAVELING ACROSS THE STONE GIANT'S BACK!!!
ARE WE GONNA LET HIM BEAT US TO DOFLAMINGO?! NO!!!
C'MON, WE CAN CLIMB UP TO THE ROYAL PLATEAU NOW!!!
...
YOU CAN DO IT, MOOCY!!
MOO—!!
ZZSH
YEAH, DO IT, BULL!
HEY, I TOLD YOU TO GET DOWN!!
AW, C'MON!
LISTEN, STRAW HAT...
HMM?
I UNDERSTAND THAT FIGHTING IS OUR ONLY MEANS OF SURVIVAL NOW.
I'VE BRACED MYSELF FOR THIS!!
?!
THE PLAN I BROUGHT TO YOU WAS DESIGNED TO CRUSH DOFLAMINGO IN A LONGER, MORE ROUNDABOUT WAY.
BUT THE TRUTH IS...
I WANT TO TAKE HIM DOWN MYSELF!!!
I LOST THE LAST TIME, BUT THAT WON'T HAPPEN AGAIN!!!
RAAAAH
YAAAH
RAHH

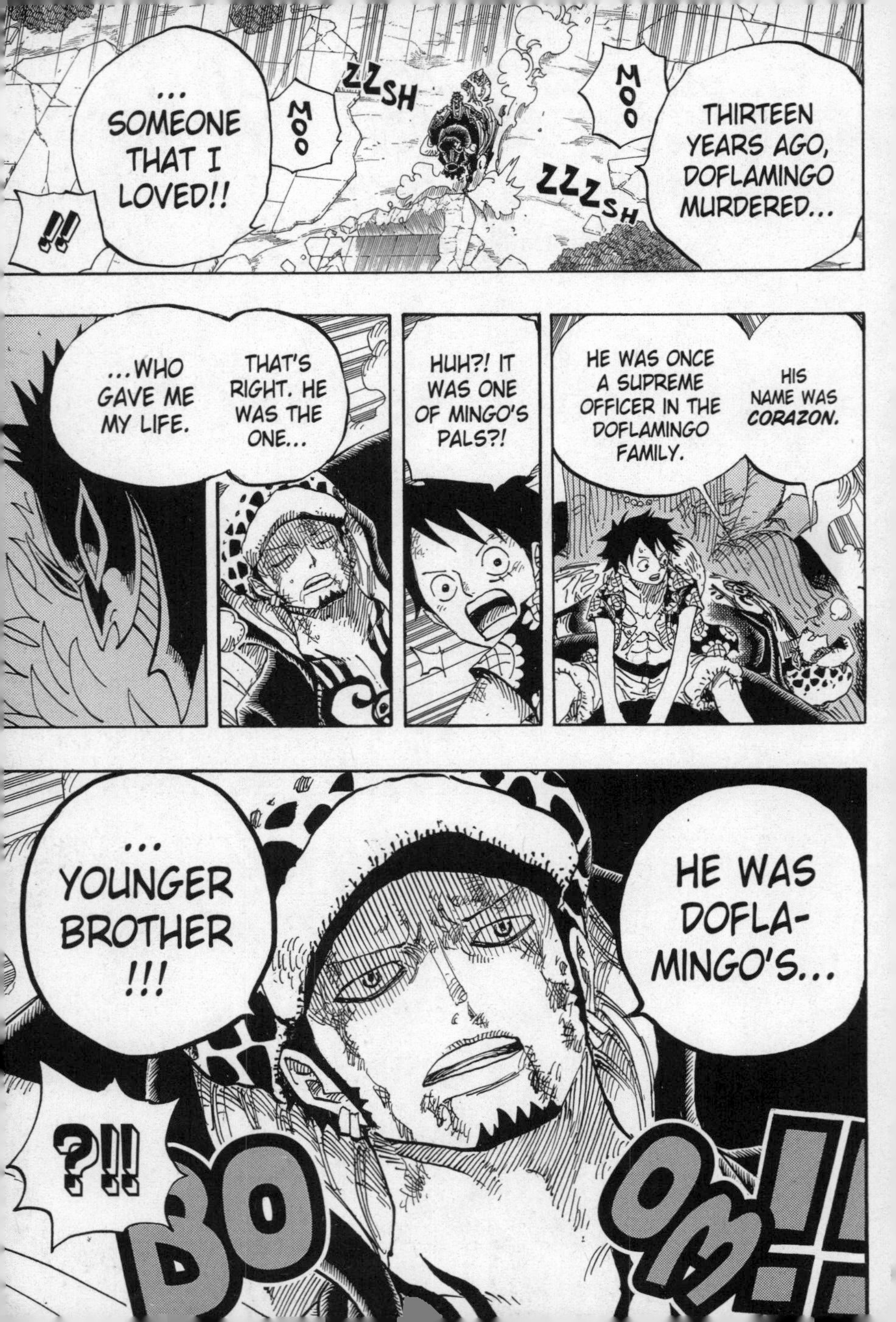
THIRTEEN YEARS AGO, DOFLAMINGO MURDERED...
MOO
ZZZSH
ZZSH
MOO
... SOMEONE THAT I LOVED!!
!!
HIS NAME WAS CORAZON.
HE WAS ONCE A SUPREME OFFICER IN THE DOFLAMINGO FAMILY.
HUH?! IT WAS ONE OF MINGO'S PALS?!
THAT'S RIGHT. HE WAS THE ONE...
...WHO GAVE ME MY LIFE.
HE WAS DOFLA-MINGO'S...
... YOUNGER BROTHER !!!
?!!
BOOM!!

Chapter 750: FLASH POINTS

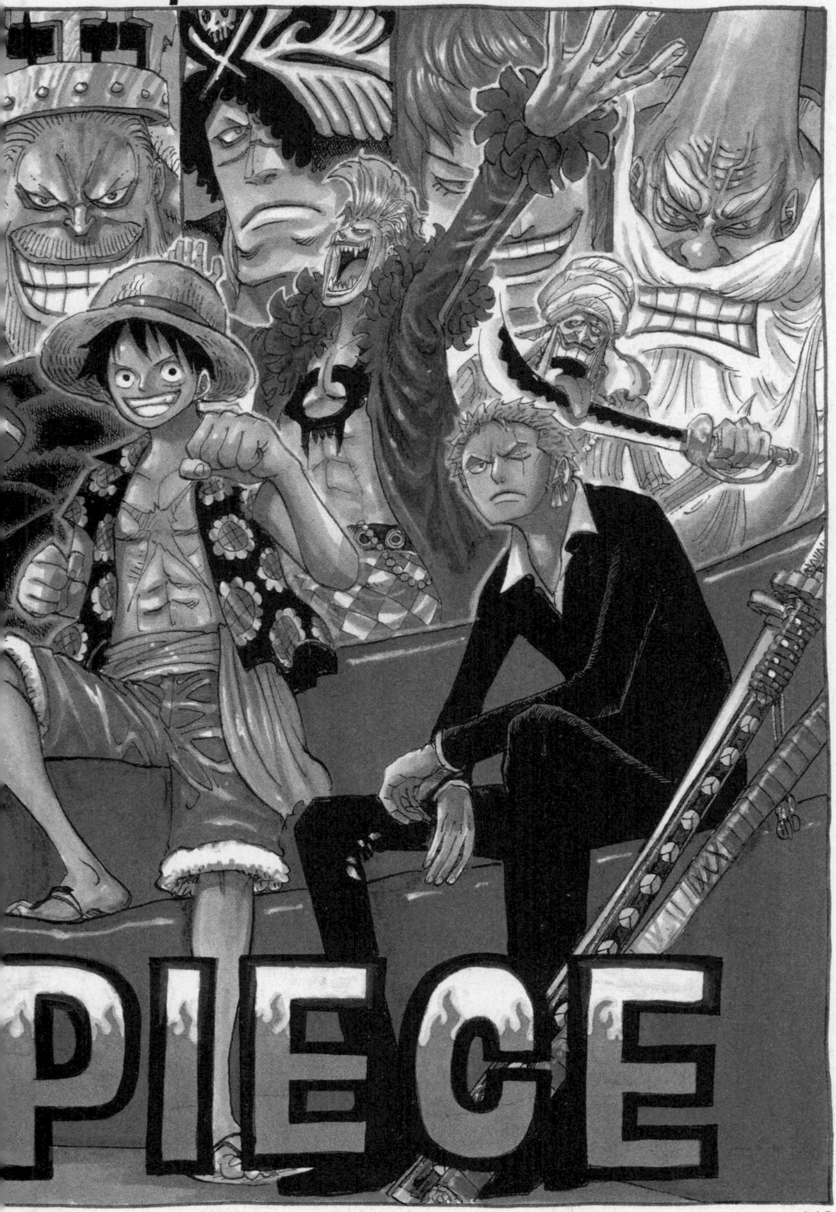
PIECE

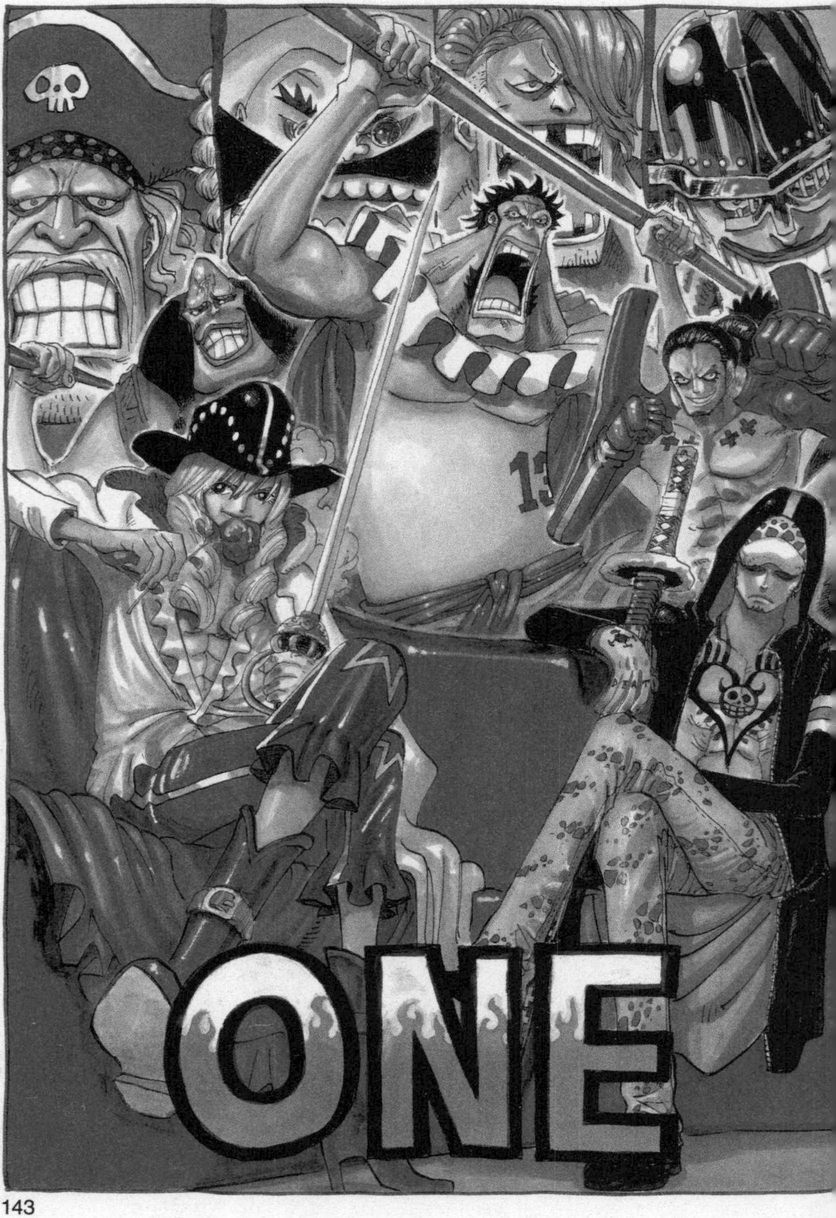
ONE

vol.75

ONE PIECE

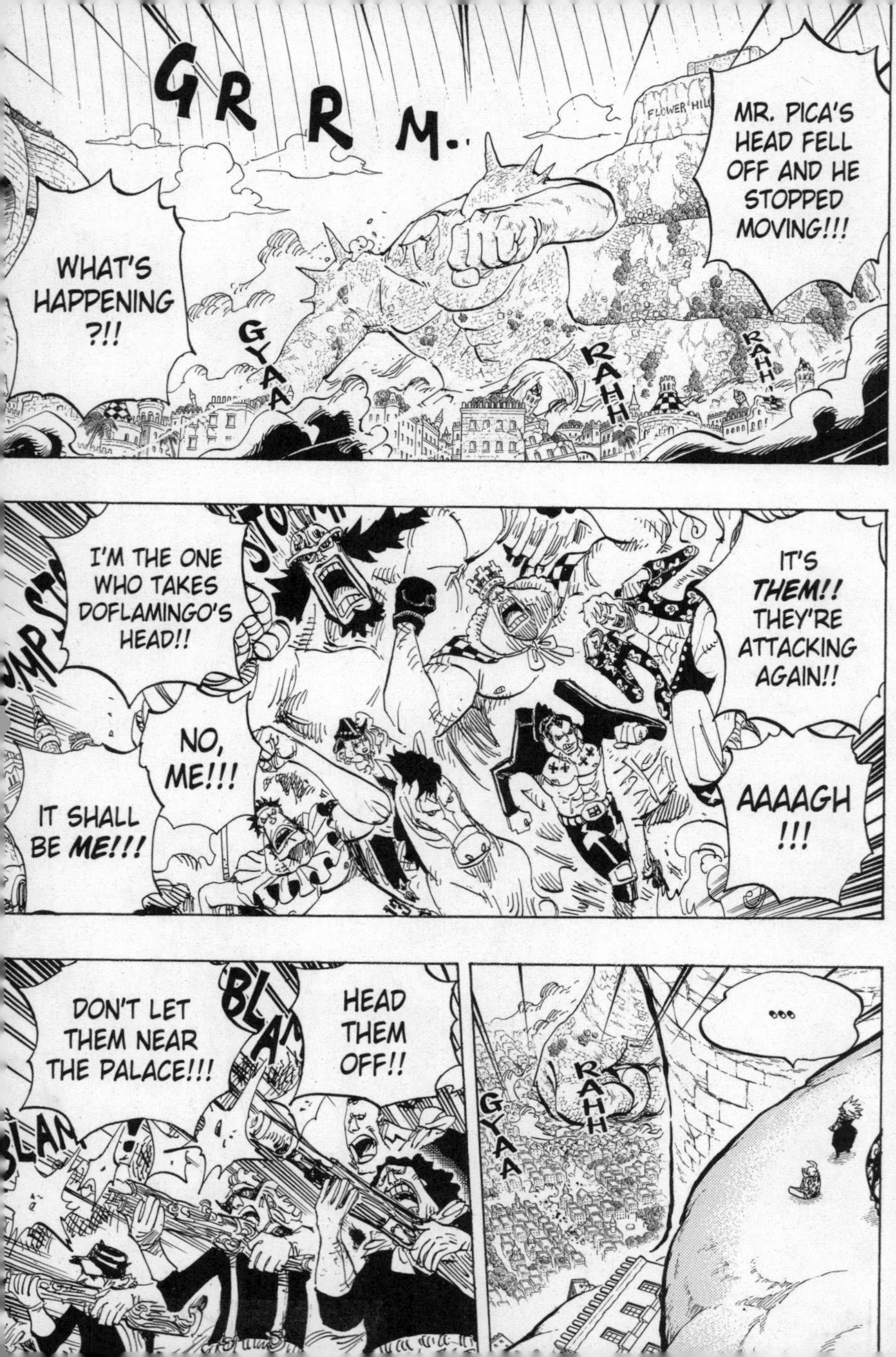
MR. PICA'S HEAD FELL OFF AND HE STOPPED MOVING!!!
RAHH
RAHH
GRRRM..
GYAA
WHAT'S HAPPENING?!!
IT'S *THEM!!* THEY'RE ATTACKING AGAIN!!
AAAAGH!!!
I'M THE ONE WHO TAKES DOFLAMINGO'S HEAD!!
NO, ME!!!
IT SHALL BE *ME!!!*
...
RAHH
GYAA
HEAD THEM OFF!!
DON'T LET THEM NEAR THE PALACE!!!

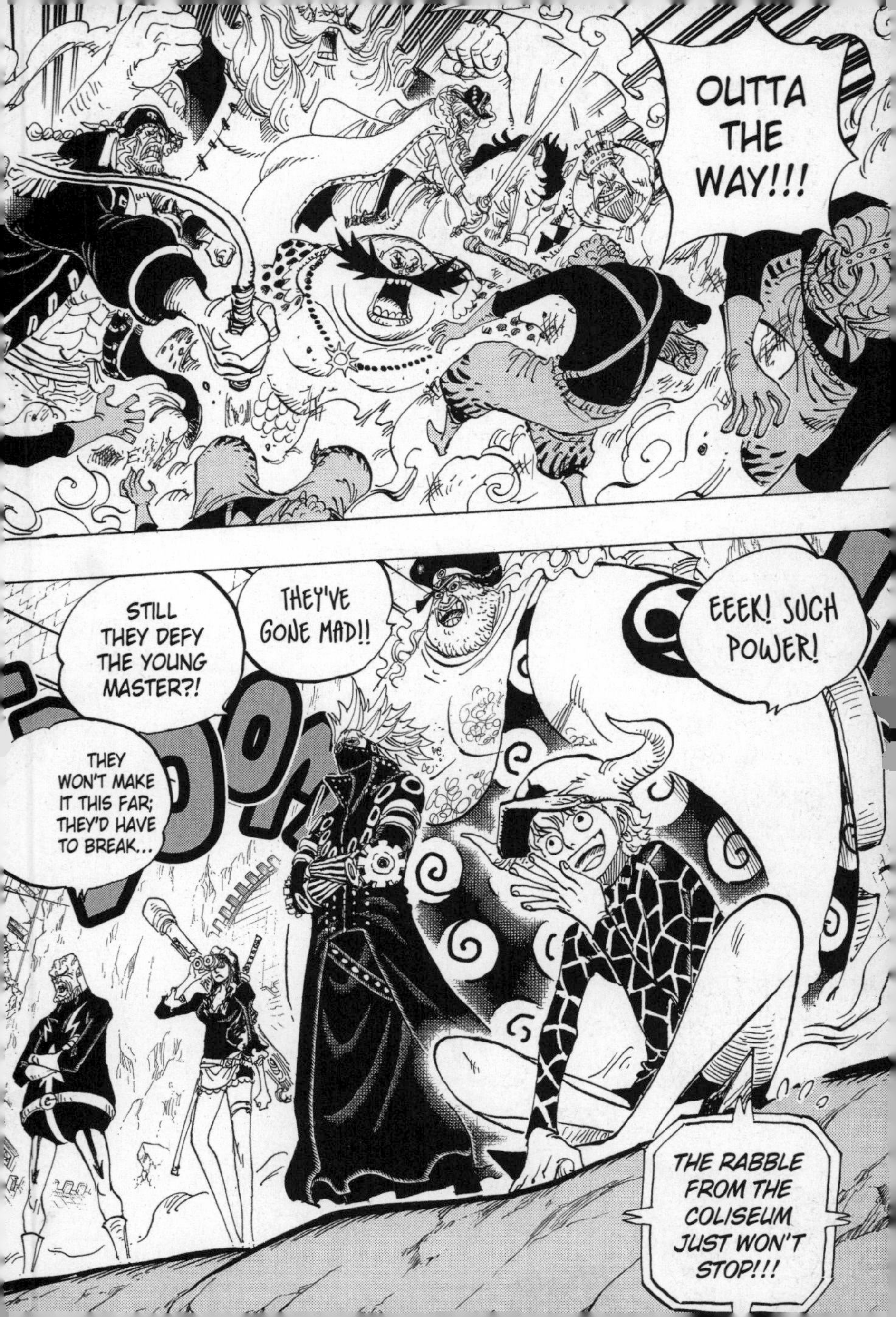
OUTTA THE WAY!!!
EEEK! SUCH POWER!
THEY'VE GONE MAD!!
STILL THEY DEFY THE YOUNG MASTER?!
THE RABBLE FROM THE COLISEUM JUST WON'T STOP!!!
THEY WON'T MAKE IT THIS FAR; THEY'D HAVE TO BREAK...

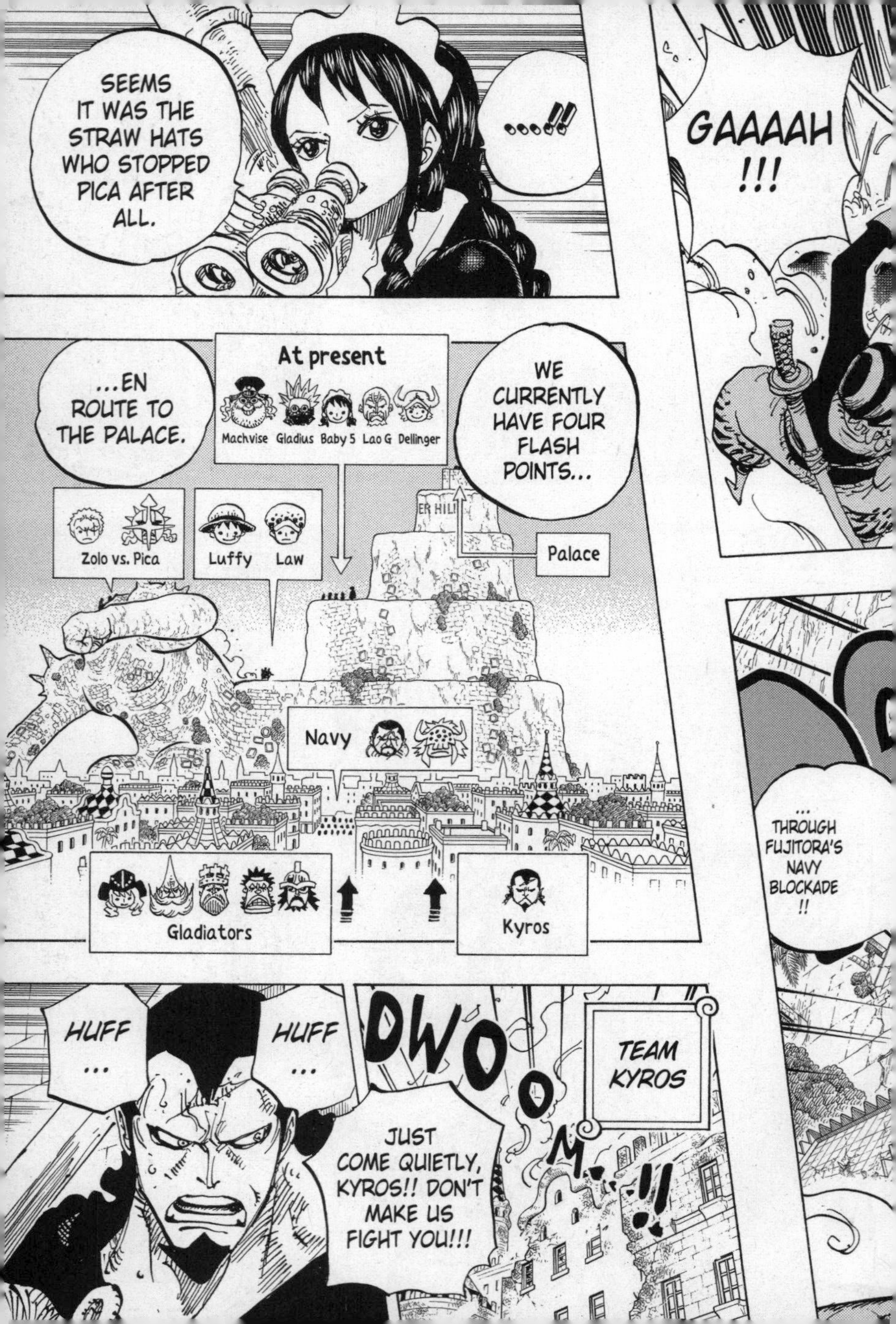

GAAAAH!!!
....!!
SEEMS IT WAS THE STRAW HATS WHO STOPPED PICA AFTER ALL.
WE CURRENTLY HAVE FOUR FLASH POINTS...
...EN ROUTE TO THE PALACE.
At present
Machvise Gladius Baby 5 Lao G Dellinger
Palace
Luffy Law
Zolo vs. Pica
Navy
Kyros
Gladiators
...THROUGH FUJITORA'S NAVY BLOCKADE!!
TEAM KYROS
DWOOOM!!
JUST COME QUIETLY, KYROS!! DON'T MAKE US FIGHT YOU!!!
HUFF...
HUFF...

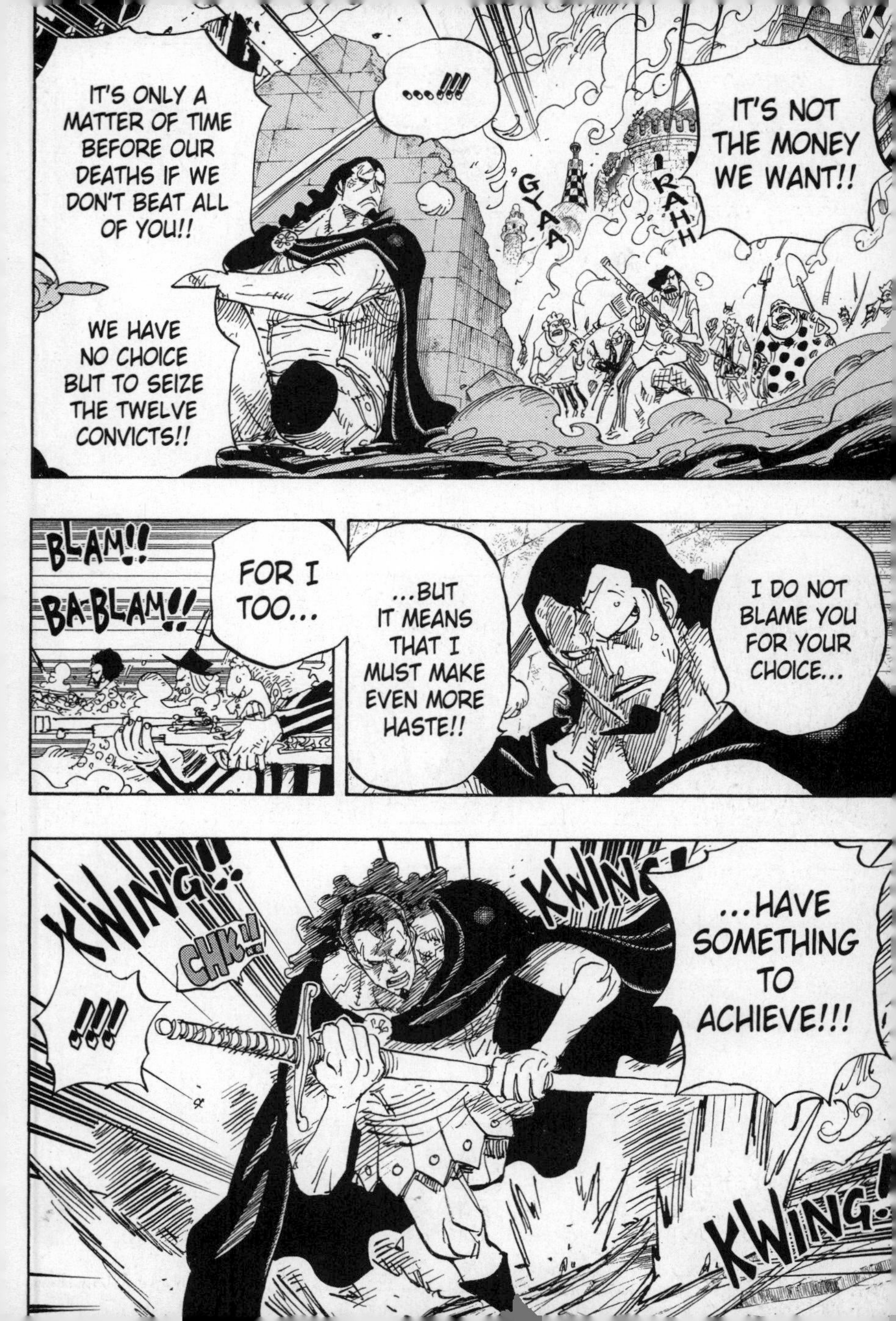
IT'S NOT THE MONEY WE WANT!!
RAHH
GYAA
...!!!
IT'S ONLY A MATTER OF TIME BEFORE OUR DEATHS IF WE DON'T BEAT ALL OF YOU!!
WE HAVE NO CHOICE BUT TO SEIZE THE TWELVE CONVICTS!!
I DO NOT BLAME YOU FOR YOUR CHOICE...
...BUT IT MEANS THAT I MUST MAKE EVEN MORE HASTE!!
FOR I TOO...
BLAM!!
BA-BLAM!!
...HAVE SOMETHING TO ACHIEVE!!!
KWING!!
KWING
CHK!!
KWING!!
!!!

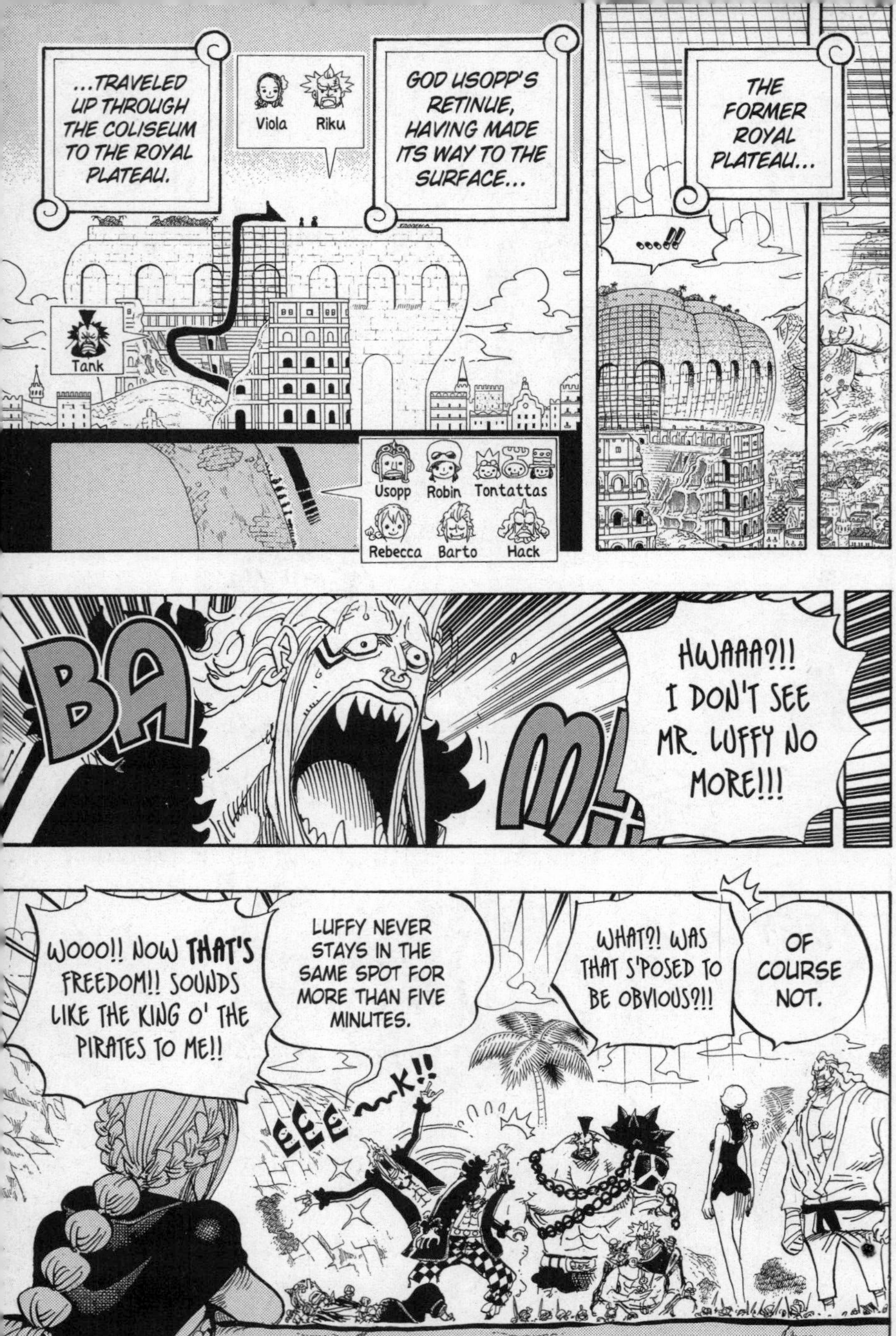
THE FORMER ROYAL PLATEAU...
...!!
GOD USOPP'S RETINUE, HAVING MADE ITS WAY TO THE SURFACE...
Viola
Riku
...TRAVELED UP THROUGH THE COLISEUM TO THE ROYAL PLATEAU.
Tank
Usopp
Robin
Tontattas
Rebecca
Barto
Hack
HWAAA?!! I DON'T SEE MR. LUFFY NO MORE!!!
BA
M
OF COURSE NOT.
WHAT?! WAS THAT S'POSED TO BE OBVIOUS?!!
LUFFY NEVER STAYS IN THE SAME SPOT FOR MORE THAN FIVE MINUTES.
WOOO!! NOW **THAT'S** FREEDOM!! SOUNDS LIKE THE KING O' THE PIRATES TO ME!!
EEE~K!!

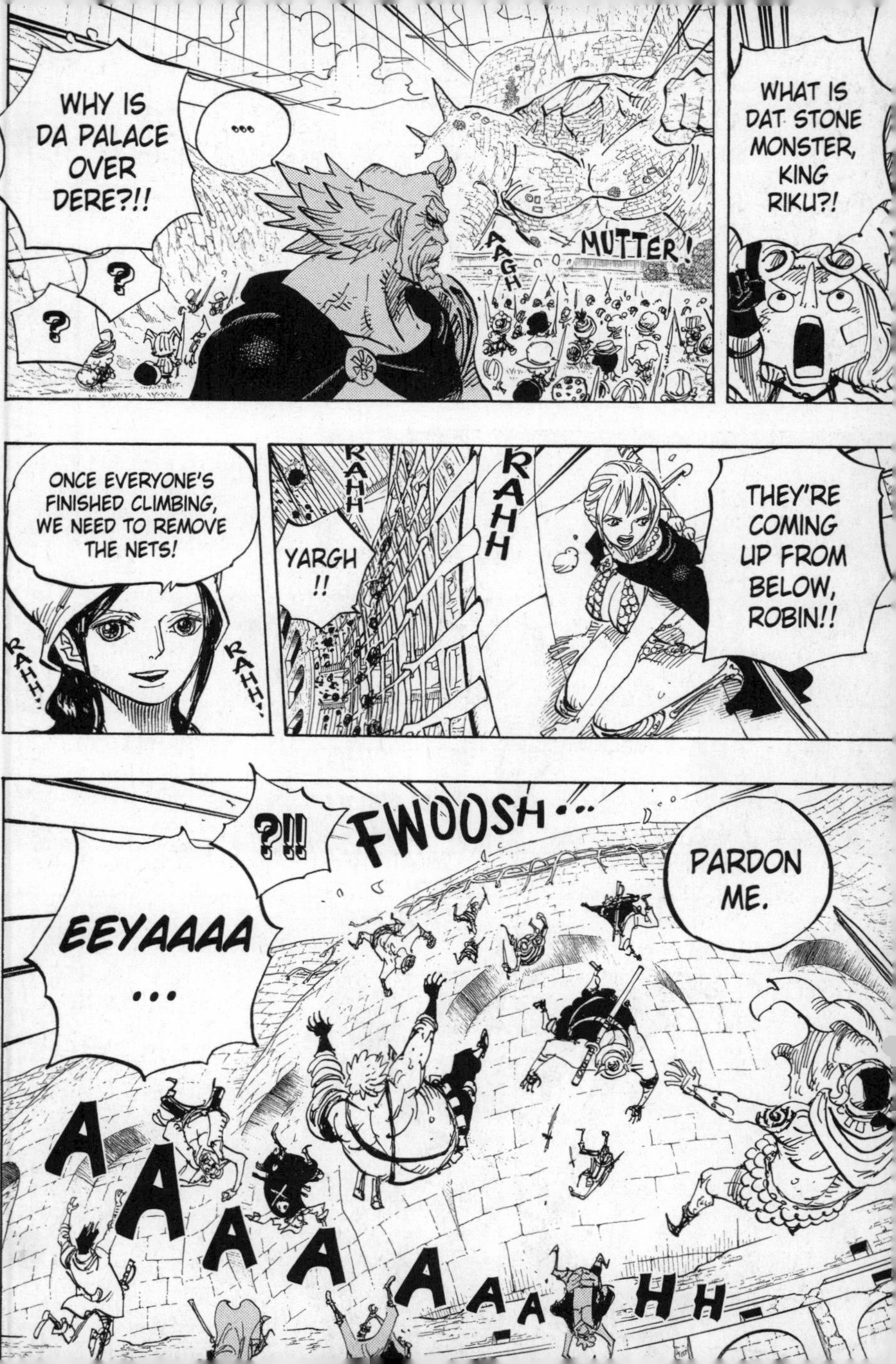
WHAT IS DAT STONE MONSTER, KING RIKU?!
MUTTER!
AAGH
...
WHY IS DA PALACE OVER DERE?!!
?
?
THEY'RE COMING UP FROM BELOW, ROBIN!!
RAHH
RAHH
YARGH !!
ONCE EVERYONE'S FINISHED CLIMBING, WE NEED TO REMOVE THE NETS!
RAHH!
RAHH!
PARDON ME.
FWOOSH...
?!!
EEYAAAA ...
AAAAAAAAHH

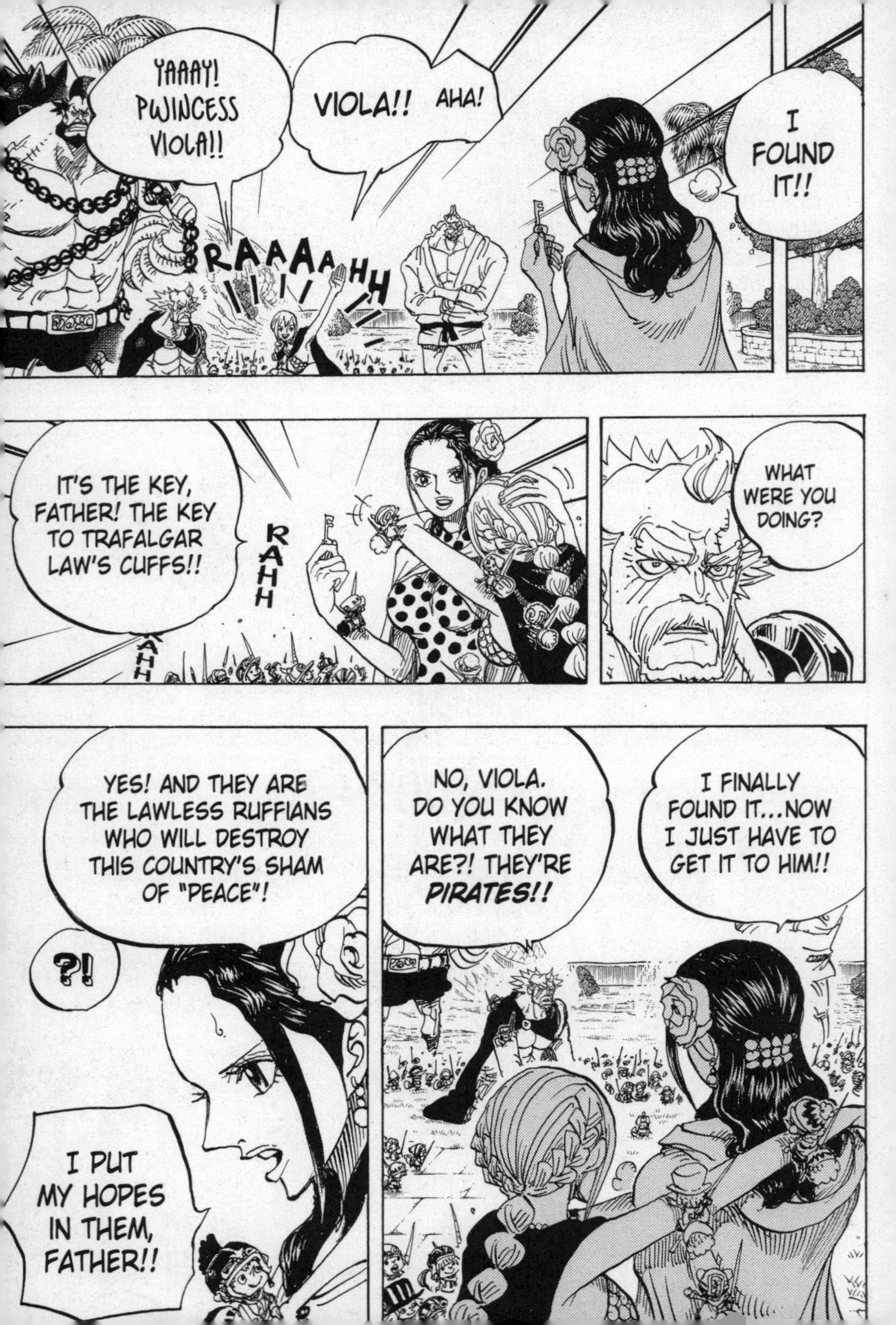
I FOUND IT!!
AHA!
VIOLA!!
YAAAY! PWINCESS VIOLA!!
RAAAAAHH
WHAT WERE YOU DOING?
IT'S THE KEY, FATHER! THE KEY TO TRAFALGAR LAW'S CUFFS!!
RAHH
RAHH
I FINALLY FOUND IT...NOW I JUST HAVE TO GET IT TO HIM!!
NO, VIOLA. DO YOU KNOW WHAT THEY ARE?! THEY'RE PIRATES!!
YES! AND THEY ARE THE LAWLESS RUFFIANS WHO WILL DESTROY THIS COUNTRY'S SHAM OF "PEACE"!
?!
I PUT MY HOPES IN THEM, FATHER!!

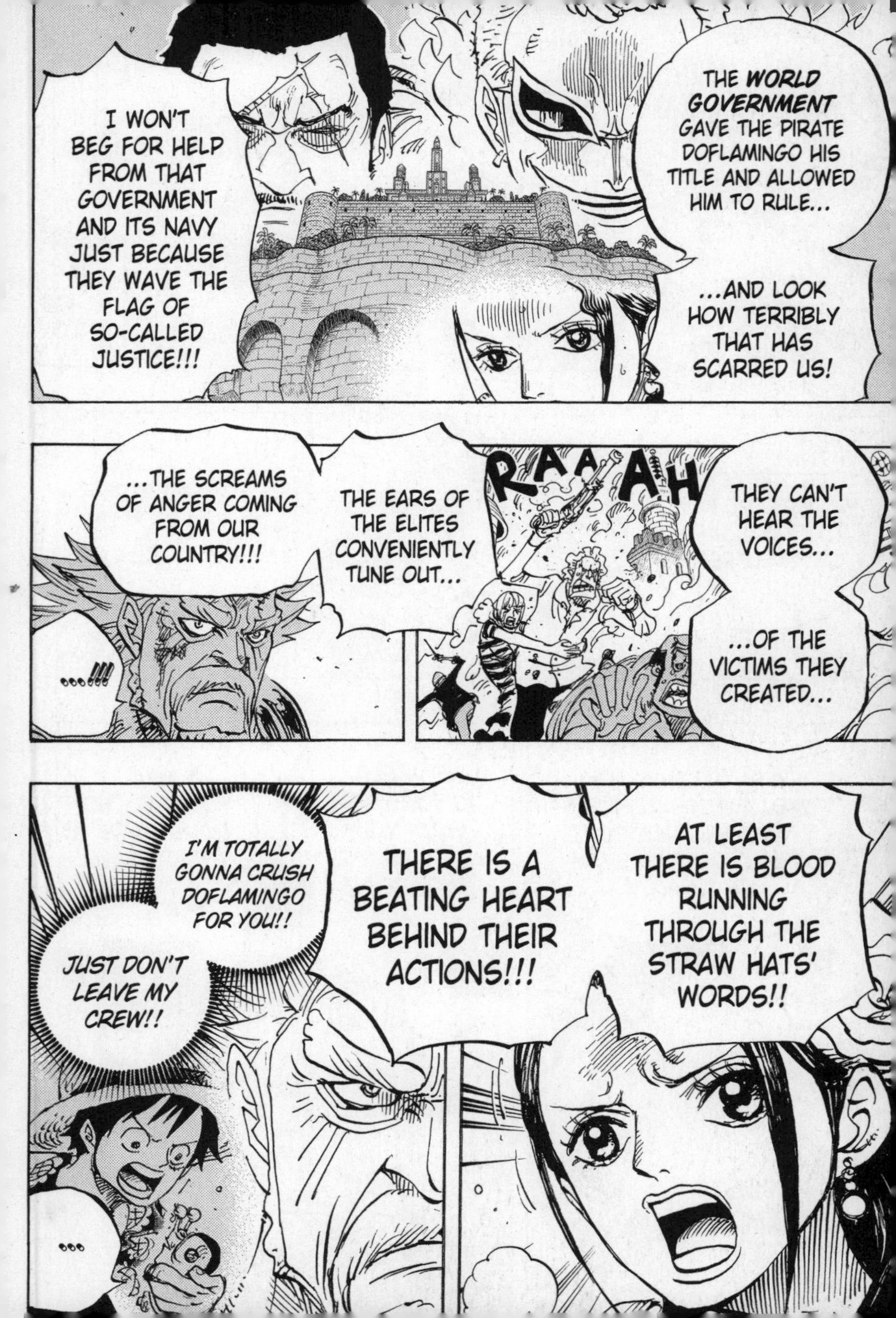

THE WORLD GOVERNMENT GAVE THE PIRATE DOFLAMINGO HIS TITLE AND ALLOWED HIM TO RULE...
...AND LOOK HOW TERRIBLY THAT HAS SCARRED US!
I WON'T BEG FOR HELP FROM THAT GOVERNMENT AND ITS NAVY JUST BECAUSE THEY WAVE THE FLAG OF SO-CALLED JUSTICE!!!
RAAAH
THEY CAN'T HEAR THE VOICES...
...OF THE VICTIMS THEY CREATED...
THE EARS OF THE ELITES CONVENIENTLY TUNE OUT...
...THE SCREAMS OF ANGER COMING FROM OUR COUNTRY!!!
...!!!
AT LEAST THERE IS BLOOD RUNNING THROUGH THE STRAW HATS' WORDS!!
THERE IS A BEATING HEART BEHIND THEIR ACTIONS!!!
I'M TOTALLY GONNA CRUSH DOFLAMINGO FOR YOU!!
JUST DON'T LEAVE MY CREW!!
...

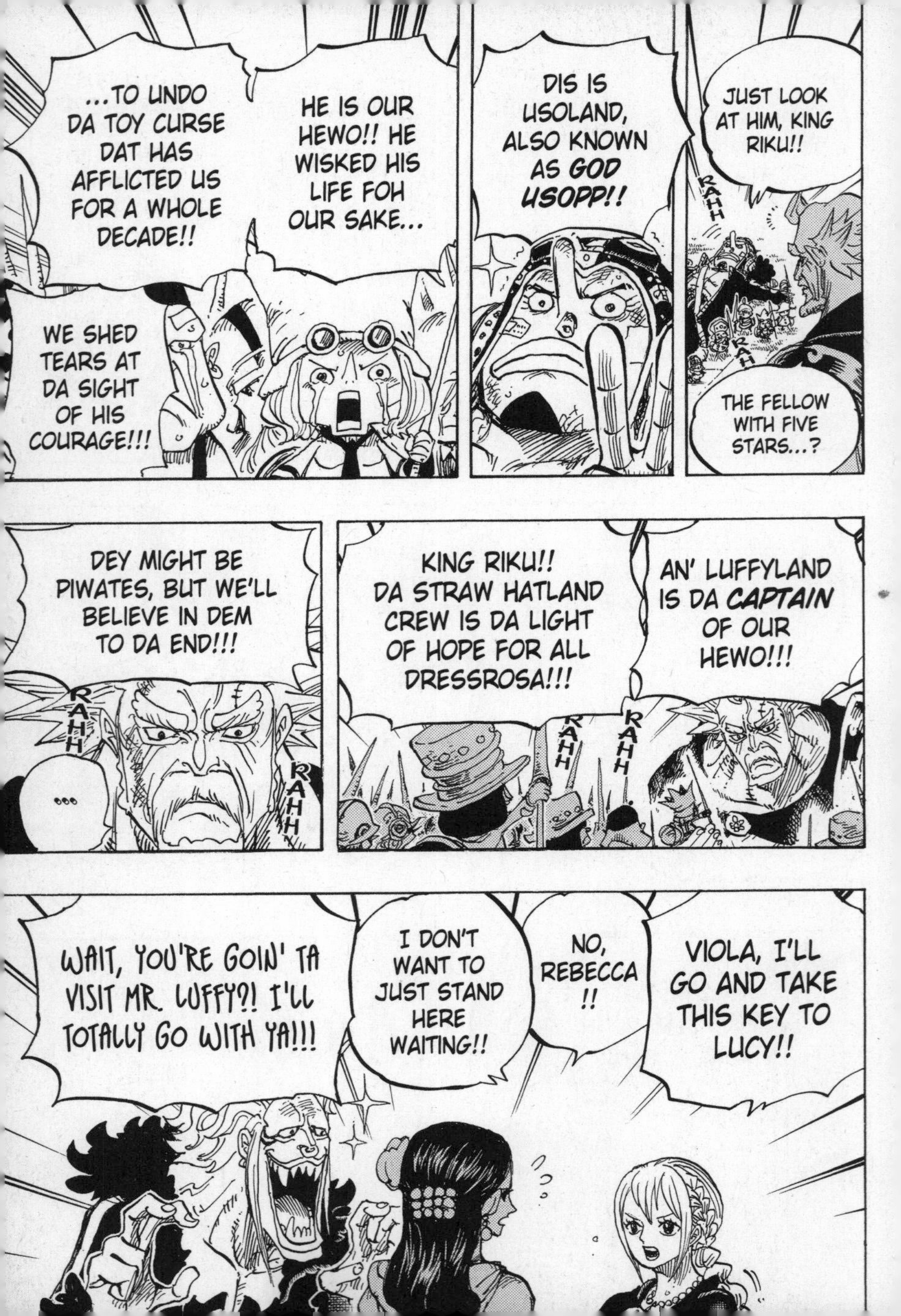
JUST LOOK AT HIM, KING RIKU!!
RAHH
RAHH
THE FELLOW WITH FIVE STARS...?
DIS IS USOLAND, ALSO KNOWN AS GOD USOPP!!
HE IS OUR HEWO!! HE WISKED HIS LIFE FOH OUR SAKE...
...TO UNDO DA TOY CURSE DAT HAS AFFLICTED US FOR A WHOLE DECADE!!
WE SHED TEARS AT DA SIGHT OF HIS COURAGE!!!
AN' LUFFYLAND IS DA CAPTAIN OF OUR HEWO!!!
KING RIKU!! DA STRAW HATLAND CREW IS DA LIGHT OF HOPE FOR ALL DRESSROSA!!!
RAHH
RAHH
DEY MIGHT BE PIWATES, BUT WE'LL BELIEVE IN DEM TO DA END!!!
RAHH
RAHH
...
VIOLA, I'LL GO AND TAKE THIS KEY TO LUCY!!
NO, REBECCA!!
I DON'T WANT TO JUST STAND HERE WAITING!!
WAIT, YOU'RE GOIN' TA VISIT MR. LUFFY?! I'LL TOTALLY GO WITH YA!!!

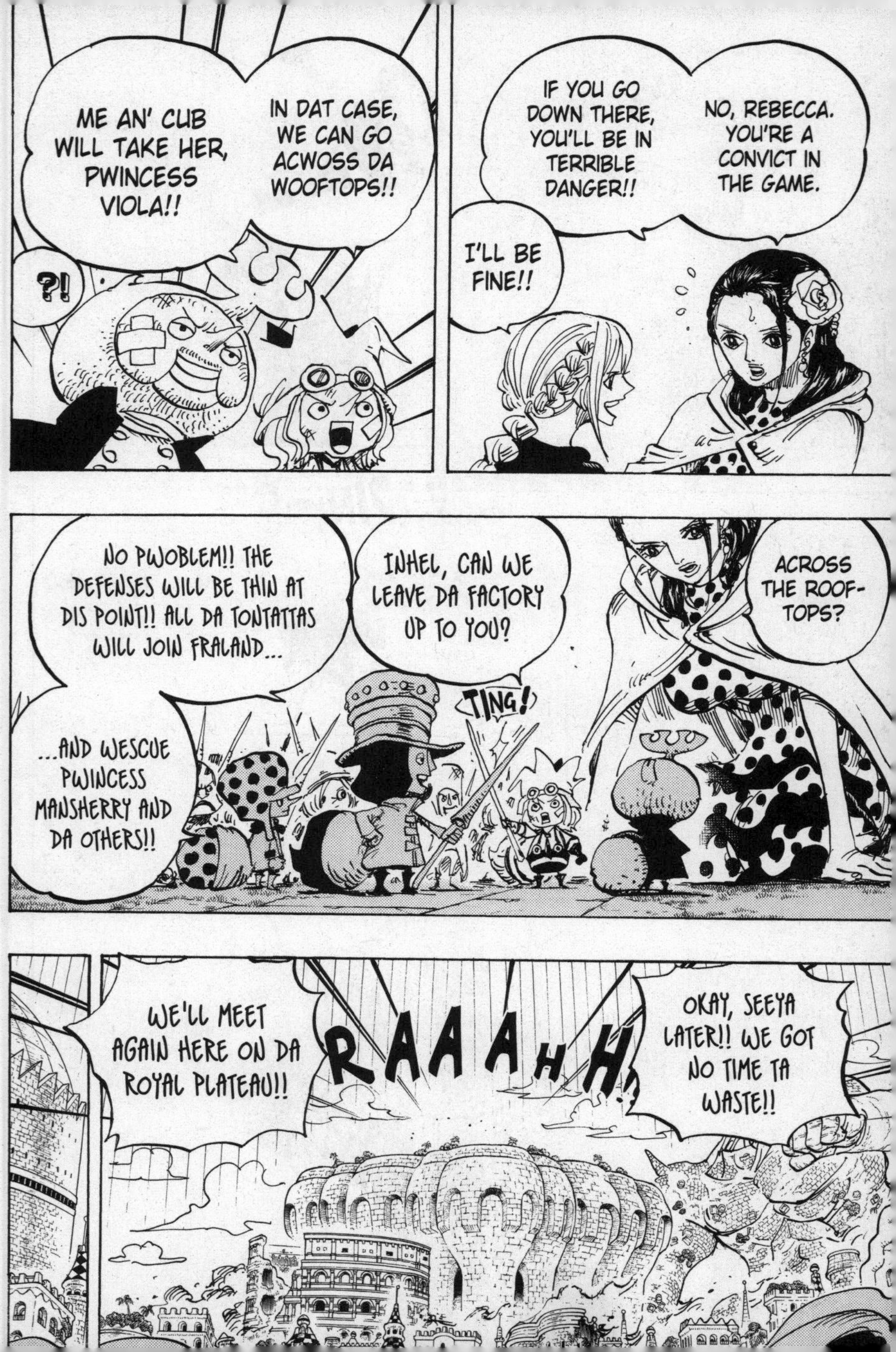
NO, REBECCA. YOU'RE A CONVICT IN THE GAME.
IF YOU GO DOWN THERE, YOU'LL BE IN TERRIBLE DANGER!!
I'LL BE FINE!!
IN DAT CASE, WE CAN GO ACWOSS DA WOOFTOPS!!
ME AN' CUB WILL TAKE HER, PWINCESS VIOLA!!
?!
ACROSS THE ROOF-TOPS?
INHEL, CAN WE LEAVE DA FACTORY UP TO YOU?
TING!
NO PWOBLEM!! THE DEFENSES WILL BE THIN AT DIS POINT!! ALL DA TONTATTAS WILL JOIN FRALAND...
...AND WESCUE PWINCESS MANSHERRY AND DA OTHERS!!
OKAY, SEEYA LATER!! WE GOT NO TIME TA WASTE!!
RAAAHH
WE'LL MEET AGAIN HERE ON DA ROYAL PLATEAU!!

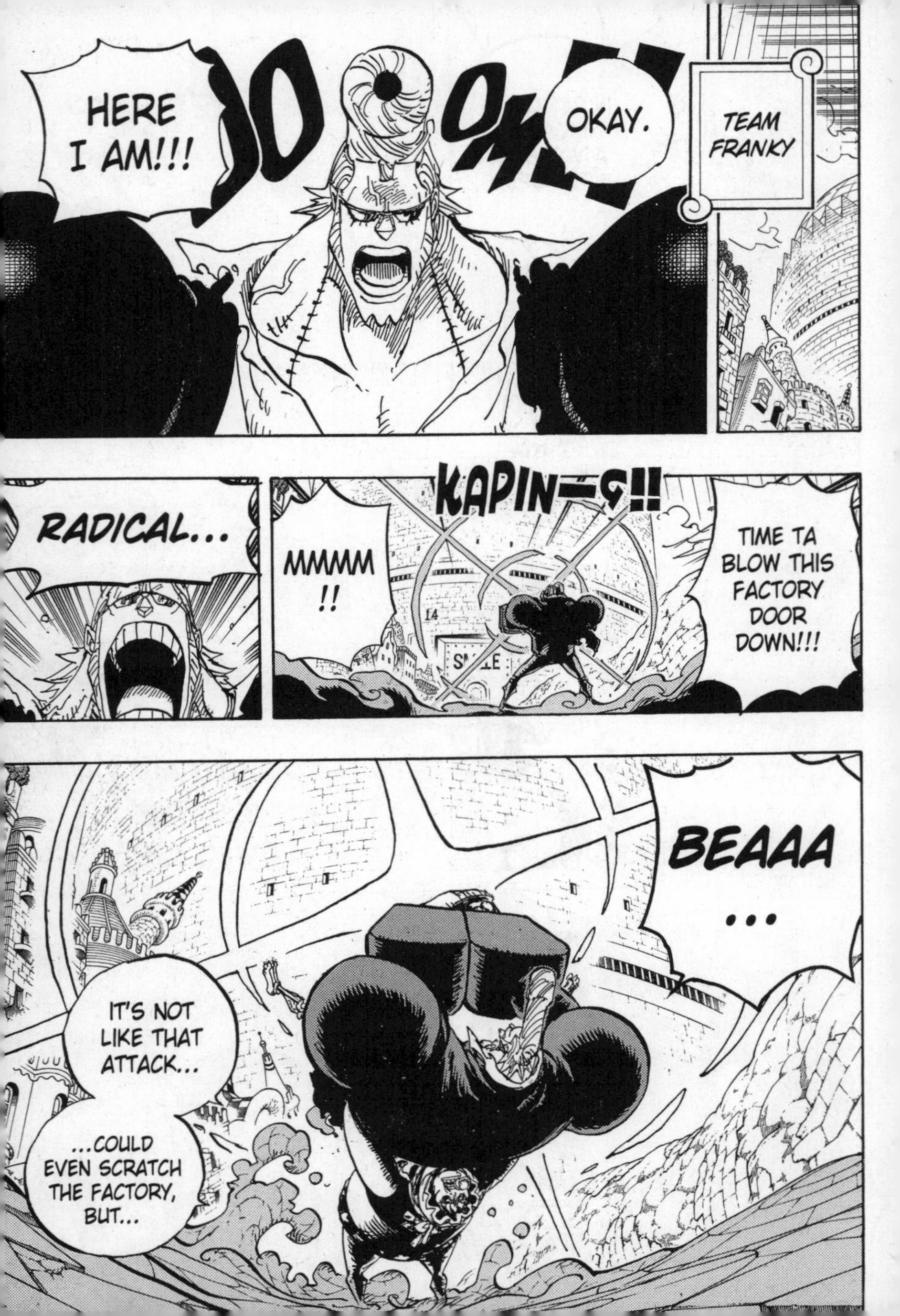
TEAM FRANKY
OKAY.
HERE I AM!!!
KAPIN—G!!
TIME TA BLOW THIS FACTORY DOOR DOWN!!!
MMMM !!
RADICAL...
BEAAA ...
IT'S NOT LIKE THAT ATTACK...
...COULD EVEN SCRATCH THE FACTORY, BUT...

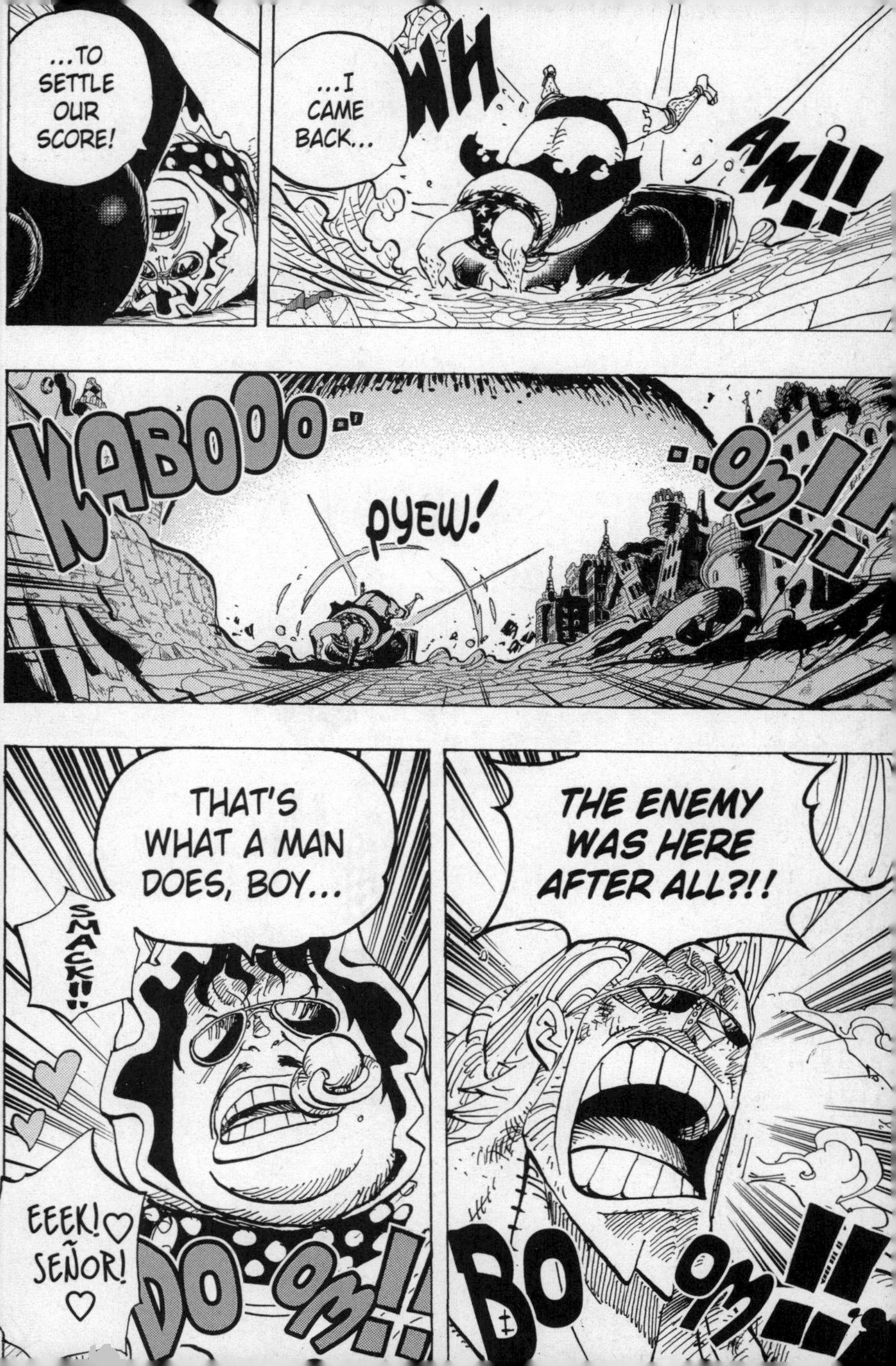
WH
AM!!
...I CAME BACK...
...TO SETTLE OUR SCORE!
KABOOO-
...OM!!
PYEW!
THE ENEMY WAS HERE AFTER ALL?!!
BO
OM!!
THAT'S WHAT A MAN DOES, BOY...
SMACK!!
EEEK! ♡ SEÑOR! ♡
DO
OM!!

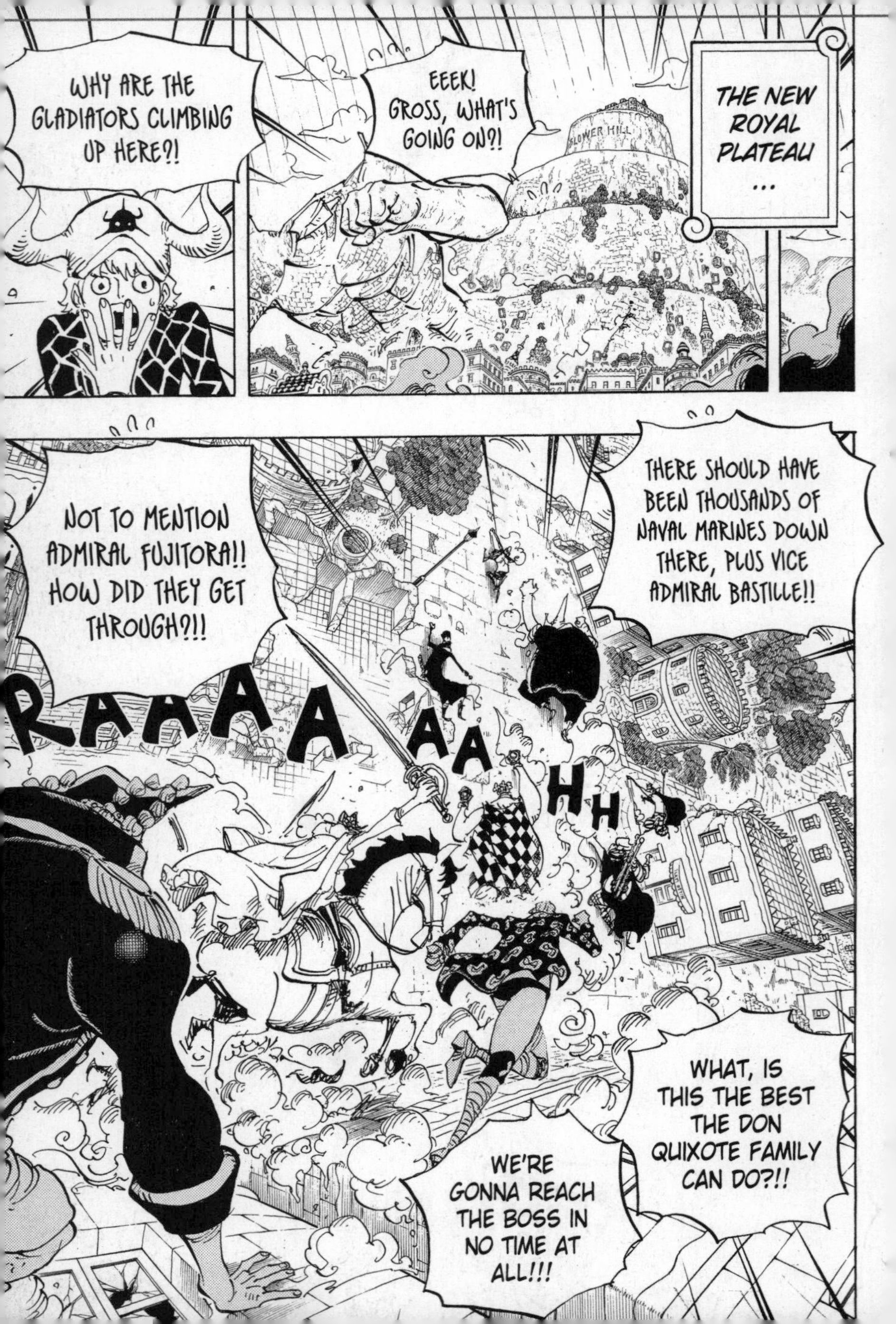
THE NEW ROYAL PLATEAU ...
FLOWER HILL
EEEK! GROSS, WHAT'S GOING ON?!
WHY ARE THE GLADIATORS CLIMBING UP HERE?!
THERE SHOULD HAVE BEEN THOUSANDS OF NAVAL MARINES DOWN THERE, PLUS VICE ADMIRAL BASTILLE!!
NOT TO MENTION ADMIRAL FUJITORA!! HOW DID THEY GET THROUGH?!!
RAAAAAAHH
WHAT, IS THIS THE BEST THE DON QUIXOTE FAMILY CAN DO?!!
WE'RE GONNA REACH THE BOSS IN NO TIME AT ALL!!!

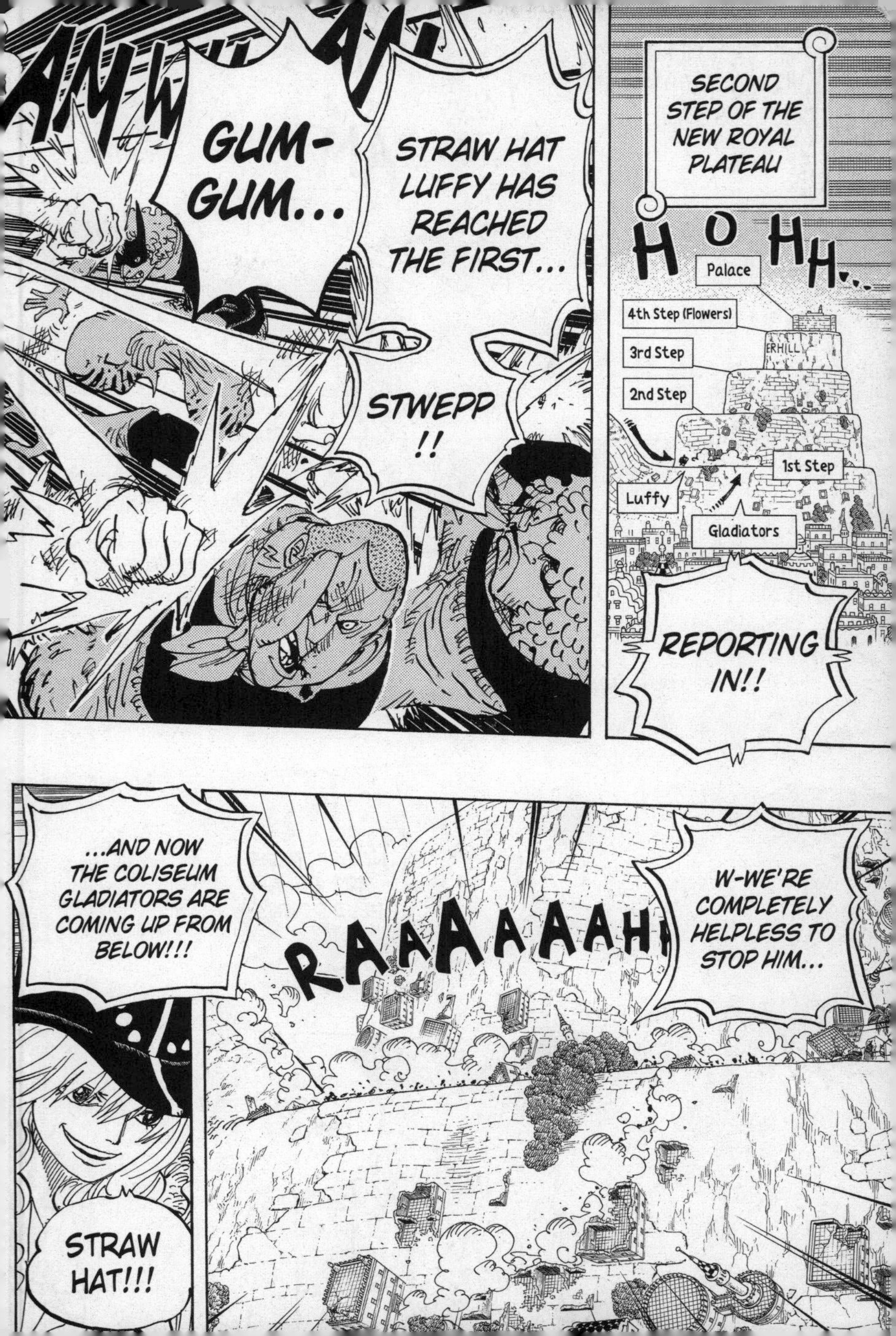
SECOND STEP OF THE NEW ROYAL PLATEAU
HOHH...
Palace
4th Step (Flowers)
3rd Step
2nd Step
1st Step
Luffy
Gladiators
REPORTING IN!!
STRAW HAT LUFFY HAS REACHED THE FIRST...
GUM-GUM...
STWEPP!!
W-WE'RE COMPLETELY HELPLESS TO STOP HIM...
RAAAAAAH
...AND NOW THE COLISEUM GLADIATORS ARE COMING UP FROM BELOW!!!
STRAW HAT!!!

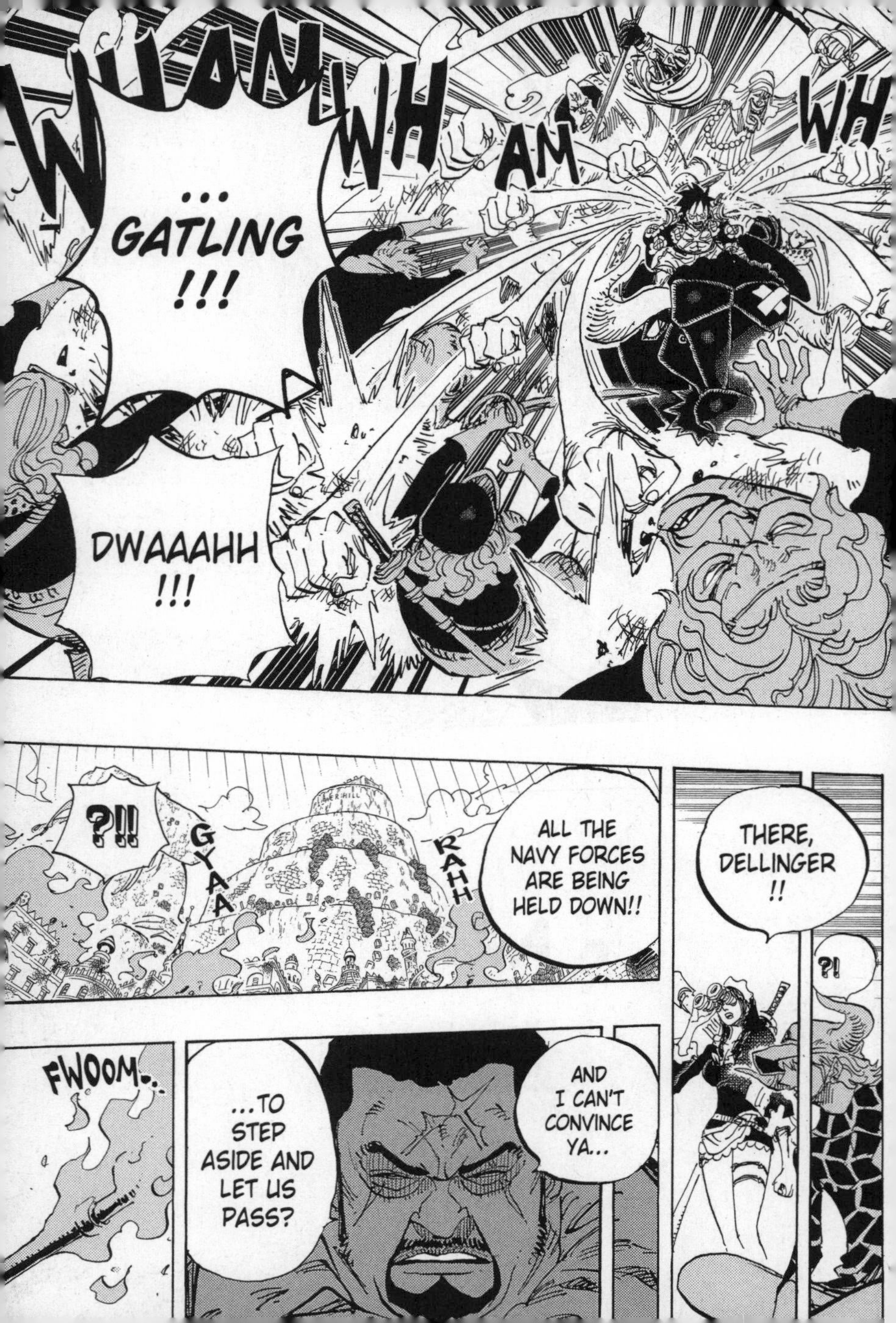
WH
WH AM
... GATLING !!!
DWAAAHH !!!
THERE, DELLINGER !!
?!
ALL THE NAVY FORCES ARE BEING HELD DOWN!!
RAHH
GYAA
?!!
AND I CAN'T CONVINCE YA...
...TO STEP ASIDE AND LET US PASS?
FWOOM..

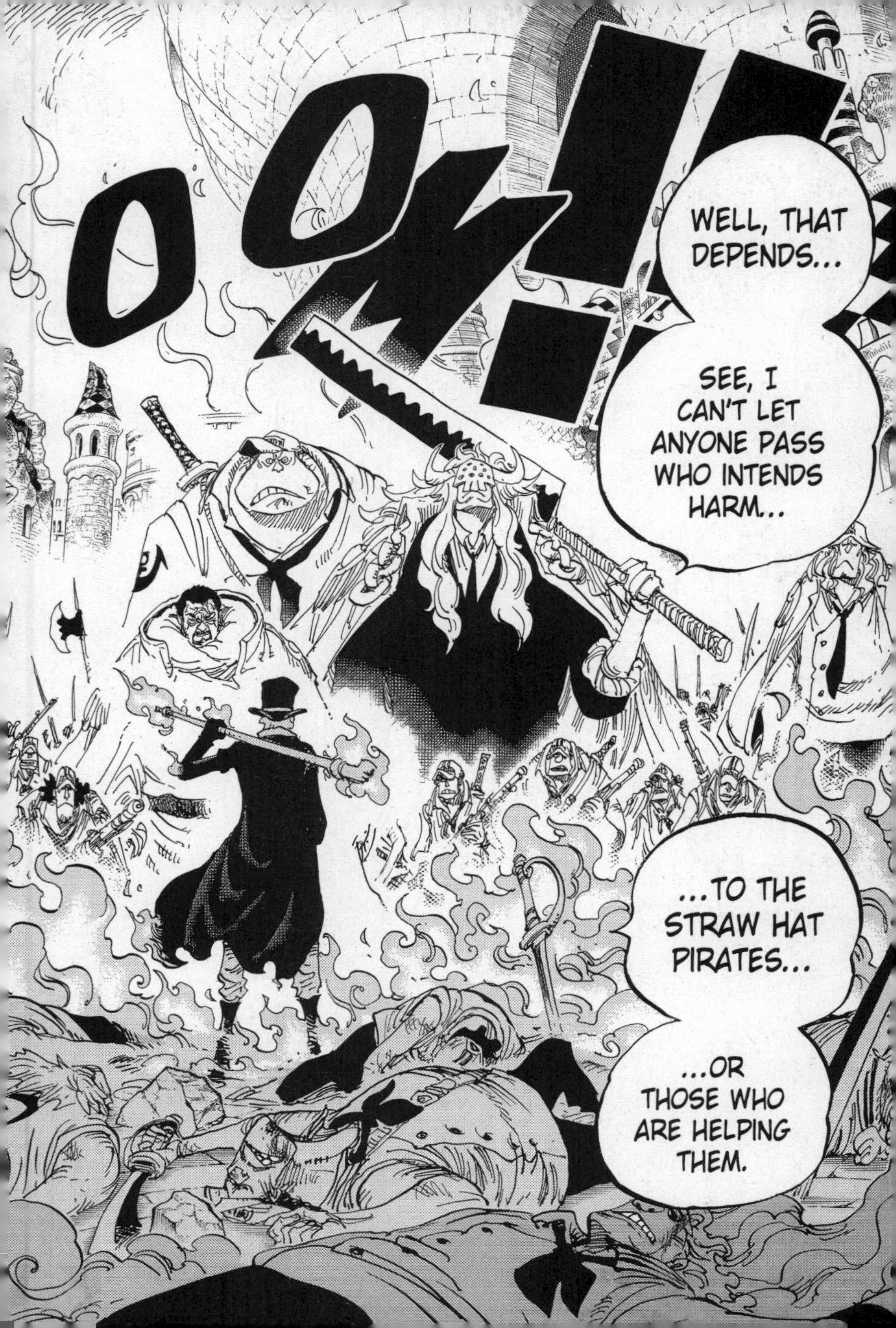
OOOH!!
WELL, THAT DEPENDS...
SEE, I CAN'T LET ANYONE PASS WHO INTENDS HARM...
...TO THE STRAW HAT PIRATES...
...OR THOSE WHO ARE HELPING THEM.

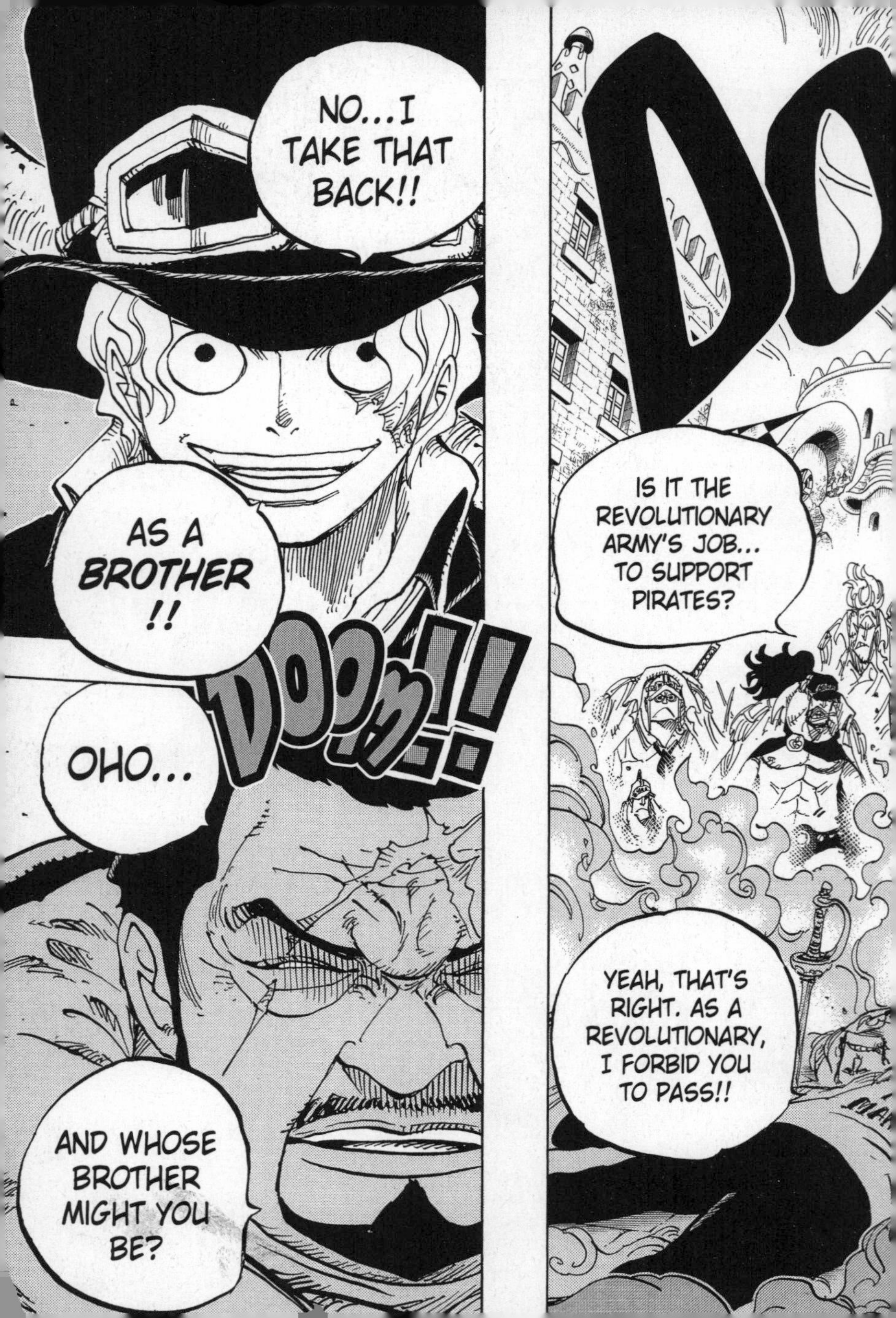
DO
IS IT THE REVOLUTIONARY ARMY'S JOB... TO SUPPORT PIRATES?
YEAH, THAT'S RIGHT. AS A REVOLUTIONARY, I FORBID YOU TO PASS!!
NO...I TAKE THAT BACK!!
AS A BROTHER !!
DOOM!!
OHO...
AND WHOSE BROTHER MIGHT YOU BE?

SBS Question Corner

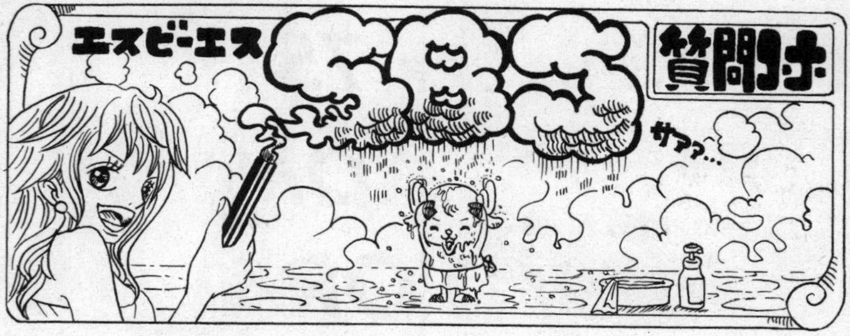
エスピーエス
SBS
質問コーナー
サァァ…

(Michi Nakahara, Tottori)

Q: Odacchi, nice to meet you! So what's Sugar's real age?! I've been so obsessed with her, Sugar's all I can think of during my exams! And I'm supposed to be preparing for college... Thanks to that, my test results were awful.♡

--Gahara

A: Ah, I see. That's too bad. If I let you in on some behind-the-scenes stuff, it turns out she can't actually be all that old. Her appearance is frozen at age 10, but her actual age is 22. She's two years younger than Baby 5. Actually, why don't I just list the ages of the entire family?

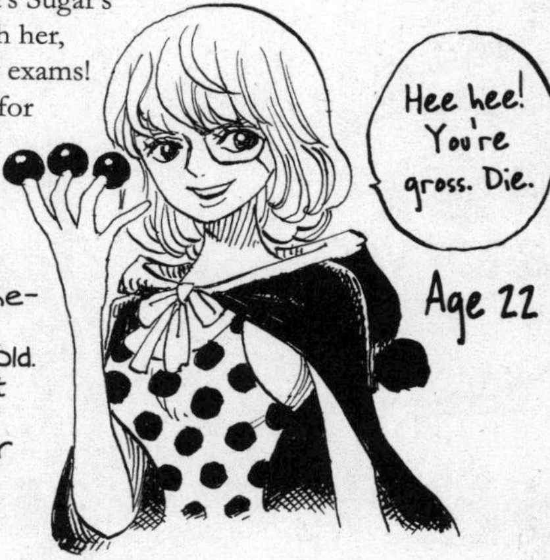
Hee hee! You're gross. Die.
Age 22

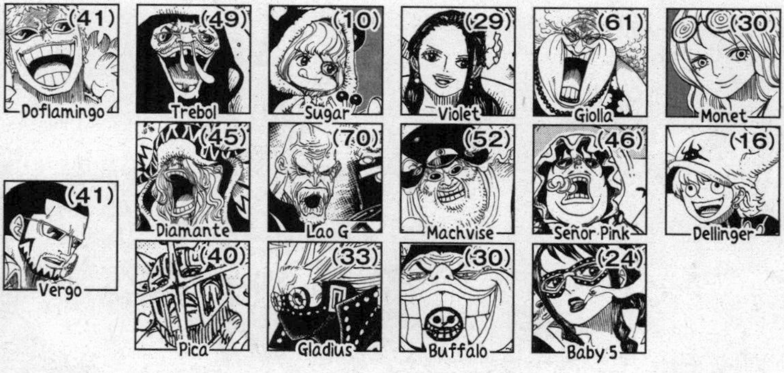
(41) Doflamingo
(49) Trebol
(10) Sugar
(29) Violet
(61) Giolla
(30) Monet
(45) Diamante
(70) Lao G
(52) Machvise
(46) Señor Pink
(16) Dellinger
(41) Vergo
(40) Pica
(33) Gladius
(30) Buffalo
(24) Baby 5

They range from their teenage years to their 70s--no wonder they're called a "family." Well, that's all the time we have. No more SBS! Look forward to the results of the popularity poll in the next volume!

Chapter 751:
SABO VS. ADMIRAL FUJITORA

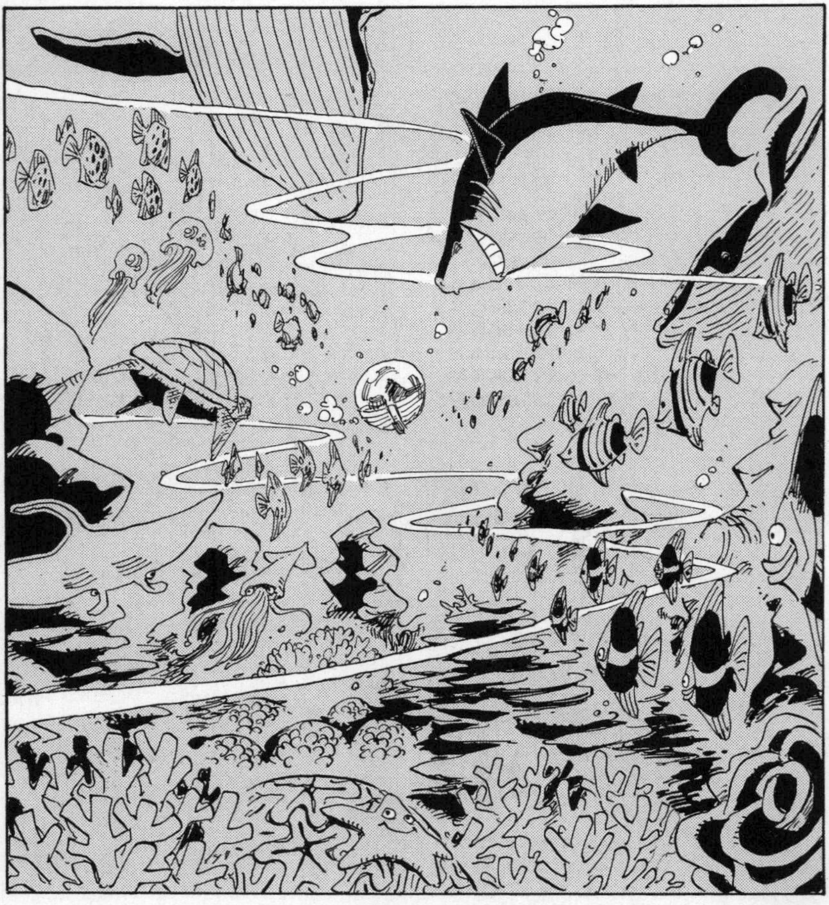

LIMITED COVER SERIES, NO. 21, VOL. 1:
"ONWARD TO MY FRIENDS"

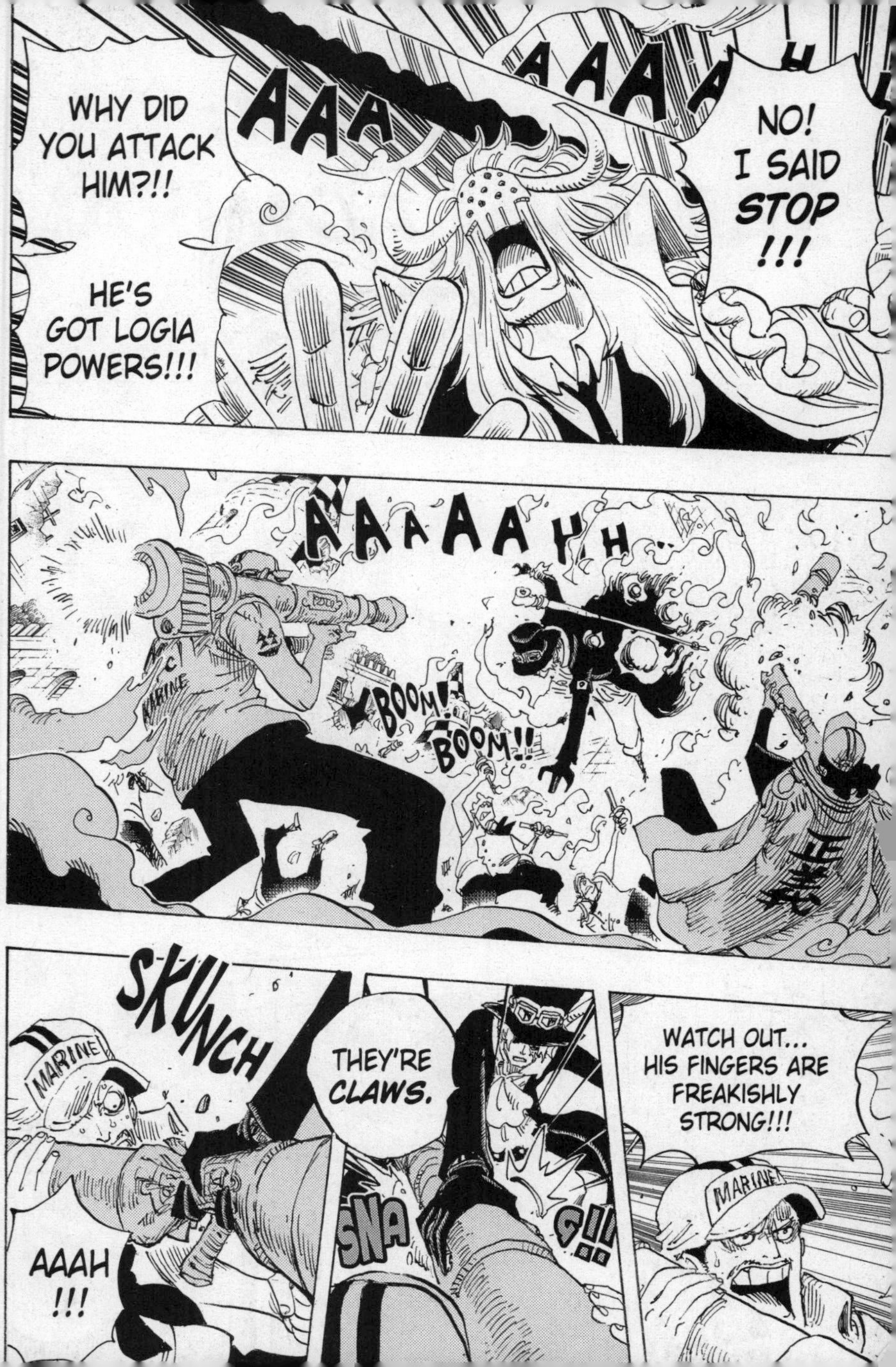
NO! I SAID STOP!!!
AAAAAAAH
WHY DID YOU ATTACK HIM?!!
HE'S GOT LOGIA POWERS!!!
AAAAAAH
BOOM!!
BOOM!!
WATCH OUT... HIS FINGERS ARE FREAKISHLY STRONG!!!
MARINE
THEY'RE CLAWS.
SNAG!!
SKUNCH
MARINE
AAAH!!!

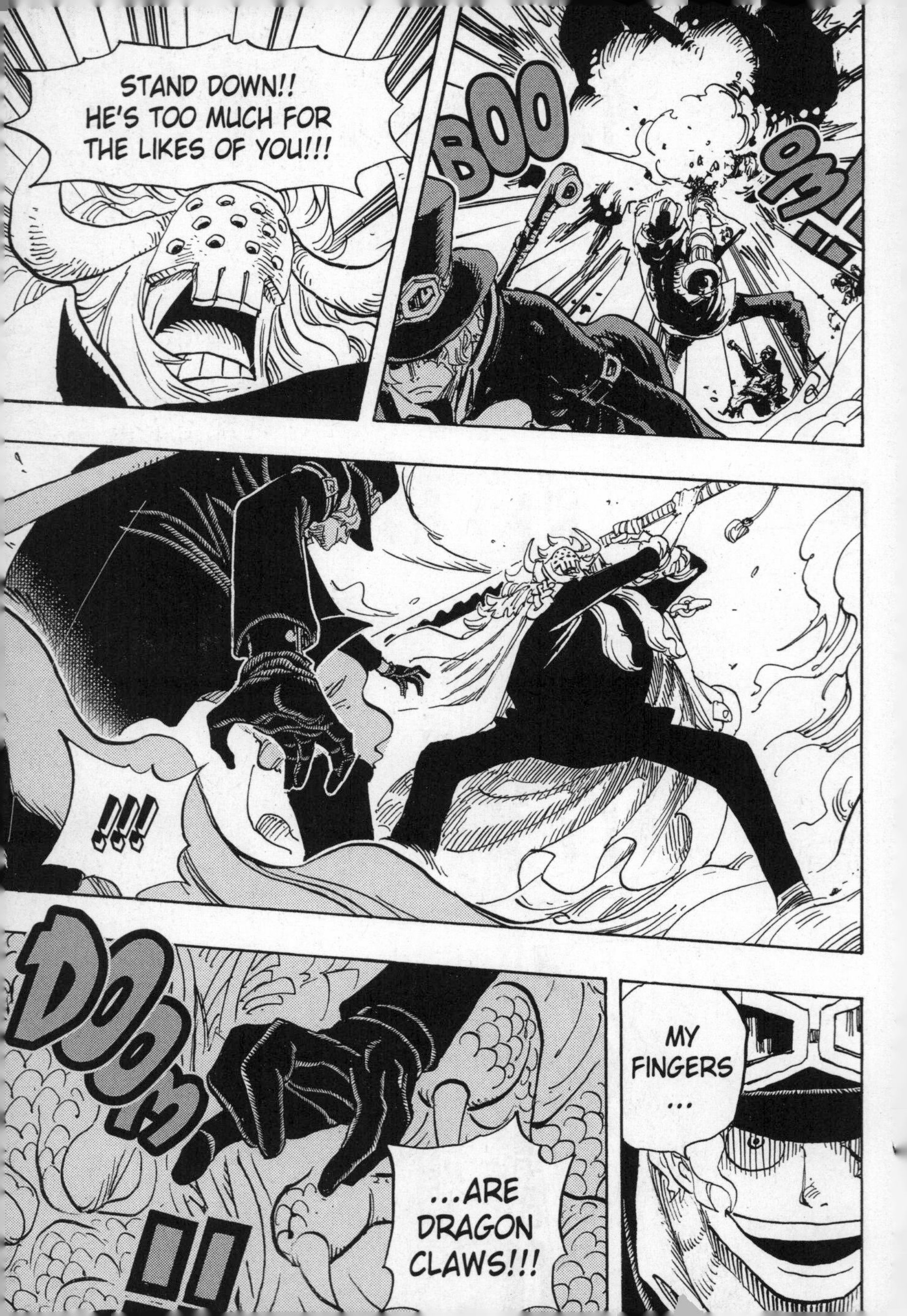
BOOOM!!
STAND DOWN!! HE'S TOO MUCH FOR THE LIKES OF YOU!!!
!!!
MY FINGERS ...
...ARE DRAGON CLAWS!!!
DOOOM!!

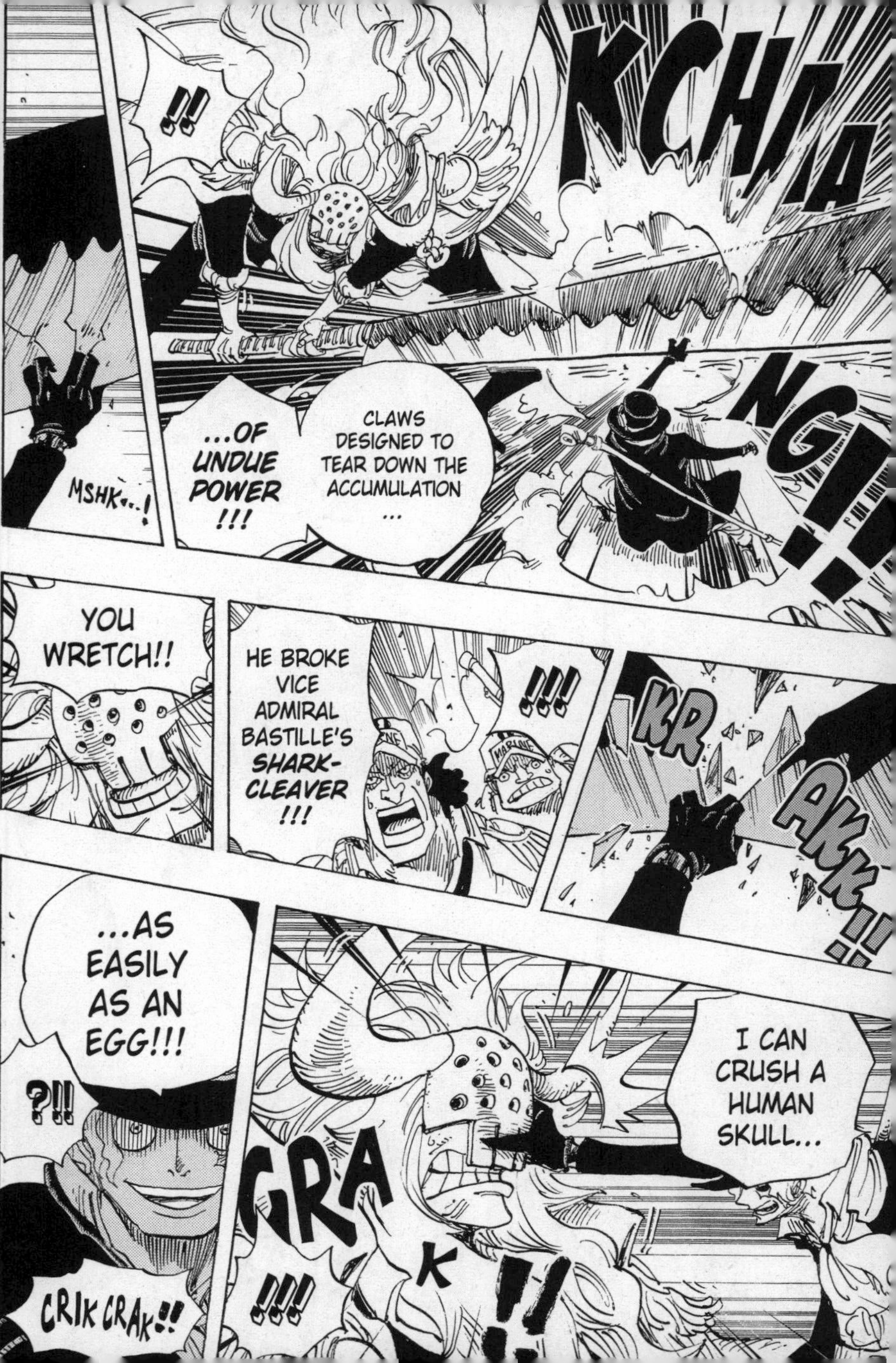
KCHAANG!!!
CLAWS DESIGNED TO TEAR DOWN THE ACCUMULATION ...
...OF UNDUE POWER!!!
!!
MSHK...!
KRAKK!!
!!!
HE BROKE VICE ADMIRAL BASTILLE'S SHARK-CLEAVER!!!
YOU WRETCH!!
I CAN CRUSH A HUMAN SKULL...
GRAK!!
!!!
...AS EASILY AS AN EGG!!!
?!!
CRIK CRAK!!

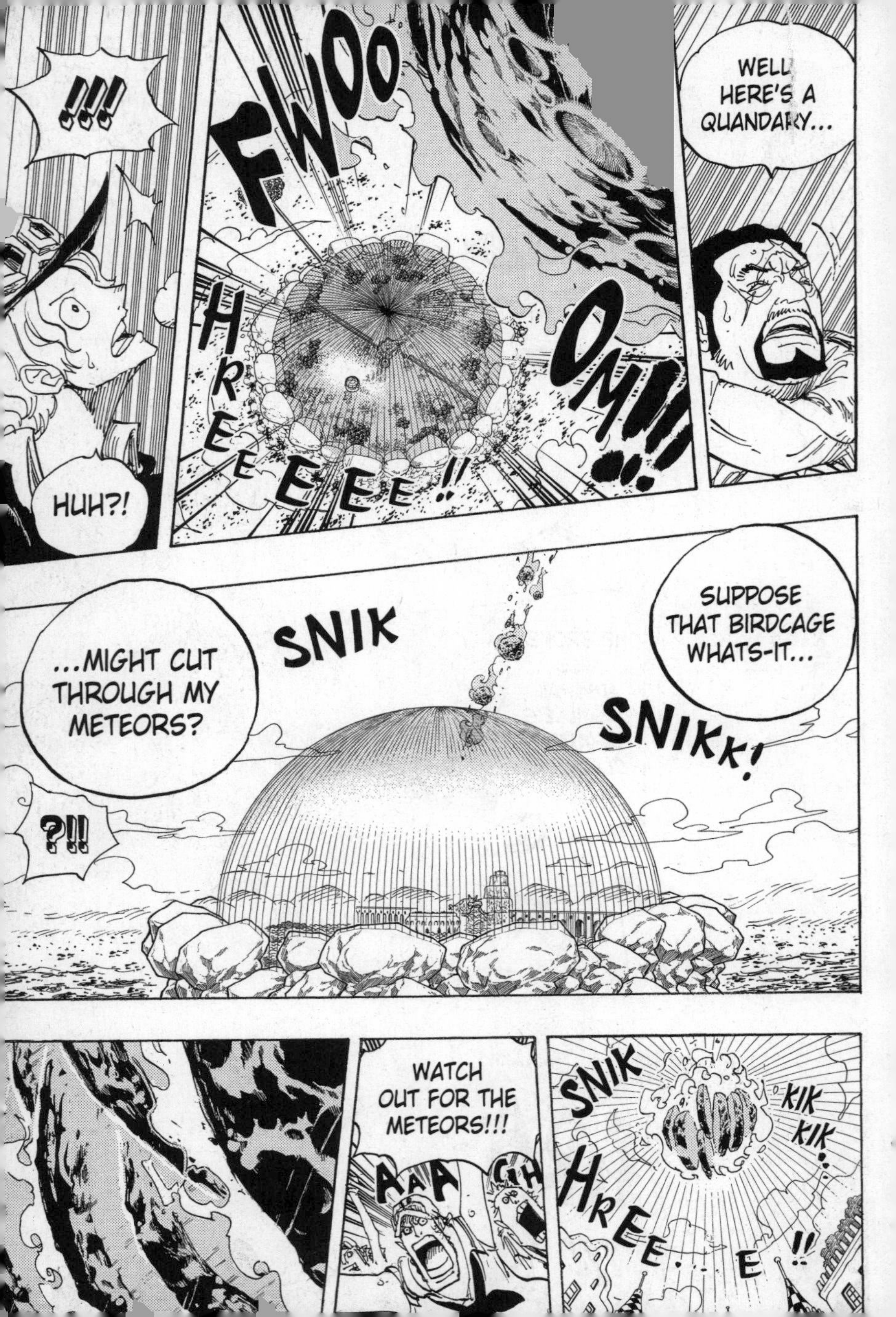
WELL HERE'S A QUANDARY...
FWOO
OM!!!
HREEEEEE!!
!!!
HUH?!
SUPPOSE THAT BIRDCAGE WHATS-IT...
SNIKK!
SNIK
...MIGHT CUT THROUGH MY METEORS?
?!!
SNIK
KIK KIK..
HREEE...E!!
WATCH OUT FOR THE METEORS!!!
AAA

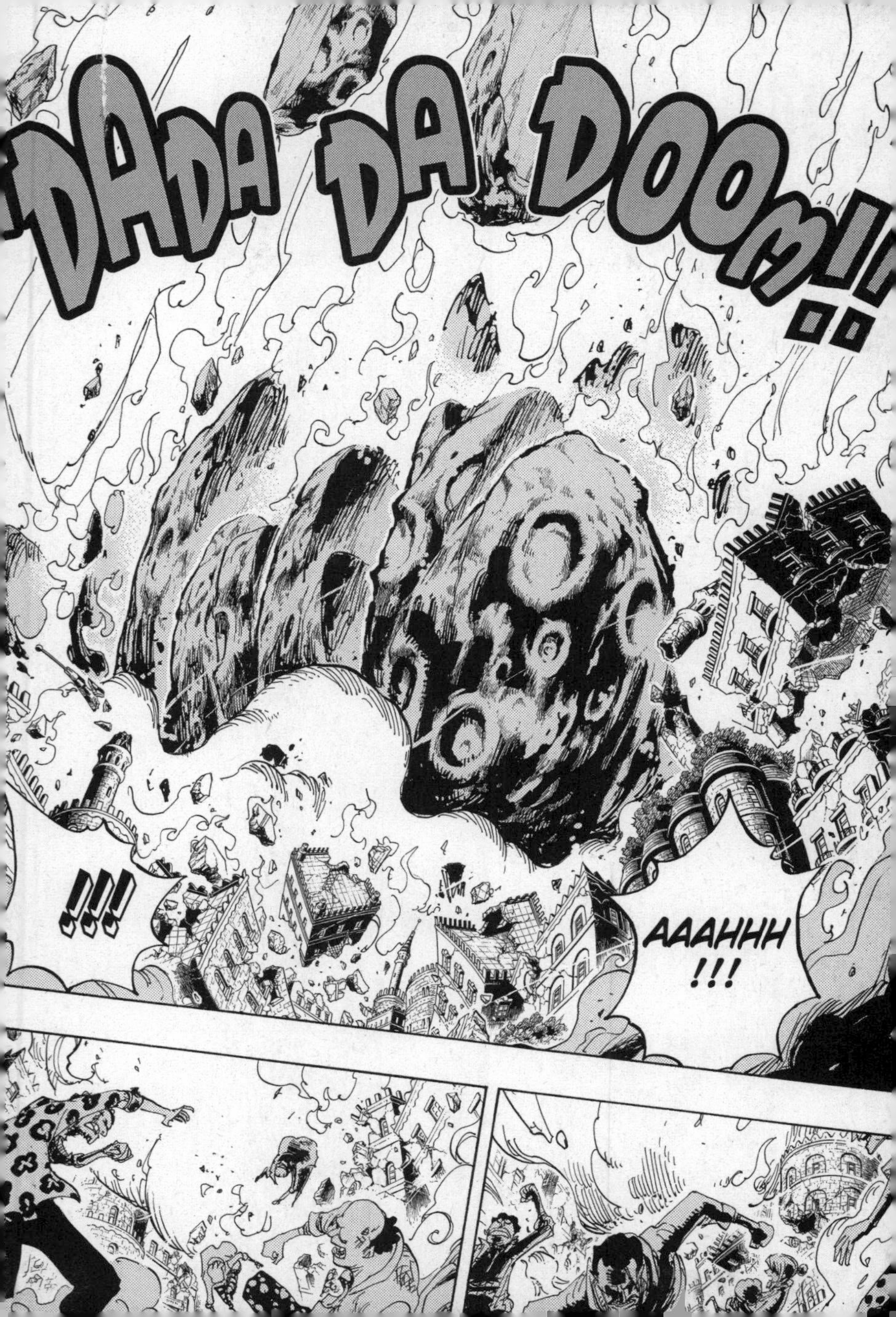
DADA DA DOOM!!
AAAHHH !!!
!!!

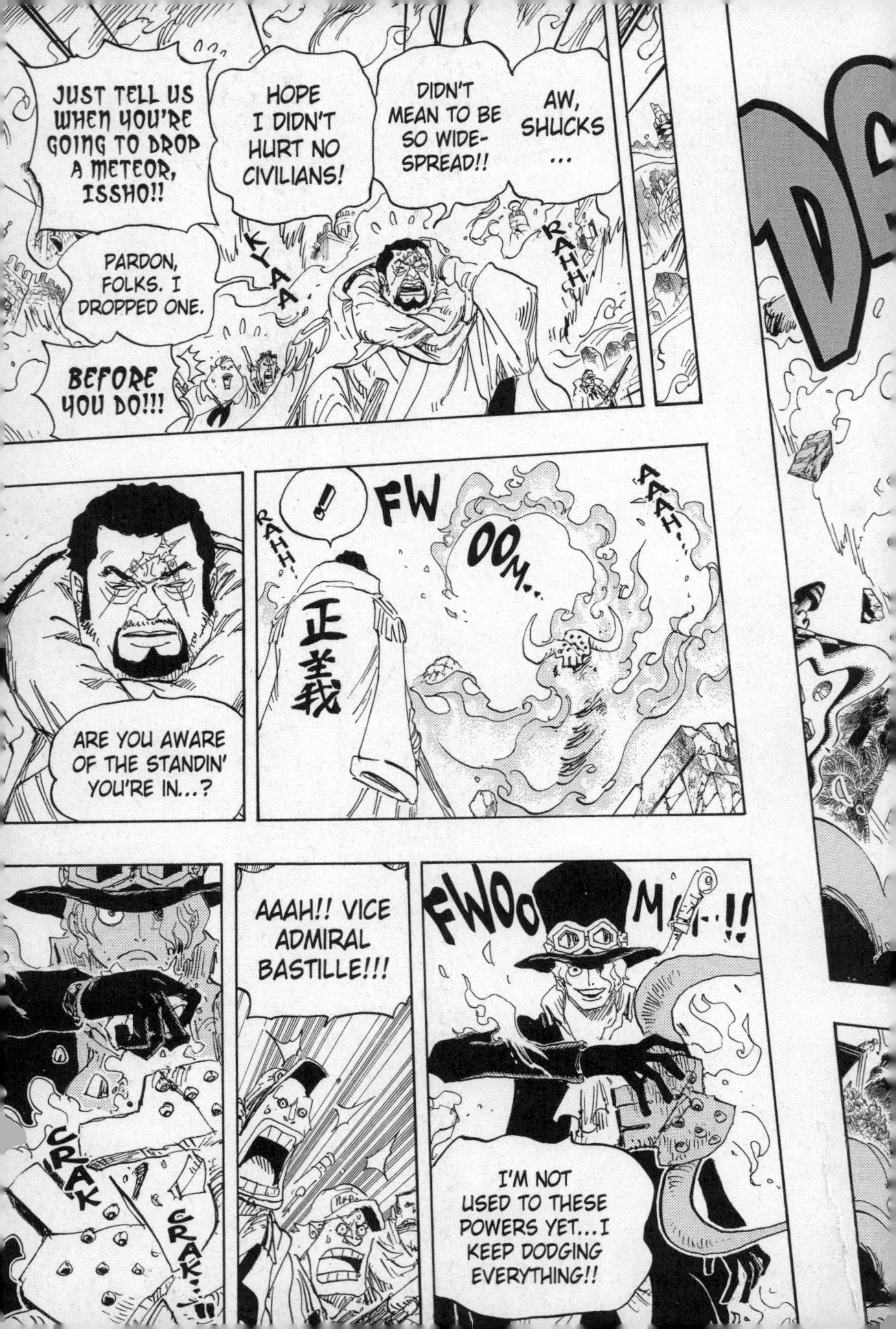
AW, SHUCKS ...
DIDN'T MEAN TO BE SO WIDE-SPREAD!!
RAHH
HOPE I DIDN'T HURT NO CIVILIANS!
KYAA
JUST TELL US WHEN YOU'RE GOING TO DROP A METEOR, ISSHO!!
PARDON, FOLKS. I DROPPED ONE.
BEFORE YOU DO!!!
AAAH...
FWOOM...
!
RAHH!
正義
ARE YOU AWARE OF THE STANDIN' YOU'RE IN...?
FWOOM...!!
I'M NOT USED TO THESE POWERS YET...I KEEP DODGING EVERYTHING!!
AAAH!! VICE ADMIRAL BASTILLE!!!
CRAK
CRAK...!!

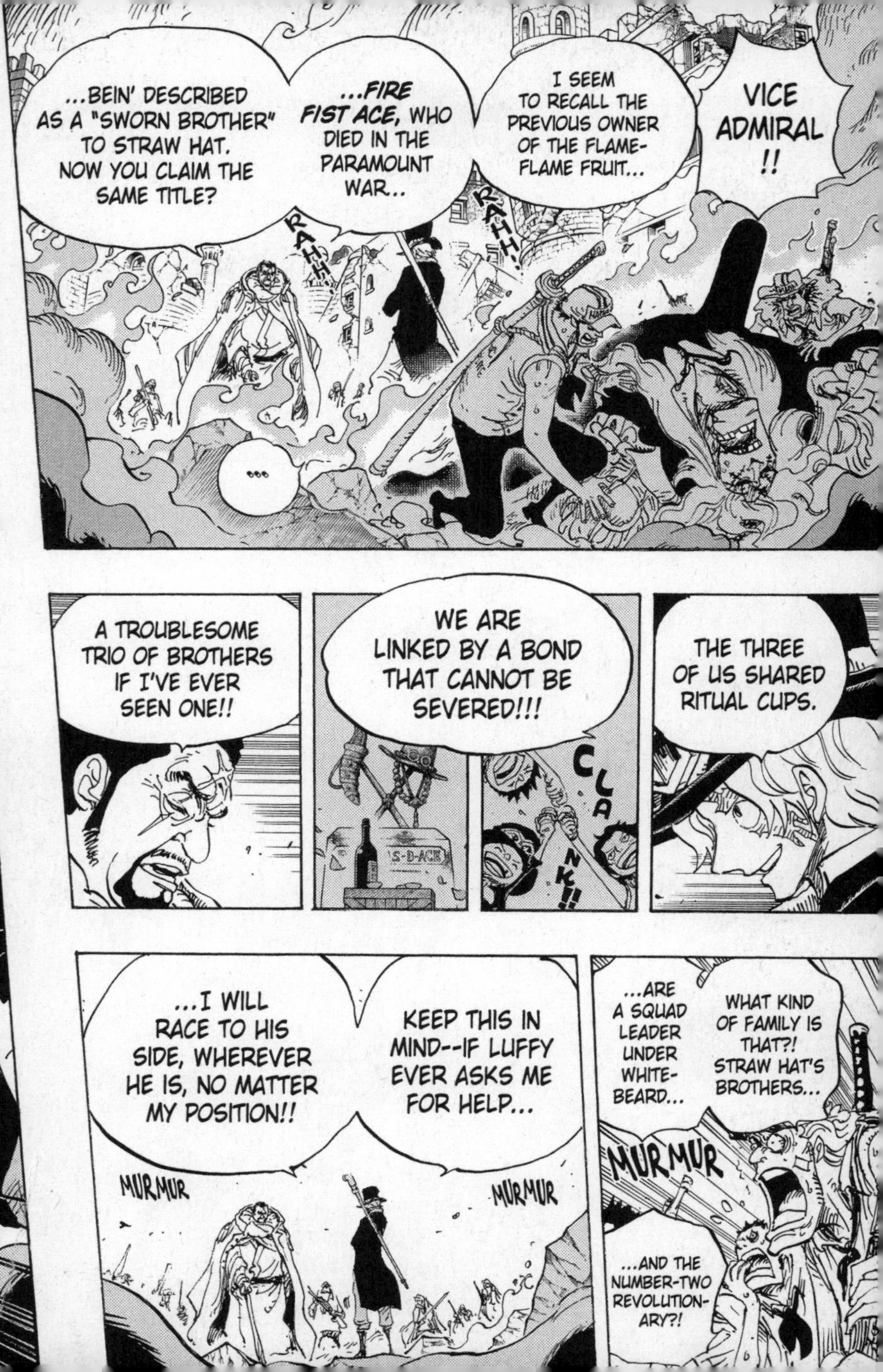
VICE ADMIRAL!!
I SEEM TO RECALL THE PREVIOUS OWNER OF THE FLAME-FLAME FRUIT...
...FIRE FIST ACE, WHO DIED IN THE PARAMOUNT WAR...
RAHH!
RAHH!
...BEIN' DESCRIBED AS A "SWORN BROTHER" TO STRAW HAT. NOW YOU CLAIM THE SAME TITLE?
...
THE THREE OF US SHARED RITUAL CUPS.
CLANK!!
WE ARE LINKED BY A BOND THAT CANNOT BE SEVERED!!!
S-D-ACE
A TROUBLESOME TRIO OF BROTHERS IF I'VE EVER SEEN ONE!!
WHAT KIND OF FAMILY IS THAT?! STRAW HAT'S BROTHERS...
...ARE A SQUAD LEADER UNDER WHITE-BEARD...
MURMUR
...AND THE NUMBER-TWO REVOLUTION-ARY?!
KEEP THIS IN MIND--IF LUFFY EVER ASKS ME FOR HELP...
...I WILL RACE TO HIS SIDE, WHEREVER HE IS, NO MATTER MY POSITION!!
MURMUR
MURMUR

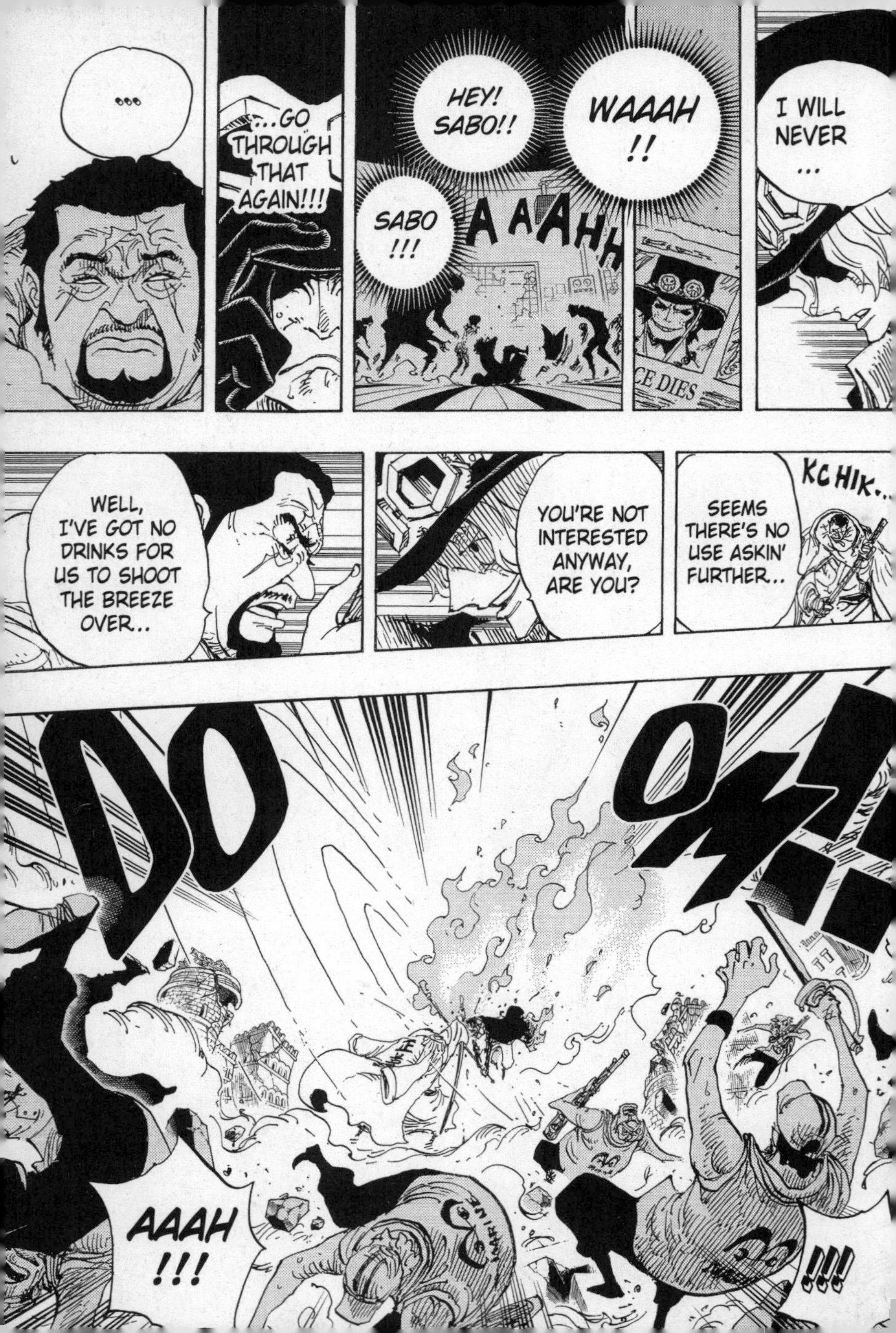
I WILL NEVER ...
CE DIES
WAAAH !!
HEY! SABO!!
SABO !!!
AAAHH
...GO THROUGH THAT AGAIN!!!
...
KCHIK...
SEEMS THERE'S NO USE ASKIN' FURTHER..
YOU'RE NOT INTERESTED ANYWAY, ARE YOU?
WELL, I'VE GOT NO DRINKS FOR US TO SHOOT THE BREEZE OVER..
DOOM!!
!!!
MARINE
AAAH !!!

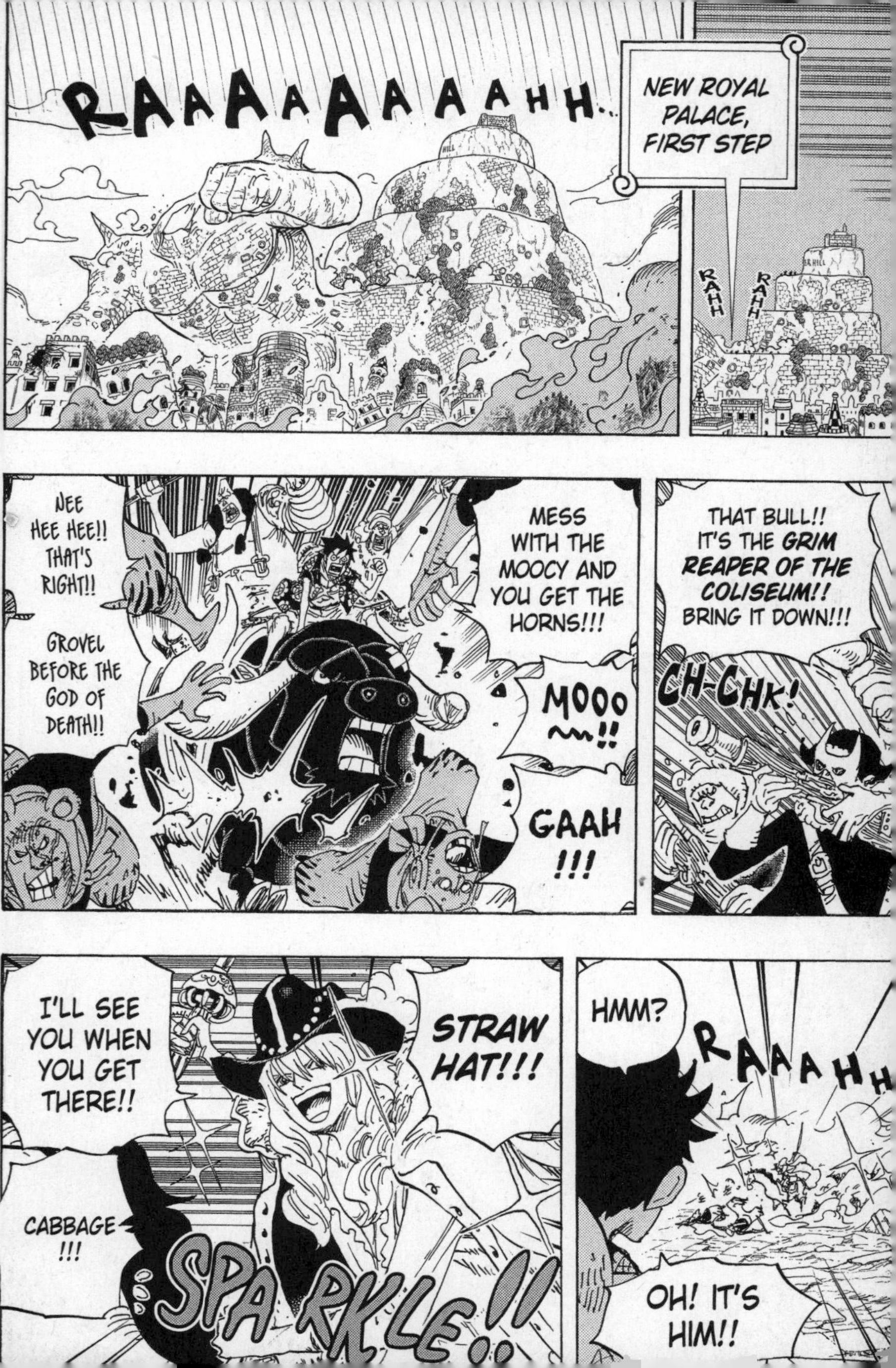
NEW ROYAL PALACE, FIRST STEP
RAHH
RAHH
RAAAAAAAAHH...
THAT BULL!! IT'S THE GRIM REAPER OF THE COLISEUM!! BRING IT DOWN!!!
CH-CHK!
MESS WITH THE MOOCY AND YOU GET THE HORNS!!!
MOOO ~~!!
GAAH !!!
NEE HEE HEE!! THAT'S RIGHT!!
GROVEL BEFORE THE GOD OF DEATH!!
HMM?
RAAAHH
OH! IT'S HIM!!
STRAW HAT!!!
I'LL SEE YOU WHEN YOU GET THERE!!
CABBAGE!!!
SPARKLE!!

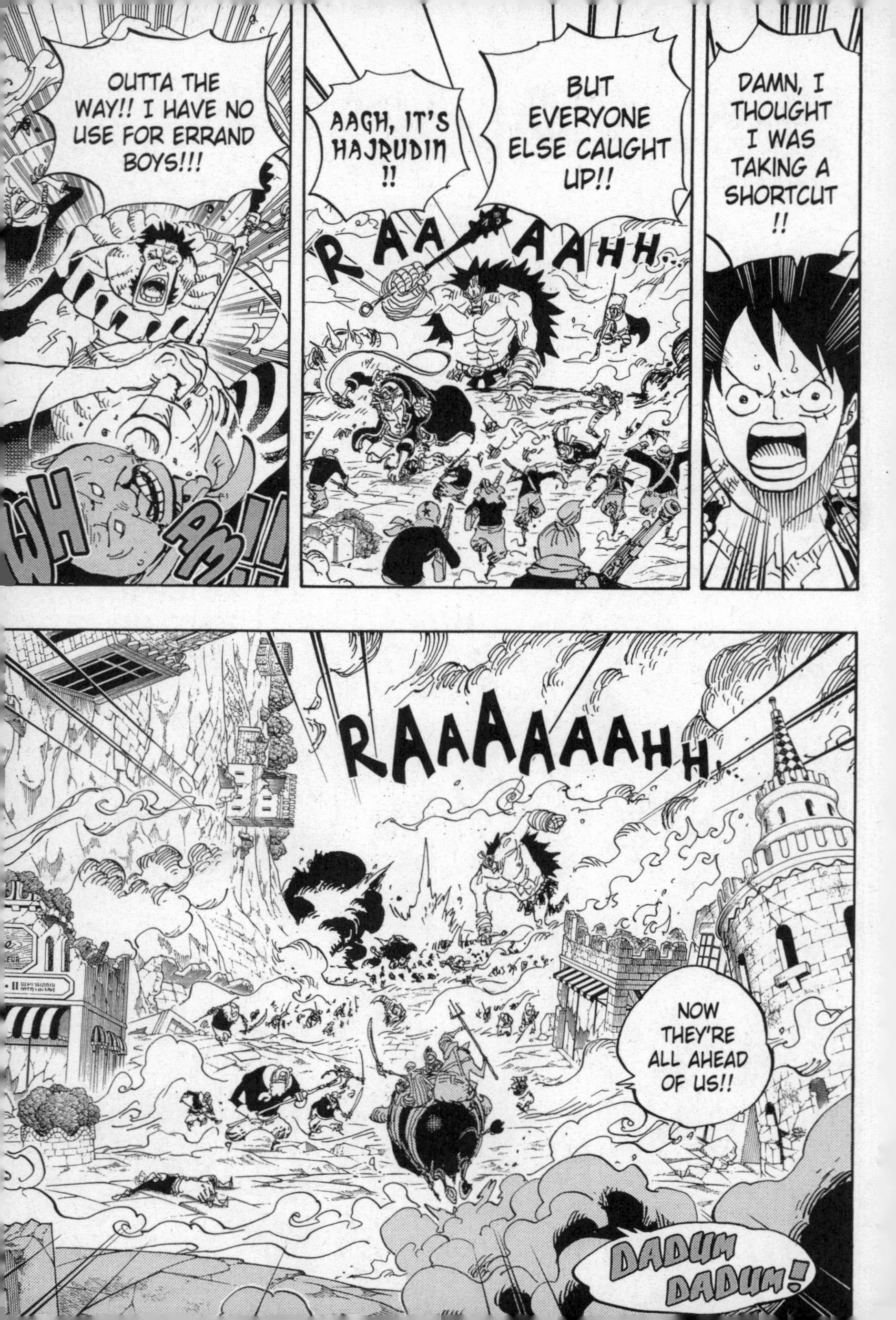
DAMN, I THOUGHT I WAS TAKING A SHORTCUT!!
BUT EVERYONE ELSE CAUGHT UP!!
AAGH, IT'S HAJRUDIN!!
RAAAAHH...
OUTTA THE WAY!! I HAVE NO USE FOR ERRAND BOYS!!!
WHAM!!
RAAAAAAAHH
NOW THEY'RE ALL AHEAD OF US!!
DADUM DADUM!

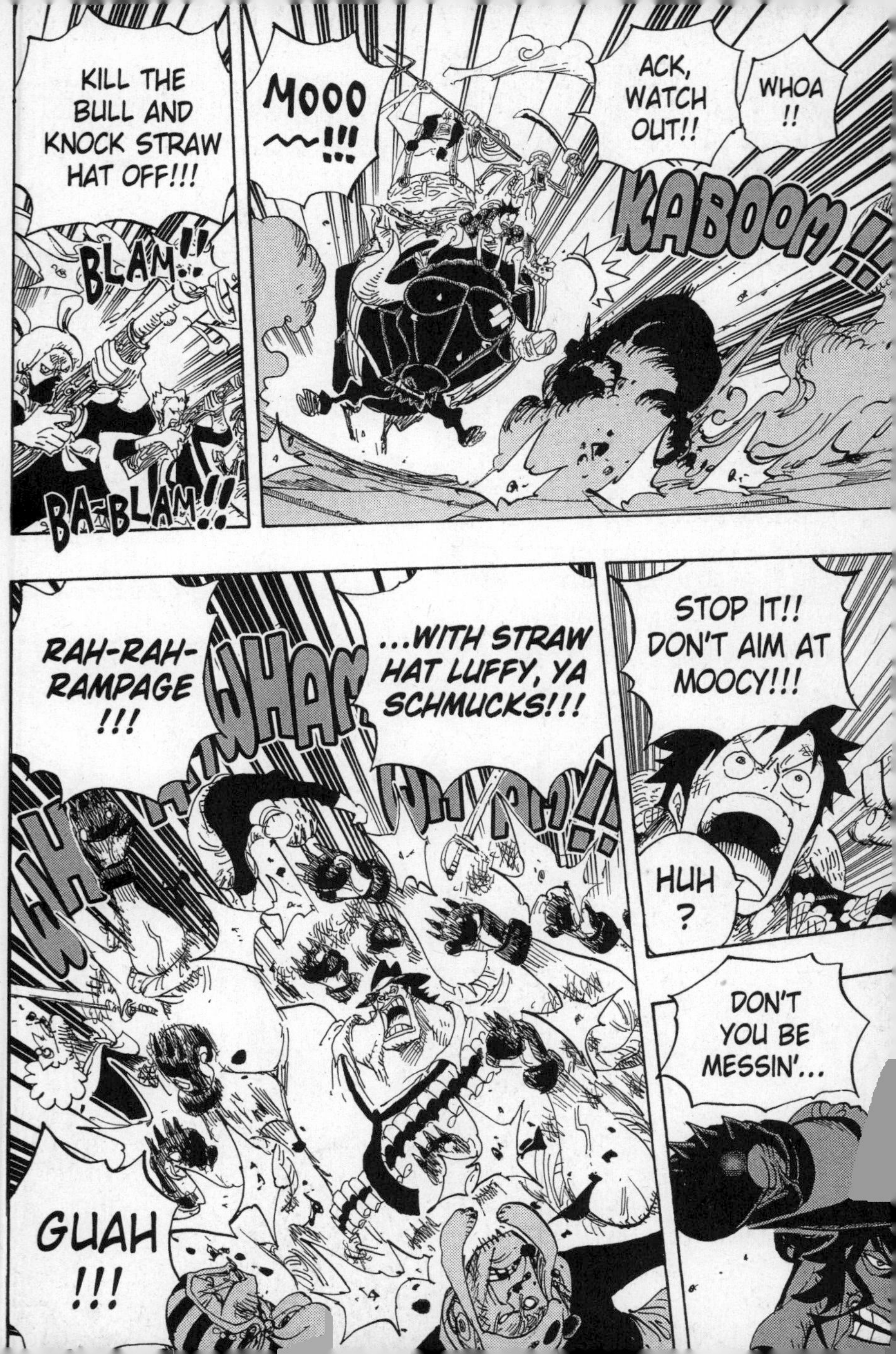
WHOA!!
ACK, WATCH OUT!!
KABOOM!!
MOOO~~!!!
KILL THE BULL AND KNOCK STRAW HAT OFF!!!
BLAM!!
BA-BLAM!!
STOP IT!! DON'T AIM AT MOOCY!!!
HUH?
DON'T YOU BE MESSIN'...
...WITH STRAW HAT LUFFY, YA SCHMUCKS!!!
WHAM
RAH-RAH-RAMPAGE!!!
GUAH!!!

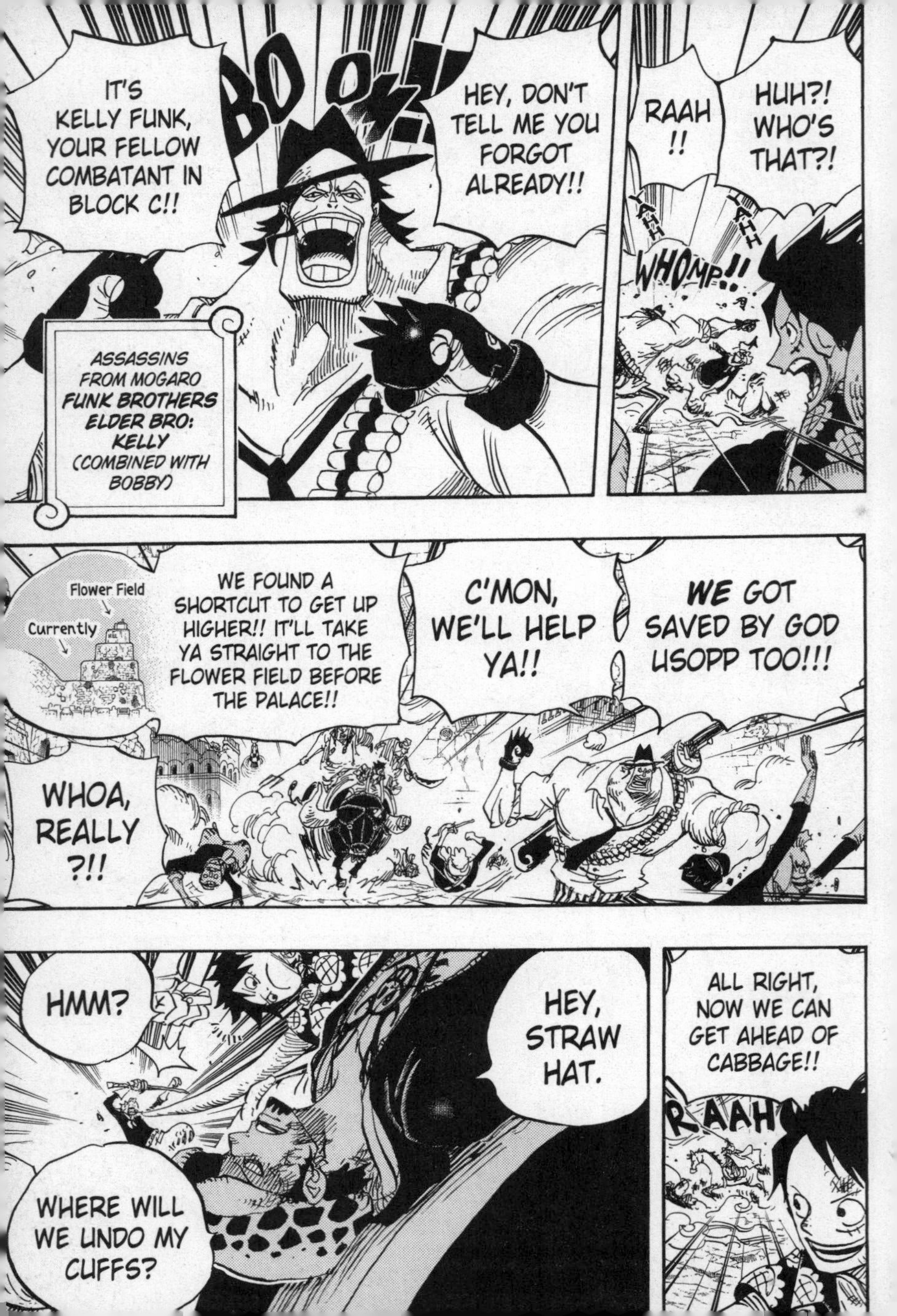
HUH?! WHO'S THAT?!
RAAH !!
YAHH
YAHH
WHOMP!!
HEY, DON'T TELL ME YOU FORGOT ALREADY!!
BOOM!!
IT'S KELLY FUNK, YOUR FELLOW COMBATANT IN BLOCK C!!
ASSASSINS FROM MOGARO
FUNK BROTHERS ELDER BRO: KELLY
(COMBINED WITH BOBBY)
WE GOT SAVED BY GOD USOPP TOO!!!
C'MON, WE'LL HELP YA!!
WE FOUND A SHORTCUT TO GET UP HIGHER!! IT'LL TAKE YA STRAIGHT TO THE FLOWER FIELD BEFORE THE PALACE!!
Flower Field
Currently
WHOA, REALLY ?!!
ALL RIGHT, NOW WE CAN GET AHEAD OF CABBAGE!!
RAAH
HEY, STRAW HAT.
HMM?
WHERE WILL WE UNDO MY CUFFS?

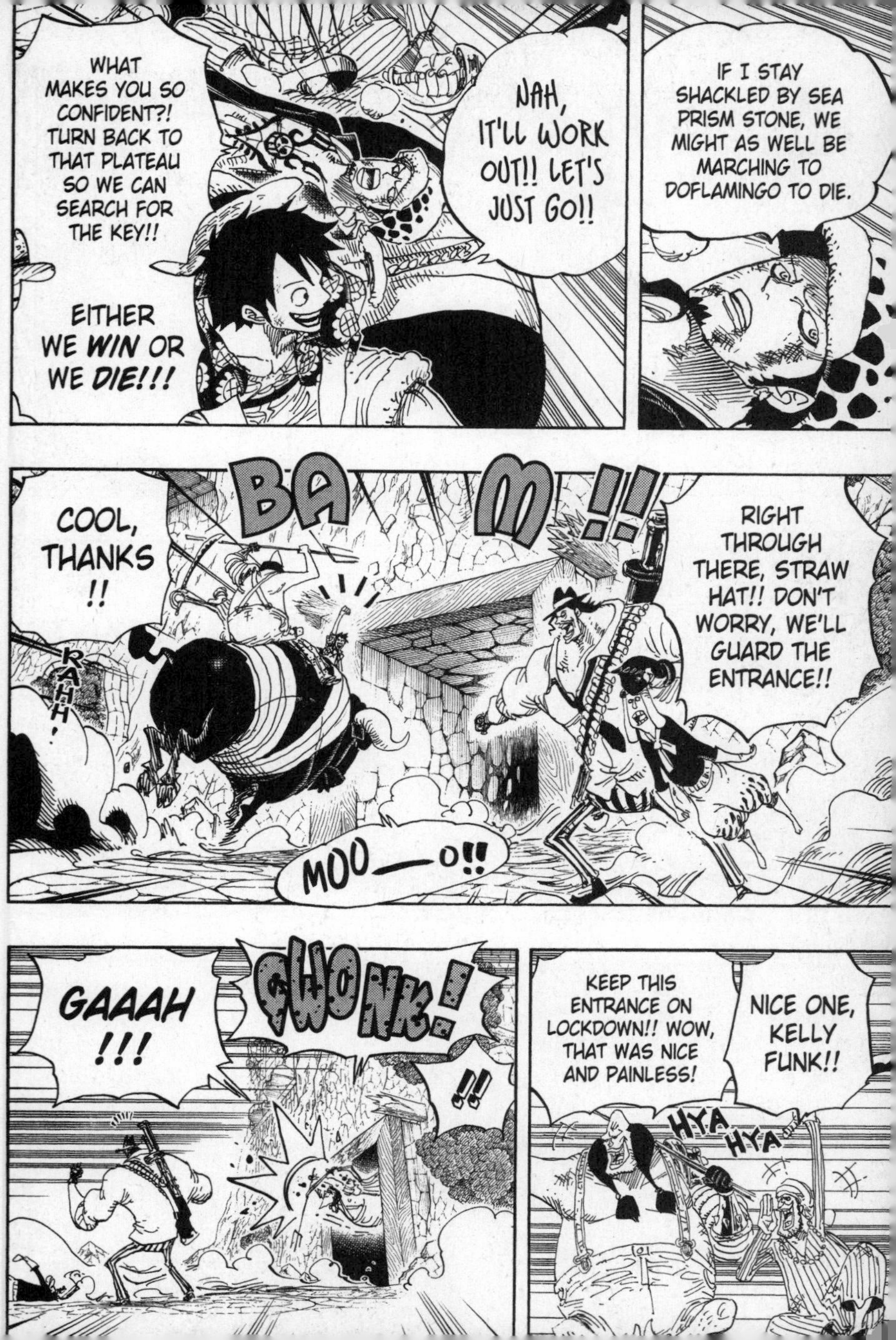
IF I STAY SHACKLED BY SEA PRISM STONE, WE MIGHT AS WELL BE MARCHING TO DOFLAMINGO TO DIE.
NAH, IT'LL WORK OUT!! LET'S JUST GO!!
WHAT MAKES YOU SO CONFIDENT?! TURN BACK TO THAT PLATEAU SO WE CAN SEARCH FOR THE KEY!!
EITHER WE WIN OR WE DIE!!!
RIGHT THROUGH THERE, STRAW HAT!! DON'T WORRY, WE'LL GUARD THE ENTRANCE!!
BAM!!
COOL, THANKS!!
RAHH!
MOO—O!!
NICE ONE, KELLY FUNK!!
KEEP THIS ENTRANCE ON LOCKDOWN!! WOW, THAT WAS NICE AND PAINLESS!
HYA HYA
CHONK!
!!
GAAAH!!!

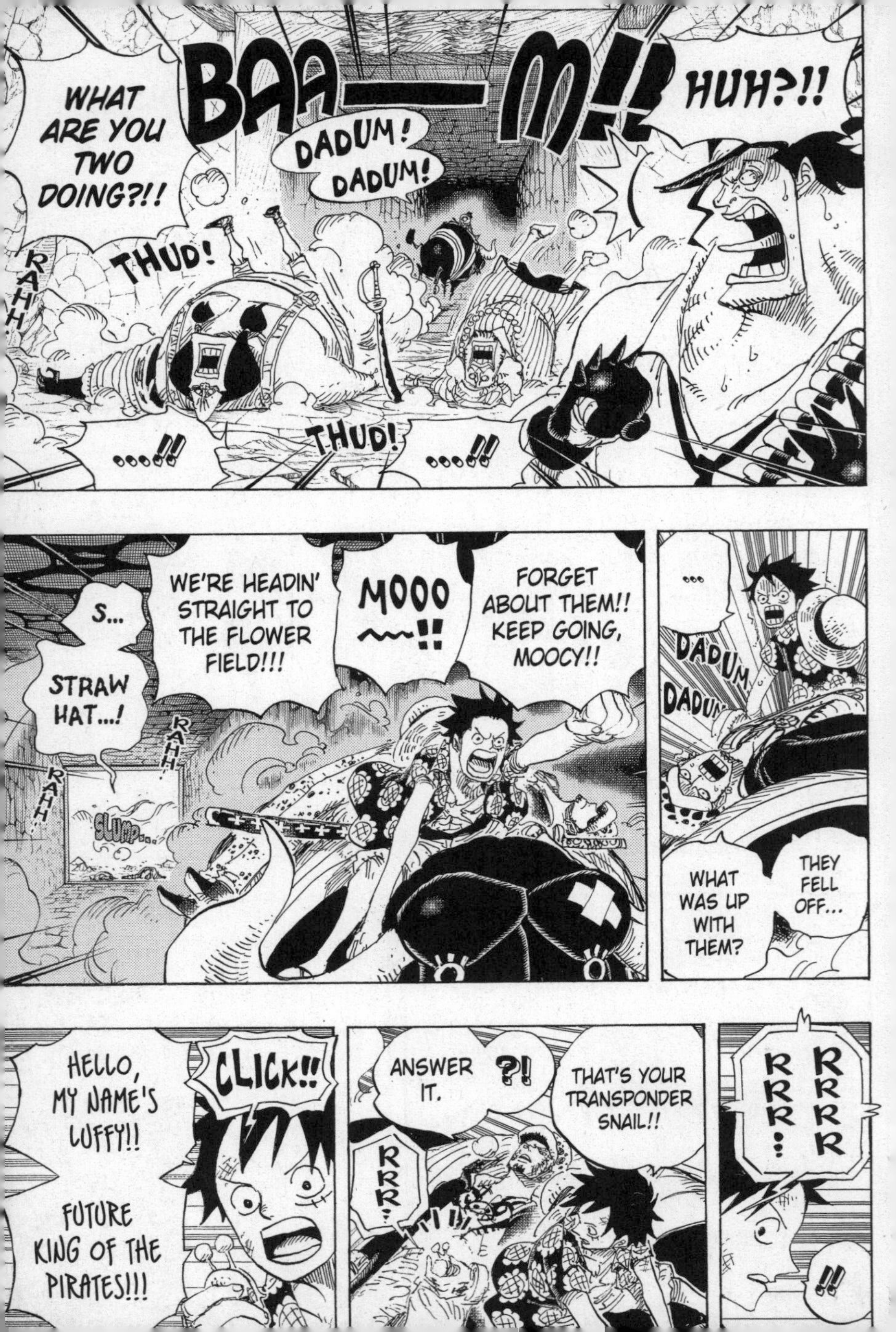
HUH?!!
BAA—M!!
DADUM! DADUM!
WHAT ARE YOU TWO DOING?!!
THUD!
RAHH
...!!
THUD!
...!!
...
DADUM DADUM
THEY FELL OFF...
WHAT WAS UP WITH THEM?
FORGET ABOUT THEM!! KEEP GOING, MOOCY!!
MOOO ~~!!
WE'RE HEADIN' STRAIGHT TO THE FLOWER FIELD!!!
S... STRAW HAT...!
RAHH
RAHH
SLUMP...
RRRR RRR...
!!
THAT'S YOUR TRANSPONDER SNAIL!!
?!
ANSWER IT.
RRR...
CLICK!!
HELLO, MY NAME'S LUFFY!!
FUTURE KING OF THE PIRATES!!!

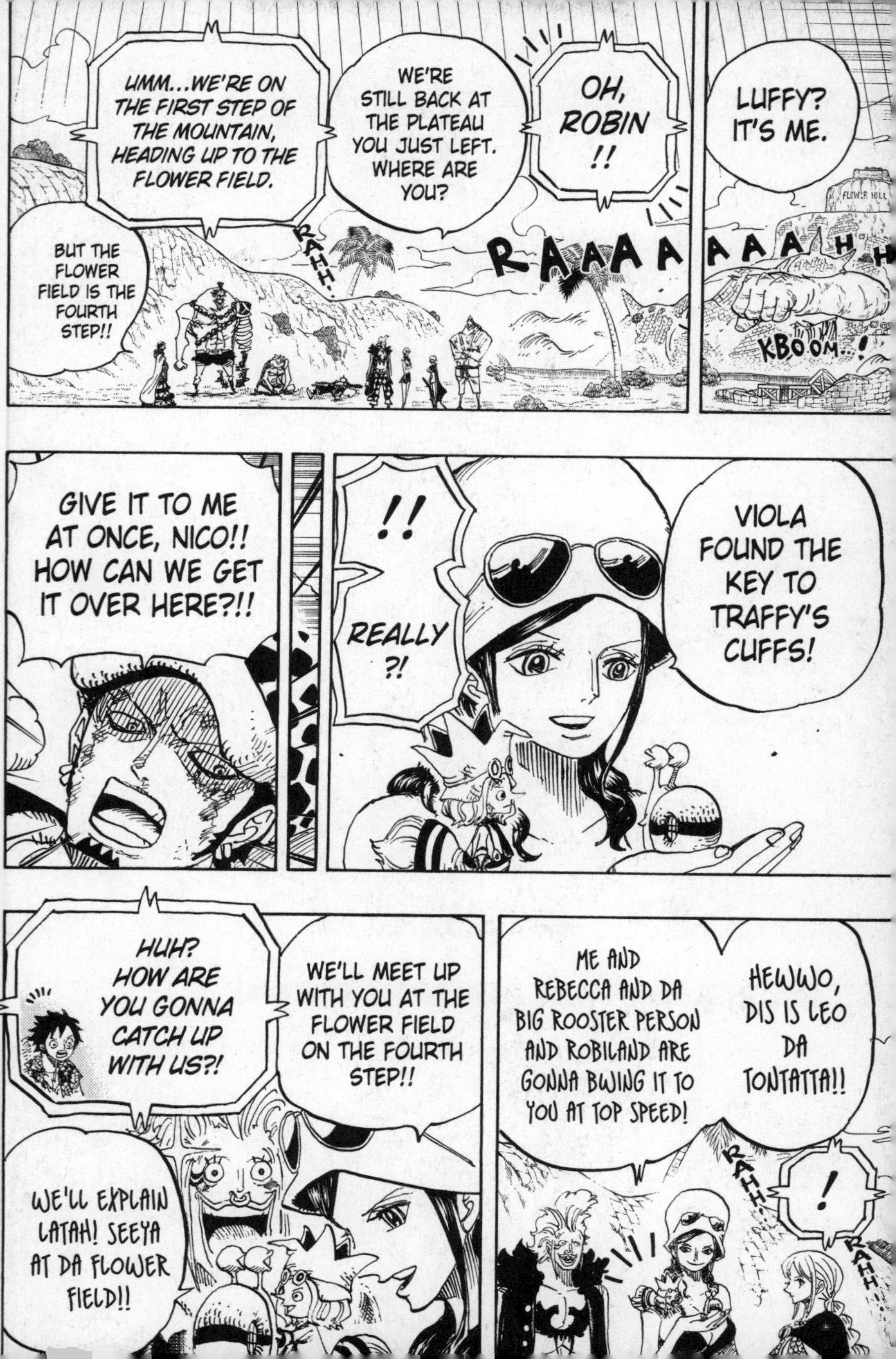
LUFFY? IT'S ME.
RAAAAAAAH
KBOOM..!
OH, ROBIN!!
WE'RE STILL BACK AT THE PLATEAU YOU JUST LEFT. WHERE ARE YOU?
UMM...WE'RE ON THE FIRST STEP OF THE MOUNTAIN, HEADING UP TO THE FLOWER FIELD.
RAHH!
BUT THE FLOWER FIELD IS THE FOURTH STEP!!
VIOLA FOUND THE KEY TO TRAFFY'S CUFFS!
!!
REALLY?!
GIVE IT TO ME AT ONCE, NICO!! HOW CAN WE GET IT OVER HERE?!!
HEWWO, DIS IS LEO DA TONTATTA!!
ME AND REBECCA AND DA BIG ROOSTER PERSON AND ROBILAND ARE GONNA BWING IT TO YOU AT TOP SPEED!
!
RAHH
RAHH
WE'LL MEET UP WITH YOU AT THE FLOWER FIELD ON THE FOURTH STEP!!
HUH? HOW ARE YOU GONNA CATCH UP WITH US?!
WE'LL EXPLAIN LATAH! SEEYA AT DA FLOWER FIELD!!

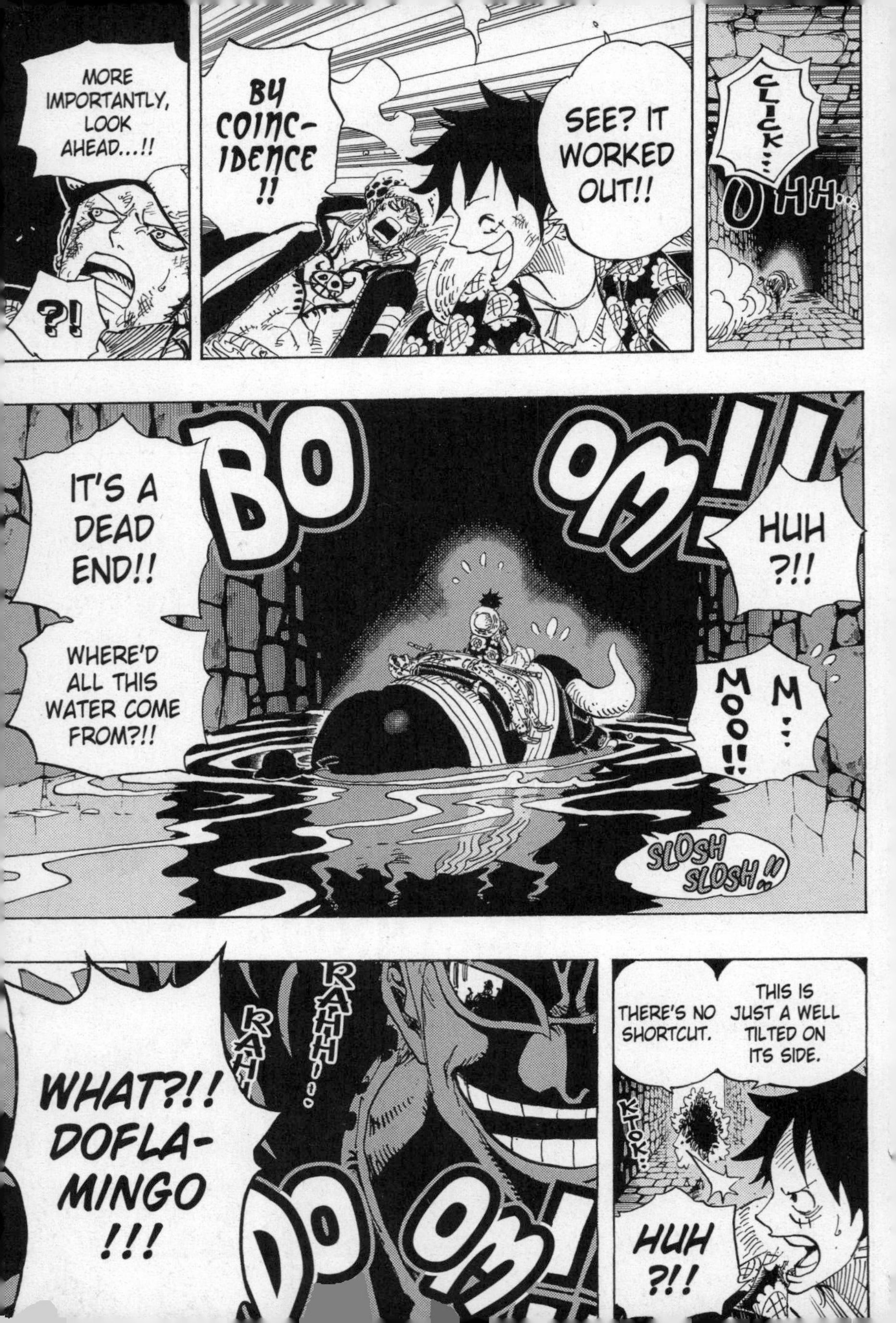
CLICK...
OHH...
SEE? IT WORKED OUT!!
BY COINC-IDENCE!!
MORE IMPORTANTLY, LOOK AHEAD...!!
?!
BOOM!!
HUH?!!
M...
MOO!!
IT'S A DEAD END!!
WHERE'D ALL THIS WATER COME FROM?!!
SLOSH SLOSH!!
THIS IS JUST A WELL TILTED ON ITS SIDE.
THERE'S NO SHORTCUT.
KTOK...
HUH?!!
RAHH...
RAH...
DOOM
WHAT?!! DOFLA-MINGO!!!

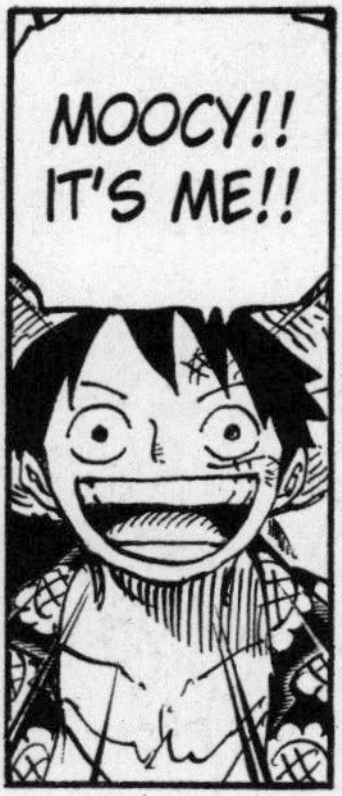
MOOCY!!
IT'S ME!!
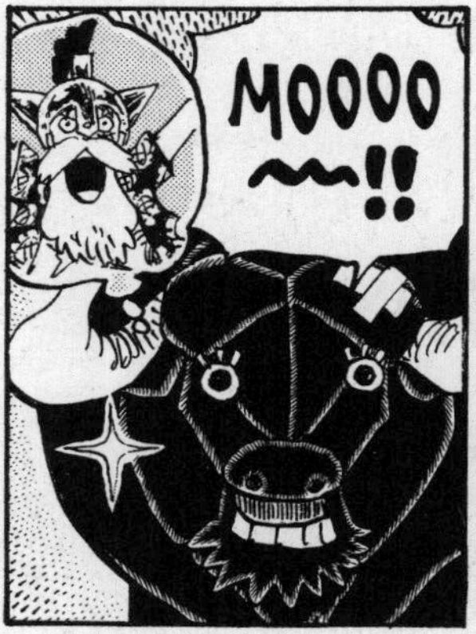
MOOOO ~~!!

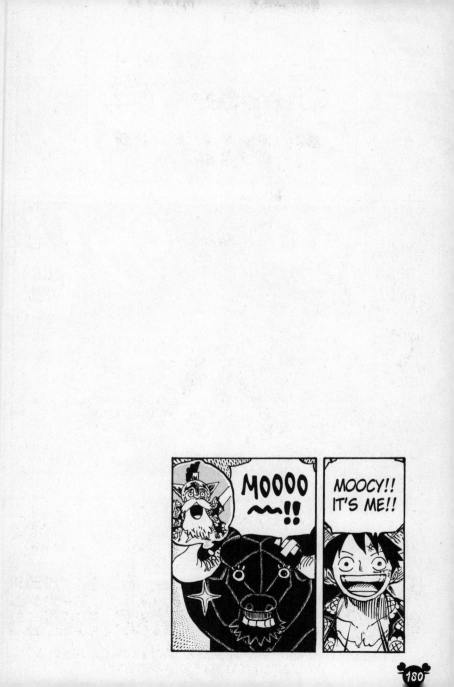

Chapter 752:
PALM

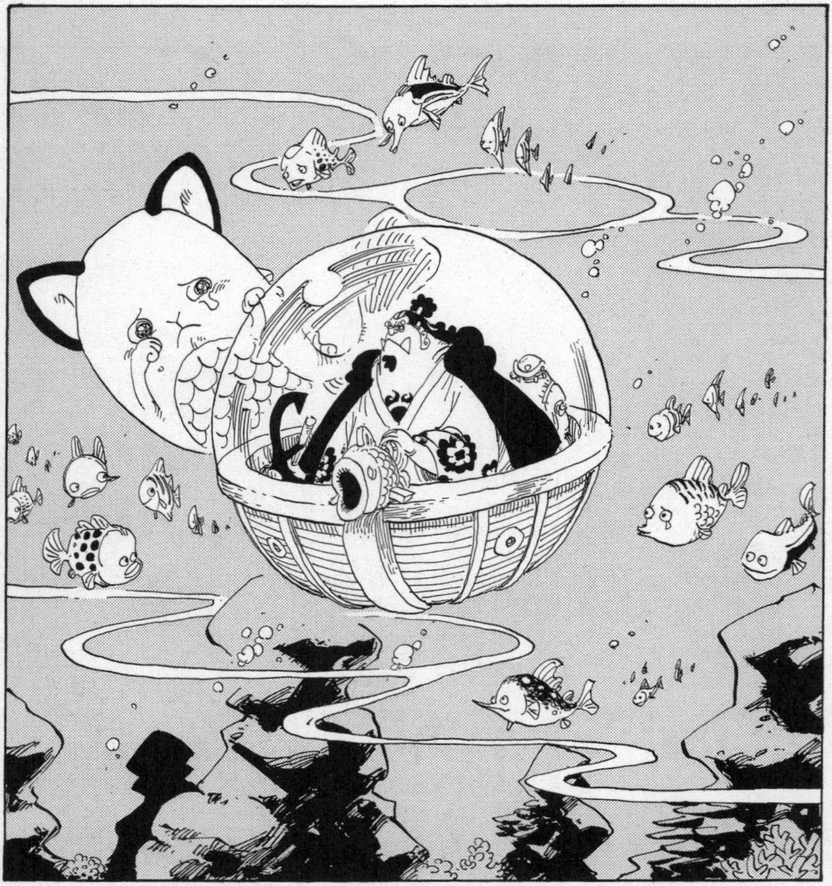

THE SOLITARY JOURNEY OF JIMBEI, FIRST SON OF THE SEA,
VOL. 2: "LOST LITTLE SEA-KITTEN"

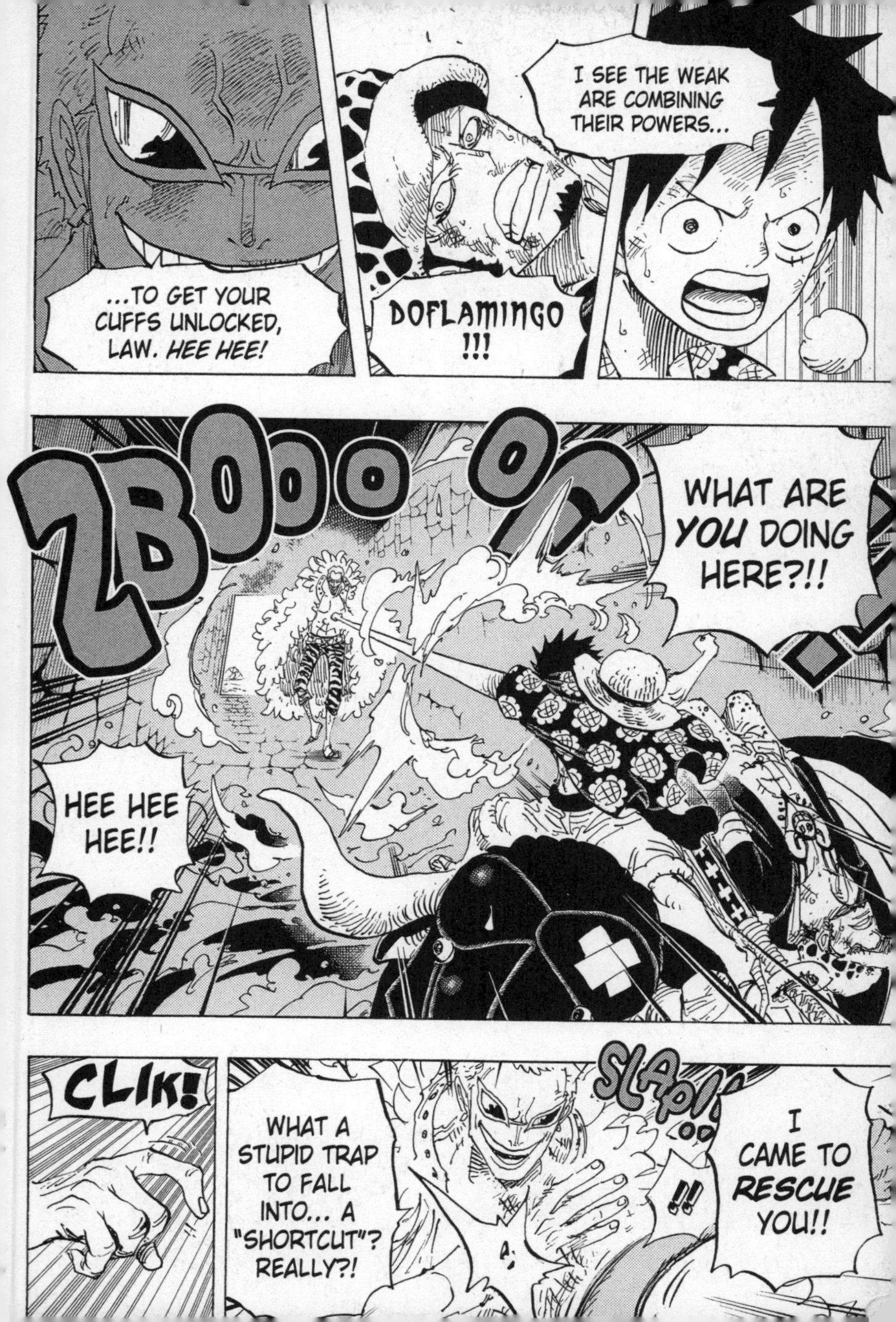
I SEE THE WEAK ARE COMBINING THEIR POWERS...
DOFLAMINGO !!!
...TO GET YOUR CUFFS UNLOCKED, LAW. *HEE HEE!*
WHAT ARE *YOU* DOING HERE?!!
ZBOOOO
HEE HEE HEE!!
I CAME TO *RESCUE* YOU!!
SLAP!
!!
WHAT A STUPID TRAP TO FALL INTO... A "SHORTCUT"? REALLY?!
CLIK!

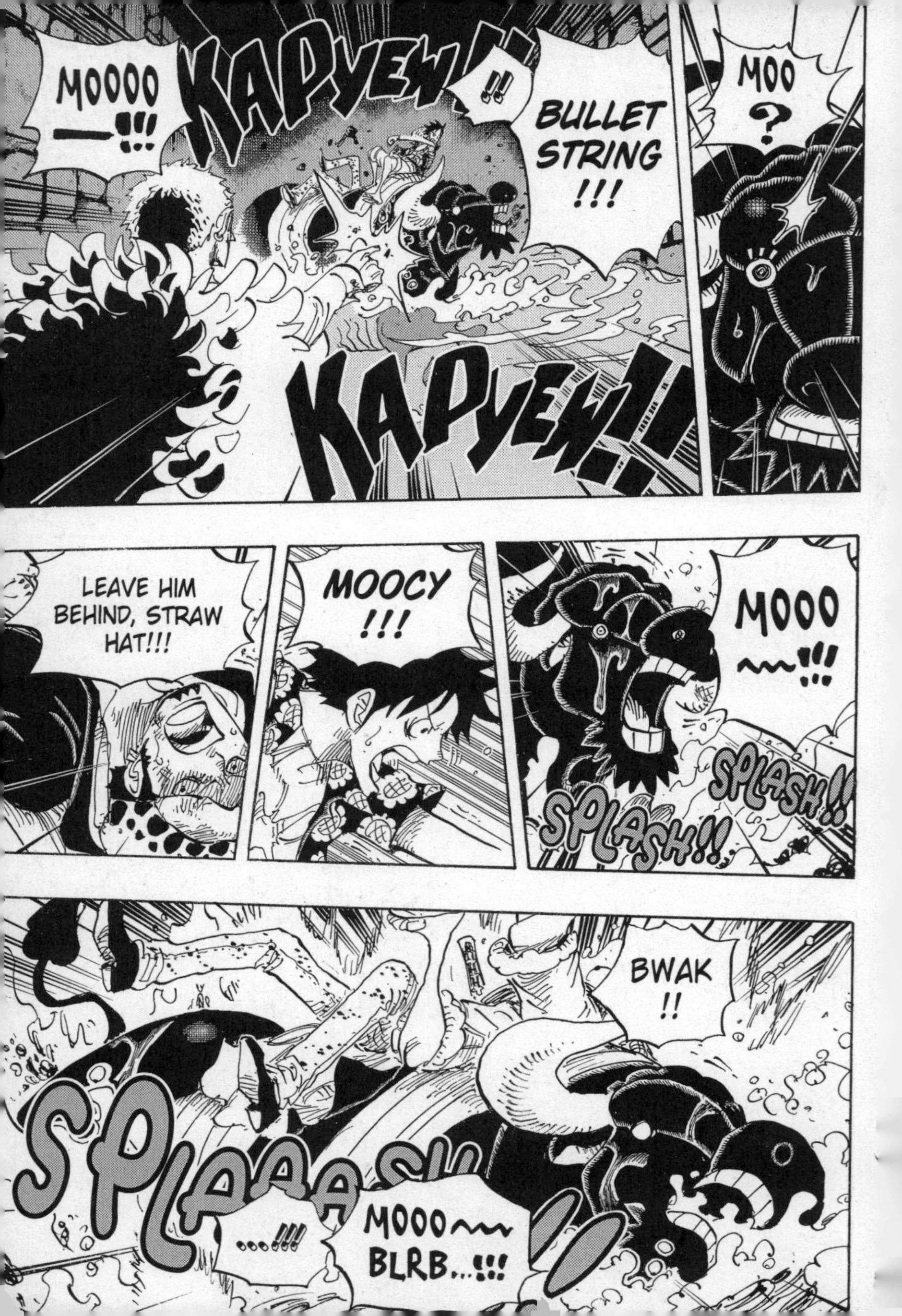
MOO ?
KAPYEW!!
BULLET STRING !!!
MOOOO—!!!
KAPYEW!!
MOOO~!!!
SPLASH!!
SPLASH!!
MOOCY !!!
LEAVE HIM BEHIND, STRAW HAT!!!
BWAK !!
SPLAAASH
...!!!
MOOO~ BLRB...!!!

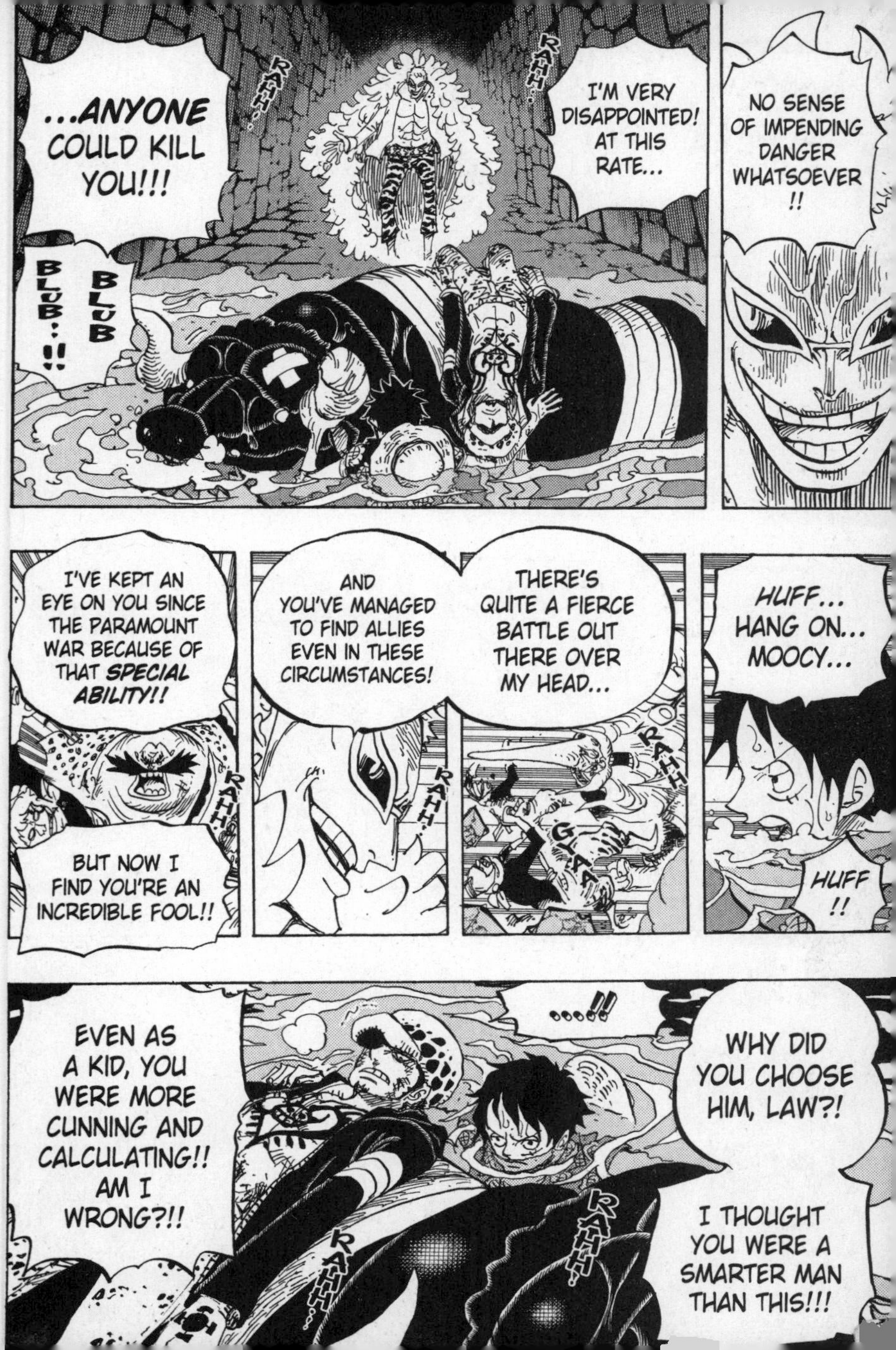
NO SENSE OF IMPENDING DANGER WHATSOEVER!!
RAHH...
I'M VERY DISAPPOINTED! AT THIS RATE...
RAHH...
...ANYONE COULD KILL YOU!!!
BLUB BLUB..!!
HUFF... HANG ON... MOOCY...
HUFF!!
THERE'S QUITE A FIERCE BATTLE OUT THERE OVER MY HEAD...
RAHH
GYAA
AND YOU'VE MANAGED TO FIND ALLIES EVEN IN THESE CIRCUMSTANCES!
RAHH..
I'VE KEPT AN EYE ON YOU SINCE THE PARAMOUNT WAR BECAUSE OF THAT SPECIAL ABILITY!!
RAHH..
BUT NOW I FIND YOU'RE AN INCREDIBLE FOOL!!
WHY DID YOU CHOOSE HIM, LAW?!
...!!
I THOUGHT YOU WERE A SMARTER MAN THAN THIS!!!
EVEN AS A KID, YOU WERE MORE CUNNING AND CALCULATING!! AM I WRONG?!!
RAHH..
RAHH..

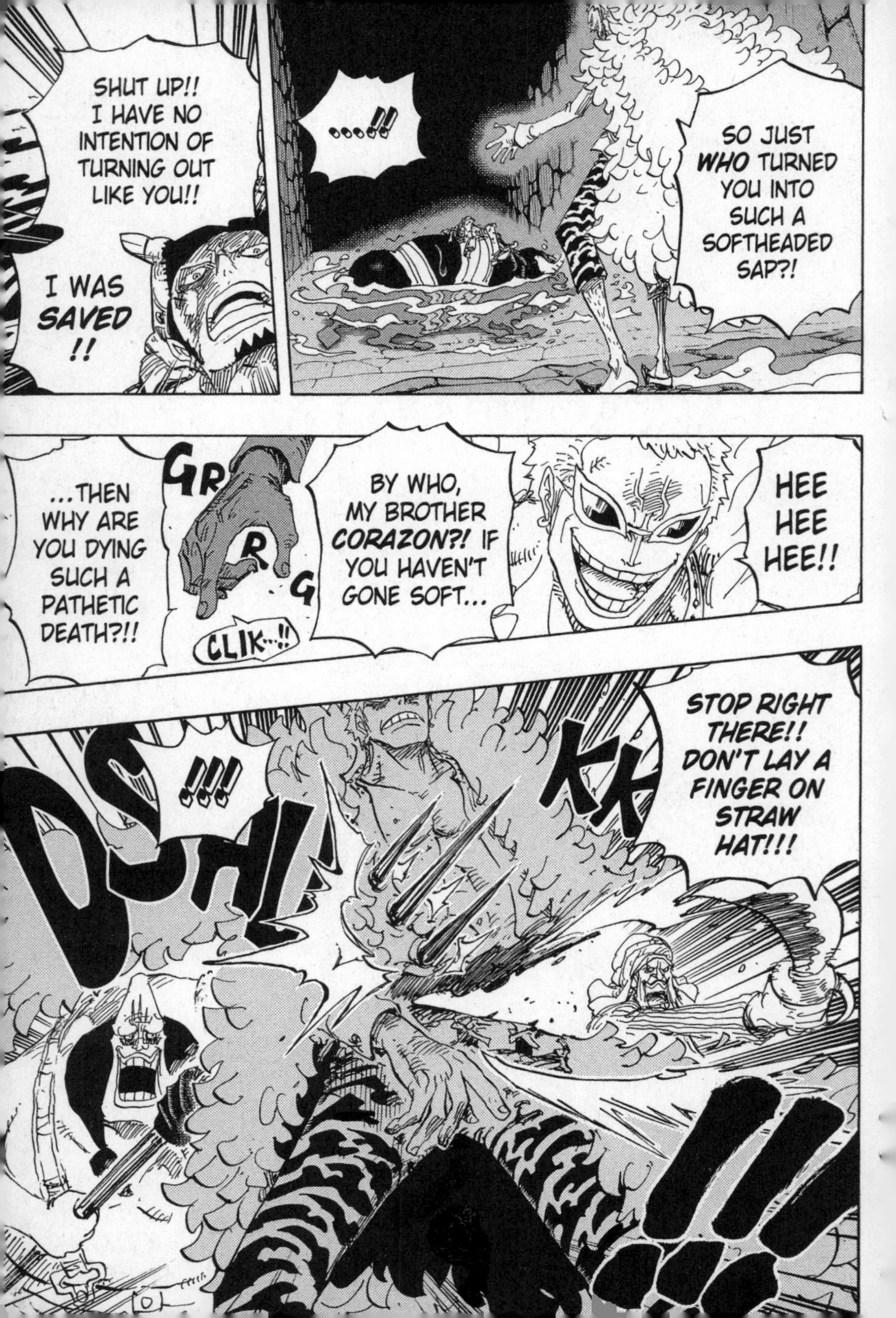
....!!
SO JUST WHO TURNED YOU INTO SUCH A SOFTHEADED SAP?!
SHUT UP!! I HAVE NO INTENTION OF TURNING OUT LIKE YOU!!
I WAS SAVED !!
HEE HEE HEE!!
BY WHO, MY BROTHER CORAZON?! IF YOU HAVEN'T GONE SOFT...
GRRG
CLIK...!!
...THEN WHY ARE YOU DYING SUCH A PATHETIC DEATH?!!
STOP RIGHT THERE!! DON'T LAY A FINGER ON STRAW HAT!!!
KK
DSH!!!
!!!

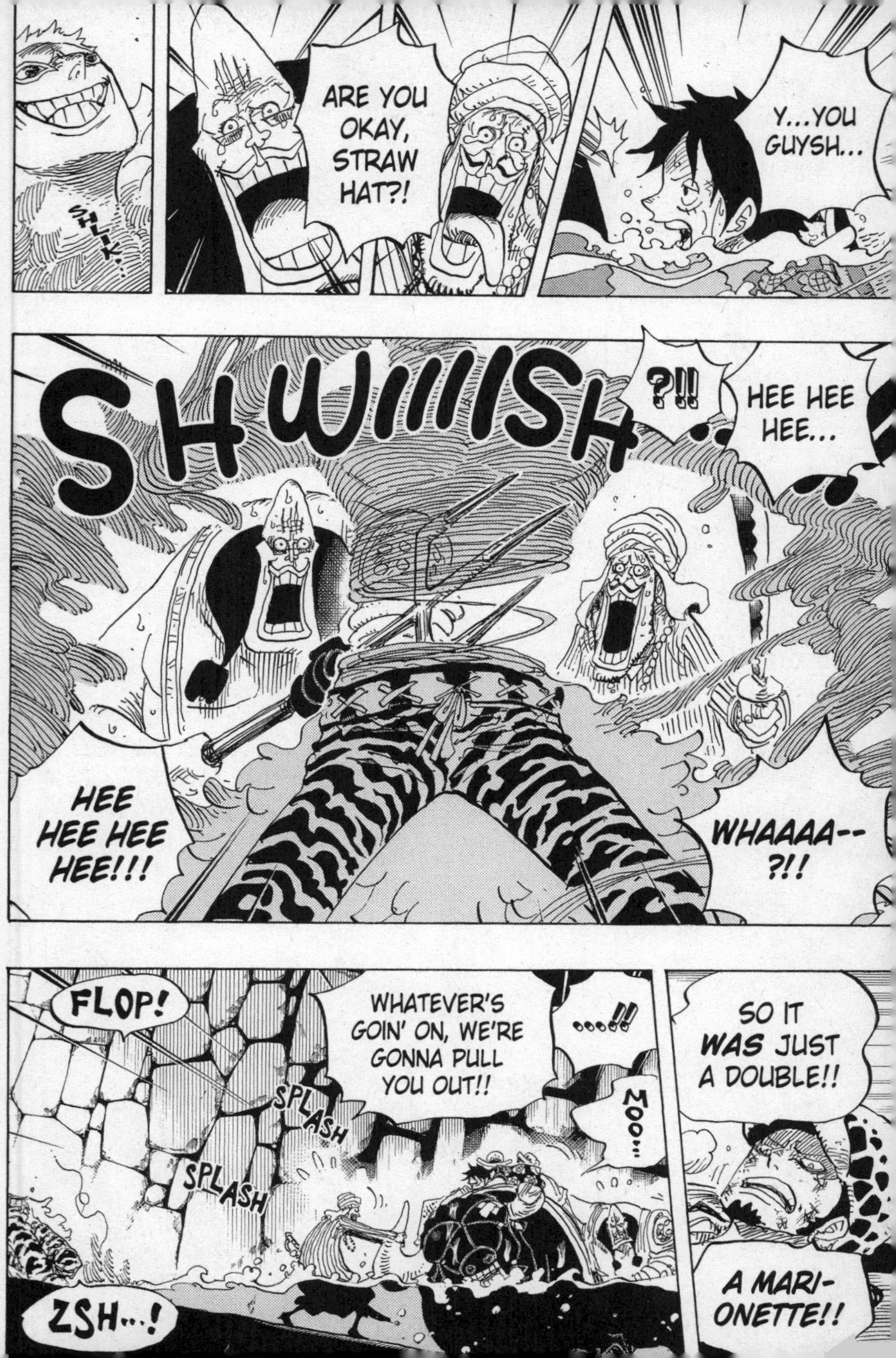
Y...YOU GUYSH...
ARE YOU OKAY, STRAW HAT?!
SHLIK...
HEE HEE HEE...
?!!
SHWIIISH
WHAAAA-- ?!!
HEE HEE HEE HEE!!!
SO IT WAS JUST A DOUBLE!!
A MARI-ONETTE!!
...!!
MOO...
WHATEVER'S GOIN' ON, WE'RE GONNA PULL YOU OUT!!
FLOP!
SPLASH
SPLASH
ZSH...!

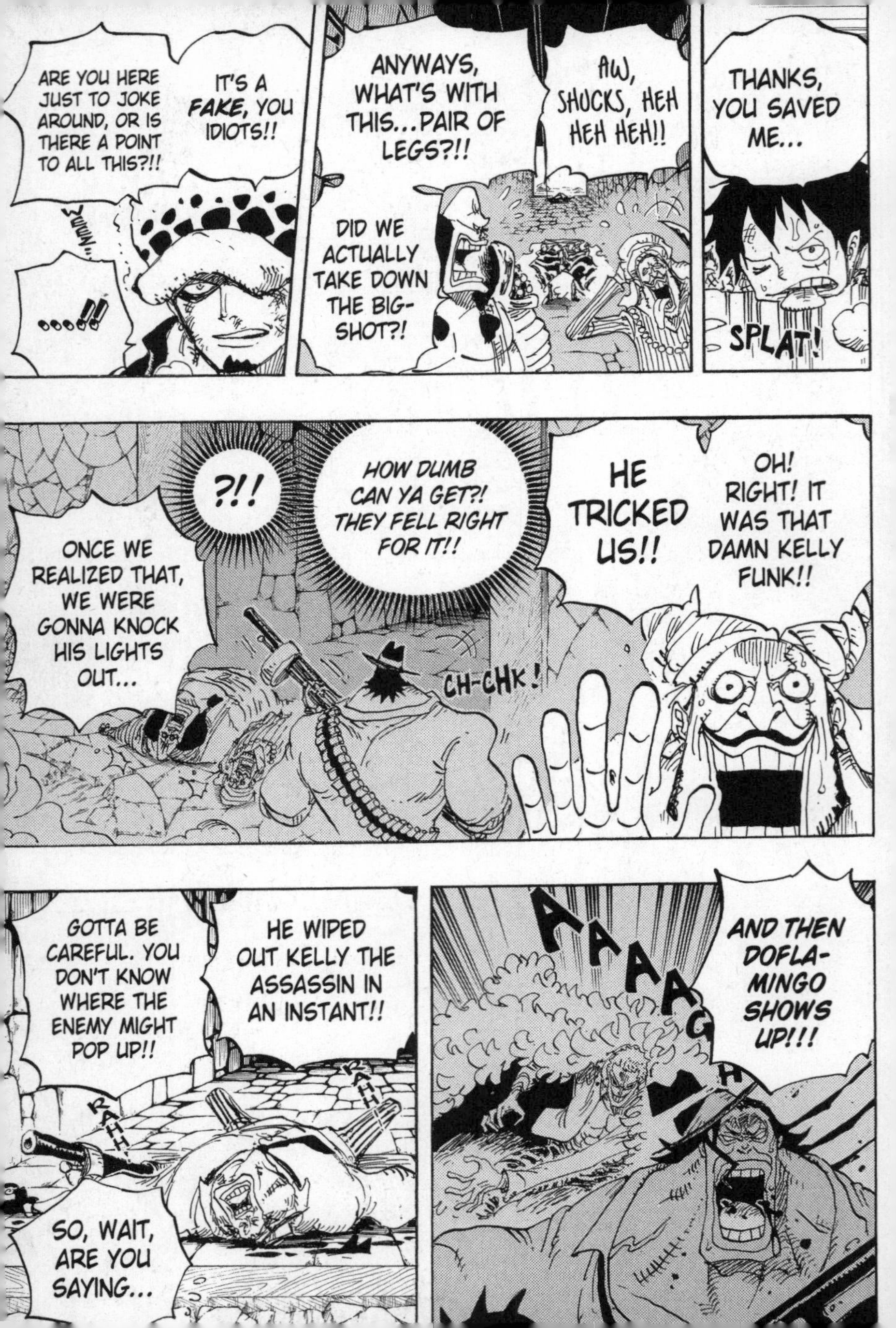
THANKS, YOU SAVED ME...
SPLAT!
AW, SHUCKS, HEH HEH HEH!!
ANYWAYS, WHAT'S WITH THIS...PAIR OF LEGS?!!
DID WE ACTUALLY TAKE DOWN THE BIG-SHOT?!
IT'S A FAKE, YOU IDIOTS!!
ARE YOU HERE JUST TO JOKE AROUND, OR IS THERE A POINT TO ALL THIS?!!
WEEEN...
.....!!
OH! RIGHT! IT WAS THAT DAMN KELLY FUNK!!
HE TRICKED US!!
HOW DUMB CAN YA GET?! THEY FELL RIGHT FOR IT!!
?!!
ONCE WE REALIZED THAT, WE WERE GONNA KNOCK HIS LIGHTS OUT...
CH-CHK!
AND THEN DOFLAMINGO SHOWS UP!!!
AAAAAGH
HE WIPED OUT KELLY THE ASSASSIN IN AN INSTANT!!
GOTTA BE CAREFUL. YOU DON'T KNOW WHERE THE ENEMY MIGHT POP UP!!
RAHH
RAHH
SO, WAIT, ARE YOU SAYING...

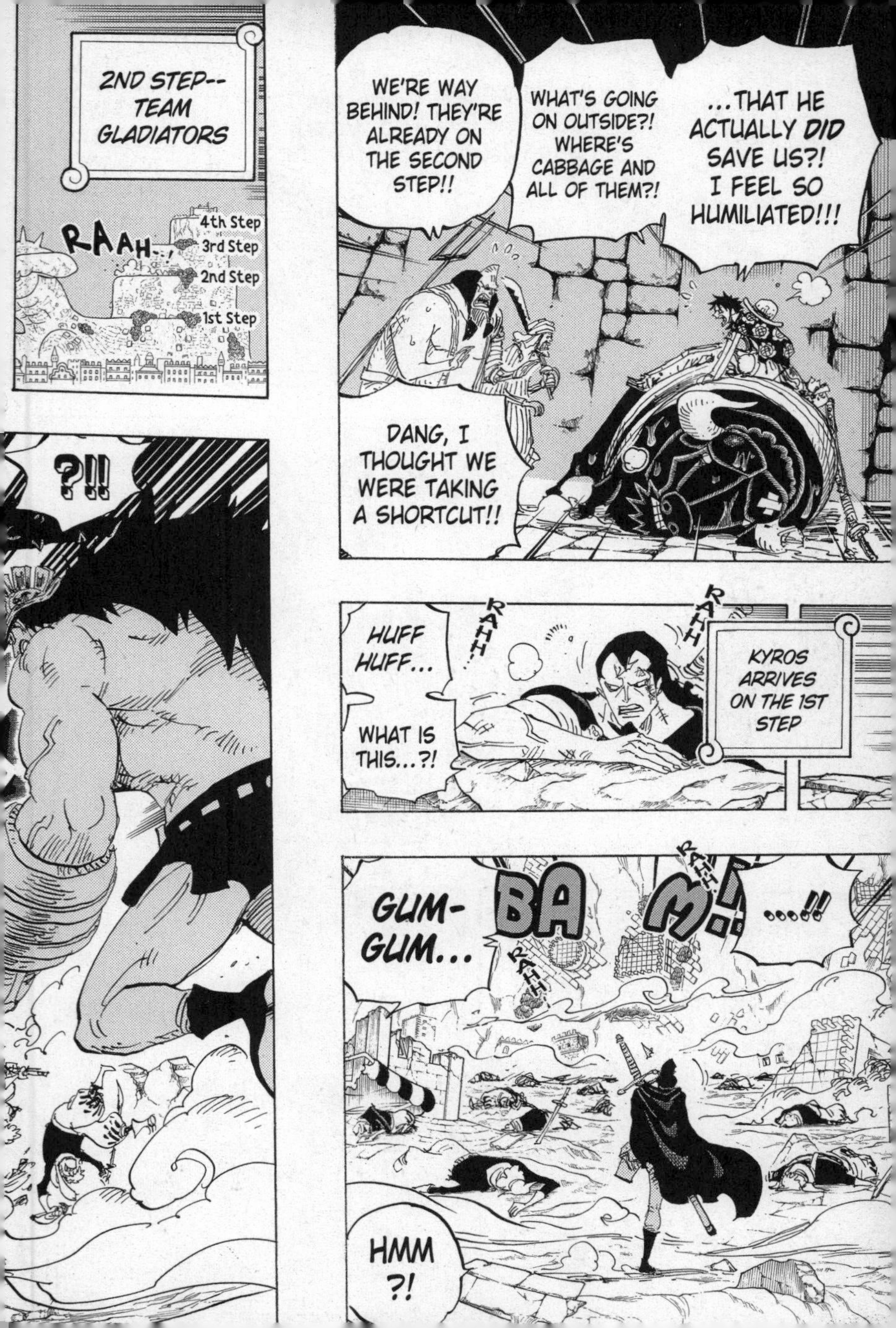
...THAT HE ACTUALLY DID SAVE US?! I FEEL SO HUMILIATED!!!
WHAT'S GOING ON OUTSIDE?! WHERE'S CABBAGE AND ALL OF THEM?!
WE'RE WAY BEHIND! THEY'RE ALREADY ON THE SECOND STEP!!
DANG, I THOUGHT WE WERE TAKING A SHORTCUT!!
2ND STEP-- TEAM GLADIATORS
RAAH..!
4th Step
3rd Step
2nd Step
1st Step
KYROS ARRIVES ON THE 1ST STEP
RAHH
RAHH..!
HUFF HUFF...
WHAT IS THIS...?!
...!!
RAHH
BAM!!
GUM-GUM...
RAHH
HMM ?!
?!!

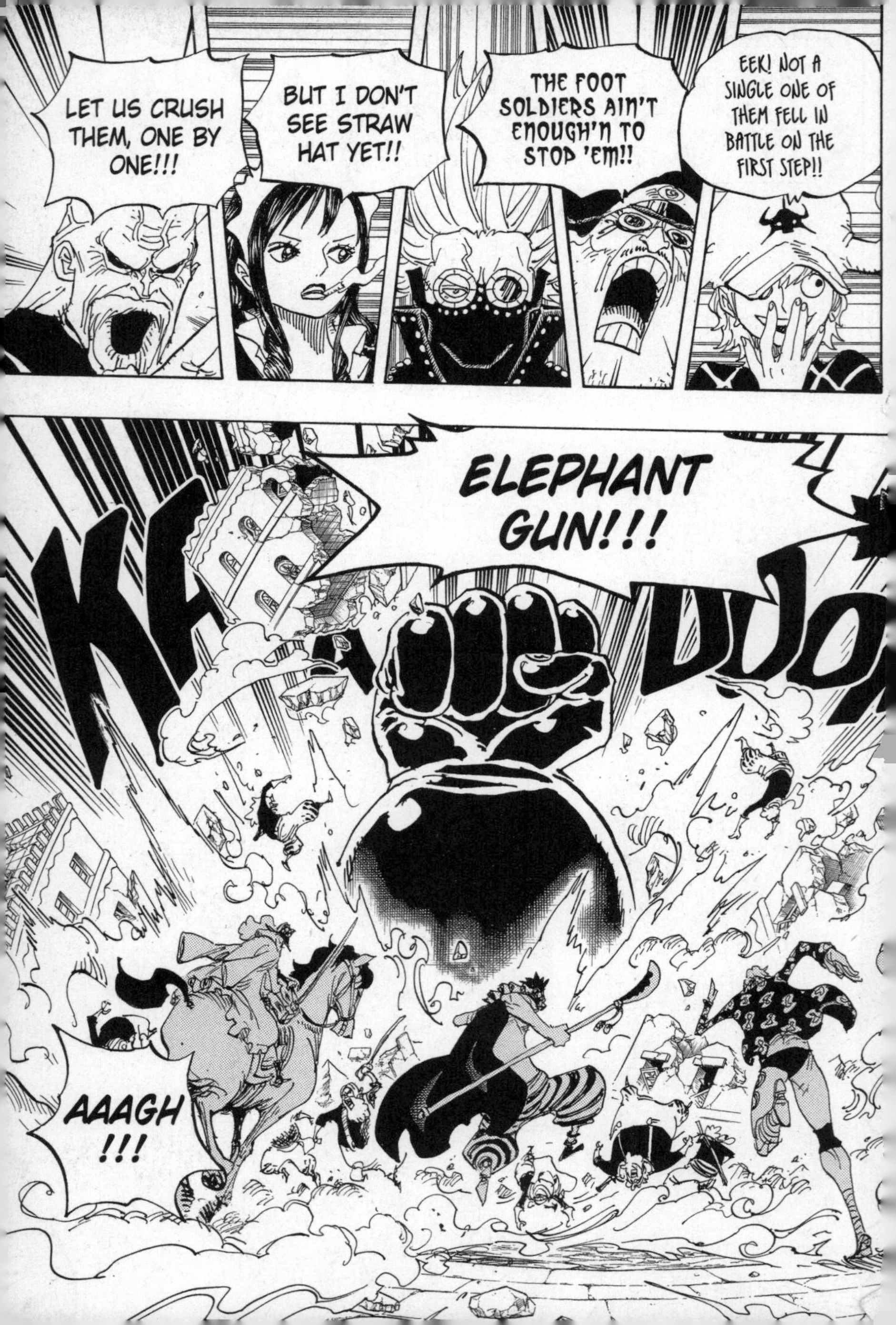
EEK! NOT A SINGLE ONE OF THEM FELL IN BATTLE ON THE FIRST STEP!!
THE FOOT SOLDIERS AIN'T ENOUGH'N TO STOP 'EM!!
BUT I DON'T SEE STRAW HAT YET!!
LET US CRUSH THEM, ONE BY ONE!!!
ELEPHANT GUN!!!
AAAGH !!!

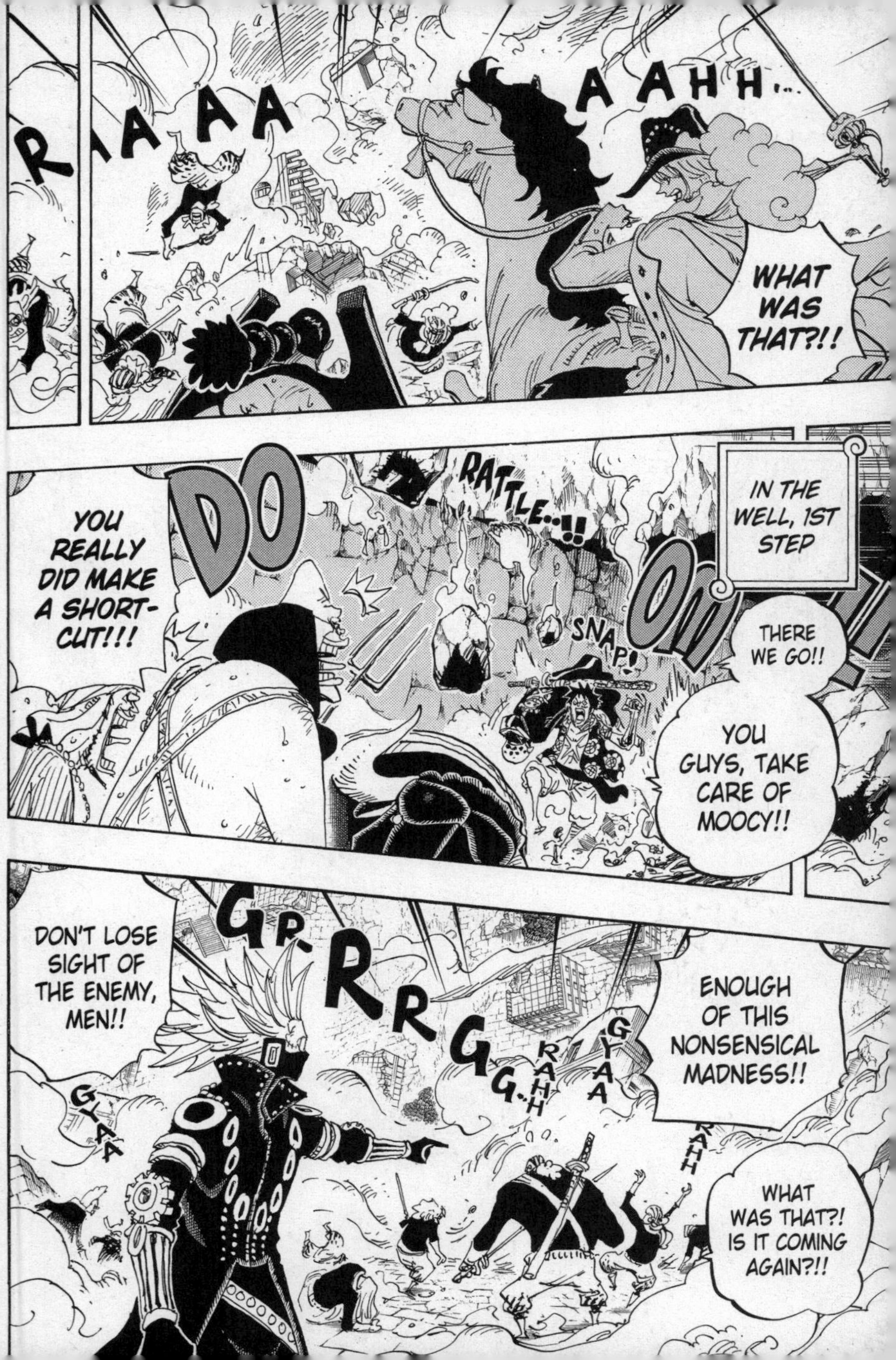

RAAAAAAAHH...
WHAT WAS THAT?!!
IN THE WELL, 1ST STEP
THERE WE GO!!
YOU GUYS, TAKE CARE OF MOOCY!!
DOOM
RATTLE..!!
SNAP!
YOU REALLY DID MAKE A SHORT-CUT!!!
ENOUGH OF THIS NONSENSICAL MADNESS!!
WHAT WAS THAT?! IS IT COMING AGAIN?!!
RAHH
GYAA
RAHH
GR-RRRGG..
DON'T LOSE SIGHT OF THE ENEMY, MEN!!
GYAA

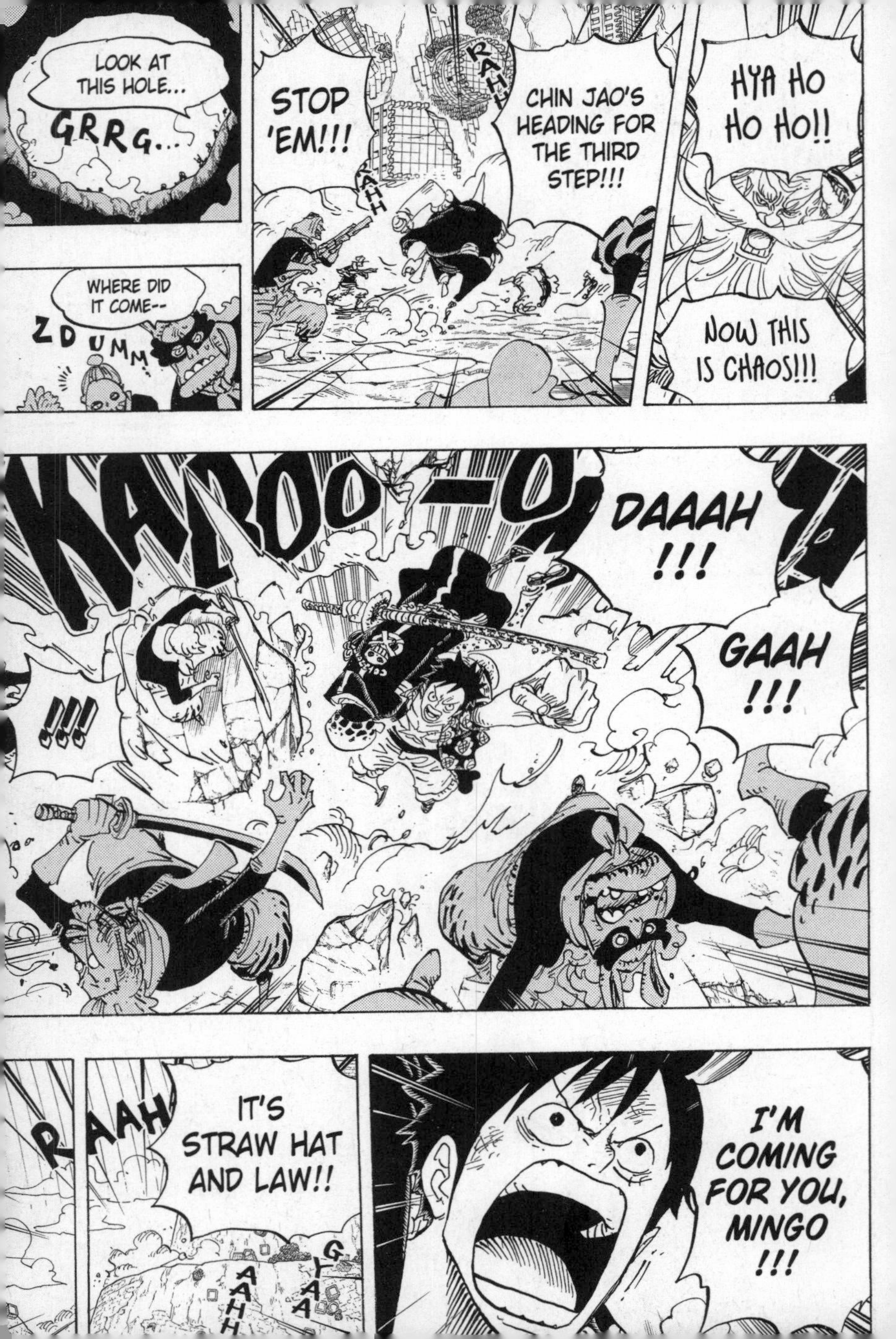
HYA HO HO HO!!
NOW THIS IS CHAOS!!!
CHIN JAO'S HEADING FOR THE THIRD STEP!!!
RAHH
STOP 'EM!!!
RAHH
LOOK AT THIS HOLE...
GRRG...
WHERE DID IT COME--
ZDUMM
DAAAH!!!
GAAH!!!
!!!
I'M COMING FOR YOU, MINGO!!!
IT'S STRAW HAT AND LAW!!
RAAH
GYAA
AAAHH

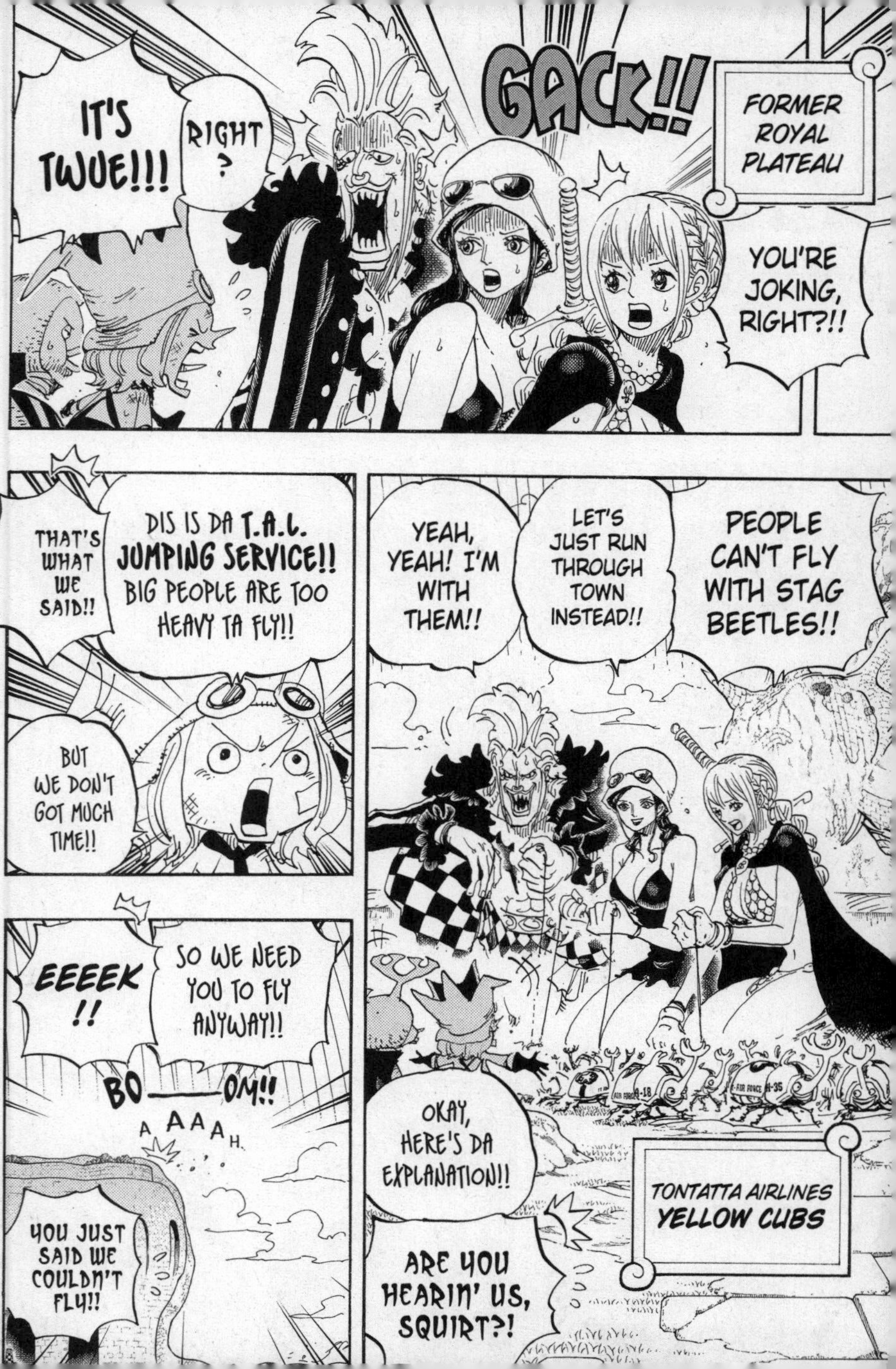

FORMER ROYAL PLATEAU
GACK!!
YOU'RE JOKING, RIGHT?!!
RIGHT ?
IT'S TWUE!!!
PEOPLE CAN'T FLY WITH STAG BEETLES!!
LET'S JUST RUN THROUGH TOWN INSTEAD!!
YEAH, YEAH! I'M WITH THEM!!
OKAY, HERE'S DA EXPLANATION!!
TONTATTA AIRLINES YELLOW CUBS
ARE YOU HEARIN' US, SQUIRT?!
DIS IS DA T.A.L. JUMPING SERVICE!! BIG PEOPLE ARE TOO HEAVY TA FLY!!
THAT'S WHAT WE SAID!!
BUT WE DON'T GOT MUCH TIME!!
SO WE NEED YOU TO FLY ANYWAY!!
EEEEK !!
BO——OM!!
AAAAH.
YOU JUST SAID WE COULDN'T FLY!!

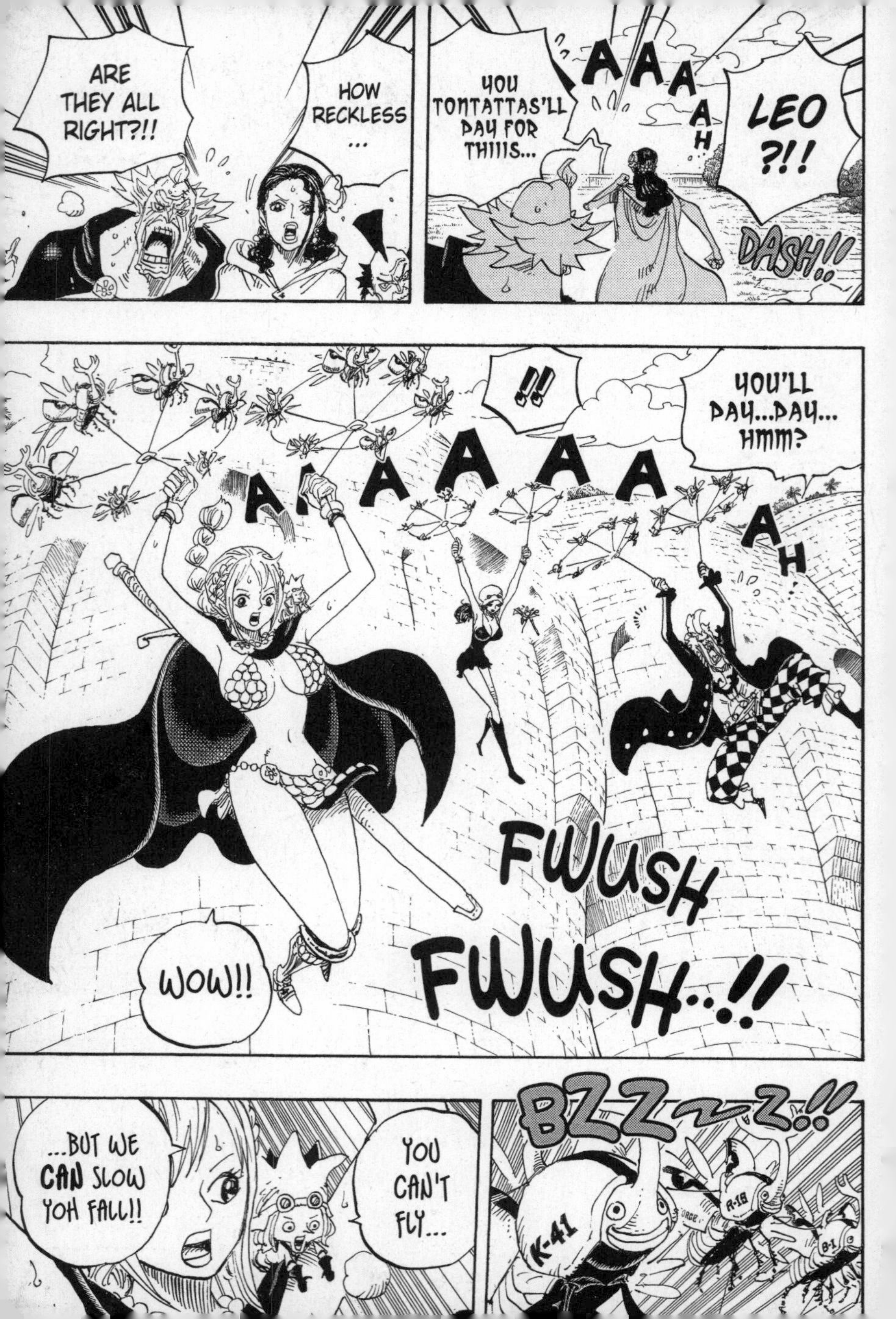
LEO ?!!
AAAAAH
YOU TONTATTAS'LL PAY FOR THIIIS...
DASH!!
HOW RECKLESS...
ARE THEY ALL RIGHT?!!
YOU'LL PAY...PAY... HMM?
!!
AAAAAAAH
FWUSH FWUSH..!!
WOW!!
BZZzz..!!
K-41
YOU CAN'T FLY...
...BUT WE **CAN** SLOW YOH FALL!!

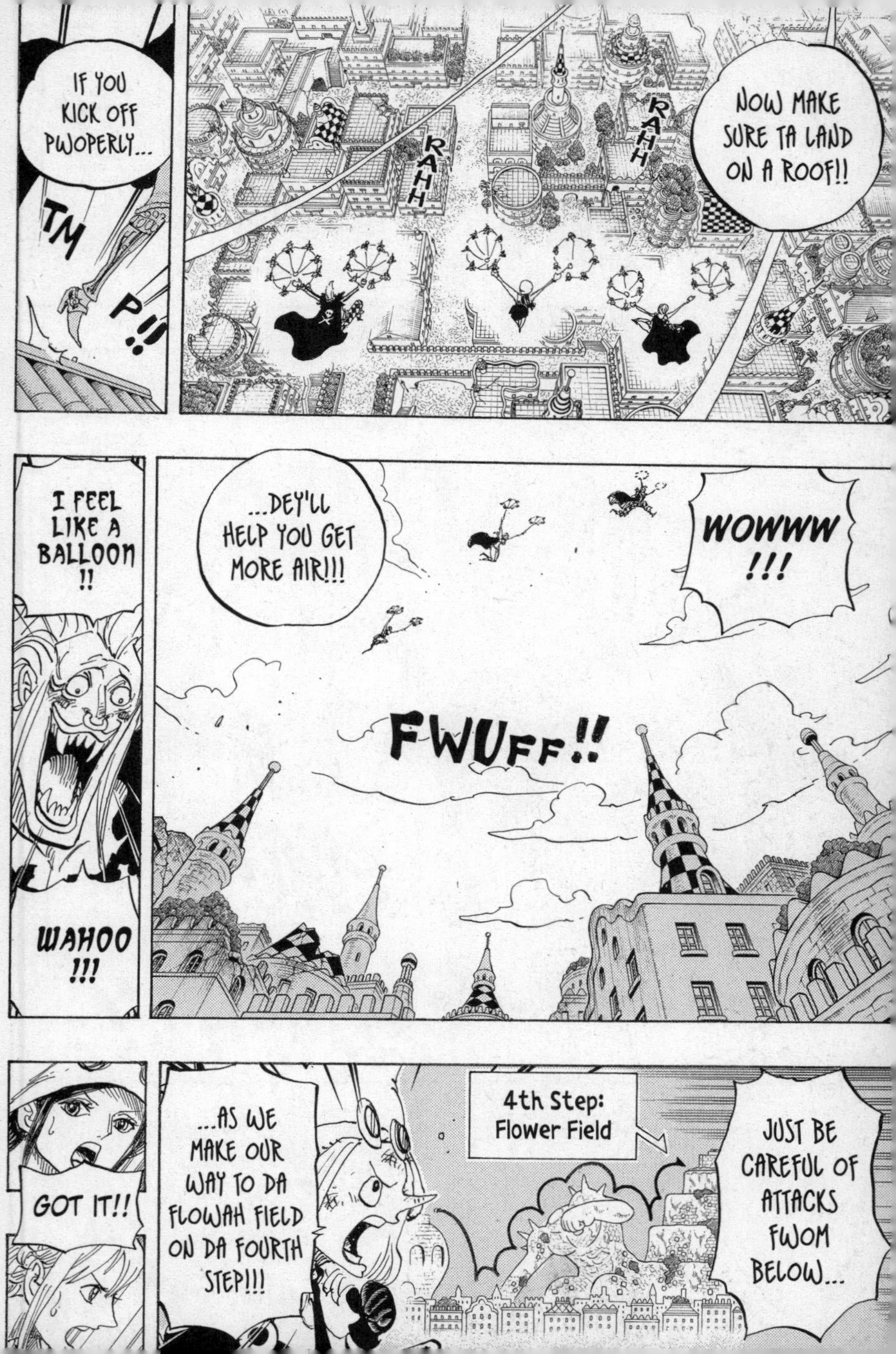
NOW MAKE SURE TA LAND ON A ROOF!!
RAHH
RAHH
IF YOU KICK OFF PWOPERLY...
TMP!!
WOWWW !!!
...DEY'LL HELP YOU GET MORE AIR!!!
FWUFF!!
I FEEL LIKE A BALLOON !!
WAHOO !!!
JUST BE CAREFUL OF ATTACKS FWOM BELOW...
4th Step: Flower Field
...AS WE MAKE OUR WAY TO DA FLOWAH FIELD ON DA FOURTH STEP!!!
GOT IT!!

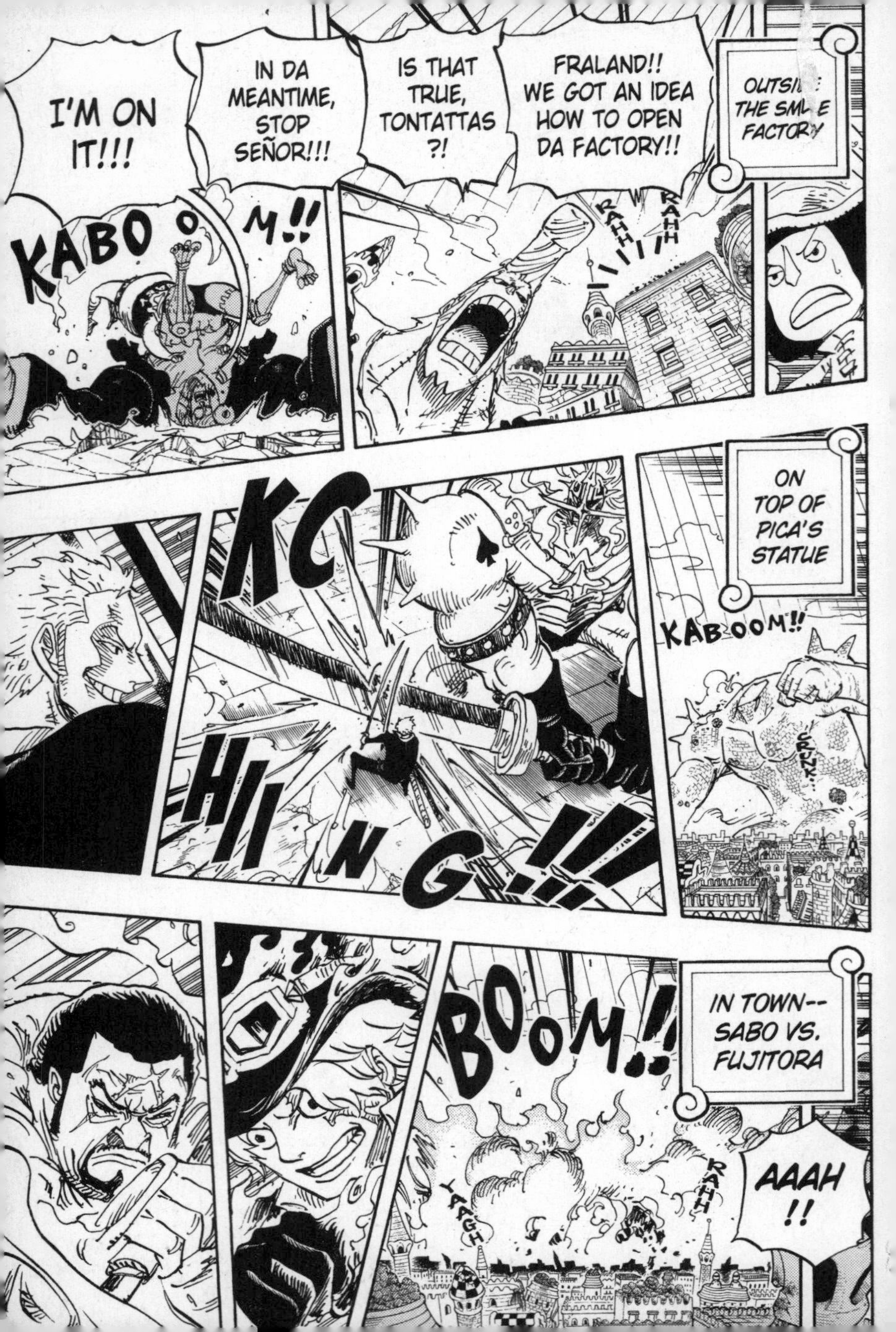
OUTSI E THE SM E FACTORY
RAHH
RAHH
FRALAND!! WE GOT AN IDEA HOW TO OPEN DA FACTORY!!
IS THAT TRUE, TONTATTAS ?!
IN DA MEANTIME, STOP SEÑOR!!!
I'M ON IT!!!
KABO O M.!!
ON TOP OF PICA'S STATUE
KABOOM!!
CRUNK...
KC HIING!!!
IN TOWN-- SABO VS. FUJITORA
AAAH !!
RAHH
BOOM!!
YAAGH

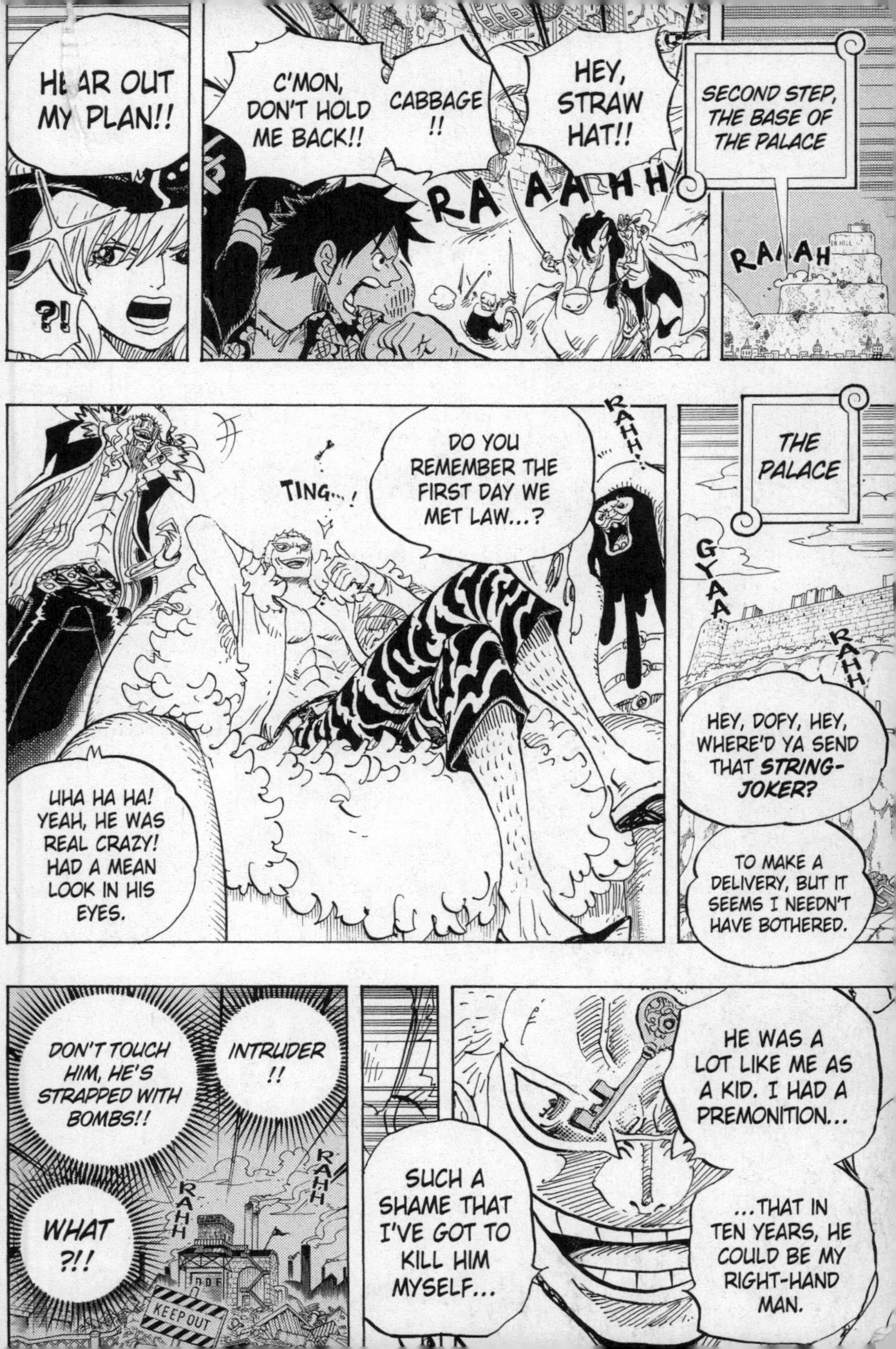

SECOND STEP, THE BASE OF THE PALACE
RAAH
HEY, STRAW HAT!!
CABBAGE !!
C'MON, DON'T HOLD ME BACK!!
RA AAHH
HEAR OUT MY PLAN!!
?!
THE PALACE
GYAA
RAHH
HEY, DOFY, HEY, WHERE'D YA SEND THAT STRING-JOKER?
TO MAKE A DELIVERY, BUT IT SEEMS I NEEDN'T HAVE BOTHERED.
RAHH...
DO YOU REMEMBER THE FIRST DAY WE MET LAW...?
TING...!
UHA HA HA! YEAH, HE WAS REAL CRAZY! HAD A MEAN LOOK IN HIS EYES.
HE WAS A LOT LIKE ME AS A KID. I HAD A PREMONITION...
...THAT IN TEN YEARS, HE COULD BE MY RIGHT-HAND MAN.
SUCH A SHAME THAT I'VE GOT TO KILL HIM MYSELF...
INTRUDER !!
DON'T TOUCH HIM, HE'S STRAPPED WITH BOMBS!!
RAHH
RAHH
WHAT ?!!
KEEP OUT